Praise for *Tesoro: The Treasured Life of a Discarded Daughter*

"In this exquisitely beautiful, haunting debut memoir, Picone weaves a personal story of familial alienation together with sharp, unforgettable portraits of Colombian social hierarchy, the American immigrant experience, and post–World War II life. The complex dance of family dynamics rises to life, instantly ensnaring readers…Picone approaches every character—even herself—with resolute compassion and unflinching honesty…Between the story's rich layers and Picone's captivating writing style, this memoir and its nuanced characters will carve a place in readers' minds. A fascinating, magnificently epic family saga told by a gifted storyteller." – Kirkus Reviews ★

"A compelling story of remembrance, redemption, and one woman's power of persistence… Each line captivates the heart. Each chapter stays inside your soul. Picone shows insightful bravery in the dramatic telling of mother-daughter dynamics in the face of Alzheimer's. Her book is an unforgettably breathtaking journey of healing, hope and love."
—Dorothy Randall Gray, author of Soul Between the Lines

"Tesoro: The Treasured Life of a Discarded Daughter is the exquisitely written story of a woman attempting to disentangle the secrets and lies of a lifetime in the hope of piecing together the fragments of her fractured family. With insight and grace, Picone braids together an absorbing narrative of her search for the truth."
—Janice Van Horne, author of A Complicated Marriage

"…The writing is superb, with an immediacy that pulls you into an intricate weaving of past and present and moves through the geography of her life…Her descriptions make you feel places. This is more than another memoir of an unhappy childhood. It is a testament to the human heart's ability to survive, forgive, and transcend adversity."
—Betsy Feist, Editor

"A gripping story of a woman's relationship to a controlling and difficult mother…I highly recommend this book for those who want to understand the impact of dementia on family dynamics."
—Dr. Darlynne Devenny, author of *Developmental Time*

"An unusual life told in lovely, resonant prose, Picone never mak or expected choice of a word, metaphor or angle on a story, but always ingly beautiful and insightful one. Proust said somewhere that literatu quality of the mirror, not the life it reflects. Picone's expert, burnish like memoir will reward you with the quality of its reflections."
—Jonathan Wallace, author of *Sex, Laws and*

Tesoro

The Treasured Life of a Discarded Daughter

a memoir

VERONICA PICONE

The events of this story are true as I lived them. Names and identifying details of some characters have been changed to protect their privacy.

Cover Design: Jacqueline Matuk
Cover Graphics: David Estrada
Cover Photos courtesy of the author

For Erik, Lilah, Elias, and Luke

and for all the discarded daughters of the world

Where there is ruin, there is hope for treasure.
— Rumi

1

Mi Madre

"*Vállase!* Leave this house and never come back. You don't belong here."

It was an icy night in New York City when my mother ordered me out of her life forever. I was seventeen and had fallen for a man more than twice my age, a friend of the family. He was kind, an artist, and devotedly interested in me, the way I'd always wanted my mother to be. It was the worst of betrayals, she said, indecent and illicit. A proud Colombian woman, Eva Dolores Reiss had not come to America to raise four promiscuous daughters, like *americanas* who knew nothing of family honor. "There will be no sexual revolution under my roof. We are decent here." I was to consider myself orphaned. Give up my place in the family. When I stepped out of our house into that February blizzard no other voice was raised on my behalf, and I didn't believe that the family I belonged to would never again welcome me.

Thirty years later and winter again in New York, my mother is an old woman and I am middle aged. Our reunion was fated a year ago by the death of my stepfather. We were polite when we were introduced at the funeral, but there was no exchange of affection or ritual of forgiveness. My mother never changed her mind. It changed of its own accord. One afternoon in her kitchen, a few months after the funeral, she stood at her pantry door, caressed my hands, and called me *m'ija*, my daughter, as if this was our custom. "What a terrible place the world would be without you in it," she said, her eyes soft with a tenderness I had never known her to possess. This glimpse into the person I had yearned for all my life pleased me. Yet, instinctively, I looked away, a child caught coveting something forbidden.

Today we sit together in a sterile conference room of a Long Island geriatric hospital. It is crowded with my mother's doctors asking about her history. A sudden, wild possessiveness wedges itself against my voice. I don't want to tell these doctors anything. I won't reduce my mother's life and its madness into a single forty-five minute interview. What I know of her now is treasure, and I won't surrender it easily. It has been too costly to reclaim her, finally. Only the howling winds rattling their discontent against the windows acknowledge what no one else will: Alzheimer's. This woman, *mi madre*, is leaving me, again.

"What changes have you noticed in your mother?" The psychiatrist lobs the question from across the room.

"Many," Julia answers. She is the eldest of my three sisters and has always lived with my mother. Like the others, she never defied my mother's edict nor came to look for me. In most of our ways we are strangers. She gives the doctors what they want. "Mrs. Reiss hasn't been herself for six months now. Her memory is poor and she is increasingly confused. She shows no interest in caring for herself or her home. It's very difficult to get her to eat or bathe. And she barely sleeps."

I am grateful Julia is here. She will take charge. It's in her nature—a true alpha, hard-wired, and inexhaustibly reactive. I watch her, fully aware that I will never get enough of watching her, for all the time lost. Her auburn hair is pulled tight away from the small, soft features of her face, so fair skinned and different from my own that no one easily believes we are related. She has no problem answering the doctors' questions about my mother's medications. Until the neurologist asks, "When was the last time your mother went out socially?" Julia doesn't answer. Maybe she's forgotten.

"On her birthday," I blurt. "A few days before this past Thanksgiving." The doctors write in their charts, and I remember that evening. It was our first time at the theater together, ever, looking like any other mother and daughter in the world as we waited for the performance to begin. She'd talked for those few minutes with a young man in the next seat about his interest in Spanish dance. She'd been gracious, as I had always known her to be in public, telling him about her Spanish and Colombian heritage with just a hint of appropriate arrogance. She went on, boasting to the young man that she'd insisted all her children get a classical education that included the arts, each of them playing at least two musical instruments, and that I had been a flamenco dancer. That prompted the man to smile at me with admiration.

Just as the house lights went down, he complimented her on having been a good mother, and she answered in a matter-of-fact voice, "No, I was not. I was a very cruel mother. I hurt my children, and they suffered. I did not know how wrong I was at the time." There is nothing about that show I remember now, only the unsettling lapse in recognition when I saw my mother as someone else.

The others turn to Julia with another checklist of questions, but the psychiatrist is impatient. He swivels in his chair and taps his gold pen. I wonder if he will take time to directly address my mother, just a few feet away, before he condenses the chaos of her world into a diagnosis his team can manage. Or perhaps he'll rely on her family's answers and the one quick glance he gave her as he entered the room. Will he detect that beneath the mismatched buttons of her sweater, her dead husband's mended pants, the layers of torn undergarments she adamantly refuses to discard, and her grown son's boyhood shoes on her feet, are the vanishing remains of another, utterly different Eva Dolores Reiss? I imagine him mentally comprising his notes: 'Patient female (78), presents as frail, disheveled, passive affect, sits with hands folded, limited eye contact, intermittently engaged with surroundings'.

It was my suggestion that we bring my mother here, the most reputable geriatric treatment center in the city. But I worry about the power of charm. This team is sure to admire and never question the seductive portrait we present—two grown sisters doing the right thing for their troubled mother. They will know nothing of my hard-won victory, entering her world anew just as my mother's mental failure grew serious. My having to convince Julia that what was happening wasn't pretense, nor in any way intentional, but serious enough to need medical attention. The doctors won't hear the school teacher tone my sister uses to address my mother, the "Walk faster!" she snapped into my mother's ear in the hospital lobby today, or her mocking nudge to me, "Let's get this thing over with. We've waited fifty years to get her head examined."

I've known rare moments of self-doubt in Julia. Even as children, when she carried the burden of parenting the rest of us, she did so with the self-imposed ferocity of an exhausted child that both reassured and scared all around her into submission. On the odd occasion when her voice would crack or she'd suddenly stop short in the midst of a show of force, she'd soften momentarily, allow the breaking of a rule, look the other way, tempting me to approach, curious for more. Today she isn't at all soft. But it's good to have her with me, the two of us together against the odds, despite my friends and colleagues who question why I'd want to, under the circumstances. I have never felt otherwise. I've only known the longing for this sister, for all of them, during the years of silence.

"Mrs. Reiss, I am Dr. Klein. I am a psychiatrist and I'd like to ask you some questions."

I catch my mother's gaze. She moves nervously in her seat.

"Who is he, Ronnie?" The roll of the first letter of my nickname announces to all the world my mother's foreign birth.

"A doctor," I answer. "He wants to get to know you, so he can help you."

"Help me with what? Am I sick?"

"Yes, Mom, you haven't been feeling well lately. You've been very sad, worried about things, confused about money. You haven't wanted to go out of the house. Do you remember?"

"No. I do not. That does not sound right." She dismisses me, looks down at her lap.

"Tell me what part doesn't sound right, Eva?" Dr. Klein slides his chair closer.

My mother looks up at him. He smiles. She smiles back. "Nice teeth, doctor." She disarms him momentarily, and we all laugh.

"Thank you," he says. "Tell me, how are you feeling today?"

"Pretty good. And you?"

"Good. Do you know where you are right now, Eva?"

"I think so. This is your office. Somebody is sick?" My mother looks around the room to answer her own question.

"Do you know who these two people are, Eva?" Dr. Klein motions to Julia and me.

"Of course, doctor. They are my daughters. Julia, the difficult one. And that is Veronica, the *bandida*." She winks at me and chuckles, as if we had a secret understanding of what her answers mean. I notice that Julia has half-turned away, looking up at the ceiling.

"Tell me about them," he says, and I feel an urge to stop him.

My mother leans in toward the doctor, as if she were telling him very important news, and points her arthritic hand toward Julia.

"That one has a good heart, but no social graces. Very rough, like a *sargento*. She drives men away."

"And Veronica?"

"Ronnie?" My mother doesn't look at me, just at the doctor. "Man crazy. Ran off when she was seventeen with a older man. Broke our hearts. She was the smartest of all the girls. She could have been an attorney, like her father. But she ran away."

"*Persona non grata,*" Julia calls out over her shoulder.

"Oh?" Dr. Klein throws me a steady-eyed glance, but doesn't pursue. "How many girls are there, Eva?"

"Four," she says. "A disgrace, I know. But I kept trying, doctor, until I finally had a son."

"And that is very important, isn't it Eva?"

"Doctor, I am South American. To me, a son is a reward." My mother sits up in her chair, her chin raised and head cocked slightly to one side, eyes pinned to the doctor's. She speaks slowly. "My father's family were aristocrats. Perhaps you do not understand this so easily, being an American. It is no easy thing to have to raise four women. No, sir. A woman must remain pure and decent so that her family name can be respected. A son is a different story. He can do whatever he wants and never lose his name. No matter how he falls, doctor, a man always lands on his feet."

Dr. Klein repeatedly nods his head as my mother speaks. I can't tell if he agrees with her, or he wants to encourage the flow of her lengthy answer.

"So you have five children," Klein says. "A nice family. You must enjoy them very much." Yes, I think, the charm is working. "Any grandchildren?"

"How many, Ronnie?"

"Three," Julia answers before I can.

Dr. Klein turns to me. "All yours?"

"I have two girls. The grandson is in Seattle. From another daughter."

"Another daughter, yes." Klein swivels his chair toward me and winks. "And smart enough to have a son." He begins to write.

"Carmela." My mother has always said this daughter's name differently from the rest, as though she were making an introduction. "A pianist. Very sensitive."

"I see. There's one more, isn't there? Another girl. What about her?"

The excitement fades from my mother's face. She shrugs and looks down again as she says, "Isabella favors her father. She despises me."

Dr. Klein is writing fast now. "Why is that?"

"Because I am not Jewish." He stops writing and puts his pen down on his clipboard. He looks up at my mother again.

"Is she?"

"Yes. She is. And Gabriel, too. Like Ben."

"Ben is your husband. He is Jewish," he repeats. "And you're not."

"I am Catholic. Raised by Protestants. But Ben liked me anyway. He married me. A foreigner, a widow, with three girls, and not Jewish." She smiles. "Poor Ben. He could have married anyone. He was a dentist. Nice looking. A kind man. Of course his children had to be Jews. They are his blood. That is his right. I sent them to Hebrew school. I made sure they learned."

"I see. A dentist. So that's why you liked my teeth." He chuckles.

"I have a good eye," she says triumphantly.

"Yes," Dr. Klein nods his head slowly a few times. "There was a first husband, what happened to him?"

"History," my mother says with a wave of her hand. I turn to look at her, feeling a jolt of anger at her ability, even now, to summarily dismiss the subject of my father, as if it belonged only to her. But I see that Dr. Klein accepts her answer. Julia has crossed her arms.

"And what about Ben?"

"He is busy at the office," my mother answers. "He is very devoted to his patients."

Audible sighs escape my sister and me at the same moment. We exchange the look that only siblings can, a mixture of contempt for outsiders and compassion for one another. It is how Julia and I close ranks, shield ourselves from the old shame of having to explain our family, and I am pleased to see we can still do it. I try to catch Dr. Klein's attention, shaking my head and hoping he'll look up.

"That's not true," Julia interrupts. "Ben is dead."

"What?" My mother looks around, pained. "Why was I not told?"

Everyone else is quiet. Dr. Klein closes his writing pad and rolls himself back to his original spot on the other side of the room. The others close their charts too.

"So," Dr. Klein says to no one in particular. "A very complicated family. Multiple marriages. Several languages, religions, cultures."

My mother does not respond. Julia and I look away. The doctor clicks his gold pen shut and places it carefully into the breast pocket of his suit jacket. He turns to his colleagues and without another word they rise and leave the room.

"What happened?" my mother asks. "Where is Ben? I have to get home. Gabriel will be back from school soon and I have to get dinner ready. He has a piano lesson today." Her voice is getting that shrill tone I hate. "*Que desgracia,*" she mutters. "What a disgrace that I never learned to drive." She turns to my sister, her oldest target and most frequent sparring partner. "I am forced to depend on you now."

"That's right. Remember that." Julia stands up, walks to the door of the room and looks out into the corridor. "Where did these geniuses go?"

"Ronnie, what is going on?"

"It's okay Mom," I say. "We'll take you home soon. You'll have plenty of time to cook."

The brief reprieve Dr. Klein's attention has offered us is over. In minutes, the void he left behind will be filled with bickering between my sister and mother. They will peck at each other like two caged birds until one gives in. Lately, uncustomarily, it's been my mother. A very old and familiar cramp grips my stomach. I remind myself that I am not a small child anymore, and that I can remove myself from this situation if I need to.

"What the heck is this?" Julia steps out of the room. Her spike heels click all the way down the hall.

"Ronnie?" The shrill is higher.

"Yes, Mom. I'm right here."

"Did Ben call?"

my hand fits right into Hers
all the way down the stairs
six flights
fast as i can to keep up with Her yellow dress
that flies
then stops in the air when She turns around
it's the best
especially when we walk along Fourteenth Street
and all the way down Second Avenue
people smile at us
first the pickle man moving the water around
in that giant barrel with the giant fork
looking to get the best dill for us to share
then we stop at Sammy's to get meat
he smiles at Her more than all the others
and always asks me to read the words
in the pictures on his walls
he says i'm a very smart three year old
when he talks he makes Her laugh
then he gets a hot dog from the big glass case
and asks does the little doll want a treat today
i look at Her and She's happy
so i say yes
if i stand next to Her
with my face right on Her yellow dress
i can hear the stiff stuff crackle underneath
when She moves
maybe She'll make me one just like it
so we can be twins
except my dark hair isn't beautiful golden
like Hers

Tribe

I saw you first, and you didn't know it. All it took was a flick of my eyes into the rear view mirror, and there you were, right between the heads of my two daughters in the back seat. I turned around, pretending to ease my car into the spot I'd found near the funeral chapel, but really to see you better. You were wearing a steel gray suit, the color of the sky that morning. Could it have been that same old one? I watched you until you passed, a bent old woman taking the place of the mother I remembered. No, I thought, that can't be her. Your blonde hair had become a shy gray bun, and you were so small. What had I been so afraid of? All those years of waiting, and just like that, only a strip of sidewalk and a piece of windshield glass between us.

I didn't say anything to my girls. What could I have said? They hardly knew you. They didn't hesitate when I asked them to come with me, but I could see they were uncomfortable. The ride into Manhattan had been quiet, without their usual talk of college life and boyfriends, and as we stepped out onto Second Avenue my head was filled with thoughts only of seeing you and the family again.

Inside the chapel an usher walked us through the sanctuary, past a group of old men in yarmulkes and prayer shawls. It was comforting to see them, which you might find odd, since I'd never seen Ben pray or be religious in any way. We reached a room that was filled with people I didn't recognize until I spotted Julia speaking to a young man. She was more womanly than

I remembered, but it was her voice I recognized—she still spoke louder and faster than anyone else. When she saw me, she called out, "Veronica! Good!" and I moved closer. My impulse was to touch her, kiss her maybe. But I held back, unsure of how she'd react, and she politely shook hands with me. She did the same with her nieces, and introduced us to the young man.

He was Gabriel. The tongue-tied little brother I'd last seen as a school-boy was now a broad-shouldered man with a deep baritone voice and solemn brown eyes. We talked nervously about how grown up everyone was, but in a few minutes no one had much to say. Julia stepped away to speak to some-one else. Gabriel began to fidget with his tie. I studied the room, looking for Carmela and Isabella. My sisters could be right in front of me, I thought, but would we recognize each other? Then I saw my girls chatting with Gabriel about work and school and cars, and in an instant he became Uncle Gabriel, closer in age to them than to me.

"¡*Qué ironía*!" I said aloud, but no one else noticed. You'd been such a powerful force, forbidding everyone in the family to see me or talk to me. Now fate had ironically thrust us together in a place reserved especially for us, the Family Room of a funeral chapel.

Julia returned and I asked her to point you out. You sat alone at the far end of the room, pressed against the sofa cushions, staring out into the dis-tance and looking lost. Julia led us to you and tapped your arm.

"Say hello to your grandchildren, Jacqueline, Lissette."

I watched the girls extend their hands to you, so ignorant of the power of their gesture and of all that had come before, of all I might have told them, but didn't, that might have prepared them for so unnatural a moment. Or could it have? Their gray Moorish eyes fixed on you like fascinated toddlers, Jackie's earthy smile, Lissette's doubting brow, their strong lean bodies and thick waves of hair reaching down their backs. Your eyes opened wide, and from your mouth came the very right words. "*Que bellas*. How beautiful they are."

I took a step closer, waited for you to turn my way. "Hello, Mom."

It wasn't what I'd imagined, in those inconsequential moments, hun-dreds of them over the years, when I'd be pulling laundry out of the dryer, say, or turning the page of a book, and an involuntary sense of wonder would intrude into my life with images of the two of us accidentally meeting on a street or other public place, and I would let myself create the script of our *encuentro*, of how we'd greet each other. Here there were no tears, no long embraces, no recriminations. Just,"Hello, Ronnie." As if we'd had lunch last week.

What would work? My hand? A kiss? I did neither, looking for your cue. You hesitated too, then tilted your head and spoke to Julia. *"Se parece a Carlota."* On another day it might have bothered me that you thought I looked like your mother. But that day you kept your eyes on me, studying me. And I let you. I didn't budge.

"Otra gigante, como Carmela." I turned to see if what you said was true, if I'd grown as much as the tallest of my sisters. But Julia shook her head. Carmela wasn't coming. She was still living in Seattle. "Still a hippie. Like the sixties hadn't ended."

I didn't have time to answer when a young woman approached with an older man at her side. She was petite, like you, with a head full of ginger-colored curls. "Rabbi Feldman, this is Ronnie, another sister." Then she smiled at me and I saw she was Isabella—sweet Isabella, her pigtails gone, but not those dimples.

I smiled back at her, thrilled. But I could feel myself racing, trying to stay ahead of what was happening. There were only snippets of information coming at me, and yet so much to take in. Your faces and voices all around me, standing with you again, included. And Ben was dead. I wanted to believe this moment was all that mattered, that I could put aside the nagging questions I didn't yet dare to ask. How well did any of you remember me? What did you know about my life? Would this be my one chance to see you, or would we have more time together later, tomorrow? Why hadn't any of you ever looked for me?

When Rabbi Feldman asked me if I'd like to say a few words about my father, I felt my face get hot. He's confused with someone else, I thought. Doesn't he know Ben was my stepfather? Hasn't anyone told him what a difference that prefix made to this family? But maybe it didn't matter to him. Maybe he didn't differentiate between children, like you and Ben had. Maybe this holy man didn't issue ultimatums that could tear the mantle of a family like the gash in the garments of the bereaved he ministered to. I looked into his sympathetic face and thought of telling him about us. Estranged, I could have said, and watched the muscles of his face contract, bewildered, the way most people look whenever I've said that word. To be cut off, I could have explained. Set apart. Made strange. To feel strange. Become a stranger. Even to one self.

The rabbi called the family to enter the chapel and we stopped to pray at the casket. Do you remember how we stood there, gathered, not around my dining room table as I had so long hoped for, but around what was left of Ben? It was only when the rabbi motioned us to take our seats that you spoke. "Is it really Ben?"

What was it about your voice? Barely a whisper, it transformed the four of us into small children looking to each other, embarrassed and confused. Gabriel was the quickest. "No, Mom. We auditioned all week to find someone to come here and impersonate Dad."

It took a second, but our laughter ripped through the chapel, and it didn't matter that you didn't get it, because we were allies again. A second later you hissed "¡*Respeto!*" and our laughing stopped instantly.

That was when it happened. The only time in my life that I forgot my children, forgot I was a mother. For the remainder of the service I only existed as your daughter and as a sister. I didn't notice when the girls moved away, as though they'd been part of the crowd of strangers in the back pews. Later I felt ashamed. It was Jackie who remarked the next day about the seating during the service. It had made her angry, she said, to watch with her sister as the family filed into the front pews—Julia, You, Gabriel, and Isabella. And there had been no room for me. I'd crossed the aisle, she said, to sit in an empty row. I told my daughter I hadn't noticed, which was true, but she didn't believe me. It was an awful thing to witness, she said, how I'd just accepted being left out. I liked that about her, about both my children, that they didn't have a clue about being cast away.

The rabbi spoke about Ben and how he'd served the community as a dental surgeon for over fifty years. My mind wandered to the last visit I had with him in his office. Did he ever tell you about those visits—the yearly checkups for me and the girls? I'd call him using the old family signal, letting the telephone ring once and calling again. He'd answer, always happy to hear from me, and give me his last appointment on a Saturday afternoon. After he'd taken care of our teeth he would walk us down the avenue to the deli for lunch. The girls loved those visits. They'd get his undivided attention and a toy for each when they were little, and later a five or ten dollar bill in each hand. He'd wink at me to turn around and let them have their secret Grandpa treat. At the deli they could order anything they wanted. "The sky's the limit," he'd say. After the girls would lose interest in grownups and talk between themselves, I would ask about you.

It was always the same. Ben would lower his head and slowly shake it, looking very sorry. "Well, Ronnie, your mother is your mother." He'd give a long sigh and I would wait for more. Then he'd raise his head and look past me, over my shoulder or at the person in the next booth, and hold his gaze there for a few seconds before he'd change the subject. I didn't insist. I understood that those were the terms of our meetings. Ben was the only one willing to defy your orders about me, but I knew he would never do anything to make things better between us.

Maybe I was wrong. Maybe one Sunday afternoon in autumn, no, in summer—you were always easier in the summer—the two of you might have been in your kitchen together, you at the stove stirring the garlic and onions for *picadillo* and Ben at the white formica table, reading to you from a Times article he found particularly interesting on socialized medicine or the perils of fluoride? The house would inhale the outside world, allowed in only at this time of the year through wide-open doors and windows, coming to join Isabella at the living room piano and up to Gabriel, studying in his room? And in the midst of it, maybe, Ben might have heeded a surge of uncustomary courage, just enough to bring up my name?

One day he didn't answer the phone anymore. I called again, then again. I called for months, years, at all hours, with and without the family signal. But he never answered. I even stopped at his office once, his plaque was still on the building, but no one answered the door.

Who was it that phoned me? Just a few weeks before the funeral, a man's voice on my answering machine saying only that Ben was very ill and was at Beth Israel Hospital. I went immediately. He was in a private room. He was lying on his side, tubes and machines wired into him, exhaustion in his eyes. I stood at the foot of the bed and said hello. He didn't recognize me at first. He thought I was Carmela and called me by her nickname, Cookie. She'd been calling from Seattle almost every day, he said, and it surprised him. When he saw it was me he tried to sit up.

"Oh, it's Ronnie. How nice."

I asked if he was comfortable.

"It isn't good." I told him my girls sent their love and missed him. He smiled, "Sweet kids." Then he closed his eyes and I couldn't do anything but stand there at the foot of the bed, looking at him, my hand tight around the bed rail between us. I called him Doc, and asked him if I could give him a hug. He opened his eyes and looked at me for a few seconds.

"No."

A second anonymous message gave the funeral arrangements. I picked a suit out of the closet, the brown one I'd bought on a whim a few months before, and pressed it myself. As I moved the iron along the cloth I came to understand something, and I was grateful. Ben had given me in dying what he never could in life: I would be seeing you, all of you, again.

I don't remember much of Isabella's eulogy for her father. It's her figure that stays with me. Proud and determined, her voice quivering but dignified, she was a blend of everything good in Ben and you.

Scenes I hadn't thought of in years came into my mind. Ben taking us on Sunday picnics to Central Park, riding in his new lemon yellow Pontiac to Yonah Schimmel's for hot knishes, his crowded waiting room where patients sat for hours knowing he'd never turn anyone away, listening to him sing *La Paloma* while you smiled, and how he loved a warm piece of Russian coffee cake.

When Isabella came to me after the service and asked if I wanted to join the family on the ride to the gravesite, I didn't hesistate. I watched her get into the limousine, Julia behind her, Gabriel holding his arm out for you, so much like his father. As I stepped into the limousine I looked up at the sky. Bright sunlight had replaced the rain. I could hear Ben telling me not to worry. "The weather is always a nice on a Jewish holiday, Ronnie."

i can see everything from here without looking up
my sisters' faces right at mine
the stuff on top of the table
and out the kitchen window
She is working at the stove
Her hair bounces on Her back
i cannot see the front of Her
like when i am in my crib
or on the big bed
and She bends over me
and down comes Her face to mine
just us under Her soft yellow hair together
now the girls make happy sounds
in the other room
She is hurrying to remove Her apron
my eyes follow Her
She is smiling She is crying She covers Her face
someone else is here
my sisters lead him in
one at each hand
laughing talking quickly
he bends to kiss Her
and empties the bag he brings
onto my highchair
little paper cups filled with something white
sprinkled specs on top like colored stars
a spoonful in my mouth cold sweet
but i don't want that
just him
near me
his hand on my head
he sings
he lifts me up
in slow motion
i want to know
i search his face
he kisses my head my eyes my mouth

he is no stranger
i am deep into his skin and its sweet smell
the only color i can see
like his soft coat
is gray

2

it has been there since i woke up
leaning against the kitchen door up against the mirror
where i look to find my friend
i don't like the *maleta*
big brown thing with a zipper all around like a snake
once She opened it up on the bed
and took out all those papers
and the beautiful white pajamas
that made Her cry
then She sat in the green chair in the living room
just sat
for a long time i wanted to climb up on Her lap
and fix Her hair with the pearly brush She likes
but She pushed me away
so i played in the kitchen with my mirror friend
close to the door so i could see Her
just sitting
until it got dark
then She got up and made dinner
but today She hasn't opened the *maleta*
it's been there all day
leaning against the mirror door
waiting
She is putting on my coat now
She is doing this all wrong
after my bath we always put on my pajamas
not my coat
She is taking a long time on each button
like She did combing my braids
She even ironed my ribbons really slow
hasn't said a word not even peek-a-boo
when She pulled the shirt over my head
not even the *zapatitos me aprientan* song
when She tied my shoes
Her face looks like maybe She's angry i can't tell
it must be a special place we are going to
if i get to wear my coat with the pretty collar

i know this place
Uncle Mickey brings us here to see the planes
but he never brought us here at night
there are so many people with *maletas* that look very fat
must have lots of papers and pajamas inside
there are other men dressed like Uncle Mickey
but Uncle Mickey's hat has more golden stuff than theirs
and he has those little gold braids on his shoulders
we like it when Uncle Mickey comes to visit
in his beautiful uniform
smelling really nice
he makes us laugh and She is happy
one of the other men has taken the brown *maleta*
i wonder why She brought it
i am glad She gave it away
She won't be sad anymore
we are walking outside now
it is cold
there is a big plane
and stairs
and lights on the ground
She is holding my hand tight
i can see very big letters but i can't make a word
I-D-L-E-W-I-L-D
there is Uncle Mickey
talking with a lady who has a little red cape on
he points to us and smiles
they are talking in that other way
She has let go of my hand
She bends down to me
She lifts me
even though She always says i am too big now to be carried
and gives me to the red-cape lady
the red-cape lady smiles and talks to me in that other way
while we go up the stairs
i see Uncle Mickey at the top
and big red letters on the plane behind him

A-V-I-A-N-C-A
he is smiling *niña bonita*
he has something in his hand *para ti*
it is a toy plane
i look back to show Her
She is not there
only the lights on the ground
Uncle Mickey takes me from the red-cape lady
i still look back
i call Her
Mommy Can't Hear You
Uncle Mickey is buckling me into a seat
Be A Good Girl And Later You Can Fly The Plane
there is a circle window
i look for Mommy
only lights on the ground in rows
i hate the smell
i'm going to vomit
i want Mommy
i cry loud
a lion roars even louder than me
everything is shaking
the lights on the ground are moving
the red-cape lady opens a little table
in front of me with cookies
like the cookies Uncle Mickey brings when he visits
he lets us open his big *maleta*
we look through his clothes until we find presents
golden bracelets from someplace called Beirut
chocolates from Rome
and once little castanets from *España*
for me and my mirror friend to dance with
i remember Mommy
i cry again
the red-cape lady opens the cookies
i don't want cookies i want Mommy
i look for Her

i will watch until She comes
She might be lost in the dark
with only those lights in rows to find Her way back
the red-cape lady brings a blanket
and covers me *duerme niña*
but no i won't sleep
i must stay awake for Mommy
Uncle Mickey is calling my name
he is laughing
he takes my buckle off and walks me
past all the empty seats through the little door
and buckles me into another chair
right next to him
there are lots of little lights and very big windows
Uncle Mickey takes his black hat with golden stuff
and puts it on my head
La niña pilota he laughs again
i watch him touch some of the lights
We Are In The Sky he says
We Are Flying he says
No More Tears Little Girl he says

La Casa

My mother's house is on a quiet street in Queens, the part of New York City that until a few decades ago was known for the dairy farms and cemeteries travelers passed by on their way out east to an airport or a Long Island beach. Such an exodus today weaves through the Borough of Houses on ribbons of highways, past Citi Field, several colleges, the birthplace of Louis Armstrong, and the highest concentration of foreign languages spoken anywhere in the world. Tucked into a northeastern pocket of the borough, her neighborhood traces the county line just before the street signs change color from green to black and the city inconspicuously yields to the suburbs. Tall oaks, maples, and birches line the roads, sloping through a maze of pampered homes and gardens, an unexpected sanctuary to species of birds and plant life just miles from the hub of the downtown Manhattan immigrant community where she once lived. What my mother likes most about it, she is quick to point out, is that in Douglaston Manor no two houses are alike. And no one is apt to visit unexpectedly.

The morning sun glistens on last night's eight-inch snowfall and tree branches along Douglaston Parkway bend low to the ground like noble women bowing to the elements. I pull into my mother's driveway as the voice on my car radio announces that spring is only a week off. Has it already been two months since the visit with my mother's doctors? I think of Jackie, my first child, how she was born late in the night on the eve of spring, some twenty-nine years ago, with the same determination as the buds that were bursting into life along with her. When she was a toddler and couldn't resist picking new flowers for me from any garden we passed, I first explained nature's cycle of rebirth to her. Her face wrinkled in worry as she asked if the buds cried when they opened, and I was never able to walk past young blooms again and not listen a little. I make my way up the long and cleanly shoveled path to my mother's front steps. On days like this I am grateful to live in an apartment building ten minutes away.

From the height of the front porch I see Julia down the street. She is pushing the snow blower along a neighbor's walkway, too involved in her work to notice me. I wonder how many other driveways on the block she's cleared. I press the doorbell of this enormous house my mother loves and I have never lived in. Chances are my mother will not hear the doorbell from her bedroom. It is at the rear of the house where she spends most of her time now.

I listen for a sound or movement behind the door, but nothing. I could knock, but the wrought iron storm gate, kept bolted, prevents me from reaching the door. I could peer through one of the large casement windows into the dining room, but the blinds and drapes are closed. I ring a third time and decide to give it another minute before making the trek around to the back, where the house is built into a hillside and the snow is sure to be deeper than my boots can handle.

The irony of the moment doesn't escape me. Thirty years waiting to be at her door; now my mother doesn't hear me. I think of those first visits I made here after Ben died, when we were granted permission—that peculiar gift of death's, when it provokes, briefly, an urgency to live—to connect. I took advantage of it, and made short weekly phone calls to her. She accepted them, pleasant, unhurried, and I came to believe I could risk a visit. At first I would pretend to be on my way to or from somewhere else, doing errands nearby. I would bring a small gift of fruit or fresh bread, something she wouldn't find difficult to receive because we could share it. Her suspicious, "Who is it?" the door would change to a happy "Oh, Ronnie!" when she heard me, then a short drumroll of clicking locks and her diminutive figure behind the iron gate, a big smile on her face. She'd say, "What a nice surprise, *mi'ja*." Her greetings to me have never ceased to be kind, and still unnerve me a little.

Those first days I simply entered the house and followed her into the kitchen. But as my visits continued, I allowed myself to gently kiss her hello.

As I bent to her I would wait for the tightening of her back and the little gasp she takes whenever she's touched. Instead, she'd laugh and say, "How did such a tall woman come from such a nothing mother?"

I was careful in those days to limit my time with my mother to twenty minutes or so. She would ask about my girls and my work. I'd ask about her arthritis, an old enemy she battled since her thirties. She'd tell me again about the hours of stretching she did to no avail and her daily dose of a dozen or more aspirin, chewed without water throughout the day. Her talk was mostly about the house and its chronic need of repair, as though, like a lover she had taken care of for years, it was now betraying her. We both avoided the subject of our separation, preferring small encouragements and kindness to drudging up old hurts. I'd end my visits saying I had an appointment to keep, and my mother would happily suggest I stay longer next time. It was our routine, and it worked, like small transfusions of courage for each of us.

As I eased into my hunger to know her world, my mother began to reveal parts of herself, and I didn't question why. I would sit at her kitchen table sipping her strong coffee and watch her negotiate the space, her small muscular body moving deliberately from one side of the immense room to the other to find, arrange, and care for her tools. Her spice cabinet, her pantry, her cupboards brimming with pots and pans, baking dishes of all sizes and types, all gleamed despite years of use. Once, she took out a very small pot and handed it to me. Her face was smug and playful, her hazel eyes darkened into smiles. "This is what I heated your baby bottle in, kiddo, when we lived in Union Square."

In time she began to accept my help with putting groceries away or folding sheets or chopping vegetables for the dinner she prepared for Julia and herself every evening. In good weather I'd find her in her garden. Thinning back her Rose of Sharon bushes or pruning the pair of overgrown magnolia trees that flank her front garden like sentries, she was another woman, unselfconscious and happy. She'd talk about her plants without regard for the dirt on her hands or the hour of day, and I allowed myself brief episodes of savoring what other daughters take for granted all their lives.

The wind picks up and blows snow into my face. I wonder if I should move from here, when I hear my mother's voice behind the door.

"*Quién es?* What do you want?" She sounds weak, frightened, her accent stronger than usual.

"It's me, Mom."

"Ronnie? Is that you?"

"Yes. Mom, open the door."

"*¿Estas sola?*"

"Yes, I'm alone. Open the door. It's cold."

It's quiet again. I wait, and another time comes to mind. A Mother's Day stored away in a place that seems improbable now, when my girls were little and my husband couldn't stand to spend another sorrowful holiday with me. Michél had decided to call my mother, without telling me, and managed to persuade her to break the seven years of estrangement already passed, and allow a visit. We'd put the children and all their paraphernalia into our car to come here, to this house I'd never seen, driven by Michél's expectations of a jubilant reconciliation. He'd read somewhere that it takes the human body seven years to regenerate its epidermis. "It is guaranteed to be good," he urged. "She has new skin now."

I remember walking in, holding one little hand in mine and carrying the baby as comfort against everything this immense house contained. My mother and Ben were home, but my older sisters were already living away. Isabella and Gabriel came to greet us, not so little anymore, but after a stern look from my mother, disappeared again. They had their studies and practice to finish, she said, expecting me to understand.

It was a brief visit, and we all behaved well. My mother barely looked at me and said very little, spending most of the time tending to her cooking and baking rituals. She was preparing meals for the week ahead, to save time and energy, and keep the gas bill down. After a few uncomfortable minutes together in her kitchen, she suggested we wait in the garden. Michél and Ben made small talk, and I was grateful to be distracted by my children. When lunch was over I couldn't resist any longer. "So, Mom, what do you think of my family?" She didn't hesitate. "Very nice. But none of this is good enough for you. You have ruined your life."

Not even grandchildren could mitigate her disapproval of me, and I was too disappointed to speak. Michél was silent too as we drove away. I looked for something good to take with me, to give to my children when they would ask about their grandmother. It was the colors, the multitude of lilac and azalea blossoms around the place that stayed with me.

"Mom," I call again. "It's cold out here."

I hear her negotiate the locks repeatedly until she gets the right sequence, and I pull open the gate. My mother is standing in the foyer, dressed in a paisley blouse and half-slip, and barefoot. The blouse is inside out, but she has managed to close most of the buttons. Her long gray hair is loose and wild. She holds up her hand to shield her eyes from the outside light and moves behind the door.

"I am sorry Ronnie. I am not prepared for company." She turns to walk away.

"It's okay Mom. I'm alone. And I'm not company." I move toward her and catch her elbow. "Come here Mom, let's say hello." I bend to her—she reaches just to my chest—and kiss her cheek. She doesn't gasp. She leans into me and begins to sob.

"I cannot find anything in this place."

"What are you looking for?" I answer calmly, knowing she will take her cues from me. She steps back, hands gripping her blouse.

"My bankbook. It is gone. I have looked everywhere."

"Maybe I can help you. Where did you look first?" I close the door behind me, remembering to bolt the iron gate to reassure her. I step into the foyer. The smell of mildew I've come to expect hits me immediately.

"Where I always keep my records."

"Where is that Mom?"

"In my room. In Ben's desk."

"Okay, show me." I leave my coat and boots in the foyer and follow my mother. We cross the wide center hall that separates the very large and very dark dining and living rooms. At the far side of the dining room the sun peeks into the small breakfast room. It was once filled with hanging plants. Now there are dozens of empty glass jars and coffee cans stacked against the walls. Just beyond is the kitchen and back stairway, the beginning of a labyrinth of rooms that spill through one another, up and down the various levels of the house.

I stay close behind my mother as we climb the front stairs to her bedroom. I am mindful that she is barefoot and unsteady, neither of which was characteristic of her before. Except for this area, the floors are bare wood or tiled with colorful ceramic that my mother had especially imported from Colombia. This is a detail she used to repeat to me during my early visits, careful to point out that she and Ben had laid those floors themselves during their first year in the house. "It kept us occupied after everything happened." I understood she was referring to the first year of my exclusion from the family.

We enter my mother's bedroom through a mirrored dressing area that adjoins her bathroom. She stops there to touch the things on her dressing table.

"It is not here," she says in a shaky voice.

"This isn't the desk," I say. "Let's look inside." I put my hand on her shoulder to guide her forward and realize how thin she's become. As I pass the dressing table I pause too, drawn like a child to look through my mother's hairpins and lipsticks, and also to brace myself for the smell that will hit me as I enter her room. Stale and acrid, it is different and stronger than the mildew smell in the foyer. Despite the exhaustive search Julia and I have mounted for its specific source, it evades us.

My mother's room is the most private of her spaces. To enter it, even with her, makes me feel like an intruder. It is as formal as the rest of the house, with its high ceiling and arched doorway. A timid light enters through a corner window, and there is nothing comforting anywhere. The large bed is unmade, with a discolored bottom sheet and a worn electric blanket thrown to one side. It is strewn with several shoeboxes, plastic shopping bags, and an accordion folder, all filled with papers and receipts. On a stand in front of the bed is an old television set that is missing its knobs. It is attached to the same extension cord as the electric blanket, in a tangle of wires that hangs behind the bed's footboard. Books are randomly stacked on the television, night tables and along the windowsill. Against the far wall between the tall chest and dresser are several cardboard boxes, bulging and partially closed, and more books along the floor. Overhead, a small crystal chandelier has only one working bulb. In the center of the room, blocking the doors to her closets, stand two long, department store type metal clothing racks. One holds Ben's suits and shirts; the other is crammed with children's coats arranged in a variety of sizes. I make my way through the clutter to the other side of the bed where there is a bit of clear floor space in front of her dresser. On it are piles of folded sheets and blankets, and next to them, a stack of my mother's largest cooking pots and her kitchen blender. Business cards are inserted along the bottom edge of the oval mirror frame that crowns the dresser.

I glance behind the pots and see what was once the focal point of the room. It is a large silver-framed sepia photograph of my mother taken when she was twenty. She is seated at the edge of a high-sided bench. Muted light falls in through a set of French doors behind her. She is wearing a dark strapless gown that shows the soft line of her shoulders. She reclines slightly onto her left arm as her other arm is raised to cross it just below a delicate diamond bracelet on her wrist. Her nails are short and manicured. Around her neck hangs a small cameo on a dark velvet ribbon. She is looking beyond the camera, head tilted away a little, her curved eyebrows and full lips unsmiling under thick waves of blonde hair. I look at it and wonder why it is that women of my mother's generation found it fashionable to have formal portraits taken of themselves, and mine didn't.

Across the room, my mother stands by her desk. It is also cluttered with papers, held down by a metal fluorescent lamp, like the one Ben kept in his office. On the wall above the desk are two small photographs. One is a close-up of my little sister Isabella, about three, sitting in the grass next to my brother Gabriel, still an infant. Isabella is plump and sweet in her checkered pinafore and braids, her face an exaggeration of delight, her eyes brilliant and mouth exploding wide open as she looks at Gabriel's very serious, bald-headed baby face. Next to it is the only thing I have ever seen that resembles a family portrait, taken by a professional photographer during my last summer at home. It is an arranged pose on the living room couch, my mother seated in the center of her five children. Ben had worked unexpectedly late that afternoon, I remember, and missed the picture taking. We look awkward, every one of us. My mother grimaces, either in anger or embarrassment. Julia sits at one end with her mouth twisted, Carmela at the opposite side, staring long-necked into space, little Gabriel is half asleep on my mother's lap, Isabella next to him holding her skirt up over her face. I am in the center, uncomfortable and self-conscious in my new haircut, a few inches apart from the others.

Taped to the wall are numerous scraps of paper. Something is written on each in my mother's writing, which has become angular and disjointed. The biggest piece, torn from a steno pad, is a list of names and telephone numbers printed in large letters with black marker. Mine is the third number, after the local police precinct and Ben's office.

"Okay, Mom. Tell me what all this is."

"My important documents," she says, bending over the bed to examine the piles of papers, most of which appear to be receipts.

"Why don't we start putting them in some kind of order. That's always a good way to find something."

"What is lost?" She looks like a confused child.

"Oh. I misunderstood. I thought you'd lost something."

"No. I am just straightening up. There is so much to do." She has picked up what looks like a small black address book from the desk, also stuffed, and held together by a rubber band.

"Can I give you some help, Mom?"

"I am looking for Ann's number. She keeps calling me but I have no time to talk to her. She must have nothing to do all day because all she wants to do is talk." She sits at the edge of the desk chair and takes the rubber band off the book, shaking her head.

"Who is Ann?" I ask.

"She is an old friend of ours. You remember. Her husband died last year. Shipping. Left her with plenty of money, but too young. That is not a good combination for a woman. Men will prey on her. She probably wants to go out dancing tonight. I have to let her know I cannot go with her. Maybe some other time. I have too much to do." My mother handles the book carefully, to not let the contents fall out. "I am not an *americana*, you know. I do not cook TV dinners or spend my afternoons playing bridge like she does. Even if I believed in having servants, the way I was brought up, I would still use my time wisely to read a book or learn something, even a new recipe for my family. Ben will not want to go anyway. He will be too tired after working all day."

I reach behind the heavy drapes, the same shade of green as the walls, and open the window blinds. Dust floats off them as the sunlight pours in, and I crank the handle on the window to open it wide.

"Look at the snow, Mom. It's beautiful." I am trying to distract her from the story she is building in her mind. I remember Dr. Klein's name for it. Confabulation. When the mind is terribly confused yet cognitive enough to realize that, it invents an explanation to fill in the blanks of data it can't retrieve. "Your mother isn't lying. She is trying to make sense out of her confusion. It's one of the brain's last survival strategies before shutting down."

My mother is flipping pages, running her finger down the names as she goes from the front of the address book to the back, and back again, occasionally adjusting her glasses. The intense concentration in her face and the angle of her small body remind me of a schoolgirl's. I look around to assess what can be cleaned up without upsetting her any further. It occurs to me, suddenly, that she is in danger, alone in this firetrap of a room with only Julia in the house, upstairs in her attic apartment.

"Mom. Turn around for a minute."

"Yes?" She looks at me with surprise, as though she didn't expect me to be there. "What is it?"

"Look," I motion toward the window. "We had a snow storm last night. Isn't it beautiful?"

"Oh, my. I hope Julia comes home soon. Who is going to shovel?"

"She's already done it, Mom. The front is all cleared."

"Who did it?"

"Julia. She's still working out there. Helping the neighbors."

"Yes," she nods her head approvingly. "She helps the neighbors." Then, with eyes wide open, she smiles impishly and says, "But not her own mother!"

"That's okay," I laugh, capitalizing on her change of mood. "Julia does the outside work. You do the inside stuff. I can help you a little. What do you plan to work on today?" I turn the dial of the clock radio on the nightstand to the "on" position. The sounds of a piano fill the room.

"Haydn," she says, correctly, and closes her phonebook. She looks at her bed, puzzled. "I was going to work in the garden a little. But this is a mess. I do not know what happened here. Someone has been going through all my things."

"Let's put some of them away, then. Tell me what to start with."

"I do not know, Ronnie. You tell me."

"Well, it looks like you've been packing. What's in the boxes?" I motion to the far wall.

"Shoes. Isabella and Gabriel's. I had to move them in here from their rooms."

"Why is that?"

"So they will not be stolen. I think there are people stealing from me, Ronnie." My mother is whispering. "They must come in when I am not home. They leave everything in such a mess."

"Oh." I search for something to say. "We'll have to change the front door locks then. I'll talk to Julia about it. Maybe we can get that done today. First, let's put some of this mess away."

"What mess?"

"The bed. Let's take these things off and change the sheets. It's a good day for that." I hand her one of the shoeboxes.

"Where does this go?" she asks.

"I think in the desk drawers. Let's look." I open the center drawer of her desk and see her bankbook in the midst of old pens, pencils and other office things. I make a mental note that I need to buy paperclips and rubber bands. I hold the bankbook up to her. "Mom, is this your bankbook?"

She stares at what is in my hand, brow creased, biting her lip.

"Ronnie!" she whispers. "You found it! How did you find it?"

"It was in the desk drawer. You must have left it there for safekeeping."

"I do not remember that. Are you sure it is the right one? Maybe it belongs to someone else. Check to see the date. It should be current."

I open the bankbook. The last entry is dated two years ago. The balance is thirty-five dollars. "When were you at the bank last?" I ask her.

She thinks for a few seconds. "Yesterday. I had them enter my interest. There should be interest."

"Yes. You're okay with this. It isn't lost." I close the bankbook and slip it back in the desk. "Help me put these other papers away, Mom." We work together. I hand her things from the bed and she puts them into the desk.

"Who took all this out of here?" she asks again and again. I notice her fingernails. They are brittle and discolored, and filed into points. When we are finished, she sits on the chair again. I look at her feet. Her toenails are worse.

"Mom, help me find your slippers."

"Under the bed. Why do you want them?"

"For you," I say, squatting to look for them. Under her bed, indeed, are the frayed yellow corduroy slippers. Behind, a stash of canned foods, kidney beans, chicken noodle soups, tomato paste, Spam, evaporated milk.

I guide her feet into her slippers. "Have you eaten anything today Mom?"

"Sure. I had breakfast. Eggs and toast. Are you hungry?"

"Yes," I lie. "Why don't we finish this and get something to eat."

"Sorry. I am afraid I cannot cook for you, Ronnie. I have not gone shopping yet."

"That's okay, Mom. We'll find something in the pantry." I pull the sheet off the bed, throw it on the floor in the dressing room, and take a clean set from the pile on the dresser. She sits, observing me as though she were first learning how to change a bed. The smell and softness of the clean linen feel good. I fluff her pillow, remembering how I did this for my children, a wave of craving for their small bodies and scents washes over me.

"Where is your other pillow?" I ask.

She shrugs her shoulders. I look behind the bed. It is there, wedged between the headboard and another cardboard box. I shake it out, slip it into the clean case and place it on the bed. I smooth down the top sheet and fold the electric blanket at the foot of the bed, unplugging it to untangle the wires.

"You are too fancy, Ronnie," she says. "It is a waste of time to care so much."

"Thanks for the advice Mom, but it's too late." I smile at her.

"Too bad. You will end up wasting your life, like me." She crosses her legs and arms and slumps in the chair, a signal that her mood is changing. I need to work fast. I make my way through the clothes racks and push one away from the closet door as I speak.

"Mom. I was thinking about you the other day. About how stylish you were when I was little. When we lived on Union Square. You had such beautiful dresses."

She is quiet. I can't tell if she has understood what I've said or not. Then she shrugs her shoulders. "My mother was very stylish," she says, staring into space. "She made sure I always had the best. All my clothing was hand tailored. It was important, to maintain appearances. One's social class. That was the way it was." She shakes her head and sighs. "*Colombia.*" The word falls out of her mouth like it always has, a mixture of nostalgia and loathing.

I have made enough room. I open the closet door, a light goes on inside. There are men's shirts and slacks hanging on the rail, an iron and more blankets on the top shelf, closed shoeboxes on the floor. I close the door and make my way to the other closet, and move the other rack out of the way.

"Mom, what was it like when you were a young girl in Bogotá?"

She does not answer. I try again. "During the time in that picture on your dresser."

This closet is cedar and larger than the other, but no light goes on when I open the door. I step inside and find the pull chord. The space is crammed with clothing arranged in sections—skirts, blouses, suits, dresses, slacks. Three closed garment bags hang at the far end, past the suits. A separate compartment for shoes holds pairs of dark-colored high heels, several open backs in reds and beiges, and an array of glittered evening shoes. Along the top shelf is a collection of pretty decorated boxes, a row of handbags, and a stack of small hats, some with netting. On a rack along the floor are more shoes, all flats, in disarray. I hear my mother's voice, muffled, but I can't make out what she is saying. I reach for one of the garment bags and unzip it. Inside are more dresses, her better ones, in wools, linens, a few velvets, each with the trademark style of her youth: long sleeves, shoulder pads, gathered waist. I lean into them, resting my cheek up against the soft material, handling the rows of tiny buttons and loops at their necklines. I linger there, close to my mother's things.

"Ronnie?"

I hear the anxiety in her voice. I take a quick glance to find a pair of slacks to put on her, and decide against it. I see several bathrobes behind the door and step out of the closet.

"Mom, what color is your bathrobe?"

"What do you want my bathrobe for?" She stands up and walks toward me, irritated. "Do not throw it away, Ronnie. I know you would like to throw everything of mine away. Just like my mother." She pulls the closet door open and grabs a pink robe off the hook. "Every time I had favorite dress, she would give it away to the poor. She did not want me wearing the same dress twice. High society. Who cares! Get out of my closet, Ronnie. I do not need your help with my clothing."

I notice, but not for the first time, my mother's phrasing. It is the result of her education in Colombo-British schools in Bogotá, where she learned to avoid contractions when speaking English. As if using them was an affront to her social class and on the language itself, one she commands exquisitely, accent and all, and has no qualms about correcting whenever it is misspoken in her presence.

"I'm sorry, Mom. You're right. You can keep the robe. It's yours. Let me see what it looks like on you."

"It is just an old thing," she grumbles and puts it on.

"Nice." I pat her shoulder gently and turn her toward the dresser mirror. She sees her reflection and cringes.

"*Que horror*! Who is that?"

"It's you and me, Mom. We're both having a bad hair day." She hesitates, then laughs, and I laugh with her. "Where do you keep your hairbrush?"

"I do not use a brush," she says deliberately. "Only a comb. A brush will cause you to lose your hair." She leads me to her dressing table and begins to comb her hair. It is tangled and dirty. I am tempted to offer to wash it, but I know better. Instead, I go into her bathroom to find a washcloth. Daylight splashes on the black and salmon-colored tiles, giving the room a warm glow. The sink and tub need scrubbing, but the bathroom is cleaner than I expected, and surprisingly, it doesn't smell bad. Inside the stall shower is another cache of canned foods and a small electric fan. There is no washcloth.

"Ronnie, that is my bathroom," she calls to me, her voice becoming whiny. "Use one of the others." Then, under her breath she mutters, "*Que cosa!* Six bathrooms in this house and people have to use mine."

"I'm not using it, Mom. Just looking for a washcloth. You have something on your face."

"Where? I do not see anything."

"It's too dark in there. If you come in here you'll see better." She comes to the sink and, without looking in the mirror, reaches for the bar of soap and washes her face. I hand her a towel. I wait to see if she will automatically brush her teeth next, or if that habit is gone too. She does, scrubbing hard and using her hand to rinse her mouth several times. I look at her reflection in the mirror while she dries her hands. Her hair is off her face, clipped back. The wildness is gone. I put my arm around her.

"Good," I say. "You look great. Don't you think?" We look at our reflection again, then at each other, and she reaches up to pat my back, in quick little taps.

"You are very kind," she says. "I do not know who you take after, in this family."

"The mailman, Mom."

She laughs hard, her head thrown back and chest bouncing.

"Okay,'" I say. "I'm hungry. And Julia will be coming in from shoveling soon. Let's go see what we can dig up in the kitchen."

"You go down ahead of me Ronnie. I need to do something first," she says.

"I'll start the coffee."

She closes the door behind me as I walk out. Her voice is back to normal. The panic is gone. It is okay to leave her, I think, and walk down the back steps of the house to the kitchen. Halfway down I stop to listen for her movement out of the bathroom. I think about my mother's remark. How the very words she once used to exclude me from the family are now transformed into affection, not by any degree of effort or insight, but by an illness.

As I enter the kitchen I realize how cold the house is. I look at the big wall clock over the sink. It is just past noon, six hours before the heat turns on for the evening. A necessary regimen, my mother insists, to allay the cost of heating the big house for only two people. I get my wool scarf from my jacket and wrap it around my neck. Coffee will warm me up. I see the percolator on the stove, an old metal drip type. I spill out the old coffee it holds, rinse it and fill it with water. I look around the kitchen for my mother's open supply of coffee, usually Maxwell House in jumbo sized cans. The countertops are covered with piles of mail bundled in rubber bands, a stack of pot lids, old copies of *Money* magazine, and a toaster I recognize from the Union Square days. Behind the sink, taped onto the backsplash, is another of my mother's lists. It is a reminder for Julia, projects she is to get done before Thanksgiving. The yellow paper is faded and the lettering is uneven. The list could be years old. Clean gutters. Repair front steps (cement is loose). Fix outside spigot near garage. Regrout all bathtubs. Trim hedges upper garden. Rehang ceiling tiles (playroom). Do Not Delay.

At the foot of the back stairs is an old green leather chair, more Union Square. It is cracked in several places, the stuffing pushing through strips of masking tape, a few sweaters and a blanket thrown on it. Behind it, strung together along the banister, is a collection of faded greeting cards addressed to my mother.

I remember seeing coffee cans on a shelf in the breakfast room, but then realize that is where my mother stashes the empties. I give up my search for an open can and look for a fresh one. I open her cabinets. Each is neatly organized, labels facing front, and overstuffed with large quantities of baking supplies, canned foods, bags of pasta in a variety of shapes, and all types of spices. In the corner cabinet, next to her glassware, vials of prescription medication, arranged chronologically from the bottom shelf up, current ones at eye level, last year's above, expired ones beyond my mother's reach. Valium, Lipitor, penicillin, Erythromycin, Darvon compound, and the newest, Aricept. On each shelf is an extra-large size bottle of store brand aspirin tablets. No coffee.

I try the refrigerator, where I keep my coffee. It is also crammed with food, tied in re-used plastic bags. I see eggs and cheese, but no coffee, and think I will make omelets for my mother and sister. The largest cabinet, the pantry, is a storehouse of baking pans, molds, glass and ceramic serving platters, bowls, and trays in many sizes, shapes and materials. One whole shelf contains neatly folded large and small recycled paper bags. Another holds hundreds of white and yellow Styrofoam trays, the packing type used in supermarkets, washed and neatly stacked by size.

I sit at the table in the center of the kitchen, sure that from here I can figure out where my mother has moved her coffee. It is a Formica table, white and oval, and vaguely familiar, but not from Union Square. I do a visual reexamination of the kitchen, but come up empty. My fingers are numb from the cold. I decide to forego coffee and begin to make the omelets. The front door opens and I can hear Julia stomping the snow off her boots in the vestibule. Good, I think, now I'll find coffee.

"My God! It's cold out there!" Julia marches into the kitchen. "What are you doing sitting in here?" I think about how my sister's delivery is generally the same, regardless of the content or purpose of her words. Somewhere between Groucho Marx and the Spanish Inquisition. She cannot, I know, stop to rest.

"I'm on a mission. Trying to find coffee."

"Coffee? I made coffee this morning." She moves to the sink, spotting the disassembled percolator. "What happened here? Did you do this?"

"Yes I did. It just needs the ground coffee. But I couldn't find it." I am working to reassure her, but I'm not sure of what.

"It's out here," she says and walks out to the mudroom off the kitchen. It hadn't occurred to me to look there. She gives a grunt of irritation. "There are at least fifty cans of coffee out here." I rise just as she returns, coffee can in hand, and both of us move toward the sink at the same time. We collide. "Never mind!" she growls and reaches for the percolator. "I'll do it."

I return to the table. I know there is no point in challenging Julia when she is like this. I look at the floor, and notice the white tiles that are cracked and have chipped corners. I think about the time it must have taken for my mother and Ben to lay all of it, while I waited for them to call.

"Did she come down?" Julia asks, her tone calmer now.

"Yes, but only to open the door for me. I managed to get her cleaned up a little. She needs a bath and a shampoo."

"You do it. She lets you do anything."

"Not really."

"Yes she does." Julia counts out eight scoops of coffee and puts them into the percolator basket. "You're the only person in the history of Eva that has ever been allowed to cook in her kitchen. I've been living with her all my life and she's never let me even peel a cucumber. You walk in here and say you're going to cook and she lets you. I have to sneak around just to make a sandwich."

"It's because I remind her of her mother, Julia."

"Yeah." She pauses, takes a tissue from her pants pocket and blows her nose, hard. "She says that all the time about you. Maybe that's it. But you know how to talk to her. I have no patience." Julia turns on the burner for the coffee and sits down at the table across from me.

"You've lived with her longer," I answer. "I had nearly thirty years away from her. It makes a difference. In some ways for the worse, and in others for the good."

"She's too much. Too much." Julia looks at the floor now, shaking her head, her hands tucked into her pants pocket along with the tissue. "She's getting worse every day. Now she doesn't come down from that room until the middle of the night. Then she starts walking around the house talking to herself. She's constantly moving food around, canned food. I'm upstairs and I hear her. The first few days it scared the hell out of me. Now I just let her do it."

"Remember what Dr. Klein said," I say. "Maybe it's time to start thinking about getting some help for both of you. Taking her to the senior center, hiring an attendant to come a few hours a day."

"She'll never go for it." Julia says. "You'll never get her near a senior center. She's too vain. She still thinks she's forty."

"We can try. If we can get her over there, just to see it, maybe she'll go for it."

"And how do you suggest we do that?" Julia gives a forced laugh.

"We can tell her we're taking her for a ride, like we did when we took her to the doctor."

"Forget it. That was a nightmare. She wouldn't get dressed. She wouldn't leave the house." Julia's voice is getting agitated again. She moves toward the stove and checks the coffee pot.

"Okay. Let's try it this way," I say. "I'll come over here one morning, like I did today. When the weather gets better. I'll get her dressed and ask her to come for a ride with me. I think she'll do it."

"Yeah. Then what? Suppose we get her there. What makes you think she'll go there every day?"

"We don't know that. We can just try. She needs stimulation and contact with the outside world. The changes in her brain are confusing her. At least we can try. Even if she goes twice a week." I can hear myself pleading, weakening. "And you need to start thinking about getting a home attendant, Julia. You can't keep this up. She needs to be supervised now. And you need time to yourself too."

"Forget that. I don't need any help." She paces between the spot she's been in and the stove. "I can handle her. She's not an invalid. And she'll never go for anybody coming into her house." She stops, gets two mugs from the cupboard and sets them on the table. Silence sits between us for a few minutes. "Dammit, the coffee's spilling!" She leaps to turn down the flame, then takes a paper towel and wipes the coffee off the range. The subject is changed.

"Did she eat anything?" Julia asks.

"Not yet. I was going to make her an omelet."

"She's very picky you know." She gets two spoons from the drawer and sets one next to each mug on the table. "No matter what I serve her, she won't eat it until I order her to. She doesn't believe I can cook anything."

"What do you make for her?"

"Sandwiches, mostly. Tuna, cheese, anything. What she likes most is peanut butter. She'll eat that in a second." Julia leans against the counter, crosses her arms and looks out the window. "That was some storm."

"Julia, we'll have to work together on her hair."

My sister's face contorts. "No. I'm not touching her hair. You do it."

"Not today. Today I got her sheets changed, and that was plenty."

"What I need is to get into that room and clean out the crap she has in there." Julia suddenly comes close to me, glances over her shoulder to the stairs behind her and whispers. "That's what we'll do. The next time you come, you distract her out here and I'll get into that cave she lives in." She is as thrilled as a child solving a riddle. "Did you see the stinking crap under her bed? It's disgusting. Disgusting! I have to get it out of here. It'll be a cleansing!"

"There's more in her stall shower," I say, laughing at my sister's delight. Julia laughs too.

"What is that? Why is she doing that?" she asks. "It drives me crazy." Despite the laughter I can see the exhaustion in my sister's face, her eyes small and the corners of her mouth drawn downward.

I use my most reassuring tone. "She doesn't know she's doing it, Julia. It isn't intentional."

"I don't believe it. She has to know what she's doing. She's no dummy." Julia walks to the refrigerator and looks inside. She hasn't taken off her coat.

"She certainly was smart," I say. "But now she's sick."

"I guess so." Julia takes out a milk container and pours some into her coffee.

"Take out the eggs and the cheese too," I say. "We'll make the omelets."

"You make them."

"Okay. You relax. You did all that shoveling. Why don't you sit down and rest?" I motion to the chair she just left. She hesitates, looks at the chair, then up at the clock.

"I'm going down to feed the dogs. I'll be back." She walks to the basement door just outside the kitchen and stops, then runs down the steps calling out affectionately to her two rescued dogs, who howl back to her excitedly.

After a few minutes, the coffee starts its dance in the percolator. I get the eggs and cheese, some butter, and find a large frying pan. I focus on the omelet, on getting the right consistency before I turn it over, cheating by using a plate. I like the silence, and immediately become aware that I haven't heard any sounds from my mother's room since Julia came in.

"Mom," I call from the bottom of the stairs. "Can you hear me?"

There is no answer, no movement.

"Mom," I call again, nearly yelling, and start up the stairs. A faint sound comes from the dining room, behind me.

"*Aquí.*"

I walk into the darkened room. My mother is sitting cross-legged on an armchair in the corner, near the window and behind a plant, her head resting on one hand. She is rocking herself, biting her lip. Her face is wild again, her eyes fixed on one spot on the floor. I walk to her, take her hand and pat it a few times. It is knarled and rough.

"How long have you been sitting here, Mom?" I want to know how much she's heard of my conversation with Julia.

"Since I came in from the garden." She does not change her gaze nor stop rocking. "I am very tired. I did a lot of work out there today. The weeds are taking over the side of the house, where my roses are supposed to be. Someone has stolen them. Why would anyone want to destroy someone else's work?" She turns her body away from the window. "Bastards."

"Mom, I'm very hungry. I've made an omelet but it's too big. Can you help me eat some of it?" I pull her gently up on her feet. She complies.

"You eat it, Ronnie. I am gaining too much weight."

We are back in the kitchen. She goes straight to the green Union Square chair and sits, cross-legged again, at its edge. I check the omelet. It is ready.

"I smell coffee."

"Yes, Mom. Julia just made some." I walk to the cupboard and get her cup, a large cup enameled sky blue, the inside coffee-stained white. "Where'd you get this cup, Ma?"

"It was Gabriel's." She smiles. "He does not use it any more, so I do. Do you want it?"

"No, no," I laugh. "Just wondering. It's so unusual." I divide the omelet into three parts, serve two into plates and leave the third in the pan, covered, for Julia. "Come over here to the table Mom. We'll eat together."

"That is not necessary Ronnie. You make such a fuss. I am alright here."

I hand her a plate and set down her cup of coffee on the counter within reach. I sit at the table with mine and begin to eat. Except for my mother's sighing, it is quiet for a while. I can hear the faint sounds of children playing in the snow.

"Mom, would you like some bread?" I remember that I've omitted her favorite ingredient in any meal.

"No thanks," she says, still at the edge of her chair, looking deep in thought. I get up and open the breadbox anyway, and put a slice of whole wheat onto her dish.

"Ronnie?" She sounds very far away, but she is looking at me.

"I'm right here, Mom." I sit again.

"Do not forget to close the window in my room. It will get very cold. We will be wasting heat."

"Okay, Mom," I answer, a spontaneous smile coming across my face. "I'll do it as soon as I finish my coffee."

"Ronnie?"

"Yes, Mom."

She rises abruptly and moves to the table, close to me, setting her coffee cup down in the center of her plate, pushing her piece of omelet and bread away, still untouched. She is standing over me, eyes as dark as night, her voice lowered but deliberate, and I feel suddenly small.

"Tell me the truth, Veronica Elizabeth. Do I have that sickness that happens to old people, when they forget everything, and die?"

I am stunned, completely unprepared for her question, for the innocence and fragility in her face, for the tenderness I feel toward her in this moment.

"No, you don't, Mom."

She exhales slowly, deeply. She has believed me. After a moment, she reaches into the pocket of her robe and pulls out a folded piece of white paper. She takes my hand and places it in my palm, and says, "Here, take this home, you need it." She sits down on the green chair again.

I thank her and put the paper into my pants pocket to open later. I hand her the plate again. "Eat some more, Mom. You should eat." She stares at the food, taking a long time before she moves her fork, pushing it around the dish with little gestures, as if she were searching for something underneath. The omelette is long cold, along with her coffee, but I know she will refuse my offer to warm them up.

Julia rushes back into the room again and goes directly to the sink to wash her hands.

"Your omelet is on the stove," I say. She takes a plate from the cupboard and serves herself, and begins to eat, standing.

"Did she eat anything?" She gives a sideward glance at my mother.

"No. Just some coffee," I answer.

"Eat!" She scolds my mother. "You're going to get sick. You'll wind up in the hospital."

"Leave me alone," my mother snaps back and turns away.

"You see this?" Julia looks at me. "This is what I get. Stubbornness!" Julia takes the plate from my mother's hand and cuts the cold omelet into small pieces with the fork. "Here. Eat. One piece." She looks at me again. "How ridiculous is this? It's all backwards now. I'm forcing *her* to eat."

"Give her peanut butter if that's what she likes, Julia. The point is to get her to eat. Don't wear yourself out." I rise as I speak and walk to the foyer to get my jacket, then back to the kitchen to kiss my mother on the cheek and say my goodbyes.

"Come back soon, Ronnie," my mother calls behind me.

"Sure, Mom. I will."

Julia has gone ahead to the vestibule. She unlocks the main door, then the iron gate. I pull on my coat and boots, and notice she still hasn't taken off her jacket. "Get some heat on in here Julia. You're going to get sick. Mom, too."

"Fine, fine. She stays up in her cave all day anyway. And I'm upstairs, or out." I walk past her, into the white, fresh afternoon. I take a long, deep breath. Julia comes up behind me. "Remember. Next time it's a search and destroy mission."

I can hear my sister's mischievous laughter as I walk down the steps and along the path to the driveway. I sit behind the wheel of my car and wait for it to heat up. I breathe slowly. I make a mental plan for the rest of the day. Gas for the car, the supermarket, the stationery store, rent a movie, call my kids, call a friend, play some Chopin, warm soup, hot chocolate and an English muffin, write a little, read, in my warm apartment. I turn back to pull out of the driveway and feel something jabbing into my leg. I reach under my coat, into my pants pocket. It is the white paper my mother gave me. Not a paper, but an envelope, folded. I open it. Inside are eight paper clips, six rubber bands.

everything is different
it is raining it is very hot and the smells are not the same
Uncle Mickey is carrying me under an umbrella
he is talking to another lady i don't know
niña niña she is calling to me
with her hands open like Mommy does
when she helps me out of the tub
niña niña but that is not my name
Uncle Mickey passes me to her
Abuela he says Grandmother
i don't want this lady i want Mommy
i push away from her hard
niña she says again turning me bouncing me
i push hard as i can and i cry
she gives me back to Uncle Mickey
niña malcriada she sounds mean
i hold onto Uncle Mickey
so he will take me back to Mommy
i make believe i am asleep
like we do when Mommy comes in to check on us
Carmela showed me
all you have to do is stare into the insides of your eyes
and lie real still is all
but i never get it right
because i laugh and Mommy gets mad
this time i do it good
and the nice little lady who put me into bed
can't tell that i am not really sleeping
Uncle Mickey told her to undress me
right after he promised me
You will go home to Mommy in the morning
if you stop crying
i watch the nice little lady put my clothes on the chair
and shut the door
i hear her talk to Uncle Mickey and *Abuela* in that other way
they think i am asleep but i am not
i am in a very big bed bigger than Mommy's

but i don't like it here i must go back to Mommy
She is waiting in the dark for me
i find my clothes i can dress myself
i get my coat on but the buttons are too hard for me
shoelaces too
i sit on the *maleta*
i will be ready
when Uncle Mickey takes me home
in the morning

Wait

It never got easier, and I never got used to it. It was the condition you forced on me, and for the thirty years that I didn't get to call you Mom, it didn't matter what I did or didn't do. I was *prohibida*, excluded from my family. Access Denied. My only choice was to forget you, or wait.

Of course there really isn't any forgetting. Not willfully, anyway. I've heard people on both sides of estrangement tell themselves that lie in order to convince themselves, to make the wait bearable. One week, one month, one year, one decade after the other. Ultimately, waiting for you became what defined me more than anything else I've done.

When you wait in silence a long time, you see, you develop this ability to exist in two places at once. It's like a part of you is drugged or drunk, and the other one functions pretty well. On the outside you keep moving, but inside you're really stopped. Not resting—I don't remember ever feeling rested. Just stopped. That was the sense I had from the beginning, from the night you told me to leave your house. I was a teenager walking out into that blizzard. I remember I didn't have any gloves, I'd left them behind in the commotion, and I really loved those gloves, a blue-gray knitted pattern I'd just gotten for my birthday from that sweet boy, Adam, who liked me so and I didn't realize it, or couldn't realize it, then. I pushed through the snow and wind as fast as I could to get away from your fury. Still, when I think about it, all this time, I've never moved from that spot on your front porch, waiting to be called back in. I looked for a pair of gloves like those for years.

It didn't fit me, being excluded. It was unnatural. I liked people. And people liked me. It wasn't that you were dead, or some awful act of fate had separated us. I had a mother, a family, and we lived in the same city, practically in the same neighborhood, close enough to run into. I mean, the situation was very strange. I couldn't see you, or share my life with you. But I didn't hate you. You wouldn't let me come home—that was *punto, final*— but you couldn't make me hate you.

So, where could I go from there?

It became my way of life. This sense that there was always something else out there, lingering, unfinished. The way you can walk back into a room, certain you've left something important behind, but you don't know what it is and you search, thoroughly, but can't find anything. A part of me was always missing. I could never relax, really, because I was expecting something, someone, to show up. So I was distracted from my real life. Always preparing to be burst in on.

I didn't know where I belonged. No one called me sister, or *hija*, or daughter. I wanted to belong to my husband, to his family, later to my work, to a lover. But I wasn't welcomed by my own people, so it was hard to claim anything as mine. With my own children, there was a part of me, even if I didn't want to hear it, that kept nagging—in the background and barely audible, but relentlessly—*This, too. Don't get too used to this.*

You probably thought it was the opposite. That I did hate you, that I was free of you, enjoying myself and didn't think of you at all. Well, you were wrong. I thought about all of you. Not together, the way other people think about family. We almost never did anything together, anyway, did we? You'd come to me one at a time, a slide show running in my mind. Sometimes in rapid fire images of Carmela at the piano, her long legs over the pedals and her body swaying like a wild bird about to soar. Or it would catch me by surprise when I'd be brushing my hair; I'd see you at your mirror, deep in thought and not even looking at yourself, your fingers moving quickly to insert those brown plastic hair pins that held your twist in place. None of you ever got any older to me, because I had no stories to go with the images.

I'd see people, strangers in the street or in shops who had something of one of you, and I'd watch them. I'd follow a young woman who spoke fast and loud like Julia, or was lanky like Carmela and had her full lips. Especially a woman who had a strong walk and great legs, whose ankles were in perfect symmetry inside a pair of high heels, making that raspy click on the pavement, like yours did. I'd go out of my way behind her, for blocks. Sometimes I'd want to walk up to someone like that and touch her arm or shoulder, just to say hi again, to hear your voices. I'd bump into them, not hard, just enough to make contact.

It's a tricky thing, you know, how a face can stay clear and fixed in your mind, and then enough time goes by without seeing it again and you can hardly make out the features anymore. It's around you, shadowing you, and you know it's there because your belly tightens or your mouth suddenly gets dry when you think of the person. But you can't find the face, not the full image, only parts. That's how it happened. It was slow, but in time I forgot what you looked like.

Sure it was lonely. Especially after Michél left. Nothing was ever simple again. A visit to the doctor was a walk through a minefield of missing information about myself, reminding me how far out of the family I was, and one with so many women in it. I remember after I gave birth the second time a nurse told me I should have used cream on my skin to avoid stretch marks. It wasn't the stretch marks that bothered me but the sting of having a perfect stranger give me that little piece of advice. And just entering a supermarket felt like the ascent of the Cyclone ride at Coney Island. I'd have one child on each hand and very little money. I could navigate pretty well through the produce and grocery aisles. But the meat case was always difficult. That frigid air would hit my face as I'd turn over one cold package after another in my search for something small and affordable, and the sight of "family style" roasts and rows of chops would weaken my knees.

An old woman approached me once to offer help. She must have seen that lost expression I wore in those days, the one I hate to see in old photographs. She was very kind, and took time to explain to me that whole turkeys don't come smaller than twelve pounds. I bought one anyway. Then I discovered that it didn't matter how much my two girls and I could eat, even on Thanksgiving. My little family hardly made a dent. The leftover bird sat in the center of the refrigerator, untouched for days, until I surrendered, bitterly, and threw it out, fixings and all, into a heavy-duty trash bag.

I was very good at keeping the whole thing to myself. There was no one else to tell, and I could fake it pretty well—I mean, being sociable when I had to be. I thought I owed that to my girls, that they shouldn't see my unhappiness. I'd be pleasant to people, keeping up a good appearance. Of course the girls saw right through me. You know, the way children do when they try to fill in for what's missing by being extra good or by misbehaving. They end up acting just like the missing people did. It's uncanny, how one of my girls could be quiet and removed like Carmela or Gabriel, and the other could be in-my-face provocative like you. They didn't do it to hurt me. I knew that, but it could make me feel small, invisible, like you made me feel. And they hadn't even met you.

It really wasn't fair to them. The girls bore the brunt of it. I was hurting, and it passed on to them. I'd say awful things. I used to threaten that I was going to leave, get in my car and go to the airport to catch the next plane out, to get far away from them. They'd get really quiet and then I wouldn't know what to do next. When it got really bad, those times when I hated the hard work that never ended, the loneliness, the worry, the managing of so much with no sign of anything ever changing, what I hated most was being me. I'd loose control and let out on the children. The smallest thing could go wrong, and that would start a spiral downward. I'd warn them first. I knew I couldn't hold on much more. I'd hear myself yell, knowing I was losing ground, getting smaller as the whole mess got bigger, until the children I loved didn't matter anymore. I'd hit, almost always Jackie. I'd hold her arms and smack her, hard, and a lot. It was all upside down, because I wanted my children to understand, to make it better, to help me somehow. All the time I'd be sobbing, seeing myself doing what I swore I'd never do, knowing all that rage wasn't meant for them, you know, it was for you. I remember how in the midst of it all I wanted was someone to appear, to grab my arms and stop me, to help. No, I didn't do the same things you did, but I hurt my children too. You know, I can still feel it in my hands now, that sting, all regret and shame and confusion.

Still, I could never do what you did. No matter what went wrong. I couldn't leave my daughters in such aloneness.

There were good days. I'd be cruising down the highway in my little two-door diesel Chevette with the wind blowing in and my girls squealing in the back seat playing some made-up game that made them laugh hard, and I'd think, go ahead, just pick up the phone when you get home and dial the number and say, "Hi, I was at the beach today with my kids and the sky was a spectacular royal blue and the water was warm and the waves were coming in big and fast and I was remembering how we used to love going to Brighton Beach and you'd spend the whole night before frying up a batch of chicken and making your great potato salad and we'd all carry the bags and coolers to just the right spot for Ben to open the big umbrella and we'd be happy for a few hours and then singing and making noise in the back of Ben's car on the way home, and I wonder how you are." Then we could all finally wake up from this awful thing and treat it like a bad night's sleep and have a normal life. On days like that, it seemed just that simple.

But I knew better. You were *orgullosa*, proud that you never went back on your word. Even if you actually missed me. I knew you. You'd have found just the right Spanish proverb, a mantra you'd repeat to yourself while you were working around your house, maybe at your machine sewing, to write me off. *Los perros ladran, pero la caravana sigue andando.* The dogs may bark but the caravan keeps moving. And you'd feel justified, even obligated, to continue to punish me. I never understood what there was in that to be proud of, but I knew you couldn't stop yourself.

It wasn't only a mother you took from me. You took my sisters too. They followed you, wouldn't talk to me, even years later when they didn't live with you. Sure, Isabella and Gabriel were just toddlers when I left, so they never really got to know me. But Julia and Carmela, weren't they ever curious about me? When I had babies? Did they even know that? I sent Ben cards both time. But I never heard from him. Why didn't he ever do anything to get us together?

Eventually even the shadows started to fade. I'd be playing something, a Beethoven piano sonata, the Pathetique, say, and it would be a few hours later when I'd realize that I hadn't thought of Carmela once, and she'd played it so beautifully. It was unnerving, like having little spells, when I'd be disconnected from feeling anything about you. Not afraid or angry, not even sad anymore. Just space. I told myself it was a good thing, that I'd finished feeling bad. It had been five, ten years already. I began to admit it to myself. This is what it would be. This *silencio*. We were never all going to be together again.

I was lucky because I had the girls to raise. Had to make sure they were healthy and well educated. I certainly followed you in that. I had my work, and I was good at it. I went back to flamenco classes. I took a few piano lessons. I even made a few friends, mostly through the girls' activities, a neighbor, one or two through work. That took time. I didn't feel comfortable with women. They seemed to know so much more than I did about being female. The incidental things, especially the stuff small talk is about, like brand names and facials. And the way most women could talk about sex, joke about it, and I couldn't. But I began to see that they cared, and they were kind to me. I still have those friends.

I couldn't offer my children grandparents or aunts and uncles, but we had friends. On ordinary days, or sad ones, or for celebrations, we were welcomed at other peoples' tables. Those hours with other families were lessons, really the only experience my kids and I had with family. I'd watch things. The mundane little rituals people have with their clans that never developed with my own. You know, how a toddler's voice rises in the same inflection as a grandfather's, or those quick private jokes that bounce between siblings and are all about family stories, or the rhythms and patterns that families have, how they synchronize tempo with one another without knowing it, and have the same gestures and postures, even the same walk as other generations. All those things that give a family its texture, I watched.

I was grateful for that. But underneath, there were some hard truths none of us could talk about. As the girls got older, they backed away from invitations to other people's homes, holidays or no. And I knew why, and stayed away too. My friends had good intentions. I knew that. But being included into someone else's family to substitute for your own inevitably draws attention to the missing. I guess the girls had had enough, especially of those hard, silent rides home when we'd all be weighted down, them missing their Dad, I suppose, and me yearning for all of you.

There were just so many of you not there. And you were so nearby. I never have found a good answer to give anyone who asks about you. Especially to my children.

Still, if you'd asked me, I would have told you. All I wanted was to see you again. It's true. You fascinated me. I never met anyone like you. Maybe everyone feels like this about their family, I don't know. I never wanted to go back to living in that fear and sadness that shrouded us, no. But there was nothing mediocre about any of you. I missed that.

It was the mixture, the odd combinations of everything, our contradictions and extremes. I didn't find that anywhere else. We were people who could spend the morning listening to the Brandenburg concertos and dance a barefoot *cumbia* in the living room at lunchtime. The languages, the personalities, how we could eat knishes one day and *arepas* the next. We didn't even look alike, any of us. I had two Catholic siblings and two Jewish ones, a dead Italian father no one ever mentioned and a leftist stepfather living under the same roof with a Presbyterian aristocratic *Colombiana* mother.

We were beautiful to look at, talented, funny and well bred. We still are. I remember at Ben's funeral, how we connected, and we all liked each other. Anyone watching us would never believe how it really is.

In all my life I've only known one person who could take off her good coat on a bitter wintry day and hand it to a homeless woman in the park, just like that, and later turned her back on her own child.

Sure I missed you. I spent my life wanting to be with you again.

No one else came close.

Tesoro
that's what Tia Elena calls me
and that's what i pretend to be when i am in here
treasure
whenever she visits she brings me a treat
usually a *dulce de coco* sweet coconut candy
or sometimes *chicle*
Mommy would not like it
She doesn't want me to chew gum
anyway i think she forgot about me by now
nobody talks about Mommy here
not since the night i came and wouldn't stop crying
one time Tia Elena brought a pink tea set
and we played with two make-believe little girls
i am happy she is going to marry Uncle Mickey
he makes her laugh the way Mommy used to
before she sent me away on the plane
the little lady Elsa was nice too
she used to dress me and make my braids
just like Mommy with the ribbons in between
and call me *tesoro* too
but Elsa hasn't been back since that day
when *La Abuela* took the big whip to her
for stealing food
the whip with long tails
i miss Elsa
i don't think she's just a dirty servant
even if Abuela calls her *una puerca sirvienta*
even if i am getting somebody new tomorrow
mostly i am glad Elsa ran away to be with her baby
when i am bigger i will run away too
and find Mommy
i'm used to it now
when Abuela puts me in here
nobody bothers me
i can just sit back here on top of these boxes
and be like hidden treasure

pretend to have golden hair just like Mommy
and wait until a fairy princess finds me some day
and i can fly back to that other place
where Mommy is
anyway the dark used to scare me
but now i can reach that string and pull on the light
you can see right through the plastic pockets
that hang on the wall
red shoes black shoes white brown
all have a number five inside
when i get big my feet will slide right to the toes
then i will put on these smooth red ones
just like Dorothy's
in the *cine* Uncle Mickey took me to
i will click my heels three times and i'll be home too
all i have to do is eat all my food like Elsa said
and not get those hives that make Abuela mad
if i do that my feet will grow
i think Abuela forgets i am in here
it is a very long time until one of the servants comes
usually it is Edoardo
i can tell by his funny walk
like he has gum stuck on his shoe
it isn't nice to laugh at him
Uncle Mickey calls him *el cojo* sometimes
and Edoardo makes a face back
when nobody is looking
he is here with the keys to let me out
by now Abuela isn't angry anymore
i can never figure it out
i think i'm being good
and all of a sudden Abuela is mad
she does not like me
Tia Elena says Abuela prefers boy children
i am glad she only uses the whip for the servants
Uncle Mickey told me
she whips them because they are not loyal

i don't know what loyal is
but i will try not to make any mistakes after dinner
when Edoardo clears the big table
and Abuela sits in the end chair
her brown hand points at the page
and she says *comienze niña*
i will read for her
from the top of the big page
all the way to the bottom
i like the words
they are the same as i used to know before
in that other place i lived with Mommy
now only Uncle Mickey speaks to me like that
i wonder
is it Mommy that sends the newspaper every day
'cause on the very top it says
the New York Times

3

Edoardo calls it the baby game
i think it's because Uncle Mickey calls me baby
but when he goes to fly the planes
Edoardo bothers me
when nobody is watching he whispers baby baby
and i get scared and run away from him
i never go through the kitchen or *el patio*
i am not allowed to because the servants live there
it really started because of me
because of that day the box came during breakfast
Edoardo brought it into the dining room
de los Estados Unidos he said to *La Abuela*
i know that is the name of where i lived before
and Abuela told him to open it
so he cut the paper and string with the big scissors
and then right there on the table he put the little box
that said Crayola Crayons and the coloring book
i know it was Mommy inside that box
but Abuela said *ahora no*
she put the Crayola Crayon box and the coloring book
on top of the book case
so i would have to wait
and i was sad but i didn't cry
Abuela really hates it
so when everybody was asleep i cried in the big bed
i really wanted the Crayola Crayons
and the coloring book
and Mommy
and all of a sudden Edoardo was there
right by my bed in the dark
he took the blankets off
and took my hand and said baby baby
and then we walked down the cold white stairs
and i was scared because it was so quiet and so dark
and we walked into the dining room and then
Edoardo reached way up on top of the book case
and got the box of Crayola Crayons

and the coloring book
and gave them to me and i held them in my hands
and then we walked through *el patio* into a small room
that had a funny bed on the floor with no legs
much smaller than my big bed upstairs
and Edoardo laid me down on the funny bed
and took down my pajama pants
and took down his pants
and then he laid down on top of me
and i couldn't see anymore or breathe
but after a while i got to open the box of crayons
and pick any page in the coloring book
we play the baby game a lot
i make sure i stay inside the lines when i color
so i will have nice pictures to give to Mommy
if i ever see her again

Primitiva

The love I feel for my mother confuses people. My children, friends, lovers, have only known me to be without her. They watched me wait for an end to the decades of separation she forced between us, no reconciliation in sight, until this. My oldest friends, especially, who held a place for me at their tables when my own family would not claim me, shake their heads now as they ask me how I am.

"You look like hell," one says, handing me her mirror when we meet at a diner for a fast cup of coffee, and prompts me to comb my hair. She misses my company, she says, and how she could always count on me for a spontaneous jaunt to a movie or a museum. I search for words she will understand. My friend has arrived at middle age carrying the weight of her widowed mother, frail now and in need of constant care. Time has crept up on them without disruption, both still as confident in their anger as in their affection for one another. Being disowned for half a lifetime was my experience, not hers. That I choose to care for my mother in her illness, under the circumstances, is an unnerving mystery my friend can't solve. The best of friends, we have no common ground in being daughters.

I apologize for being unavailable. "I have to do this." I say. Her face still bewildered, I hear myself change the subject to the recent renovations in her apartment.

A newly converted Catholic friend leaves me a daily message, a voice mail welcome home after what has become my routine of long workdays and late afternoon visits with my mother. Nothing like her usually buoyant "Hey, it's me," these days her voice is strangely quiet, more befitting a condolence call. It lingers in my apartment, reciting a scripture passage, a prayer, an occasional poem. Each evening, I make a mental note to thank her, soon.

The friend who knows me longest extends me an open invitation to stop by for a home-cooked meal, coupled with urgent reminders that I get enough rest and eat well, because she knows for sure, I'm not. "What are you doing to yourself?" she demands. Her voice flattens into her teacher tone and she informs me that not even women with husbands or lovers to support them, like her and unlike me, devote this much time to their aging mothers. I think about how good it would feel to be sitting with my friends on the old wicker chairs in the back porch of my country house, drinking wine if it were a summer evening or warm tea in the fall, our conversation focused on what we once believed were the insoluble problems of child-rearing and love affairs, instead of this.

These are good women who care about me, who know me well. Their loyalty proved my early distrust of women false. My friends know my gratitude is deep. So I can see what their cringing faces say when they ask me about my mother and I speak kindly of her. It is their silent outrage against her that hangs between us, made dense by their reluctance, now, to cross the line and say what they are thinking. Indeed, their most common expression of encouragement to me through the years, "You're a miracle," (implying that the odds were against me, that I could have become a sociopath instead of a mother, therapist, good friend), seems ready to be replaced with "You're a fool." Their restraint, I know, is hard earned.

My younger daughter has no such trouble. "She was such a horrible mother," Lissette remarked during an early spring lunch the other day. We were cramped in the tiny kitchen of her new apartment in the city, her first since she left home, and she stopped in the middle of chopping salad vegetables to look straight at me, her gray eyes darker than usual. "Why do you do it, Mom?"

The question nags for an answer, as much in the unnatural disconnection of my daughter for her grandmother as in the protective attention of my friends. I should seize such moments to explain myself, my mother, and this ironic turn of fate. But I don't. Instead, I bow to a stronger force in me.

"Anticipatory grief" they call it. It is an honorable label for what I feel, recently provided by the speaker at the monthly Alzheimer's Foundation support group. A kind-faced man with a soothing voice I could have listened to for hours explained to the group of newly converted caretakers. From beginning to end, he said, this long goodbye can last more than a decade. And the highest risk is not to the patient, but to the family. Stress. Exhaustion. Lowered immunity. Compassion fatigue. Pendulating emotions. A tendency to isolate. Each stage, as bad as it is, will leave us wishing for its return as the disease moves on.

I sat in the circle of caretakers that evening—aging spouses, siblings, adult children—all wearing the disease's handiwork in our still-ready-for-battle shoulders, permanently creased brows, half-closed eyes, crossed arms and legs. Each took a turn voicing a variation of a loved one's deterioration, some quickly, others awkwardly, more than a few using up more than their share of time. One man nearly whispered when he told about his kind and pretty wife of forty-two years who had become a total stranger, a frightening, abusive woman whose condition had defeated him more powerfully than any other event in his life. When it was my turn to share I couldn't lift my eyes from an arbitrary spot on the carpet near my feet, afraid to look away from it and lose the one spec in the room I could claim for myself. All I wanted to say was Private—Keep Out.

It surprised me then and still today, this now chronic unwillingness to explain myself. I cannot find the language, or the desire or motivation, to include anyone in this. Not fellow caregivers, not my friends, nor my daughters. Unlike other hard times in my life, this thing with my mother doesn't move me toward anyone, even the most tenderly offered refuge. It is a barren territory I inhabit these days, a place I did not enter voluntarily, and despite their good intentions, no visitors are welcome.

I look into my daughter's eyes and feel inadequate. I want words. There should be a book, I think, one I could hand her. I've always found solace in books—when I nursed my children alone, when I was going through the divorce, when I didn't know how to manage money. A book would help me explain myself now, make my daughter and my friends understand. But I can't think of one. I've seen the dozens on bookstore shelves explaining the disease, each with descriptions of how the amyloid plaques and tangles are devouring my mother's brain. I've read many of them. I know how Alzheimer's is irreversibly erasing her references to everything she is and was. I've considered the lists of the dos and don'ts of caretaking, and their reminders to make time for myself first. I've poured through tender stories of adult children and spouses who stand close by, helplessly, and witness the disintegration of a loved one.

But my story isn't tender. I am not losing a loving mother. I don't feel helpless. I am responding to something even more primitive than loss. I am greedy for what everyone else I know rightly takes for granted. The elixir I have spent my life searching for. I am awkward at it, traveling without a map and within earshot of a ticking clock. No matter. At last, for whatever time is left, my mother is mine to own.

I answer my daughter's question. "She is my mother," I say. "And I am her daughter. Nothing changes that." Lissette's face is still, except for a small pout forming on her lips. A tinge of confusion enters her eyes, giving her the look she'd get when she was eleven or so, sitting at her desk confronting a new science assignment. She turns back to her chopping board and says, "Be careful, Mom. She hurt you so much."

Nos Vamos says Tia Elena
A Los Estados Unidos
A La Mami she says and smiles at me
she is making piles of clothes on the big bed
my shirts my skirts my socks my dresses
piles just like Rosario the Monday woman makes
when she comes with her daughter
they wash clothes outside in *el patio*
i hear the water running and i watch
her daughter scrubs the clothes
Rosario hits them with a stick
they sing pretty too
Rosario and her daughter and the cooker woman
when they're done washing they sit at the old table
over by the mango trees where it's not so hot
they talk soft then loud then they laugh
and when they catch me looking they call me
and i run fast as i can across *el patio*
they don't mind if my feet are up under me on the chair
and i don't have to be quiet
and we eat the delicious meat and rice
and when the cooker woman slices the *aguacate*
she lets me sprinkle the salt on
and they give me baby bananas all i want
or they take one of the mangos from the tree
and slice it for me to eat
it is sweet and the juice runs down my face
they start to iron the clothes and teach me to sing
quien sera la que me quiere a mi quiere a mi quien sera
Rosario tells her daughter to dance with me
she puts her hands around my waist and shows me how to move
pa'lante atras pa'lante atras
i never get hives when i eat with the Monday women
Abuela cannot know they are nice to me
she will call them *negra asquerosa* and whip them
still i would like to tell Tia Elena about it
while she is putting all those clothes without wrinkles

into the brown *maleta*
Niña Nos Vamos she says again and hugs me
she waves her hand at me and says *Adios Colombia*
i am not sure if it is true
but it might be like the first night
when i was three and i believed them
now i am bigger i am five
and i must be careful
not to be tricked

Union Square

Yes, I saw Isabella again. She arranged it, a few weeks after the funeral, a weeknight supper at a local tavern. You remember the place, down the block from Ben's office, although I can't picture you ever going inside. Just the two of us, she said, and she was emphatic about the time—six on the dot—because she had an important meeting the next morning.

I was early, so I decided to take a walk. In a few days we'd be turning the clocks back an hour, and the sky was streaked in vibrant pinks and golds. Still, I hated the thought of four hard months of winter looming ahead. I began to circle the block, missing the slow sunsets of summer. I thought about Isabella. She'd sounded so grown up when she called. Here I was, passing the old buildings and shops where our history began. I wanted to catch a handful of it, hold still for a while. Was it foolish to hope that tonight could be a new beginning for us? I could be the big sister again, spoil her in ways I hadn't had a chance to, take her to lunch, shop for clothes, spend hours talking about men, or hairdos, the kinds of things sisters did. But I was getting ahead of myself. We hadn't even had our first conversation. What would we talk about? Where do you start a dialogue after a lifetime of separation? Maybe I could tell her stories about these streets, the old neighborhood where she and I were born.

I stopped at Manhattan General Hospital, renamed now and part of a big city hospital. I peeked inside the lobby. The marble staircase was there, and I could see all of us sitting on the steps, four sisters in size order, little

Isabella on my lap in that red corduroy jumper you made her, matching ribbons looped into her braids, our eyes glued to the elevator doors, waiting to see you and Ben bring us, finally, a baby brother.

You remember that Russian coffee cake Ben used to bring home by the box-full on Saturday nights after work? The bakery was still in business, smelling as good as ever, so I ordered two pieces wrapped separately, and made sure to carry the little boxes carefully. One for Isabella, the other to take home.

At Ben's building all the window shutters were closed, the whole place dark, even the three floors above the office. I wondered which window was Isabella's. Maybe she'd taken the front studio apartment on the top floor, the sunny one I'd fantasized about in high school, when I'd imagined myself living there after graduation. I'd spent hours decorating the place in my mind, careful not to need much—a small bed against the wall, a bookcase and a few plants, a turntable. I'd have an upright piano and full-length mirror for practicing my *quebrada* turns. And right in front of the window, a writing desk.

Yes, I could tell Isabella about these things. I'd tell her how proud her father was on that day—was I eight or nine?—when we first saw his office. It was before you two were married, before the babies came. Julia and Carmela and I waited on the sidewalk together, looking at Doctor Ben like he'd just opened the door to paradise. He told us it was the first piece of property anyone in his family had ever owned, an 1859 brownstone, with the whole first floor for his practice instead of the old downtown walk-up with a leaky roof. I'd tell her about the history lesson he gave us, lengthier than his usual Depression era stories, as he let us in. Can't you hear him calling out to us over the noise we made tromping up and down the stairs and running through the empty apartments? "Girls, you're walking into history!" I'd been so impressed, because we were learning about the Civil War in school that year, and for weeks I found a way to bring the word "antebellum" into every conversation. I liked the way it rolled off my tongue. And whenever I said it, I could claim Ben as my own a little.

Isabella would enjoy hearing about the rest of that day, too. How we all sat around Ben's just-delivered mahogany desk following his plan for doing his change-of-address announcements. He'd read aloud from a list of patients' names, using different accents or singing renditions of *La Paloma* and *Bei Mir Bist Du Shein* to keep us going while you addressed envelopes and Julia stuffed a card into each. Carmela got to tear stamps off the enormous roll that spilled onto the floor and hand them to me. And I licked and pressed them on, careful to keep each stamp straight on the corner of the envelope like you'd said so the patients would know that Dr. Reiss was a meticulous dentist, until my tongue was so coated with glue that I couldn't speak anymore, and we all laughed harder than I'd ever heard us laugh. When we finished Ben took us down to Chinatown to eat, and we sat together at a big round table. Do you remember that you asked the waiter to remove all the silverware, because you'd brought your own?

Those were good stories. Any daughter would want to know them. Surely Isabella would enjoy them. But as I turned back down the street I changed my mind. Maybe it would be best to let dinner develop its own conversation. These stories could wait a little longer, until Isabella and I knew each other better, when she would ask about our history out of her own curiosity.

I'd seen her do that before, in the limousine on the ride back from the cemetery. She sat next to you. She asked how you and her father had met. I could see from the flush in her face that it was the first time she'd asked. You kept the mood light, giving her simple answers.

"He had a very nervous patient who could not speak English. I overheard from the waiting room and offered to translate. Then he offered me a job."

Toward the end of the ride Isabella turned to me for a minute and asked you how old I was when you and Ben met, and when you said "Still in diapers," her brow crumpled, as though she were realizing it for the first time.

I was back at the tavern door, glad Isabella had kept her word. It was the last thing she'd said after the funeral, when we said goodbye hailing cabs on Houston Street. "I'll call you. We'll get together again." I said I'd like that, very much. Then her boyfriend—I forgot his name—stepped over to me and quietly told me that I should keep in touch, because he'd noticed Isabella was comfortable with me, and that made him happy. She had very few friends, he said. A sister would do her good. It left me wondering why he'd said it like that, as though she didn't have other sisters. I'd wanted to blurt out, me too! but the first cab came by and she took it, looking small and tired in her business clothes. I went home feeling her embrace, replaying her words. Anyone watching us would believe her, I thought. Even that taxi driver up front. Not me.

She was standing at the bar. The acrid stench of smoke and fermented beer was the first thing that hit me as I walked in, and it took me a few seconds to make her out in the faint light. I waved to her. She gave me that wonderful smile of hers that both my daughters have, and walked to me. She was in jeans and a sweater, looking much younger than she had at the funeral. "Hi there." She reached to kiss me. "I just got here."

How nice this is, I thought, and let my hand touch her shoulder. I told her I'd gotten there early and had taken a walk. A waitress sat us in a corner booth and took our drink order, a Manhattan for Isabella and cranberry juice for me. Isabella seemed surprised.

"No alcohol?" I explained that I was driving. She made a little sound, part grunt, part giggle, and asked me, "Where?"

I said home, to Queens, and she giggle-grunted again, and her shoulders shook the way Ben's did when he laughed. "No. Where did you walk?"

She raised her eyebrows when I said I'd walked around the old neighborhood. "What for?" As soon as I said 'history' I was sorry. She scowled and held up one hand as if to shield herself from the word. "Please. That's one subject I've had enough of."

I'd ruined it all in less than a minute. I should have waited, the way I'd planned, felt her out a bit. Why had I even hinted at the past, instead of leaving it alone?

Isabella opened her menu. "Where do you live, anyway?" I was about to say I lived a few minutes from your house, but I thought twice. How would I refer to you? Isabella and I didn't have a common word for you. Mom, Mother, even Our Mother sounded unnatural. Those were words I hadn't used since I was a teenager. I began to say I lived near Queens College when a chatty couple sat down at the next table. Isabella took no notice, but I wanted them to move away, to have nothing to distract us from each other.

"What about your kids? I saw them at the funeral. All grown up. Do they live with you?" She was curious about where the girls had studied, if they'd gone to college, what neighborhood in the city they lived in. I answered all her questions. When I said they lived on the Upper East Side she nodded approvingly, and again when I said I'd made sure they'd learned music.

Our drinks arrived. I watched myself play with the plastic stirrer in my juice. The old feeling of being measured was creeping up on me. I reminded myself that my sister was showing interest in my life, we were still talking, and it was good. We gave the waitress our cheeseburger order and Isabella took a short sip from her drink.

I asked her where she went to school. "Austin." She giggled again. "I majored in English Lit. A great waste of time and money. It did me no good. When I graduated I moved here into Dad's building. I taught for a while, at a junior high school in East Harlem. The kids wanted nothing to do with English, or me. All they wanted was drugs and sex. I got out of there fast."

I asked her if she liked children and she said no, she didn't, and never wanted any either. It didn't make any difference when I told her she might feel differently about her own. She seemed to force a laugh and said, "No, no. No way am I passing on the lunacy of this family." I could tell it was a well practiced answer, but her voice had slowed and her eyes looked sad.

Our food came and while we ate I asked her about her apartment. She'd taken the front rooms on the top floor. She'd moved in when you and Ben were in the midst of your divorce, when she couldn't stand living at home anymore. She'd only begun renovations a few months before Ben got sick, breaking through and into the rear apartment, putting in a new kitchen, new wiring and floors. She planned on living there for a long time, she said.

I aksed her how often she went back to Queens. "I'll never go back to that house. I want to be as far away as possible. I've lived here with Dad and Gabriel, each of us in our own apartment. It's been peaceful for the first time in my life."

It was then that I understood that she didn't see you, and hadn't seen you in a long time. "I have no interest in her. None. I was polite at the funeral for Dad's sake." Isabella sat up and placed her hands on the table, stretching her fingers wide. She looked straight at me and spoke quickly, as though her words crowded her mouth. "I only got two good things from that woman. Her brains and her passion. The rest of her I can live without."

I didn't want to defend or condemn you. I wanted to help my sister, soothe her a little. She seemed too young to be so angry. We'd had a difficult and hurtful mother, yes. But it wasn't all bad.

"Really? You could have fooled me."

She took a hard bite of her hamburger, then another. She finished swallowing and opened her napkin to clean her mouth and hands, then folded it carefully and laid it next to her dish. When she spoke again she wasn't louder than any of the other voices in the room, but she had a severity that surprised me, as if she were making a controlled, terrible announcement into a microphone to a large group of people, her jaw set and tight, head bowed a little.

"That woman was great to strangers. She was a monster to her kids. And especially to my Dad. I never want to see her again."

We were opposites, I told her. She couldn't wait to leave home, I'd been waiting to be allowed back in. Isabella ran her hand through her hair and let it rest at the base of her neck. Her eyes were glaring.

"Well, lucky you. You missed all that, didn't you? You just ran away with that older man you'd been whoring around with who got you pregnant, didn't you?"

A million pin pricks rose between my fingers. I wanted to reach over the table and cover her mouth, stop her. I couldn't decipher which of her points to address first. How could I prove her wrong? Whatever Isabella knew about me had to have come from you, from Ben, from some angry distortion of the truth. Her idea of who I was had endured thirty years unchallenged: Veronica, the foolish, corrupted sister who had walked out on her.

It wasn't like that at all, I said. There was more to it than what she'd been told. But her eyes didn't change. They had you in them—the mother you were in your wild rages, savagely staving off some imagined enemy you'd been fleeing all your life, stronger than any person or logic or good intention you might have had. You'd sacrifice your own children to it. Even the medications Ben prescribed hadn't helped. Once it triggered you, nothing was safe, nothing was sacred. It ruled you the night you threw me out of your life. I was seeing now that the damage hadn't ended there.

But as I sat across from my little sister, I couldn't pretend. I'd known that fury too. The kind of rage that bears down on reason. The kind she was feeling now. Maybe she'd lived her life trying to contain it, as I had. I looked at her and wondered what she would do if she had small children pulling at her right then? I remembered the pain in her voice a few minutes before, swearing off motherhood. I saw how damaged we all were and I felt like weeping.

Isabella didn't answer right away. She spent the next few minutes poking her fork into her French fries, her little stabs more awkward than angry. She kept her eyes down. "Well, that was the story I heard about you."

So I told her the truth, that I hadn't been pregnant and hadn't run away, but that you'd ordered me to leave. She listened when I said I didn't really know why, that I'd spent a long time figuring that out and I'd concluded it had been your only option. You didn't know any other way to do things. You were scared that I had ruined my life. Everything sexual scared you. I'd disobeyed your rules. Rules from another time and place that you were loyal to, and I hadn't cared about.

Isabella pushed her dish away and clasped her hands together. "She was insane."

I reminded her that this was a hard time for her. Her Dad had just died, maybe it wasn't the best time to speak about these things. Maybe we should wait. She leaned back against the booth. She ran her index finger around the base of her glass, slowly, and gulped what was left of her drink.

"I wish her a slow and painful death."

The waitress came and no one spoke as she cleared the table.

"So. About you." Isabella's eyes were wide open, pupils dilated as she stared at me. It's the liquor, I thought. "I hope you know that you're not in the will. You got nothing. None of you did."

I felt ambushed. By sweet Isabella, the person I'd least expect it from. I wasn't after an inheritance, I said. I hadn't come for that. I'd believed her invitation was about something else.

"You hurt my Dad." She was all business again, the way she'd been on the telephone. "He said you called him at the hospital all the time, every day, asking for money. While he was sick and dying. He felt betrayed. Especially by that whole ridiculous father thing of yours. After Dad raised you, all you could do was hurt him. I'll always hold that against you."

I hated myself for not having a quick answer. I wanted to shoot something back at her, hurt her. I was standing in that hospital room, Ben saying no to my offer of a hug. A stream of rebuttals ran through my head. Who said this? Certainly not Ben. I loved him. He knew that. If you knew me you could never think such a thing. If you knew me.

For a few seconds the chatter of the couple next to us and the noise in the rest of the room seemed louder than it had been, as if I were privy to every conversation, until slowly the sound drifted and I was in a sea of silence. There was nothing I could do. Nothing would make my sister believe other than what she did at that moment.

I thought of getting up, leaving. But the waitress returned, offering us a last chance for desserts. We both declined. I asked for a check. Then I turned to Isabella. She'd shifted to the corner of the booth. Suddenly she looked scared. I told her I was sorry that she believed those things, and that she had the wrong idea about me. She finished her drink. "Well then, that will be too bad."

I envied her directness. I envied her clear, entitled anger and her ability to speak it. I waited for her to signal what would come next, the two of us sitting silently, avoiding each other's eyes, the tavern sounds in the background. I thought about my walk. About all the things I'd wanted to say to renew our sisterhood. I thought about what Isabella had been in my mind all those years, her image frozen as the baby sister, innocent, curious, easy to please. I saw you and Ben dancing in the living room, Isabella standing in between, her little arms stretched up, laughing in delight and expectation. I hated you both for whatever you did or failed to do that made all this happen.

After a while I spoke, asking if I could see Ben's office for the last time. She hesitated, then it looked like she'd softened. "All right. But it isn't an office anymore. It was all taken apart when Dad closed his practice. He lived there when he couldn't do the stairs anymore. He died there."

We walked up the block in silence. When we reached the office she let me into the vestibule while she looked for her keys. I listened for the outside door to fall hard on the stopper and ease slowly the rest of the way into the frame. It hadn't changed. The front room, what used to be the waiting room, was empty, with only an easy chair and a dimly lit lamp in the far corner, and a small side table with a phone and answering machine on it.

"This is where Dad spent the last year or so. He'd watch people through the window and listen to the radio. He never really answered the phone, unless it was me or Gabriel calling. Or the technician who came to do the dialysis."

Yes, I said. I knew what she meant. I'd tried to reach Ben many times, but he never answered—this family with its fear of phones. One of her little giggle-grunts escaped her. "How would you classify it, Ronnie? Telephobia?"

We both laughed, hard, and the last two hours hadn't happened. Isabella turned on the other lights and showed me the two rooms, empty now, that were once his operating rooms. She pointed out where Ben had collapsed on his way to the bathroom and died. She took me to his consultation room. His desk was still there, bare, and not so big.

I followed her out into the hallway and waited as she turned the locks.

"You can't come upstairs. I had the floors done yesterday. They aren't dry yet."

I didn't believe her excuse, but I understood she'd done as much as she could. I told her again that I'd come only to see her, and it had been enough. She reached her hand out to me as if to shake it, and I remembered the little boxes I was holding. I handed one to her and said it was a piece of Russian coffee cake. From her Dad. We didn't hug. We didn't kiss the way we did earlier. But she smiled.

Several times during the next few weeks I called and left simple messages for her, but Isabella didn't answer her phone. Finally, just before Thanksgiving that year she called and invited me to her place for the holiday. I was thrilled. When I asked what the girls and I could bring, she hesitated. She hadn't expected me to bring the girls. The invitation was just for me. I told her that I'd never had Thanksgiving dinner and not invited my children. She was quiet again. Then she said she'd never thought of me as a mother. It would be too many people in her small apartment.

I never heard from her after that.

i have fallen asleep
up against her soft furry coat
the one Uncle Mickey brought
from someplace called Argentina
Tia Elena is stroking my hair
she whispers in my ear
Tesoro despierta niña despierta
she wants me to wake up
Ya llegamos
la Mami
la Mami
we are in a car
we are stopping
i know this place
i know this door
i walk fast
past the others
way ahead of Uncle Mickey and Tia Elena
i know these steps
and all the steps
up there
Mommy
and Her golden hair
i am home
i am safe
with You
You
Mommy
with You
and never
i will never
be bad
again

4

when it rains we play the window game
Julia invented it
and she rules when Mommy is at work
she says our living room has the best view
we're the top floor of the tallest building
on Union Square
Carmela and her get to lean way over
but not me
they can see down Sixteenth Street
it's a street with no trees Mommy says
i'm not allowed to lean out
so all i get to see is Klein's department store
and just one side of the park where we play
except when the men with loudspeakers are out
dirty *comunistas* Mommy calls them
then we have to stay inside all day
Julia hates it so she makes up games
she always gets to say *When*
and *Yes that's him* or *No that's not him*
You idiots look for a cream-colored suit
Tall and very handsome
there are lots of people and it's hard to look so fast
i say *That's him* and i'm sure i win
but Julia says *No bean brain that guy's too short*
it's a hard game because the rules change every time
and i don't know what we're looking for
Carmela tried to change the game
but Julia got mad and punched her and said
If you don't like it lump it
once i saw a tall-cream-colored-suit-man
but even that time she said *No not him*
He's supposed to be coming around the square
Julia talks very loud so i just stay quiet
but i keep looking at the corner
where all the people come around the Square
and i wonder if his face
will look like the man in the little round frame

Julia keeps on her side of the dresser
and nobody better touch
Carmela almost found him once but Julia said
No he's old by now look for somebody old
so last time i saw a man with a cane
and Julia really yelled hard *Stop you idiot*
and she looked like she was going to cry and said
He's not coming you morons he's dead
then she closed the window real hard

Tango

My daughter's warning of a few weeks ago about how hurtful my mother can be has prompted a mental dialog we've been having, especially at moments like this. I am adjusting my body to support my mother's weight against my left side and counting steps aloud as we make our way into the Bayside Senior Center. The innocent advice of youth, I say to Lissette in my mind. As if being careful in love of any kind were possible.

It has taken months to get my mother here, despite Dr. Klein's now old suggestion that she get exposure to social stimulation while she still can. We have waited for a break in the cold weather, and in the paranoia that hallmarks my mother's illness. Alzheimer's has worsened her usual fear of people and places. Finally, my sister has agreed to give it a try. Without Julia's participation and approval, my mother would never leave home.

My mother takes small steps, lightly tapping each foot before setting it down, as though she were repeatedly ascending a curb only she sees. The red sling-back heels she wears don't help, but they mark a splendid victory for her, of the kind she hasn't experienced lately. This morning's hour-long vying with Julia for control over how my mother would dress—just stick on slacks and sneakers for Chrissake!—ended with an ironclad declaration from my mother, "I'm not dead yet."

I feel my mother's small body, dense and hard, and the sting of her fingernails digging into my forearm. "It's going to be okay," I reassure her in this absurd reversal of roles that makes me remember my first day of school, when I clung to her just as hard. "If you don't like it, we'll leave immediately. I promise."

The Senior Center borders the Long Island Expressway. I have driven past it often and thought it was a library. We make it inside, where a large woman sits behind a desk, a stainless steel relic from the gray-flannel-suit era of the fifties. It is covered with stacks of pink flyers I can't make out upside down and an open box of mailing envelopes the woman is sifting through. Her pixie-cut dark hair is peppered white to match the frames of her thick glasses and the print on the housecoat she wears. Behind her is a brighly lit corridor, and to her right, a row of tall, artificial plants. Over them comes the voice of a man, loud and amplified, shouting instructions through an even louder rendition of "Hernando's Hideaway".

As soon as she sees us the receptionist jumps up to walk around the desk with an outstretched hand and a bouyant Good Afternoon. Her eyes move quickly between my sister and me, then settle on my mother. "Welcome. I'm Jody. And you must be Eva?"

I am impressed. This place is well organized, I think, if they remembered to arrange a personal greeting like this two days after I made the appointment.

"How do you know my name?" My mother is not questioning, but accusing, and she tightens her grip on my arm.

"We've been expecting you," Jody says, and takes my mother's loose hand. She pumps it vigorously, making my mother's bony wrinkled arm look like a slinky toy. The woman moves to Julia, smile still wide. "Mom is going to have a great time here, don't you worry." Julia takes a step back. Jody pats my hand hard, and winks. Another woman, in her twenties, emerges from the corridor. "Oh, and here's Annette," Jody says, sounding like a television game show host. "She will be our guardian angel for our little tour today." Annette wears a similarly patterned housecoat, pastel-colored. Her smile is lovely, but not as wide as Jody's.

My mother notices Annette and drops my arm. "Jackie? What is my granddaughter doing here?"

"No, Mom," I correct her. "This is Annette. Jackie works someplace else. In Manhattan."

"So what the heck am I doing here, then?" My mother looks around the room, her nose wrinkled to meet her brow.

Julia says, "You're looking around. See if you like this place. So you don't sit at home rotting all day and night."

Jody, still smiling, nods to Annette, who picks up a pink flyer.

"Here we are, now. This is our schedule."

"I need to see that," Julia pulls a flyer from the pile.

The voice behind the artificial plants shouts. "Slow, slow, quick-quick-quick. Again! Slow, slow, quick-quick-quick."

My mother's eyes get wide. "Someone is dancing?"

Without waiting for an answer, she pushes past the two smiling house-coats and around the shouting potted plants, pulling me with her for support. We enter a room lined with bookshelves. It is very large and harshly lit. It could be a library. There are a few tables along the far wall, where the windows are, and where half a dozen old men are playing cards. No one in the place is under seventy. At each corner of the room is a large, circular table, where groups of elderly women sit looking through newspapers. In the center of the room stands a line of people, eight women and one man. All are paying close attention to the owner of the loud voice shouting instructions.

My mother stands very still, watching the dance teacher intently. "*Tango*," she announces, as though she's solved a riddle she's worked on for days. Her face is relaxed and she is smiling. "Too bad he does not know what he is doing." She shrugs her shoulder. She could be talking to me or to herself, I can't tell. She is radiant.

I look for Julia. My sister is standing off to the far side of the room, talking excitedly with Jody and Annette, pink flyer waving in her hand. I am about to call out to her when my mother pulls at my arm again. She moves us toward the middle of the room.

"Wrong!" she calls out to the dancers, the hard roll of her first sound pushing off her tongue to cut through the music like a whistle. Everyone stops and turns toward us. "You have to slide along the floor," she says, slapping her free hand on her hip with indignation. "Take long steps. It is not a mambo!"

Swiftly, my mother lets go of my arm, pivots to face me, places her right arm around my waist and takes my right hand. I tower over her. Yet, with a certainty my body instantly remembers, I am willingly and completely at her mercy, sure that in this at least, I am safe with her.

"*Sígueme*," she whispers, commanding me to follow her lead.

Hernando's Hideway has ended. A new tango melody fills the room.

I am standing still in my mother's embrace, my body framed, my weight carefully shifted onto the balls of my feet so that my upper body is leaned into her a little. My eyes are lowered to just beyond the line of her shoulders, I rest my head, chin straight, on the silky waves of her hair. My hands are ready: right palm lightly touching hers, the other near the nape of her neck, fingers poised. I brace my arms and give just enough resistance to anchor myself and give her leverage as she turns her shoulders slowly, hips squared with mine, and takes me with her as she descends. She extends one leg and places the rim of her foot precisely at my instep as she closes the middle fingers of her lead hand around mine. I read her signals easily. I am not thinking, only responding. The music releases us, we are in motion.

I am eight years old. I am fifteen. I am fifty. I follow my mother, my earliest teacher, letting her take me fluidly around the room, our Union Square living room. Seamless from beginning to end, and familiar, my mother's lead is strong, certain enough, tightening her hold around my waist to swerve me into the figure eight *ochos* or pressing into the small of my back, whispering "*prepárate*" into my ear to bring me into a forward dip. She is adjusting her lipstick in the mirror, beautiful in her black satin dress and stiletto heels, golden hair pinned up and ready for an evening out with Ben. She is smiling at her daughters, saying, "Dancing can never hurt you." We are okay. We are happy.

The music stops. My mother lingers on her spot. "*Bien,*" she says, and releases her hold. She smiles up at me and says, "I still have it, kiddo." It was one of Ben's pet names for her, and she cocks her head in self-congratulation. I raise my arm around her shoulders and press her close to me, gently, wanting to hold on longer, but she turns away. She looks around the room and stops when she sees the potted plants. She squints hard at them.

"What kind of nightclub is this?" she asks. "Lousy atmosphere."

She moves toward the plants. I stay close behind, intoxicated from the dancing and now confused by the lightning-speed changes of the past few minutes, not sure about her balance. There is a small commotion. The instructor and his students are approaching us with compliments and applause, frail because of their age, but eager with questions about how long and how often we have danced. My mother stands before them, gives the group a quick look and retreats. I bring my hand to her elbow and she shifts her weight onto me. The suppleness of her body has gone. She is heavy and hard again.

"Get me out of here, Ronnie," she calls over her shoulder.

"Sure, Mom." We start walking.

"My, what a surprise!" Jody reappears. "I've been watching you from my little corner back there." She motions with her head back toward the front desk area as she advances, her hands crossed high on her chest. "Isn't it funny how you can never tell about people?" Jody is the television announcer again. Maybe for a children's show. She stops near us and makes eye contact with each person in the group, except my mother. She gets to me and winks. "You were keeping a little secret, weren't you?" Her question isn't for me. "Eva, Eva. You didn't tell us you were such a great dancer, did you?" Jody hooks her arm onto my mother's free one and tugs at her, so that my mother is pulled between us.

"Everybody," Jody announces. "This is Eva."

My mother quickly frees herself and makes a sucking sound against her teeth. Jody doesn't seem to notice.

"Eva has come to join our center. And boy, isn't it a good thing today was Dance Lesson Day?" She reaches for my mother's free hand and is about to pat it. My mother snaps it away and glares at her.

"Leave me alone, lady!"

Jody throws me another of her enormous, rigid smiles, the clench of her jaw wide enough to show every one of her teeth. She motions to me. "And this is her daughter, Vanessa."

"Her daughter," a woman in the group echoes, nearly whispering, as if she were looking at a puppy. "How nice."

"Veronica," I correct Jody. "I'm her daughter, Veronica."

I pronounce my name slowly, giving each syllable equal stress, so this common mistake won't happen again. It is something I learned to do in seventh grade, after I complained to my mother for picking a name that people never remembered, and she said it wasn't her fault that *norteamericanos* are too lazy to pronounce any word with more than three syllables in it. It was shortly after that when she began to call me Ronnie. I hated it instantly, but she kept it.

Another woman in the group calls out. "Wonderful! A daughter who dances with her mother."

The dance instructor moves next to my mother, replacing Jody who excuses herself with a grin. "I'll leave you all with our Maestro, then." Up close I see that the man is younger than I'd first noticed, in his early forties, with a thick head of white hair. He looks very proper in his starched shirt and dark vest. He is wearing elevated dance shoes that are badly scuffed at the toes.

"Bravo, Eva," he says, bowing to her a little.

My mother waves him away. "Forget it, Mister. I have nothing you want." She shoots a pleading look at me, motioning with her thumb that she wants to leave. Mister comes close to me and puts both hands on my shoulders. He has a wide Jody smile, too, but he is missing all his back teeth.

"Bravo to the daughter as well," he says in a smoky voice that doesn't really need a microphone. His breath is stale, but his dark eyes sparkle. Others echo him. I look around the group of nodding, approving old men and women. I am unexpectedly pleased and decide to enjoy the moment. I smile back at them.

A rapid, hard clicking sound travels across the floor. I hear my sister's entrance before I see her. She stops abruptly in front of me. "What's going on here?" The group disperses. Julia shoots a glance at my mother and back at me. Her eyes are excited. She is holding two small cans in one hand, jiggling her car keys in the other. "Yapping? Is this what you've been doing all this time, Veronica?" Julia's voice is an tricky mix of playfulness and sarcasm, and makes me think of the way an alcoholic ex-lover of mine would toy with me after a few drinks, a preamble to the rage that would ensue after he'd had a few more, and how my throat would close up in the confusion of finding the right answer to stave off what was coming. I know Julia doesn't really want an answer to her questions. She has something of her own to announce.

"While you've been out here wasting time, Miss, I've been busy." She has used the code word, *Miss*. The unmistakable signal, learned at the hands of the nuns that educated her, that she is the Big Sister. She leans forward, raising the two cans in front of me. "Ensure!" She gloats and laughs victoriously. "A meal in a can for old people." Julia gives me a playful, hard shove, the way she did when we were children. It jolts me against my mother, setting her into motion once again, toward the exit.

"Don't shove me, Julia." I say it calmly, fighting the urge to join her play, shove her back, harder, for all the times I didn't dare to. She ignores me and goes on. "I have to get one or two of these into her every day. She won't eat what I cook anyway."

My mother stops walking. "You can cook?" She jerks a shoulder and twists her face, mocking. "Since when?"

"You see?" Julia's face is changed. The playfulness has soured. Her voice is cracking. "I'm nothing. You're the only one she eats for. She loves *you*, Veronica."

I want to have a quick answer for her, something that would rid us of this rivalry that shows up more and more frequently lately. But I am stuck between my sister and my mother, pulled by one and pushed by the other. I can't think fast enough, except to change the subject.

"Did you see Mom doing tango?"

"Who cares?" Julia turns away, leaving a wide distance between us.

I try again. "She danced, Julia. It was like magic."

"I was busy, see?" She lifts the cans again. "I didn't waste time like you." She has reached the lobby area a few steps ahead of us, and begins to button up her coat. She holds her mouth hard, twisted to one side of her face. I reach the front desk with my mother and ask Julia, "Where did you get the Ensure?"

She doesn't look at me. She speaks to the wall across from us, as though we were speaking on the phone and not next to one another. "That woman, Nannette, Paulette, whatever her name is. I told her to show me the rest of this place. They have stacks of this stuff in the kitchen. She gave them to me."

"*Vámonos*," my mother cuts Julia off. "I have work to do at home. Have your fun on your own time."

I look around for Jody, who I last saw walking down the corridor. No sign of her. "Julia, what about the bus?" I ask. "Did you arrange anything?"

"Forget it." She still talks to the wall. "This is like nursery school. They want to pick her up at ten in the morning and drop her off at two thirty." Julia talks faster and louder. She doesn't care who's listening, particularly my mother.

I say, "It's only two days a week."

"It's not happening." She turns to me and slams the two cans in her hands down on the desk. My mother startles again.

"This is important for Mom, Julia."

"Are you deaf? I said no, Miss. This is not going to work. There's no way I can get her on a schedule."

"*Ordinaria*," my mother throws her verdict in Julia's direction. Then she turns to me. "Where did such a creature come from? No softness."

"I wouldn't talk," Julia lobs back.

I notice I'm clenching my teeth. I pick up a flyer from the desk and give it to my mother to distract her. She takes it and looks at it. I'm hoping she can decode the words. "Mom," I say. "That was some tango you did. You were a star." My mother looks at me blankly.

"What tango?" Julia asks. She has leaned against the wall, arms crossed over her chest. Her tone has lowered a notch. "Nobody did a tango."

"She did, Julia. With me. Out of the blue, she just started leading me."

"What are you talking about?"

"She even got a round of applause. I thought you were watching. The dance teacher was giving a tango class and…"

"Tango, to these people?" Julia twists her face in disbelief. "Veronica, please. You'll fall for anything." She is moving, taking little steps, unaware that she is making a full turn as she speaks. "You call that a tango teacher? What kind of dancing do you think they do here? It's like the living dead."

My mother looks around. "Who's dead?"

I look back for Jody again. I want to finalize things before my mother completely closes off on her own, or in reaction to Julia. I don't see her. My mother tugs at my sleeve. "*Ya.*" She's had enough.

I ask my sister, "Do we need to see Jody again?"

"What for? I already said she's not coming to this place, didn't I?"

"*Ahora mismo.*" The tug is harder.

"Okay, Mom's had enough. She wants to leave. Let's talk about this later, Julia."

"Nothing to talk about. Get that through your thick skull." Julia walks to the glass exit doors, her hands ready to push them open. "This place doesn't suit her anyway."

"It's for stimulation." I say.

"Stimulation? What stimulation?" Julia turns and squares off. This close, I notice how fair her eyebrows are, almost invisible, giving her a ghostly look in her anger. Her face and eyes are fixed on mine, only her lips move, pulled taut when she speaks, the words catapulting out of her mouth, landing on me hard. I begin to feel small, very small. It is the most familiar feeling I have with my sister. Being overpowered. "You see something going on here, Veronica? What, Bingo? Reading the paper? People sitting around yapping?"

I do a quick mental review of what's just happened, to find the thing that triggered Julia's mood. Maybe I can diffuse it. She makes a sharp about face and pushes the exit door open. "This place stinks. Just another racket to get money from old people."

I try logic, hoping to stop her from leaving. "Julia, Medicare pays for the bus service. The center itself is free."

"Free?" She hangs on the door. "It comes from the taxes you pay doesn't it?" She spots the two cans she left on the desk and walks back in to pick them up. "Whatever genius told you about this joint doesn't know *her*. She'll never go for this. I'm leaving."

My mother pokes my arm hard with one of her brittle fingers. "Now," she says.

"Don't do that!" I push away from my mother's jab. Her arms drop to lean on the desk. My voice is scolding, the way I spoke to my children when I'd reach my breaking point. I have never used this tone with my mother before. She frowns, looks at the floor and mutters to herself.

"*Que desgracia.*" She's had it. She sounds hopelessly beaten. Her words grate at me now as much as when I was a child, when I tried just as hard to help her, and couldn't.

"I'll be right back." I turn away fast and walk down the dark corridor to find Jody. I hear Julia behind me jiggling her keys, my mother still muttering. I can feel my stockings against my skin as I walk, thick and irritating. They are the cheap brand, rough to the touch, that I bought at the gas station convenience store in a rush yesterday. Rushing. That's all I do lately. Rushing to get to my mother's house when she or Julia calls. Rushing to work, because I can't wake up once I finally fall asleep, hours after I go to bed. I want to rip the stockings off, tear them into shreds. My ears pound. I want to make it to the room at the end of the corridor before I break down. I don't want to cry. Not in front of my sister and mother. If I can only find smiling Jody to get this over with.

I doubt my own perceptions. Who was the woman dancing with me just a few minutes ago? My mother—this mother—which mother? I want that feeling back. That shift into another state of mind that happens whenever I start to dance, the flood of anticipation, the few seconds of real time that stop time, changing all the ugliness in a room, in people, into sheer pleasure. In a few hours it will all be different. I will be laying out an outfit on my bed, built from the bottom up, starting with the shoes. A pair carefully picked from the dozen or so I keep displayed, for my benefit, on a shelf in my bedroom. Reds, blacks, skin tone, bronze metallic, in leathers and suedes and patents. Three inch professional heels with ankle straps to support my fallen arches. A skirt and leotard, varying styles, but always black, and sparkling costume jewelry. At the top, intricate rhinestone hair clips from Asian specialty stores in Manhattan, wholesale and plentiful, waiting in velvet boxes on my dresser.

Twice a week, maybe more, no matter what, I dance. In warmly lit festive places around town where the rush of music and well-dressed, good-smelling people greet you, ready and willing to take regular life off your hands and check it at the door. If you're a good dancer you don't miss a number—tango, rumba, merengue, salsa, bachata, swing, hussle, sometimes a waltz. After a few hours you're covered with sweat, you go home exhilarated without having said more than hello-yes-thanks to people who are always happy to see you, hold you, and know your body's reactions and rhythms better than a lover. Fully clothed and anonymous, all your senses plugged in to a hundred people—what you're called, what you do, what your friends see, who your family is—all irrelevant.

"Are you and Mom ready, Vanessa?" It's Jody, in the middle of the corridor.

"Yes." A sigh escapes me. "We need to go." I turn and walk back with her to the front desk. My sister and my mother are just as I left them.

"All righty, then," Jody says. "Did you like our center, Eva?"

"It's okay," my mother doesn't look up. Her voice is faint. "I have things to do at home. I need to get back."

Julia says, "She can't handle this. It's not for her."

"Oh," Jody looks confused and turns to me. "Maybe another day? She enjoyed the dancing."

I watch my mother. She glares at Jody, not recognizing her. Jody persists. "She was our star today."

There is a long silence. "The women in our family dance," I say, and hear conciliation in my voice. I am remembering my mother, her mother, my sisters. I remember that when I dance, I dance for them, with them. "It's like a religion."

"Miss," my mother sounds alert again. She looks straight at Jody. "I married two professionals, you know. Both great dancers. The first was an attorney. He left me with nothing." She waves her hand back toward Julia and continues. "Just three monsters."

"That witch." Julia pushes the glass door hard, making it rock back against its frame. As she passes me I see tears spill from her eyes. She takes big steps, digging her high heels into the ground as she goes. Her words trail behind her. "She never has anything nice to say. Let her rot."

My mother accepts Jody's help to get around the desk and latch onto my arm. I say goodbye to Jody and leave her with her smile. We reach my sister's car. I help my mother into the front seat. I strap the seatbelt around her. She reaches for my hand and squeezes it.

"Ronnie," she says. "That place is full of old people. It's not for you."

stuffed four Band-Aids into my front packet
in case i fall
two for those long stingy scratches i get on my hands
the others for my knees
today i put my skates on fast
and got the key before Carmela
she always takes too long
getting her feet in between the red hooks
then Julia gets p.o.'d with the waiting
and when it's finally my turn
they go ahead without me
today i got a head start around the square
and waited for them in front of Ohrbach's
i didn't hit any bumpy parts on the sidewalk either
Julia showed me how
you have to stay inside the safety zone lines
where it's all smooth black pavement
so we can skate down Fifth Avenue without falling
of course nobody ever tells not even Julia
we would never get permission again
if Mommy knew we skated
all the way to Washington Square Park
especially off the sidewalk
so Julia made the rule
to not put on our skates until we get to Fifteenth Street
there's a lot of traffic there
so Mommy can't see us or hear us
Carmela doesn't think it's a real sin to do that
she says it's like a trade
'cause on days like this
we're not allowed in Union Square Park
even though it's right there across the street from us
those men stand around and take up all the room
all they're doing is listening to other men
who shout stuff into a microphone up on the stage
they don't skate or play anything just stand there
so Julia begged Mommy

she promised she would watch me
if we could go outdoors
and walk to Washington Square Park instead
God doesn't mind says Carmela
we pretend we're walking downtown
and it keeps Mommy from worrying
there's no sandbox or monkey bars
in Washington Square Park
but i like sitting on the edge of the big circle
sometimes Julia says to take off our shoes and socks
and we dip our toes into the water
and listen to people playing guitars and violins
or watch the little kids with fathers
walk around the edge of the circle
holding hands so they don't fall in
Julia likes to skate around the circle as fast as she can
she never falls and doesn't even mind all those cracks
in the six-sided shapes on the ground
she gives a little hop whenever a big one is coming
and that makes her ponytail fly up in the air
and she looks just like she's falling from the sky
i can tell it's time to go back when Julia says
Race you around the outside
she always gets to pick home base
but it's always the same spot
the bench on the street that goes downtown
the opposite way from Union Square
Julia says if you follow that street all the way
it takes you right to Mulberry Street
right to the Café Roma
right downstairs from Nonna's house
but we couldn't skate that far

Witness

I've always been lucky like that. The right people came into my life at the right time, just when I needed them, during all those years when you wouldn't have me. A teacher, a boss or two, a doctor, a kind stranger who took special interest in me, stirred me to keep moving and led me in the right direction. Not family, but the closest thing to it I had available. They witnessed my life.

Professor Chandler convinced me to go. Otherwise I would have skipped the whole graduation thing and stayed home, like I did when I got my Bachelor's. I was already thirty-two, the oldest student in my program. Except for Emma Jordan, who was seventy-six and already a practicing therapist for decades. Emma kept saying she wanted to see an M.S. next to her name on her business card before she died, and she was going to her graduation, no matter what. But I wasn't used to celebrating my own success. And anyway, for all the weight you'd placed on education, you still wouldn't be there.

I met with Chandler every Tuesday afternoon for half an hour before class. He supervised my fieldwork. During that last year, I was interning one night a week with illegal aliens who were homeless, women living at a shelter in Flushing, not far from the college. Before that I'd worked with pregnant teenagers in an alternative-school program, and with battered women at a police precinct. In the mid-seventies there weren't many support programs for women in Queens. An intern was always welcome.

There were photographs on the walls in Chandler's office, some with him standing in the midst of a group of smiling young men and women, his students. A few were holding certificates or awards, grants they'd won to start up women's shelters, food banks, a mobile crisis unit, a drop-off site for parents on the verge of abusing their children. It reminded me of Dr. Mayes, who delivered my girls. He had a wall in his office too, covered with pictures of all the babies he'd helped bring into the world. Chandler was the first man I'd ever known who was actively helping to change conditions for women. I admired him.

He didn't talk much, and he moved his slender frame slowly. But Chandler had a straightforward, quiet way of looking at a person that shut the rest of the world out. It took getting used to, sitting with him, having someone's complete attention like that. Especially a man's. In the beginning I spent a lot of time avoiding his eyes, staring at the nameplate on his desk, Dr. Richard Chandler, Chairman, until I got to trust him enough to look back.

Some of what I knew surprised him. Like when one little girl I worked with kept getting into trouble in school for refusing to change into her gym clothes. I thought it might have been a signal of molestation, and I was right. Or when I'd translate a remark a client made, like *Hay algo en el canto de la cabulla*—There's more to this than meets the eye—he was delighted that I spoke three languages well enough in which to counsel people. He'd nod his head a few times and smile.

There were a lot of things I wanted to tell him, things the work was triggering me to look at. Especially about you. Some of the situations I was hearing about from clients were like ones I'd lived through myself. More than once, I was close to telling him that I was scared, that I was hurting my own children, too.

But I didn't speak about it. I didn't want any of it there. Not in school, where I always did well. Chandler thought so highly of me and of my work. I didn't want to mess things up with my awful story. He must have sensed it, that I held back. After all, he was trained to. But he never pried. We'd talk about my case notes for most of the time I was there, and then he'd be quiet for a few uncomfortable moments while I collected my things. I knew he was waiting, giving me time to talk, but I couldn't.

I felt ashamed. Here I was being trained to help clients open up, to be vulnerable and honest. And I did it well. Children, men, and women of any age, any race began talking to me, and before long their hearts were wide open. But with him, I'd say "Thanks, Professor," and keep things business-like. Every now and then I'd hear him in class saying it was impossible to be an effective healer without going through the process yourself. I thought for sure he was saying that to me.

Chandler wasn't an easy teacher. He expected a lot of preparation, which meant hours of reading late into the night. It was the beginning of the fiscal crisis in the city and a lot of the faculty had been let go. His practicum classes were a mix of students from several graduate disci-plines—social work, psychology, and counseling—all eager to outdo each other as we replayed and analyzed case histories. We weren't competitive, but we were a motivated group. It was Chandler. He got people to work harder. He had a sense of balance about him. Steady, no temper or ego. He knew when to apply pressure and when to stand back. And he had confidence in us.

He had these sighs. They were his hallmark. Long before grades were handed out, people coveted a Chandler sigh. He would stand at one side of the room, paying close attention, his hands in his pockets, or arms casually crossed, stroking his white sideburns. If he interrupted, it was to quietly remind us to stop and follow our instinct, or, if we were stuck, he'd raise a critical question we'd overlooked. When he was pleased, or moved by what he heard, he'd lean his head back a little and his nostrils would flare wide to inhale, deep and slow, then he'd exhale the same way, and the hiss of his breath would still the room until he spoke. "Good work, people."

I liked him from the very beginning, at my admissions interview. He was different from the other faculty on the panel who had questions about my ability to maintain a full time teaching job and do graduate work as a single mother. He turned away from them and looked right at me. "You have stamina." And he smiled.

Chandler made little concessions for me. I never asked for them. I never thought to. I would never do that—ask for help. I didn't think I'd get it. I never asked you for any, no matter how hard it got. My kids were still very young, and I was bringing them on campus with me in the afternoons. I'd find an empty classroom for them to stay in and leave them with cookies and their homework, and a boxful of colored chalks they could use to their hearts' content while I went to meet Chandler a few doors down. When his lecture class started I'd make sure to get a seat in the back of the room near the door to keep a ready ear, and check in on the kids a few times during the class. They were good like that, my girls. I expected to hear them making a fuss or fighting, but they never did. Not in public. Even though he saw me do it, Chandler never questioned why I left the room so often.

During the two-hour dinner break between classes I'd run out and take the kids home. It was just a ten minute drive, which gave me enough time to fix something to eat, check homework and get them bathed before the sitter arrived. That's how it was, three times a week. If it all worked out, I made it back just in time for the second class.

A lot of times it didn't. I'd hit traffic, burn dinner or forget to have someone's school trip money ready. It meant a lot of advance planning, and those were days when getting a few extra dollars together meant I wouldn't eat dinner. Or a variety of mini-crises might erupt just as I was getting ready to go back to my second class. A sudden stomach ache, a lost schoolbook, an escalating fight I'd have no time to mediate. Or the baby sitter would be late—the pretty Trinidadian teenager who lived in the apartment next door with her own single mother. She was sweet, but mostly interested in keeping her long, artificial nails shaped and painted in brightly colored patterns that always found their way onto my kitchen table as well. She was all I could find and afford, and the girls liked her. So I'd walk out fast when she arrived, loaded with two arms full of books and enormous guilt.

When I'd get back to class, I'd sit for a few minutes, deaf to what was happening around me—the small talk among my colleagues that I never joined. I was too full of remorse, for the harshness I had shown my kids, the sudden rages I'd get into, the screaming, the threats, the cursing, the slaps that would leave one child scowling and fist-clenched, and the other sucking her thumb in tears. I was sitting in graduate psychology classes, where I felt competent and intelligent. I was compassionate to other people's troubles. But I hid a lot. I felt like a fraud. And I was so tired all the time. I was becoming you. That was when I needed a mother most.

One afternoon after his lecture Chandler asked me to join him and the group at the dining hall. I made my apologies and told him I couldn't. He offered to bring something back, and I said a black-coffee-no sugar would be great. But he looked puzzled, so I told him why I couldn't go, about my kids. He was surprised, and wanted to meet them. I walked him to the empty classroom, where Jackie had drawn a mural along the front blackboard of her favorite preteen subject—a bride, in a splendidly detailed gown of stars and sparkles, standing in a meadow of wild flowers. Lissette had fallen asleep head-down on one of the desks, thumb in mouth.

If he disapproved, Chandler didn't show it. Instead, he talked with Jackie, asking about her picture, the colors she chose, and how she came up with the scene. When Lissette woke up, he made her laugh, congratulating her for being smart enough to come to college at the age of eight. The next week, he had arranged with another professor to have my kids be part of a reading teachers' practicum down the hall. The teachers loved having real kids to work with, and my kids were delighted to be the center of attention. Each night that semester, when I'd make the return trip after the break, a cup of coffee was waiting for me on his desk. Black, no sugar.

On the last day of classes Chandler didn't exactly smile, he looked a little sad actually, but he gave me a strong handshake, and held onto it. He said, "You've worked damn hard for this." I didn't want to let go. Then he took one of his deep breaths and just about ordered me. "Veronica, go to your graduation."

I listened to him. I ordered the cap and gown and filled out a return address envelope for the diploma. And I ordered the tickets. Five per graduate. I thought about who to invite. My two kids, for sure. You? But it had been fourteen years already. My sisters? I didn't know how to get in touch with them. And I had no close women friends.

So I asked the man I'd been seeing on and off for a few years. He'd called a few months after Michél left, and had been a former friend of ours. He was recently divorced himself, and asked me to lunch. You would have pegged him immediately with one of your sayings—*lleva la musiquita por dentro*—he keeps his melodies on the inside. But I didn't see it like that, not then. He was elegant and brilliantly educated in Italy. An evening with him could be filled with Puccini and readings from Dante in *terza rima.* He drank vintage wines, took me to foreign films and liked tango, but would never dance it because of his dislike of Argentineans. He was determined to amass a fortune in real estate before he turned forty, and spent much of our time together teaching me to manage money I didn't have. Above all, he had a penchant for secrecy and infidelities. I'd once found his mysteriousness attractive, exciting. In time I swore I'd never say his name again. But none of it mattered the day I called to invite him to the graduation. He was very pleased for me, glad to come, and would bring his teenage sons too. That made five.

When the cap and gown arrived in the mail, I took my time ironing the pleats and primping up the collar. I wore it over a cool summer dress with my best pair of heels, and the pearl ring Michél made for me when Lissette was born. The girls took turns styling my hair, Jackie insisted I wear lipstick, and Lissette painted my nails lavender, to match the collar on the gown. They put on their best summer dresses and good shoes, and got pansies from a neighbor's garden for me to hold.

I don't remember the ceremony. It was hard to hear over all the talking. I hadn't imagined the crowd. Hundreds of graduates seated in the center of the campus, a small stage for the faculty up front, more seats with families in back. It was late June, and the sun was beating down. No matter how hard I tried to find their little blue dresses, I couldn't see my kids in that sea of people.

A very nervous young woman sat next to me. She complained for most of the first hour that the collar of her gown kept shifting around to the back of her neck. It was because she couldn't keep still, but I couldn't tell her that. I finally helped her hold it in place with a one of the straight pins from her corsage. It didn't help. Every few minutes she would jump up and wave at someone, usually her father, and yell. "Daddy! Over here!" Or she'd pose for her boyfriend who periodically appeared in the aisle next to us, camera ready. I don't think I ever got her name, but I still remember his. "Gaaaaary!" She'd cross her legs or stand up on her chair in her high wedge heels. "Get one of me like this."

She was a nervous talker, and I was grateful for her because she kept my mind off you. All that morning I'd wondered what you'd say if I'd called you. I would have heard that hello of yours that was more a question that a greeting. I'd have started with "Mom it's me, Ronnie," and maybe you'd hang up before I'd have a chance to say "I'm graduating today." Or maybe you'd barrage me with insults like the time I called after my honeymoon when you said I should consider you dead and never call again. Or, if you were somehow okay with me, it would be too late to invite you.

I talked to her, the perky girl. She had green eyes and freckles along her cheekbones. Underneath the mop of brown hair that hid her face, she was cute, cheerleader cute. She asked me what my major was, but before I could answer she told me hers, Exercise Physiology, pronouncing it as if it were her name. And I thought to myself, of course.

I let her talk herself out, to see if it would calm her. I like to think of her as my first client as a professional. She told me about how she'd wanted to be a high school physical education teacher all her life. Nothing else. After that she went on about her engagement, the ring Gary gave her a few weeks ago, and the evolving wedding plans.

She eventually exhausted herself, and the news reached us from people in rows ahead of ours, who could hear, that graduates' names would be called off in groups, by discipline, and that we should stand when we heard ours. The crowd was slowly quieting down, and as I waited I thought about it. How when I was a kid I'd wanted to fly planes, like Uncle Mickey, but girls didn't become pilots then. Or how I'd wanted to be a dancer, but you wouldn't allow it. And I'd thought about writing, like my English teacher Mr. Howard thought I should. But I'd gotten married instead.

"So anyway, what was your major?" When I said it was psychology, she frowned. I could never do that. Listen to people's problems all day. "You must be a good listener." I laughed, and told her it was a prerequisite, to life.

It had been Nora Boorman's joke. She'd say it every time she'd call me into her office for senior staff meetings, in her Swiss accent, waving a finger in the air as she walked by my desk. "Come, come now. And take notes. Plenty of notes. I count on you to listen." Nora was a chemist, the product manager of the cosmetics division of a large pharmaceutical company. I was her summer secretary. She'd asked me more than once to stay on with her after the summer was over. She would train me to be her assistant. I would make lots of money. But I turned her down. The business world wasn't for me, especially the world of fashion. And I only had one more semester left to finish. "You're a temporary secretary right now, but you'll go far. You are a good listener."

Nora was too. She'd heard me one night, when I'd stayed late to type a final paper for the next day's class. I'd thought I was alone. The place was empty. I was working fast, wanting to get home soon. Something went wrong, the typewriter ribbon broke. I went to get a new one in the supply room, but it was locked. I sat down again and looked at my half-written paper, and I lost it. I was sobbing when I heard someone speak. "Whatever it is, don't waste your life on it."

I looked up and saw Nora sitting on the edge of my desk. I wanted to disappear. But she kept talking, her voice gentle, different from the executive tone she used all day. "Most people avoid it. Don't you. Find someone to talk to. A professional. You're a smart woman. You're still young. And you're going into the field yourself. You know what to do."

I felt horrible, but relieved. I wanted to hug her, the way I used to want to hug Blanche DeGrab at my piano lessons. I think you would have liked Nora. She was smart and independent, with a big heart. And way ahead of her time. You would have said *para buen oido, pocas palabras*, for a good listener, few words.

I began to apologize. I told her I was just very tired and had a lot to do.

"Open the yellow pages. Find a mental health center near you. Make an appointment. Otherwise, no matter how far you get, it will sabotage you in the end." She put her hand on my shoulder, which made me cry again. "It's an act of courage to get help. I did it myself." Then she walked back into her office and quietly closed the door.

It took me a few days before I made the calls. Only one person called me back, a Clinical Social Worker. He asked me a few questions. He sounded kind, easy to talk to. He suggested I come in for a consultation, some tests, before we go any further. I said I would wait until I finished school. When I'd have more time. In a few months.

"Listen!" The young woman next to me was pulling on my arm. "It's your turn."

The voice on the loudspeaker announced the Department of Social Sciences. "Will all the candidates for the Masters in Science please rise." It was Chandler at the podium. I couldn't see him, but I knew his voice. I stood up with the others and listened for my name. I looked around for my kids again. I thought of you again. I touched the tassel on my cap, ready to move it over. I thought of the social worker. I thought of calling him back. Soon.

Mommy makes us all get dressed up
and takes us on the subway
even though i am past six now
i have to go under the turn-thing so we save money
we get off at Centre Street
and pass the big police station
then at the corner by Café Roma
Mommy stops and says the same thing every time
Pórtense bién
i want to tell Her that we always behave good
but She stays at the corner watching us cross
over to the brown door with the 194 on top
the buttons on the wall don't have names
but Julia knows which one to push
then her and Carmela run down the skinny hallway
and they begin to climb
there are so many steps more than in our building
they wind around and around like they never end
i can see Carmela's shiny black shoes above me
i wonder do they hurt like mine
since mine were hers before and hers were Julia's
our feet are very noisy
it's like playing follow the leader
and Julia is on top making an echo *Hurry Hurry*
i look up to find her
but there is only sunshine in my eyes
now i see her and Carmela too
looking over the banister to me
Nonna's waiting Hurry
and yes she is
standing at the door with her arms out
giving kisses all over your face
we run inside
to see the treats on the dining room table
strufoli millefoglie and little *canoles*
we know before Uncle Paolo says it *They're for later*
so we play with the brown beads

that hang near the kitchen
then wind up the little piano on Nonna's bureau
and watch it make the song over and over
we go into the big white bathroom
and laugh at the bathtub's little feet
and peek into the room with the big bed nobody uses
Uncle Paolo tells about the opera songs
that come out of the phonograph
he sings them too
his voice is loud and you can hear it all over the place
then he starts Monopoly with the girls in the parlor
i can't play i'm too little
but i get to help Nonna make her sauce
she puts her apron on me
and we squeeze tomatoes in our hands
she stands me on a chair
and lets me mix the big pot
then we wait for it to cook
Nonna takes me into the room
with thread things in all the colors of a rainbow
up and down the wall
i push the pedals on her machine
while she puts beads on the beautiful bride's dress
I make one like this for you sometime she says
Nonna speaks just like shoemaker Joe
on Fourteenth Street
it smells so good here
when we sit down in the kitchen to eat i am happy
Nonna Uncle Paolo Julia Carmela and me
we go into the parlor
to watch Lassie on the television
and we look at the pictures
under the glass top of the little table
when Ed Sullivan begins Nonna calls me *Veni qui*
i go to her chair by the window and sit on her lap
she points to the big picture on the wall
Il Tuo Padre

Non Dimenticare
she's telling me it's my father
and i should never forget
i stare at the tall man standing in the picture
in a cream colored suit
and i think how strange
that Mommy stays downstairs

5

this time the sister lady surprises us
Skipped to the third grade she says
i think it's because i learned all my times tables
just like Mommy said i should
once before after i got home on the plane
She took me to see another sister lady
who had long beads on her skirt
like the ones at Nonna's house
and a bonnet on her head like a baby doll but black
and a little bit of red hair looking out from underneath
she's the one that said *No room*
Let her finish first grade in public school
and Mommy got real mad and took me to PS 19
i cried when Mommy left me there
so hard i couldn't see the other boys and girls
but the days we played the blue bird game were okay
Mommy told Julia to give me extra homework
and Carmela to teach me prayers
and every morning when Mommy made my braids
She tested me
when I got the answer right She was happy
Learning is the most important thing She says
No one can take it away from you
i will help Mommy
we will show those sister ladies yes we will
that just because a person speaks with an accent
doesn't make Her ignorant
and anyway She was a citizen before She came here
not like other people who come here hungry
muertos de hambre
and live in the welfare building down the street
so this time we go back
and the sister lady asks me to read and do math
then she looks at me for a long time
and goes into another room with Mommy
now i'm skipped
Mommy says *Por supuesto* like She expected it

from now on She says i must do the talking for Her
because i am *Norte Americana* and have no accent
things will be easier for us that way
Mommy doesn't have to take me anymore
i get to walk to school with Julia and Carmela
i know the way by heart
down Sixteenth Street to the cobblestones under the el
past the Quaker church and the scary church
through the park right past the sandbox
over to Fourteenth then to First Avenue
it's a long way and the girls walk ahead of me laughing
it's always about boys who stand in the park
or in front of school
Julia says Mommy can't know about the boys
and I better not tell
but it's not fair Julia always tells
if we don't practice piano a whole hour
or if homework isn't finished before she starts dinner
i always get my stuff done but not Carmela
then there's a war with Julia trying to hurry her up
and they pull each other's hair
sometimes there are even worser wars
when Mommy gets home from Her job
at Dr. Ben's
and Julia tells
She takes the strap the one She calls *la penca*
and makes Carmela pay for being a lazy *desagradecida*
ungrateful girl who does not appreciate
how hard Mommy works
to bring food to the table
what makes Mommy the maddest
is that Carmela won't eat
and she takes too long to chew
longer than the timer Mommy sets on the table
ticking and ticking
we're not allowed to talk
because that makes Carmela eat slower

so when Julia and i finish everything on our plates
we can leave the table but not Carmela
nothing can make her swallow
not even the syringe
Mommy keeps it in the pretty white box in the drawer
Dr. Ben brought it one day
to give us vitamin B shots
I was brave and didn't cry
and when he put it away he said
Never touch it because it could break
but even if Mommy brings it out
and puts in on the table in front of her
Carmela still doesn't swallow
she takes so long that Julia and i are gone to sleep
Carmela is still sitting there asleep with her food
and the strap on the table in front of her
and the timer not ticking anymore
and Mommy in the green chair fixing socks still mad

Delicioso

"*Delicioso.*"

My mother's face is a mosaic of little pleasures as she pronounces the word, a welcome change from the increasingly haunted look Alzheimer's has given her face these past months. Her kitchen is cold and I purposely wear a turtleneck and wool socks to visit her on this mid-June afternoon. She doesn't notice. Her eyes are closed and relaxed, her mouth stretched into a full smile as she chews, moving the food around slowly, savoring each mouthful of the *arroz con pollo* I brought her. She looks more as if she were fantasizing the experience than actually eating the rice and chicken.

"*Eres Carlota Barragán,*" she says. It is her ultimate compliment. In my cooking, she says, I am her mother, and her mother's mother before her, reincarnated.

I am uneasy with her remark. This invitation to ancestral connection, to take my place in the line of women of her family, floats before me, shapeless. I am curious, stirred to belong to something bigger than the two of us—an identity beyond the one of estranged mother and daughter that we have carried too long. But, like much of this newness between us, it is not easy to leave the place of separateness I have been accustomed to.

"*Gracias,* Mom," I say, fidgeting with the collar of my sweater.

In all her life my mother has spoken very little to me—less than a paragraph of sentences—about her ancestors. What I knew of *la abuela* Carlota

I gleaned firsthand from the two disturbing years of my childhood I spent with my grandmother in Colombia. She was dark, I remember, in beauty and in temperament, either unpredictably animated or taken to silent, brooding periods. The few visits she made to us were in my early adolescence, when I made great efforts to avoid her piercing eyes as much as possible. *Piel canela*, she would call me, and I would shrink from her attempt to link my cinnamon coloring to hers.

I knew my two handsome *tíos*, my uncles who were both airline pilots and dropped in on us, unannounced, and departed just as quickly. My mother's brothers were total opposites of each other. The short, blonde Uncle Mickey was quick to play and easy to hug. For days after he'd leave, his *Maria Farina* cologne filled the apartment, setting my preference for the gifts I would give to the men I would love later. *Tío Agustín's* brown-skinned hands held open the books he'd bring, anxious to teach me a new word, a poem, a phrase that turned in English or in Spanish to delight him. He was tall and lanky, a gentleman whose black hair and eyes sparkled and became my standard for the way a man should groom himself.

Being with the uncles made it seem like nothing before had ever existed. There were no accounts of family history, tales of wild adventures, or personal disgraces, no mention of homeland politics or traditions. No photographs. No heirlooms. It was the family condition—no one spoke about the past.

But their visits brought ease to my mother's usually stern face, and so, to me. There were hours of conversation and the sound of men's voices made everything good with our world. For a few days my mother's laughter mixed with her brothers. When *la abuela* joined them in their *visitis*, her cooking filled the apartment with the delicious aromas of *arepas, buñuelos, sancon-cho*, corn cakes, bean fritters, and vegetable stew with plenty of cilantro. And later, in the living room, the inevitable dancing to the latest *merecumbé* or *porro* in the uncles' collection.

Once they left, no mention was made of them again. The music, the smells, the crowded rooms, were changed back to wait for another visit. If there were letters or calls, my mother never shared them. Her life returned to its insistence on routine and obedience, and long silent evenings where the only communication among us was the sound of a Bach prelude, Chopin waltz or a Clementi Sonatina someone practiced on the living room piano.

On rare occasions, while she made my morning braids, my mother made reference to the women who came before her, and it intrigued me. The

usually rapid tug of her hands on my hair would ease, and she might unchar-
acteristically pat my head a few times, hard and awkwardly. "You have the
silky hair of my mother's family," she'd say. I never saw her face from where
I sat on the floor in front of her, and nothing about her voice hinted at any
emotion. If I pressed her for more and asked for a name or the color of their
hair, she wouldn't speak. The braiding would quicken, and after a pause,
she'd change the subject.

Once or twice, she did answer me, uttering a few words I would hang
onto like a miner follows a vein. *"Mujeres muy sufridas,"* the women suffered. They were strong characters, stronger than the men. *"Y todas baila-
ban,"* and they all danced. Her hands pulled harder and faster as she laced
the colored ribbons into my braids, silent again until she finished. Then she
whispered angrily under her breath, as though she'd forgotten I was waiting
for her daily blessing, *"Una desgracia ser mujer!"* What a disgrace to be a
woman.

Now I watch my mother across the table and wonder at this dis-
dain she has felt, always, for being a woman. I want to reassure her, tell
her it's all right, no danger in having passion, sensuality, pleasure. The
world is different today, and haven't we each paid an awful price for
all her terror, our life together so long interrupted? What she feared for
me, I want to remind her, is exactly what she's feeling now as she tastes
my food.

"Veronica Elizabeth," she says. The use of my full given names signals
something important is coming. "You are the only one of my four daughters
that can cook." She holds her plate out to me for another helping. There is a
playful, impish look on her face. *"¿Como es eso?* How come?"

For a second I am thrown by her question. After all, I have no way of
knowing whether my sisters cook or not. But then I get it. And she sees me
get it. It is our own private joke.

"Herencia," I answer. My heritage.

We break into laughter together. The more she laughs, the more I do,
and the funnier it gets. In seconds we are open-mouthed and raucous, rocking in our seats, tears streaming down our cheeks. It is splendid, filled with
recognition and satisfaction, both of us enjoying the irony and the unexpected delight in being mother and daughter, still.

I am relieved to see my mother happy, however short-lived it may be.
Just a few hours ago her voice was shaky when she called, asking me to come

by. She'd forgotten the previous, identical four calls she'd made, just minutes apart. She needs to move something downstairs, she said. Something that is too heavy for her.

I wait a few minutes to let her finish her meal. My mother is eating her old way, the way I love to watch. She holds her utensils reversed from *norteamericanos,* the fork in her left hand and knife in her right, always. With the attention of an artist at work, she slides her fork through the mound of rice on her plate, separates a small amount and presses it against her knife until it settles on the fork, then turns her wrist slightly to shift her grip and the direction of her fork as she lifts it to her mouth.

It is a complex maneuver she does meticulously, never spilling a kernel of rice. It is the way my uncles ate, and my grandmother, the way she taught me to eat, but I don't anymore. Neither does she, usually. While she chews, mouth closed tight, her utensils rest in her fingers mid-air above her plate, like a drummer listening for a beat. When she is done swallowing, not before, she begins again with another forkful of rice.

"Mom." I wait a beat for her to look at me. I know that changing the subject now will be like abruptly changing a television channel, her clarity will be gone, she will be confused again.

"What is it that you need me to help you move?" I ask.

"Let me think," she says, biting her upper lip.

"You said it was something downstairs. Something heavy."

"Downstairs," she echoes me. I can see her mind scanning, working hard to retrieve the information. I think about Aricept, the drug she is on, that is supposed to delay the progression of the disease. I wonder if it responsible for this interlude of clarity she—we—have been having today. She lays down her knife and fork parallel to each other across her plate, to signal she is finished.

"I wish Ben was here," she says. "He would know."

I decide not to mention that Ben is dead.

"What?" I ask, gently. "What would Ben know?"

"He knew everything." She smiles at me. Even her eyes smile. "He always did."

On pure impulse, I choose to stay with my mother's reality, whatever it may be. And to tap into it. Wherever it may take us.

"Mom. Tell me about Ben. From the beginning, how did you meet?"

Mommy will kill her i say again
and again Sister Claudia asks me
why Carmela won't stop crying
even Julia says *My mother will kill her*
so she sends us to get our schoolbags
and empty them onto the big table in her office
but it's not there
because Mommy gave us each our bankbook
one dollar in each like She does every Thursday
and now Carmela's is missing
Sister Claudia doesn't know about Mommy
what she's like when She gets mad
she tells us to go retrace our steps all the way home
Julia takes the curb side of the street
i'm on the inside and Carmela in the middle
Julia says we better check the trash cans
Carmela says probably somebody found it already
and is at the bank right now
taking out the forty-eight dollars
and i say let's pray to Saint Anthony
maybe it's a nice person that finds it and will return it
we're up to the Quaker church and nothing
Carmela says she won't go home she'll run away
i tell her please don't that we'll keep looking
we've crossed the el
and we're up to Washington Irving High School
we check the doorways where the bums sleep but nothing
we check the refugee hideouts between the buildings
where we take shelter from the cold and snow
on the way home from school
just like people escaping from communists or fascists
Carmela says they suffer like we do
we only have one more block to go
but Carmela won't move
she's crying and shaking and i'm afraid
because even Julia is quiet
i start crying too thinking about what Mommy will do

it will be worse
than when Carmela stuffed food in her clothes
and threw it down the toilet
or when she gets nauseous and vomits
because she can't eat anymore
and Mommy holds her down on the floor
with her face in the vomit
when Mommy gets mad like that
i eat Carmela's food to save her
and sometimes i feel like i'm going to vomit too
Mommy puts me by the window in the living room
and opens it wide and says *Breathe Breathe*
almost like She's saying a prayer
and i do and i pray to the Virgin Mary
and i hold back the vomit
but it's very hard because my heart beats real fast
and i sweat
but this will be worse
Mommy says She never forgives
not when it comes to money
Carmela is always losing things
She will kill her this time
now we are all crying
and someone says *What's the matter girls?*
it is a policeman
he helps us look for the bankbook
and says he'll walk us home
but Carmela won't move
and when he asks why i say *Mommy will kill her*
and Julia says *Shut up* to me
then the policeman says *Don't worry now girls*
and he walks us home
Go on up everything will be okay he tells us
all the way up the stairs
Julia calls me a *Big mouth brainless numbskull*
when we get inside Mommy is not home
it its very quiet and everyone is acting strange

Carmela looking in the bedroom even inside our bed
Julia watching by the window to see if Mommy is coming
then Carmela is crying again
and we're all sitting together on the sofabed
then the doorbell rings it's the policeman
Julia lets him in there is a lady with him
she is beautiful and has blue eyes
and sounds just like the Father Knows Best mom
A social worker she says when Julia asks who she is
and Carmela starts to cry again
Keep your traps shut says Julia
but when the beautiful lady
asks me to show her my arms and legs
i do
and when she asks me how we all got those marks
i tell her
and Julia keeps saying *Shut up*
but i don't
i show the beautiful lady where Mommy keeps the strap
on the nail by the window
because i don't want Mommy to kill Carmela
the lady wants to know about the locks on the phone
and why the wire on the tv is cut off
i tell her Mommy has a special plug
and only She can put it on
so we can practice piano
and do our homework
and not be ignorant
when the lady and the policeman leave
Julia says *You're in for it now Miss*
and bites her nails
Carmela says let's hide under the bed
we put on our dungarees so the strap won't hurt
and we crawl under the bottom bunk and we are safe
until Mommy comes home
and Julia tells Her everything
then Mommy comes into the bedroom

and says *Come out here*
Carmela is crying and me too and we stay put
i can see Her shoes
the brown high heels with the pretty buttons
and i see Her walk back and forth then stand still
it is very quiet and we don't move
then Mommy goes out to the kitchen
the social worker lady and the policeman come back
and they talk with Mommy with the door closed
they are in there a long time
Carmela is wishing they will take us to live with them
when they come out the social worker lady smiles
she puts one of her white glove hands on my head
and says *You're a brave girl*
after they leave Mommy stays sitting at the kitchen table
and i am watching Her from the sofabed
She is not moving only looking straight out the window
later She turns around and looks at me and says
Traitor

"It was *coincidencia*. I met Ben *por suerte*. Destiny. Julia was in first grade. The school required a note from the dentist. I did not know any dentists in the area, so I asked the nuns. They recommended Dr. Reiss. They spoke very highly of him, and they all had good teeth, I could see that. I notice teeth right away when I meet someone, you know.

"The next day I went there with Julia, up on the second floor over a tailor's shop. I saw in the waiting room that there were people who did not speak English. Imagine, the Lower East Side of Manhattan, you had every ethnicity there. Jewish, Italian, Oriental, Black, Puerto Rican, Polish, Hungarian. Everything. Except Colombian. People here in New York had not even heard of Colombia then. It was better to say I was from South America. Most *norteamericanos* did not know geography; they still do not. They would say stupid things like, 'Do you speak Colombian?' as if it were a language. Or, 'You speak English so well for a foreigner.' I always felt like saying, *Idiota*—I have been speaking English longer than you have been alive!

"But I was too well educated to belittle myself, so I showed them their stupidity in another way. For the ones I could help, like the Italians or the Puerto Ricans, I translated. That is what happened at Ben's office that first day. I helped him with a few of his patients. Ben did not have a drop of prejudice in him. He was a tolerant man.

"He must have been impressed, because on the next visit he asked me if I would like to work for him. I thought about it. I had three little girls. I was separated and had to go to work every day. It was easier for me to get to Ben's office that to mid-town, where I had been working at an insurance company, in the Mony building. And taking that subway every morning, always late because I had to walk all the way to the school on First Avenue with the big girls, then drop you at the baby sitter a few blocks further. *Que cruz la de una madre*. What a nightmare. So I said yes. That is how it began.

"I liked him right away. So clean, kind to everybody, and a hard worker. He would never turn a patient away. Even if it meant staying late, until eight or nine at night. If you came to him in pain, he helped you. People waited to see him for hours, you know. Right to the end of his practice. When they did not have money to pay, he gave them a year, or he accepted other things as remuneration.

"Like the baker on First Avenue, Veniero, way back when he started, would bring him boxes of pastries in payment. Ben would laugh, there was so much of it. Later, when Veniero became successful, that man sent Ben a big rum cake every year on his birthday. You remember. Ben would bring it home for all of us.

"Anyway, I knew he liked me. I had to be smart about it. No man would want a woman, an immigrant, with three children. Plus I was not Jewish. He knew about Julia from the beginning. When I started working I told him I had another child. That was Carmela. I was afraid to tell him about you. But one day he saw me on Second Avenue pushing the baby carriage with you in it. He did not care. He loved you instantly. He used to carry you everywhere. He called you China Doll because of your eyes, so small and dark. We would even go to the movies with you. You were a good baby. Never cried.

"At first he asked me to lunch, on Fridays, when the office was closed. Then we progressed to dinner. Ben was a very shy man on a one to one. That's why he was almost thirty and still single. When he did not have that dentist's gown on, *mi' jita,* he was very uncomfortable with people. But he loved to dance, and when he saw I was a good dancer, he took me every week to Roseland and other nightclubs around the city, especially uptown, in Harlem. Lindy, jitterbug, tango, cha cha, merengue, anything. Except that crazy one, the fox trot. I could not do that one. But we had fun.

"It was not long before he said he wanted to marry me. I did not have a divorce yet from your father. It was Ben who said I was in limbo, not married, not single. What is the protection in that? I wrote to my mother and asked her about it. She said as long as my decision to stay in the United States was firm, and the relationship with Nino, your father, was irreparable, I should get a divorce.

"You know that meant I could never go back to Colombia, because a divorced woman may as well be dead there. She is worse than a prostitute. No one will look at her. I knew I would never go back there. What for? A pain in the neck is what! From people straining to look up and down at each other. They cannot help it. It is a phony life. Being measured all the time. What class you belong to, what family, what country club, what bank you use, who sews your clothes. Go back to that? *Cuando San Juan agache el dedo!* Not till the cows come home.

"Here in America people are more real. They are cold and indifferent and undereducated compared to what is expected of even a peasant woman in Colombia. But Americans are less complicated. No one bothers you. You can live next door to someone for twenty years in New York City and still not even get a hello or a drop dead. But no one is asking you about your pedigree or keeping score. You do not have to worry about maintaining your social class. In Colombia even the restaurant you choose depends on class. Good riddance. I knew I would never go back.

"So I spoke to an attorney and he filed papers against your father. Ben said he would marry me as soon as the divorce came through. But he was not brave. Nine years. He made me wait nine years. We even broke up several times. As soon as he heard I had another *admirador*, he would come back. There was never any doubt for me that it was Ben. He was the man for me. But if he was not going to make up his mind, I was not going to sit around waiting, wasting my life.

"I could have made another choice. There was a writer, Fernando Hernandez, the poet. You may remember him, you were about five years old when we met. He was handsome, with dark hair and dark eyes, and that beautiful dark skin. *Muy indio*. Erudite. An intellectual. But poor. I had not expected to meet anyone. It was during the breakup Ben and I had right after that miserable trip to Mexico. Fernando's sister had been a classmate of mine in Bogotá, one of the few loyal friends I had. She came to live in New York and I was so happy to see her. She introduced me to Fernando. He was a very sensitive, passionate man. Sweet. He used to write me poems and sing to me. I was still a young woman. Fernando was kind, a gentle man who found beauty in everything around him. He wanted to marry me, without any of the fear Ben had. He loved you girls. He loved me, without reservation. But he had no financial security.

"So I wrote to my mother and told her my dilemma. She was a very practical woman, Carlota. As long as you are going to stay in the United States, she said, you should marry an *americano*. She never wanted me to marry a Colombian, or any Latin. Sooner or later you will be hurt, *te la hacen*, she would say, either they are womanizers or they want to own you. And she never wanted me to be limited by Colombian society, the way she was. She wanted me to have freedom, to be able to have choices in my life, and that is what America is. I turned Fernando down. Love alone does not feed babies. He cried when I told him I was going to marry Ben. Did I miss him? Every day, for a long time.

"Ben left me waiting at the courthouse twice. Until ultimately he did not have a choice anymore. When I told him I was going to have a baby, he gave in. It had happened before, you know, and he convinced me to get it taken care of. It was against the law then. Even more than that, nobody spoke about it. Those were different times. He did not know who to get, and he would not ask anyone either. He was terrified that it would jeopardize his practice if anyone found out, or if anything happened to me. So he suggested I ask my roommate Madelaine. She was from Mexico, in her early thirties like me. Do you remember her? She was your godmother. I met her right after you were born. Your father was gone. She needed a place to live. I needed the income. She came with me to the church on Fourteenth Street, La Virgen de Guadalupe, just the two of us, to baptize you. She used to carry you all the time, *consentièndote*. She loved babies. She did not have any of her own.

"So I asked her to help me. She found a doctor for us. Ben closed the office for the first time in his life, saying he was going on vacation. Some vacation. Madelaine took care of you and your sisters and we drove in his new car, that yellow Pontiac that used to make you nauseous, all the way to Mexico. Five days of misery. *¡Que desastre!* Hours and hours on the highway. Then those awful winding roads of Mexico. Some dingy office with this doctor I did not even know, did not even see his credentials. He could have been the *carnicero* in that town, who knows? I should not speak ill of butchers. There was Sammy on Second Avenue who was so sweet. He liked me. Every time I went in with you girls he gave me a break on the meat, giving me a little extra, or free bones for soup. He was a big flirt, but so what? I flirted right back. You do anything to survive and feed your children.

"On the way back from Mexico, two days after the procedure, I started hemorrhaging. But I did not want Ben to stop in any unknown place. Poor Ben was driving like a crazy man to get back fast. I waited until we got to New York and I went to Dr. Berry. What a wonderful man he was. He said I was lucky. Things could have been very bad if I had waited any longer. All that endless driving in that car. It is funny how you hated that car. You used to throw up in it all the time. Maybe it was because you sensed the *desastre* of that trip in it.

"No sir. I wasn't going to go through that again. I was having this baby no matter what. So he finally married me. On his day off. Would not even take a vacation day for it. Poor Ben always worried about his patients. So one Friday morning I put on my gray suit and sent you to school. Then we met at the courthouse and got married. The next day he went right back to work, like nothing had happened.

"Ben was a good man. But always scared. Scared of the stock market crashing again any minute, scared of anyone seeing us together when we went on a date, scared to tell his family we were married. He was already a grown man, forty years old, a professional. He had bought the building for his new office by the time I had Isabella. We had a two-year-old baby and he was still staying at his mother's house after work. *¿Qué es eso?*

"Finally he took one of the apartments upstairs from his office. But that was no better. I was living on Union Square with his baby, and he would come to visit us after he finished work, late in the evenings, then leave in the middle of the night so you girls would not see him. This is a married couple?

"His mother used to come to the office. She lived just a few blocks away. I guess she was lonely for her son. It was strange, because she had her other son, Morris, twelve years younger than Ben. She never doted on him like she did with Ben. My mother was like that with my brother Mickey. Ben's mother used to come around just to sit in the waiting room every afternoon, just to be with people and listen to conversation. She must have been very lonely after her children grew up.

"She had a husband, Abe. Such a good man, gentle, quiet, always friend-ly. But Miriam preferred coming to Ben's office to being with her husband. We would chat. One day she said to me, 'Oh, I hear a baby crying.' It was Isabella in the back room. You remember, there was a kitchen and eating area, with a big room, enough for a playpen. Just like in his old office, when I started working for him and you were a baby, and you stayed in his back room too.

"I said yes, Miriam, it is my baby." By then I was already expecting anoth-er child. Gabriel. I still worked for Ben for a few hours every day. He would not hire anybody else. Did not want anyone knowing his business. On the week-ends Julia worked for him. Then you worked for him too, correct? Anyway, that day his mother must have heard the baby moving around in her playpen. What else could I do? When I brought Isabella out she made such a fuss. "What a beautiful baby." She must have said it a hundred times. She wanted to carry her, so I let her. She asked if I ever took the baby to the park, because she liked going to the park in the mornings, and she could meet me there. So I did. I would meet her every morning before going to work. Can you imagine that? Miriam was playing with her own grandchild and did not know it.

"The situation was getting absurd. 'What is this?' I said to Ben. But he still would not tell his mother. We could not go on living in that small apart-ment, me with four children. I had had it. He was not doing anything about it, so I had to think of a solution.

"Once I got the idea there was no stopping me. I packed the baby up, pinned a note on her coat that said 'Hello I am your granddaughter

Isabella' and sent Julia to Ben's parents' door. I told her to ring the bell
and watch until someone opened, then to leave the baby there in her carriage. About an hour later I got a call from Ben. 'How could you?' He
was very upset of course. Furious. All I said was that we could not go
on like this. Five minutes later I get a call from his bosom buddy Sidney,
the attorney. Telling me I had caused the family mental trauma, that if
anything happened to Ben's mother or father I would be sued. Go ahead,
I said.

"Of course I did not care, because I did not have anything to lose. I was
not scared of that Sidney either. He had tried to fix me before Ben married
me. The day before we finally went to the courthouse for the ceremony,
after all the patients were gone, Ben tells me I have to sign a paper. That his
lawyer had advised him he needed a prenuptial agreement.

"I was so hurt. It was one of those moments of deep betrayal that one
never expects from a person you love. Here you are carrying his child and
about to be married. But I said Yes, Ben. Then he dictated the thing to me
right there in his office while I typed it on his Underwood, the manual one,
making all that noise. I signed it. It said I would relinquish all my rights to
any of his assets, both those he acquired before the marriage, and any acquired after the marriage. Then he listed every possibility, his practice, bank
accounts, real estate, insurance, stocks.

"I knew I was signing away my financial future. But I signed it. I was
pregnant, already had three children, and most of all I trusted Ben. I knew
he would never hurt me once the child was born. I knew he would be a good
father. He was a good man. Just scared of everything. So I signed it, in du-
plicate. He did not even give me a copy. One was for him, the other for his
lawyer. I was so hurt. I could not stop crying.

"The only record I had of that agreement was the carbon paper.
Something told me to keep it. Your father taught me that at least! Always
keep a record of what you sign. I guess it paid to marry a lawyer first. When
I got home I called the lawyer I used to get a divorce from Nino. He told me
to re-type the agreement on a piece of paper, have it notarized, put it in an
envelope with the carbon paper and mail it to myself, certified. He said I
might need it someday.

"The next day I put on my gray tweed suit and we met at the courthouse.
And we got married."

Dr. Ben is so nice
i don't think he knows about Mommy
he surprised us once
it was on Wednesday when we had released time
and i got to walk to his office by myself three blocks
Mommy was helping the patients
She looked so pretty in Her white uniform
talking sweet like She used to before
i didn't mind waiting in the back room
i got to watch the whole Lone Ranger and Felix The Cat
then Dr. Ben came in and said
Help me get something from under this table
and there was a box with a puppy inside
we call him Hamlet because Julia liked that name
it was in a story she read
about a prince whose father died
she can read all the hard words eighth graders get
and she gets to wear stockings to school
Carmela too she's in seventh
if they behave they go to dances in the school gym
and i get to help them set their hair in big rollers
i pass them bobby pins
and they open them with their teeth
which is bad to do Dr. Ben says
Dr. Ben tells us about taking care of our teeth
we get to sit in his office chair
he rides us up and down
and puts the fireman's hose in our mouth
and sprays water
then the elephant's nose sucks it up
and we get a toy every time
Mommy says he is the best dentist
that's why all the nuns go to his office
even Sister Claudia
she doesn't like me i know it
because on the first day
she put me all the way in the back of the room

which didn't work because i couldn't see
so Mommy took me to get glasses
then Sister Claudia had to put me in the front row
that made her change her seating chart
and she didn't like that
she doesn't look at me
even when i get gold stars for spelling
or when i almost won the math medal
except for Billy Cunningham
i got just as many hundreds on my tests as Billy
but Billy has a mother and father
they talk with Sister after Sunday mass
all of them together
anyway i guess that's why he won the medal
Sister always has us say a prayer
for dead mothers or fathers
except for mine
i haven't told Mommy
that Sister Claudia doesn't like me
but i had to tell about the red ribbons
Mommy put them on my braids
and tied a big bow on the tops
when Sister sees them she says *Come Here Miss*
in that mean voice and points to her desk
so i go up there and she says
What color ribbons are you wearing
which was obvious
but i say *Red* not to be disobedient
and she slaps me on the face
The color of communists she says
Take them off
i don't turn around but I can hear the kids gasp
and I know communists are bad
they want to drop surprise bombs on us
that's why we practice the shelter drills in the hallways
now they'll all tease me and call me commie
i know Mommy will be very angry

about me losing my ribbons
and my braids all coming undone
and me looking like an *india salvage*
and maybe hit me or send me away again
but when Mommy asks me i don't want to lie
i don't want to be a sinner
so i tell Her what happened with Sister Claudia
and afterwards She is very quiet the whole night
next day it's my turn to do math at the blackboard
and there's Mommy at the door
in Her Special Day grey suit
Sister Claudia goes out into the hallway
she is out there with Mommy a long time
then she comes back to her desk
and gets the red ribbons and gives them to Mommy
everybody sees it
after that Sister Claudia says over and over to me
You have a wonderful mother

"Life is funny. Sidney Cantor had formed an opinion of me that I was some kind of monster. But after Ben's parents found out about us, and they did not collapse, Sidney invited us to his house in Long Island. When we got there, all of Ben's family and friends from the neighborhood were there. What a surprise. Ben did not want to come out of the kitchen at first. He was so angry at Sidney. But Sidney said, 'Be a man.'

"Ben told me years later that I had made him grow up. He thought his parents would hate him. They did not. But they did not like me much. It is understandable. They were old. I was Christian, plus I was from a different culture, divorced, three children. His father, Abe, never said a mean thing about anyone. He was a tailor, from Poland. Miriam was an Austrian Jew. She had an older sister, Beatrice, a nice woman, but the two of them were the only ones left in her family. The rest died in Europe in the Holocaust. Miriam and Beatrice never got along. I liked Aunt Beatrice. When I told her I was Ben's wife and that the baby was Ben's, she said God had blessed us. But not his Mother. Miriam never liked me. I took her son away from her.

"Ben worked too many hours. He was too interested in making money. Even his brother Morris used to tell him to get out of the office and go to his family. It would be nine and ten o'clock before he got home. But he grew up in the Depression. He could not help it. When he bought this house it got worse. He never stopped worrying about money.

"He only spent money freely on his mother. Everything was Mama Mama Mama, a real mama's boy. I married two of them! No luck with mothers-in-law. Both of them the same baloney. They wanted their sons for themselves. Forever. I am not like that with my son. I have no power over Gabriel. I do not tell him what to do or who to marry or anything. I guess I only did that with the girls.

"That was not the only similarity either. According to what I see, I married two sex maniacs. The first one could not resist an attractive woman no matter where or when he saw her. And Ben could not live without sex every day. What is it about men? They never calm down. Even years later, he was still making demands on me, incessantly.

"We bought this house. I wanted a big house. I was fed up with living in Jackson Heights. Those attached houses, everyone knowing your business. Anyway, after you ran away—well, after you left—then Julia and Carmela left too. It was very hard. We did not expect it. Ben and I cried together in that bed for months. It was time to change. So we found this house. We loved it here. We had privacy.

"By the time Isabella and Gabriel were teenagers I got tired of being a slave to housecleaning and taking care of children. I waited until Gabriel started high school, and I found a job. Ben was still giving me the same allowance I had agreed to when we got married. Forty-three dollars a week. That was my salary when I had stopped working for him at the office in the 50's. From that I paid for the three girls' piano lessons and dance lessons, clothing, little extra things. I tried never to ask him for money for you three. Of course he provided the house. And the food. He bought all the food, every Friday. He could keep track of the expenses that way.

"But now it was 1975. I never had money for myself, or to save. Plus everything was in Ben's name. If something were to happen to Ben, I would be out in the cold. He did not even have life insurance in my name.

"I always listened to radio shows that gave practical advice. Especially that one, Rambling with Gambling. It got me thinking. I began to ask Ben for an increase in my allowance. I was not getting any younger and I was worried about my future. He refused. I felt humiliated. I needed spending money. I had been a good wife. Faithful, took care of his office, his home, his children. I felt used. I had tried in every way not to be a burden to him. I never wanted him to throw in my face that he had taken care of someone else's children.

"I had become very frugal. I recycled everything, before it became fashionable. I had learned to sew. I made new clothes for the little ones from the clothing you girls had outgrown. I bought day-old bread. I baked cakes instead of buying. I kept most of the lights out in the house to save on the electric bill. All this to save him money, so he would see I was a good wife.

"Ridiculous! Here I am married to a dentist, living in a mansion, but worse off than when I lived in Union Square. I had nothing of my own. So one day I told Ben that I only wanted one thing from him. I asked him to add my name onto the deed to the house. He refused. So I got a job.

"Sometimes I would be tired, working all day, coming home to prepare dinner, do the dishes, waiting for him to get home at nine or ten, get lunches ready for the next day. Before I knew it, it would be eleven-thirty at night. He would already be sleeping. I would go in quietly, exhausted. The minute I would lie down, he would feel the mattress move and say 'Hi Honey.' Right! Hi Honey. You know what he wanted. Sometimes I would sleep on the floor, to avoid waking him up. I wanted to sleep. Rest. To be left alone from his desires.

"Eventually I felt so betrayed by him. I had trusted Ben to take care of me, and that after all our years together he would see that he could trust me to be his ally, that he would know my loyalty by now. But he did not. All he wanted me for was his gratification. I was only a sex object.

"I had had enough. I saw all these other women in the world who did absolutely nothing for their husbands, with cleaning ladies and long nails and new clothes all the time, spending their husband's money like water. All right, that was not my way, to take advantage like that. But here I was doing my best to raise his children to be intelligent, cultured, well-mannered. When I asked him to put my name on the deed to the house, he refused and would not budge. It was something a normal man would do without having to be asked, I took another room and put a lock on it. That was the beginning of the end. He said without sexual life there is no marriage.

"So he went to his friend Sidney. He filed for divorce. It was such a farce. All because of sex and money. Here he is telling the judge in court that I refused to have sex with him and that he had to move out to avoid the fighting. Yes, we had terrible fights at the end. Ben was never a man to have a temper. But you know me, when I am pushed against the wall, *olvidate!* Forget it. I had begun to lose respect for him. I was desperate. No matter how I asked him, *a las buenas o a las malas*, kindly or in anger, he still said No.

"What a fool. What would it have taken? Putting the name of your wife on your house with you? This is too much to ask? After all the papers I had signed my name to, now he refused this. It did not make sense to me. It was okay with him to put my name down on his joint returns to the I.R.S., which I had to do blindly. Every year he brought home the prepared forms and put them down on the kitchen table for me to sign, but I never was allowed to read them. He had a blank piece of paper covering everything but the line I was to sign.

"Did I do it? Yes, I did. I trusted Ben. But not after he refused to put my name on the house with his. I had no safety left.

"After that last awful fight we had I guess it was all over. He was coming home later and later. It would be eleven o'clock before I would hear the car pull into the garage. Then he would stay in the basement. I would call down there and say 'Ben? Aren't you coming up?' But he would stay there until I was already asleep. Everything had changed by then.

"I had always looked forward to him coming home every evening. In the old days, when we first got the house, it was my favorite time of the day. We had time alone. We even took showers together, after the children were asleep.

"But by now he stayed out more and more, I guess to avoid the topic of the house coming up. Which I became more insistent about, the more he avoided it. *Se encontro el hambre con las ganas de comer.* As we say, hunger met appetite.

"I thought I would convince him to see my point. One night I went down to the basement after him, to talk. He would not talk to me. He walked upstairs and I started to argue with him in the kitchen. He would not answer me. The silent treatment. Then he went into the bedroom, which I did not use anymore, and locked the door. I was so angry. I went into the bathroom crying. Then I got the key and opened the door myself.

"¡*Que ironia*! It was me who had the lock put on that door in the first place! To keep burglars out. Now he pretends he is sleeping and I go over to wake him and does not answer me. So I remembered that we kept a bedpan under the bed because of his bad kidneys he had to use it sometimes in the middle of the night. I got so mad looking at him pretending he was asleep like that. I went to the bathroom and peed into the bedpan and then I threw it at him. That was the proof that he was not asleep, because it did not hit him, it went all over the bed but not a drop on him.

"Some aim I had! He was furious. I had never seen Ben like that. He jumped out of the bed and came at me with his fists up in the air, like a boxer. So ridiculous when I think of it. What was he thinking? Was I another man his size that he should box with me? The next thing I knew he had me on the ground and punched me. He was strong, Ben. He knocked my bridgework right out of my mouth. My face was all black and blue for more than a week. After all the trouble he had gone through to make me those bridges, too. I was not an easy patient.

"I ran out of the house to the neighbor and she called the police. When they got there, I went back to the house but they said I should not press charges. They just said some foolish things about this being a respectable neighborhood and Ben being a professional man, maybe we should go for counseling. Ben was terrified, his hands were shaking. I did not want him to lose his license to practice dentistry. The police officer suggested one of us leave to avoid more fighting. So Ben left. He went back to his office and lived upstairs again, like before we were married.

"Even in the divorce he did not have the courage to be genuine. During the whole divorce procedure he came home every weekend and slept in my bed. He said he missed my cooking. *¡Imagìnate!* I guess that proves the saying about the way to a man's heart.

"There we were in court one day and his attorney, Sidney, making motions about the premarital agreement and little did he know Ben had driven me to the courthouse that morning. It was so offensive that it became almost comical, you know.

"At one point I asked my attorney if I could speak on my own behalf. When the judge said yes, I stood up and said, "Your honor. I did sign that premarital agreement. I loved my husband and I trusted him to take care of the children and me. And did you know that the defendant slept in my bed last night?"

"Well, that created some commotion. Sidney was ready to kill Ben, he was so angry. Such lies. That is why Isabella will not speak to me. Ben had her convinced that she should leave the house and go live with him in Manhattan after he left. She was just a teenager at the time. Of course she would choose to be with her father. She loved her father. I understand that.

"Me, she hated. Because I was the warden. I had to keep the home up and force the children to practice, to study, to be educated, and to never have to depend on anyone for money. She is independent now, and that piece she owes to her mother, whether she faces it or not.

"Poor Isabella. Hating her own mother. One day she found something in Ben's car that belonged to me. And all that time he had not told her that we were seeing each other. Like I was 'the other woman.' Together on weekends, in divorce court during the week. *¡Que locura!*

"In the end he wound up giving me the house. I did not ask for anything else. Not alimony or support or anything. I just wanted a roof over my head. Look how much it cost. Breaking up the family like that. All because he would not put my name on the deed with his. That is all I took from him. Just my house.

"Ben wanted to marry me again. He called me every day, right to the end. 'I miss the food, I miss the house, the garden,' he would say. I would never deprive him of that. He was my husband, even after the divorce. He said it had all been a mistake, that Sidney had pressured him to file for divorce. I believe him. Because when Sidney was dying in the hospital from brain cancer, Ben did not go to see him. Friends since childhood. It was not like Ben to be that way. But he said 'Sidney has paid for what he did to you.'

"How ridiculous. The whole thing. *Nadie sabe para quien trabaja.* All the money and power in the world, like Sidney's millions, cannot save you from dying. I was stupid, yes. Impetuous. But it is in my nature that when I am offended, I am *intransigente.* It is in my blood. Latin people are very easy going, but do not offend us! I do not think Americans understand that, they do not take offense the same way we do.

"When Ben asked me, I should have said yes and married him again. I missed him. He was a good man. Only he was so scared of life. Held onto money like it was sacred. Now I am like that. I became just like him. He even apologized to me, a few months before he got sick. 'I treated you so badly. I gave you so little money.'

"*¿Ya para qué?* You know, right until the last week of his life I cooked for him. I sent him his meals, with Julia. Poor Ben. I did not want his money. I wanted him to respect me. And protect me. Too late now. I miss him though."

I look up at my mother's kitchen clock and see two hours have passed. She has talked steadily and clearly, the words coming to and from her fluidly. She is every bit as smart and alive as when she was my young mother, when the sound of her flawless but accented English would have made me cringe. I feel proud of her. She has given me more than I asked for. She has emptied herself. As if today was the appointed time for it, the right time. The Story of Ben Day.

There is calmness on her face. But she is tired and it is growing dark. Soon, the Sundowning will begin. She will grow restless, fearful, and reenter the confusion that is her usual world.

I say, "Let's go downstairs and see what needs to be moved."

I follow my mother down the string of steps leading to the basement of her house. She is walking slowly but knows where she is headed. There is loud barking. She reassures me that the dogs are in the garage, leashed and waiting for my sister Julia to return. She clicks on the dim overhead lights as we go. The air is thick with mildew and the smell of dogs. My mother walks to the door of a storage room, reaches into her pants pocket for a key and unlocks it. She looks around furtively, then pulls the door open fast.

"I have to be careful with everything, Ronnie." She sounds scared, pained, almost whining. "They are stealing everything. They break in at night and take things." And then I remember that Julia mentioned she was secretly emptying out rooms, methodically ridding the house of what she calls the crap heap. "By the time I'm finished there will be enough to fill two dumpsters of useless stuff," she said.

But my mother does not know this. I must choose between reassuring her that thieves are not entering her home and protecting her from taking offense at being overridden. Both will add to her anguish. Neither will lessen her confusion. I decide to distract her instead.

"What is this room, Mom?" It is one of several storage rooms in the big house I have not seen. My mother pulls on the overhead light chain. The room is the size of my bathroom, with wooden shelving along three walls with peeling paint. There is a badly stained sink with large jugs of liquids in it. A few chipped enamel basins sit on a bottom shelf, and what looks like a large box rests at the top of another.

"This is the photography room," my mother says. "Gabriel uses it for his hobbies." She is running her hand along the shelves, talking to herself. "Poor kid, he never gets out, always busy, always studying."

"What are we looking for in here?"

She turns to me, a look of surprise on her face. She winks at me, extends her arm and points up at the box on the top shelf.

"*Eso*," she says. "*Bájame eso.*"

I follow her instructions and bring the box down. It is lighter than it looks. It is not a box at all. It is an old suitcase. Beneath a film of dust it is brown leather, smaller than I remember, with a wide zipper around its perimeter. "*La maleta*," I whisper in awful recognition.

"It was yours. When you went away to Colombia." My mother uses the edge of her blouse to wipe off the dust on the handle. "Take it with you. I want you to have it."

"What's inside?"

"Old things. You keep them now."

She runs her hand across the top of the suitcase, feeling the leather. I let my hand follow hers to pull on the zipper. It makes a thick purring sound. She helps me pull the top open. A pungent, citrus smell fills the room. Inside, folded carefully into individual clear pastic bags, are all my dance costumes. The ones she made for me.

something is wrong
my sisters are not here on the corner
like they are every day talking to boys in their class
today there are no big kids at all
not even in the candy store
where Carmela buys us a hot chocolate
with money from her babysitting job
if she has enough money we get an English muffin
with lots of butter and we share
maybe they got detention but it's been a long time
and all the kids have gone home
maybe it is released time but today isn't Wednesday
it must be that i forgot something
maybe i should walk to Dr. Ben's office
it is three blocks and i know how
even if it still is scary to cross by myself
i do what Mommy said
walk next to a kind looking woman never a man
until i get across
but today it is hard to keep up
our desks had to be emptied for housekeeping
Sister said *All books and personal belongings*
must go home
my school bag is very heavy
i am okay on the avenue
but not Tenth Street
it is very long and has no stores just tall buildings
so i must drag my school bag on the sidewalk
and i can't even play the games Carmela makes up
on Saturday mornings
when we walk to Third Street Music Settlement
we see who can count the most squares
not stepping on a line
the winner gets to pick the candy bar at the store
and we share it
when Carmela wins she picks Almond Joy
and Julia picks Chunky

which is hard to break so we take bites
but i pick Mounds i like the coconut
Mommy and Dr. Ben can never know
about us eating candy
it's our secret
Carmela knows what's coming
blocks before we get there
without even looking at the street numbers
she knows when it will be the shoemaker
or the Second Avenue Deli
or the Saint Marks Theater
or the Chinese laundry
or Sammy's Butcher store
i know when the Yiddish Theater is coming
it has pictures and there is an actress Molly Picon
whose name is almost like ours
i told Dr. Ben about it
but he said probably it is just a coincidence
and that Miss Picon is a very famous woman
sometimes he goes to see her in shows
i can see Second Avenue now
and Dr. Ben's windows up on the second floor
there are no kind looking ladies crossing so i will wait
i drag my school bag to the curb and sit on it
a man is coming
he walks funny
like the monster on television
like the one Carmela pretends to be
when she comes out of the shower
he is closer now
i think he is the monster for real
he stops and looks at me sitting on my schoolbag
Can I help you little girl
he sounds like the monster exactly
he is Frankenstein
i scream
Don't be frightened child he says

i scream some more
Frankenstein is coming closer
putting his hand on my head
i will be taken away and cut up into parts
i scream again
and someone says *Leave that child alone*
it is a kind looking lady
she is hitting Frankenstein with her newspaper
i run behind her
Frankenstein and the lady are talking
she says *So sorry Mister Karloff so sorry*
Frankenstein looks sad and walks away
the kind looking lady helps me across Second Avenue
and tells me
i just scared a movie star

Work

The truth is, I've never had trouble finding work. It's been a running joke in my life, that the abundance I didn't get in family I was given in work instead. But I'm not sure you have a right to ask me about how I managed, considering that you never bothered to find out how I was doing. You probably believed I'd married rich and was okay. Michél wasn't rich, but money wasn't something I worried about. Not until the divorce. I didn't retain any wealth from my marriage; just most of the responsibility. Thanks to you and how you trained me, I had office skills, and for those years while I went back to finish college, they came in handy. A few weeks after I graduated, I answered a newspaper ad. The city school system was doing emergency hiring of bilingual staff to comply with new federal laws. I hadn't intended to work in education, and didn't have the training. I'd studied political science and languages, and before that, music and dance. I had other things in mind, like writing, or working for an international firm. But the summer I got my bachelor's diploma I was alone with my girls and needed a job as urgently as the school system needed me. I could write and read Spanish and Italian well, so I took the test. A month later I was hired as a grade school teacher, *en español*, given a provisional license, and sent to a part of the world I'm sure you've never known existed.

It was only an eighteen minute car ride from my Queens apartment to East New York, Brooklyn, but I may as well have been assigned to another country. I'd never seen a place like it. Union Square and Second Avenue were nothing like Livonia Street or Linden Boulevard. Empty lots covered in trash and old tires dotted the landscape like pieces of a perverse Monopoly game, each contained by a high fence, as though the mounds of rubble needed guarding. In between, the remnants of buildings that once stood tall waited for something better to happen. Every few blocks the burned carcass of a car sat on a sidewalk. The only break in the vague shades of brown on the horizon came from the electric-lemon-yellow of the corner *bodegas*. You could buy groceries and beer there, and tickets for the *lotería* in San Juan or Santo Domingo and New York's lotto. All on easy credit, for a fee, provided by the welfare check-cashing service the bodegas offered if you stepped inside, where the stink of exterminator fluid hung on every shelf.

If you looked at an aerial photograph of the neighborhood, you'd place it just a few parkway exits away from the Long Island suburbs where most of the school's staff lived. But you wouldn't see a park, library, supermarket, drug store, movie theater, or clinic anywhere around. You wouldn't see many people moving through the streets either. Especially not children. Just twice a day, they'd congregate at the one place that connected East New York to the world outside. School.

It was the mid-seventies. You would remember, the time when New York City was on the verge of bankruptcy. City services were cut drastically. The worst hit was taken by the school system, where thousands of teachers were fired overnight. The position I was hired for had been newly created under a federal grant, and was exempt from the city's budget problems. It was my *destino*, as you might say, to enter that workforce when morale was at its lowest. My timing couldn't have been worse. The last person any of the teachers wanted to meet was an idealistic newcomer walking in to replace one of their experienced and now unemployed friends. To make things worse, mine was the only job that was secure, because of the funding source.

It rained the first day, in heavy downpours. My battered old Chevy stalled just as I turned onto a side street near the school. *Un viejito* with a Dominican accent appeared and helped me push it to the curb. When I left it there he said he'd keep an eye on it for me, and blessed me because I was a teacher. By the time I walked into the building I was soaked and shaking. But no one, not even the security guard, noticed me.

That's the way it was for a long time. The principal and his secretary were besieged by legalities and district politics, and had very little time or inclination to speak with me. Teachers complained within earshot about my license, saying it was a sham because I hadn't been required to complete the same course of study they had. They resented the program I worked in. It catered to illegal immigrants, they said, and the money it cost would be better served rehiring their friends who'd been fired.

I tried not to take it personally, but it wasn't easy. In the teachers' lounge someone would invariably tell me all the seats were reserved, but no one else came to fill them. Important information didn't reach me because my mailbox was overlooked when notices about special events or new procedures were distributed. The union rep did speak to me once, and got me to join the union. But months passed before I realized he hadn't given me enrollment papers for my benefits plan. And no one came into my classroom to supervise me, except for the once-yearly compulsory observations.

Worse, there were no books for my students. I was told there was no money allotted for my program, bilingual education. Of course I believed the administrators. I was new to the system and hadn't yet learned to question authority. I asked a teacher across the hall if I could see her teacher's manuals, but she made excuses. I went to the district office a few times, and the best offer I had was for a pile of outdated math workbooks I could take if I was willing to carry them back to the school. I did, and decided to work alone and stop asking for help.

I'd been assigned a combined third and fourth grade bridge class. Some of the children were violent, completely out of control, and nothing I did was working. For a week or so I hardly got any instructional time in. Then I thought of Sister Claudia, who managed to keep order in her classroom without even raising her voice. I imitated her. I adopted that stern look of hers and tried to exude the silent power she projected. Even without a nun's habit, I realized the children responded well to me when they sensed I cared about them. I made trips to the book room behind the gym and the teacher helped me dig up expired books to use. I read everything I could get my hands on about bilingual education and planned every lesson, in two languages. I worked the children hard, the way you did with us. They learned. They liked school. The administrators took notice. So did my colleagues. I was rated an excellent teacher.

Over the next few years more bilingual staff was hired. The culture of the school grew more polarized. The more vocal bilingual staff complained that they felt shortchanged. Money wasn't being distributed equally among programs and Hispanic children were being deprived. Senior people, mostly white, felt imposed upon, betrayed. Suddenly it became a common thing for people on both sides to approach me. They complained about everything from the imbalance of supplies to program assignments to the number of difficult children per class to parking spots in the schoolyard. They were convinced every malady was based on favoritism and racial bias against their own group. A few tried hard to persuade me to side with them against those they considered the "enemy." Latinos assumed I sided with them. Whites assumed, because I didn't fit their image of a Latina, that I'd be on their side.

It felt like home. Split down the middle, both sides fighting. Things peaked one spring when the supervisors of both groups separately brought it to my attention that I'd made a terrible mistake completing a new Faculty Ethnic Survey form. I hadn't selected *Hispanic*. I hadn't selected *White*. Instead, I'd made my pencil mark next to *Other* and written in *Mixed*.

I could hear your voice. You would have been horrified, telling me to make a fuss over the *ignorancia* of whoever designed the form. Couldn't a white person be Hispanic? Or a Hispanic be Black? What about most Hispanics who have Native American roots? And, I wondered, how would Isabella and Gabriel be classified in such a survey? Jewish, White, Hispanic? *Other* worked for me.

You would have suggested I quit. But I couldn't afford to care about politics. I needed the job, the family medical coverage. Most of all, I liked working with children. I was in a position to do good or great damage. With a child, I couldn't pretend and succeed. They could see right through me. I had to be real, work hard, be prepared. And I admired the families, especially the mothers. Most of them were single, like me, far from home and alone. I could see the pain in their faces, but very few were bitter. They trusted me with their children, and I took that seriously. No matter how bad I had it, especially with money, I could look at the hardships these women faced and see that I had advantages in my life that I was very grateful for. They taught me what real generosity looked like. It wasn't unusual for a child to bring me food, a piece of cake, rice, or a *pastel,* in appreciation. I knew each time I accepted a gift that it was given at great sacrifice.

So I stayed. After a few years, the city's finances stabilized. The principal broke down in his office one day, right in the middle of lunch, and was replaced. Another group of newcomers came into the system from the newly created Special Education division. They became the new target for the disgruntled people on staff. I finished graduate school and moved into the mental health staff. By the time I left there, my colleagues had come to respect my competence enough to stop into my office with their personal problems. They'd forgotten all their prejudice.

you can tell Mommy is in a good mood
when She makes French toast
i get to help
sometimes i dip the bread in the egg
and pass it to Her then She puts it in the frying pan
the whole place smells delicious
and Carmela likes it too so no wars
there is never war when Dr. Ben comes
he brings us coffee cake and milk
or for a special treat Carvel brown bonnets
then we all go for a ride in his new yellow Pontiac
Mommy and the girls love it
but the leather smell makes me car sick
i know it would be a very bad thing
to vomit in Dr. Ben's car
he has to stop all the time so i can breathe into a bag
but he never gets mad
we go to Central Park and have a picnic
with salami sandwiches or the potato knishes he brings
Dr. Ben pushes me on the swings
when he gets tired Carmela pushes higher and higher
she won't stop and i get scared
Julia says a little girl went flying over the top and died
but she and Carmela stand up and swing real high
i like to watch them they look like giant butterflies
their hair goes out way behind them they flap their elbows
and they can stop and jump off real fast too
Dr. Ben always says *Watch Out Girls Don't Break Your Leg*
when he is with us we are safe and Mommy is happy
She gets dressed up and makes hairstyles like in the movies
the French twist is Her favorite
Dr. Ben calls Her Lana Turner and She laughs
it feels just like Dr. Ben is our daddy
but i know he really isn't
so today when i am dipping the bread in the egg
i ask Mommy where is our father
She looks surprised and says *He's Dead*

then i think about Jeannie Ryan
her father died last week
and our whole class went to the funeral mass
and Jeannie went to the cemetery with her mother
so i ask Mommy where is my father buried
it seems like She forgot the answer
because She looks like She it trying real hard to remember
Julia pulls my braid and says *Nosy body*
and Mommy says *Far away*

6

Mommy looks very pretty
Her hair is up and She's wearing Her gray suit skirt
Carmela and i are wondering where She is going
it is a school day and a Friday so Doctor Ben is closed
Her face is all scrunched up
like when the radio gives bad news
and She'll stop ironing or chopping onions
or whatever She's doing
She'll look at the radio as if it's a person talking to Her
and She gives a long sigh and tells Julia
If I'm not back in time you make the noodles
we can tell Julia knows what's going on
because she's quiet
i hope Julia makes pastina that's our favorite
when Mommy walks Her skirt opens a little in the back
the same as the lady who came to see the walls last week
her skirt was brown not gray and she wore little glasses
So sorry to bother you on a Sunday morning
her husband was a great artist
they lived in our apartment before us during the war
and he painted pictures right on the walls
could she just take a look she asked
so Mommy let her come and walk through
there is only wallpaper now no paintings
but she was very thankful
when she left Mommy said *Pobre Mujer* and sighed
i wanted to tell the lady we have wars too
but instead i watched her skirt open and close
now Mommy is giving us a hurry-up-and-eat look
but it's soft boiled eggs today
i hate swallowing the white part all slimy and stringy
Carmela hates it too and pokes at it
we use pieces of whole wheat to wash the egg down
and just as i'm dipping into the yolk
Mommy walks away
like She forgot all of a sudden about watching us eat
She is standing at the mirror

i watch Her tie the bow on Her blouse
She opens the closet door to get Her shoes
and nobody is saying a word
so i say where are you going Mom
She puts Her feet into the black patent heels
and She says
To get married

Corrientes

R ain has been coming in through the dining room ceiling all morning. In the forty minutes I've been here my sister hasn't stopped cleaning, until now. Julia is leaning on the handle of her mop, lost in thought. She is barefoot, in snug khaki shorts and a tank top, a film of perspiration coats her sunburned neck and shoulders. In a faint voice, as if I weren't standing here, she repeats something I've just said. "That's right. You never lived in this house." My sister has forgotten, out of habit, I think, that for most of our lives I haven't been welcome in the house she lives in.

Julia glances at me from across the room and shifts her weight, looking like she is going to say more. Instead, she lifts the bucketful of murky rainwater next to her and walks with it, setting it down in front of me without a spill. I watch her bend to wring the mop head, hard, the muscles along her arms and back are taut and distinct, and although almost no water comes from it, she twists the mop once more in the opposite direction. Julia isn't a large woman—she has my mother's frame and is inches shorter than me even when she's in her high heels—but there is a nearly impenetrable quality to her body that matches the uncompromising way she can move through a room filled with people. When she is upright again, I try to read her face. Is she annoyed, embarrassed? That was a rare glimpse of tenderness she offered a moment ago. I'm confused.

Julia pushes her mop, working backward and away from where I stand. She's already cleaned this side of the room and now she glides over it again in quick, side-to-side strokes. I take a step out of her way to avoid the light spray of water that bounces from the floor onto my open-toed shoes. "Bad leak, huh?" I hear myself being careful, as I am with everything I do around Julia. Our reunion is still new, unsure.

I clasp my arms behind me and wait for her cue. She doesn't answer and doesn't stop moving. A muffled drumroll of rain stutters across the roof. All that is left of the intrusive rush of water that earlier made its way down the wall and along the baseboard the length of the room is a small puddle near my mother's massive Barcelona dining table. I'm glad my mother hides in her dementia, closeted in her room, unaware of her flooded house, unable to worry herself sick or start a quarrel with Julia about why it happened or how to fix it.

A few feet from the kitchen door, Julia stops to lean on her mop again. Her eyes are lowered. She is still silent. Only her chest moves, rising and falling in slow, deep breaths, as though she were preparing to hold in the air in her lungs for a long time. What could she be thinking? I listen to the rain. We are a strange sight. Two women standing in this enormous room, heads down, sighing. Someone watching might imagine we are looking for something we've dropped, or maybe, praying. I want to move closer, offer to take a turn with the mop, touch her arm in solidarity. But I hold back. I've never seen Julia welcome affection or help, from anyone.

This is a peculiar stillness we share. I can't remember another time when we've been quiet together. It feels all right, nearly peaceful, as though we've been given permission, finally, to simply be. Maybe we need this time, this space, for what we've just bumped up against—those decades of absence between us neither of us has mentioned yet.

Julia is the first child. She holds her place clearly, unequivocally. With just her tone of voice or change of expression I can feel miserably misunderstood or entirely reassured. I know her as my mother's helper and companion, another parent, someone I learned to fear and obey early. The very things that once by necessity made her more than a sister make her less than one now. I want to remind her about sisters, how we are familiar in a way we can never be with others. But Julia and I have arrived at middle-age bound in childhood postures and images of each other that never evolved. This nervous politeness we've fallen into isn't helping. I want to know what her life has been about, if she's ever been in love, or in trouble, or ill. And, after all this time apart, how much does she know of me?

We don't ask these things. We stand in this damp, quiet room in my mother's deteriorating house, behaving ourselves as we honor old family rules. I tell myself to let it be. Can't this be enough, standing side by side in the silence, just sisters? Isn't this better than all the years of waiting?

Julia heads for the puddle. As she pushes her mop she takes me by surprise and says, "We lived in the other house then."

"That's right," I say. "In Jackson Heights. You'd just finished college and I was seventeen." I tell myself to wait. But I can't resist. "Do you remember that night?"

"I don't spend time thinking about that stuff. You do."

"There was an awful blizzard."

"Really?" I can see her face now. Her brow is creased, which makes the pale reddish hairs of her eyebrows stand on end.

What does she remember about that night? Was she there when my mother ordered me to leave, told me that I couldn't come home again? In all the commotion, I don't remember seeing Julia. Has she forgotten what led up to it, how it all started a few months before, with the blind date my mother arranged for her? A foreigner, a Middle-Eastern artist and businessman, and she hated the idea immediately. When he came to pick her up she refused to leave the house with him, until my mother directed me to go along. It was with me he flirted all evening—the first man who ever did, and I was smitten. Did she hold that against me? Did she find out later, like my mother did, that I'd been meeting him secretly? And that last night, when he came back with his offer to marry me, was Julia up in her room listening? Did she hear our mother's blind rage, his insistence, my pleadings? Did she watch from her window when I stumbled out into that storm? I want to hear Julia's side of it. What was it like to have had her sister declared off limits, forever? Most of all, why did she obey that rule, faithfully, for nearly thirty years?

I take a breath and ask, "Did you ever wonder what happened to me?"

"You eloped."

"Eloped?"

It is my mother's word. It riles me to hear it, like a sudden burst of sand blowing in my face at the beach. It is the word my mother uses to explain, and to avoid explaining, to anyone who asks, why we'd been apart so long. The touch of romantic adventure it conjures up usually draws a sympathetic glance from the listener toward my mother and a suspicious one toward me. It is an image so deliberately different from what really happened that I can never muster an answer of my own, my mouth filled with sand. She's an old woman, I say to myself. She's lost her reason. There is no point in correcting her.

But this is Julia saying it. I never expected it from her.

"I didn't elope, Julia." I want my sister to understand, to be my ally now, because she wasn't then. "I didn't get married for months after that."

"That's not the way I heard it," she says.

"Weren't you there that night?"

"No. I was not."

"So how do you know what happened?"

Julia stops and looks directly at me for the first time. She brings one hand to her hip. "When I came home from work that night you were gone. Ran away. Left everyone in shock. You let yourself be seduced and ran off with that man. It nearly killed her." I watch little lines of entitlement form around my sister mouth as she speaks. "You made your choice," she says.

Everything else I know about navigating through life doesn't work here. I want to shake her, make her see. I want my sister to know what really happened that night. How it became the demarcation line, the before and after, of my life. The time when I lived inside a family, filled to the brim with them, the good and bad, the everything of all of them, when I was one of them, hoping it would get better. And the abiding sense of being split that pervaded everything I did afterward, even to this day, distracted always by a persistent yearning for the reunion I waited for, stood vigil for, even as time played against me, *esperando*, waiting to be allowed back in.

I lean against the wall I'm near and dig my fingers hard into the palm of my hand to stop the tears I feel coming. "But it wasn't a choice, Julia. It was an ultimatum. And I was only seventeen years old."

Julia lets the mop handle rest on her chest and raises both arms to gather and clip her hair in a jumble onto the crown of her head. It gives her a primitive, ceremonial look, a tribeswoman wearing native headdress.

"Well," she says. "As it turned out she was right, wasn't she? Your husband didn't stick around and you ruined your life. She couldn't do a thing to stop you." A quick, forced laugh escapes her. She is mocking me, or my mother, I can't tell. I don't care. I want her to stop.

"It's not that simple," I say. "Not any simpler than when she was right about you and Neal." I regret my words as they leave my mouth. Julia's eyes are wide and her mouth hangs open. She either didn't expect me to speak, or the answer I gave. I steel myself. My sister and I are determined, each in our own way, to change our tangled history.

But Julia misses a beat. Her shoulders drop. She nudges a renegade strand of hair away from her face. "So what?" she says, softer. "That's how she was. You should have known that. So should I. Once she made up her mind, the woman never budged. Never. Even if she was wrong. There was no way to win with her." Julia makes a full turn away from me, back to her mop. Over her shoulder she says, "At least you didn't have to put up with this nightmare all your life."

I stand, contrite and miserable, watching my sister, seeing clearly for the first time how we have lived mirror images of each other's lives. It was Julia who eloped, just weeks after I left, with Neal. The marriage ended quickly and, except for those months, Julia never really left home, never had children, never lived alone.

Even if I can find the right words, it is too late for talk. Julia is done. In a second she is in her full voice, getting louder with each twist of her hands around the mop. "This is a curse! Every month it's another disaster around here." She props the mop against the kitchen doorframe and lifts her bucket. "This stinking flooding is the worst of all." She scolds the house, head back, as though she expects an answer. "Anything else?"

I tiptoe over the wet floor to reach the kitchen door and hold it open for her. She moves through and into the mudroom. Neither of us speaks as I grab the mop and move ahead of her. I open the garden door and she steps out into the rain. She empties the bucket into the storm drain. When she comes back in I hand her the mop. She puts it into the bucket. I silently offer her a kitchen towel. She takes it, slings it over her shoulder, washes her hands at the sink, and dries herself off.

When she's done she walks back into the dining room. I watch as she gets a portable fan from the corner and turns it on. The breeze is a relief inside this soggy house. She pulls the heavy drapes and the room seems even larger. I look up at the ceiling, to the football-size hole along the crown molding that shows an exposed beam above. It is where the rain began its morning course down the wall. The leak has slowed to a single sporadic drop. Below, further along that side of the room, my mother's sewing machine stands, open and threaded.

I leap toward the machine. "We better move this," I say, and quickly swing the console cover over it. The calligraphy lettering has faded, but I can still make out the gilded "SINGER" across the polished black arm of the machine. I run my hand on it and feel suddenly comforted by this old habit of my mother's, that she's always kept her sewing machine handy, ready to quickly mend a garment or alter a hemline for her family. Or to invent something new from something outgrown, the way she did late at night in our Union Square days, when I shared her sofa bed across from her machine, and I'd watch, wrapped under a blanket, while her foot pushed the cast iron pedal driving the purr of the motor faster, slower, stopping, lulling me to sleep, making it safe to finally close my eyes and leave my tired mother to her reverie.

I see my grandmothers. *Nonna,* stitching beadwork on wedding gowns in her Mulberry Street sewing room, the favorite room of my childhood. *La abuela,* sitting at this very machine during her visits, the only time I felt it was okay for me to approach her, to watch her cut a piece of cloth into a garment and leave a finished dress or pair of pants for each of us to wear long after she was back in Colombia. I wonder, did these two women ever meet?

"I'll do that," Julia says. She pushes past me and in one motion lifts the machine and swerves through the side door into the adjacent breakfast room. I follow her. The floor is dry here.

"Mom doesn't try to use it anymore, does she?"

"No," Julia grimaces. "She just stays up in her room."

For a second I wonder how much of our talk has reached my mother. Then I remember, she wouldn't be able to follow it anyway. "Maybe we should cover it, in case the water comes in again."

"There's no leak in here," Julia says. But she goes back into the dining room and returns with a flowered plastic sheet, maybe an old tablecloth. She flings it open, I catch the bottom end and we slip it over the machine. We tuck the ends in, careful to wedge the corners under the legs.

"Damned roof," Julia groans. "We've had half a dozen people in here over the years. They promise they can fix it. They always lie. They see there's no man living here, so they take advantage. It's the same every spring. The stinking water comes back in. You should have seen the basement last year, before we got the new drains."

I stand near a small café table. The window sills that line the room hold small plants Julia has brought in to replace the empty coffee cans and jars my mother mindlessly collected. Julia pulls out a chair and tells me to sit down. She reaches for the stack of store-bought cake boxes on the table and opens one. The smell of cinnamon reaches me.

"It isn't Russian coffee cake," she says, and smiles. "But it will do." She darts back to the kitchen announcing, "I need coffee!"

I sit and look out the two large picture windows that frame the room. The rain has stopped, the sky is clearing. I see my mother's pear tree, her two magnolias, her irises readying to open. Her garden is loyal, even in her absence. I hear the birds and their commotion. I listen to Julia clanging metal as she prepares her favorite drink. My heart beats fast. Tears well up again. This time I don't hold them back.

Julia returns with two coffee mugs and two dishes and puts them on the table. She folds paper napkins, sets out a spoon and fork for each of us, and sits down. I wait for her to look at me.

"It's like Nonna's little room," I say.

She nods and takes a long sip. "With all her sewing threads on the wall. And the mannequin. And the sunlight."

We are quiet again. We inhale the aroma of cinnamon and coffee.

Fridays after school we go to the A&P under the el
Carmela and i pull the cart
Julia holds the black wallet with the list and money
she knows where everything is around the store
and how to pick fruit without brown spots or holes
Carmela and i always look at the T.V.Dinners
she likes the picture on the macaroni and cheese one
i like it too
especially the way it has separate places for everything
and the little piece of cake just the right size for kids
but Mommy thinks frozen food and cans are bad
so we can't get any
except three cans of tuna and vanilla ice cream
Doctor Ben is always talking to Mommy
about ways to cook easier
and making things Carmela will eat
but Mommy says people in this country are lazy
and don't know anything about nutrition
and will eat anything that's wrapped
americanos ignorantes who will be very sick some day
from not eating fresh food
She is afraid we will have poor blood and get polio
so every morning we take a vitamin
and every Thursday is cod liver oil day
when we get home from school there's the bottle
on the kitchen table
Mommy pours one spoonful for each of us
and gives us a piece of lemon to suck on
it's very disgusting to swallow and hard not to vomit
we hold our noses not to smell it
but then we get liver for dinner and it's the worst day
Fridays are good
because Mommy makes tuna salad and egg noodles
and Saturdays *arroz con pollo* we like the yellow rice
especially the burned part at the bottom of the pot
the other days aren't so good
Mondays meat loaf

Tuesdays chicken
Wednesdays leftovers
Julia says she could do the shopping by memory
it's always the same every week
one day Mommy gave us something from a can
Doctor Ben brought it
Fruit Cocktail he said
we each got a little cup for after we finished eating
but Carmela took some with her meat
and she swallowed real easy
so Julia and i tried it too and it worked
when Mommy saw it worked She put it on Her list
now we can swallow anything Mommy makes
real fast even liver
as long as we have fruit cocktail to make it go down
we call it Carmela's miracle
on the way back from the A&P
Julia and Carmela take turns
one block each pulling the cart
and i carry the eggs and bread
Julia gets mad because the cart is too heavy
she says curses and that she is not our slave
when we get to our door she curses even more
carrying it up the stairs
Carmela pulls from the top and Julia is underneath
i hold the doors and act as lookout
Carmela says 101 East 16th Street isn't our real address
that it's really 36 Union Square
because our building is really two connected
and that's why each floor is so different
first you come in the lobby
then there's long white steps
where there are usually lots of men by the mailboxes
Julia says they are having a union meeting
in the big room
Mommy tells us to never speak to those men
just keep going don't even look at them

you turn left and up the dark steps to the second floor
where the wierdo people live
that's what Julia used to call them
until last Christmas when they invited Mommy and us
inside their apartment
it was gigantic and so pretty
there was a big real tree growing in the living room
i never saw a tree like that indoors
but no Christmas tree
and lots of books in shelves all around
and they have a piano with a tail
Mommy called it a Grand
they ask us to play for them
Carmela played her Bach Prelude and Fugue
Julia played Golliwog's Cakewalk
and i played the Tales of Hoffman
it is a really nice melody even though it makes me sad
the lady gave us a song book
and the man gave us cookies
they even asked us to show
how we slide down the banister
but Mommy wouldn't let us
She says we have to behave like ladies
even with the beatniks
we have never seen the people on the third floor
those are offices with the doors closed all the time
you have to walk down the hall to the next stairs
that's where you have to be real careful
just in case there is a bum sleeping on the floor
we have to jump over him real fast and quiet
and it's really scary that the bum might wake up
while you're in midair
once you make it to Mr. Durant's on the fourth floor you're safe
he is the super he gives us light bulbs for the hallways
and sometime brings up fried chicken his wife makes
Mommy says he is our black saint
because once She felt really sick during a blizzard

and She was alone
and there were no taxis or ambulances
so Mr. Durant walked to Fourteenth street
in all that snow
and found a man
a perfect stranger
who drove Mommy to Bellevue hospital
and i was born

Dream

I had the same dream for years, into my thirties, that I'd discover a door in the living room of our Union Square apartment, between your sewing machine and the old upright piano, and I'd walk through into a room I hadn't known was there all along, crowded with fine old furniture, large, solid wood tables and chests, and I'd run my hand over them to feel the different grains, ignoring the Do Not Touch signs that were placed all over. Way in the back, he'd be standing there. A tall man in a cream-colored suit, one hand in his pocket, looking at me. But through all that furniture, I couldn't make my way to him.

Nino was brilliant, you said, handsome and very kind. He died a long time ago, and I should leave it alone. I didn't need to know any more, you said, in that unyielding voice of yours. As if it was enough, as if I should have let it be, like the others had, and never mention him again. But I was curious. Why wouldn't I be? Your silence about him was impossible to ignore. I only heard him mentioned once, when you were arguing with Ben. He said Nino was a swindler who had taken all your money, and you went into the bathroom and cried for a long time. Ben's voice was crude and mean. I can't remember another time I ever heard it like that. I worried because he was holding baby Isabella in his arms while he yelled. I didn't understand at first. I'd never seen you withdraw from a fight before. It took a few seconds until it registered that Nino was my father's name.

I wanted to follow you, to be with you behind the bathroom door, on your side of something I didn't even know about but I could see had broken your heart. But my twelve-year old feet wouldn't move from where I stood at the far side of the kitchen, my eyes on Ben as he paced back and forth. His words weren't meant to hurt me, I'm sure. He couldn't have known he had stepped on a minefield—a child's curiosity about family secrets. But Ben had torn something away, exposing me as the child of someone he looked down on. I wanted him to take back what he'd said, right then, because I believed in Ben, and there was no way for me to know if what he said was true or not. After that I was never easy around him again.

Every so often Julia would change the usual muttering she did under her breath when she was angry at you and declare *Nino isn't really dead* and slam the bedroom door or kick a chair, swearing *He'll come back someday to save me from this hellhole!* I didn't know what to believe. When I got a little older, I figured out she would say that just to make herself feel better. She'd been his daughter the longest. She was nine when Nino died. She knew him, even more than Carmela had, so she missed him most, I told myself, and that was what made her so mean.

The only picture we had of him was on Julia's side of the dresser. A plain round silver frame resting on two pea-sized orbs, a perfect fit inside my hand. Mystery spilled out of that photograph, like that melody that now and then came up late at night into our apartment from one of the floors below us, the bewildering sound you complained about because it kept you tossing in your sleep and you could never figure out its source. Was it one of those overnight tramps that slipped into our building, maybe, and settled behind the lobby staircase with his horn, his mute fit in snuggly to keep the music just inside our orbit without causing a fuss, his sliding tones ascending to each floor, melismas slipping under doors and back down again, breaking the silence around us one sweet note at a time?

Nino, patient like that tramp, resting inside that little silver circle, in Colombia maybe, sitting like no man I'd ever seen sit, cross-legged and elegant in a dark cane armchair, one hand on his knee, the other slung over the chair's side, his long fingers reaching toward the checkered floor, his shirt loose and open around his slender neck and strong chin, his features soft and symmetrical around the straight line of his nose, the only hint of tension the two small creases around his mouth. Nino, always waiting, disregarding everything else around him to look straight ahead, his eyes serious, sure, ready to listen to everything I needed to say. I used to run my finger around the edge of that little picture when no one was around, and cover up the line of his crossed leg and wonder what it would have been like to climb onto his lap.

Things got even more confusing when Ben moved us out to Queens. I suppose you wanted to forget Nino and Little Italy and Union Square. You wanted us to forget too. I can't blame you for that. You were starting a new life with a new husband, new children. But I didn't belong to Ben; that was clear. I hadn't been part of your old life with Nino and my sisters either. And I'd lost sight of Nonna and Uncle Paolo when our trips to Mulberry Street stopped. I was an outsider among you. It wasn't long before a vague, persistent longing took root in me. Moving away didn't stop my wondering. It fed it.

I wanted Nino to be real. I wanted to know ordinary things about him, the kind of things you only know about people when you live with them. I would look at other fathers with their children, especially Ben with my little brother and sister, and wonder what my father had been like. If his voice was deep or nasal, or how he looked standing on a line or walking down the street, what the smell of his skin was, how he held a fork, or what his handwriting looked like on a shopping list. When I was in dance class I'd think of him watching me, the tall silent man by the door, and that would make me work harder at arm positions or at cleaning up my footwork. I'd practice my Czerny finger exercises and my mind would wander. I'd imagine what he would have been like coming home, hearing me play the piano. Would he smile and give me a hug and say something kind? Would he have been quiet and sullen and walk past everyone without a word, on edge, like you? And I had other, bigger questions. How did you meet, two people from different parts of the world? How did he die? How did he feel about me, the third child, another girl, still in a high chair the last time he saw me?

My sisters weren't any help. I couldn't talk to Julia. I learned to stay clear of the temper and name-calling that usually followed my asking her about lesser things than our dead father. And whenever I mentioned Nino to Carmela, she became quiet. A look would come across her face—the one I'd see on you late in the afternoons when you finished work and sat down for a while in that green kitchen chair of yours—as if she was tracking something far out in the distance, absorbed by it, disconnected from time and place. After a while she'd come back, and she'd stutter hard to say, "I d-d-don't remember him."

It wasn't until high school that I ever talked about it. I met Amy, Elyce, and other girls who would mention their dead fathers in the middle of an English class or across the lunch table. It was a relief. I could say "my father is dead, too," out loud and not feel ashamed, or worry that I'd be up next to be teased—what I saw happen often enough in previous schools—for being one of the unfortunate children. We were the kids who recognized something in each other eyes that other kids avoided, sadness perhaps, locking our gaze whenever adults asked a bit too kindly about us, or about how our mothers were doing, then shake their heads as we passed. We were the boys and girls for whom nuns whispered extra prayers at daily mass and encouraged our classmates to do the same, as if we had a condition to be pitied and feared, contagious, and that we should strive to somehow overcome. I suppose, in the fifties, being fatherless was just that.

All the same, I wasn't equal with other girls. They knew details about their fathers. They could tell stories they'd heard or remembered about their dads being in the war or owning a grocery store or teaching them to play the cello or beating up their mothers. I didn't. Nobody I met was as ignorant as I was when it came to fathers. I didn't even think to make things up.

You don't get it. You can't. You had your father in your life. You knew him. You talked to him, watched him eat, heard him give you advice, tried to impress him. At least I suppose that's true. Maybe you hated him, I don't know. You didn't say much about him either, except that he was a Spanish aristocrat who was very serious and died just before Julia was born. Even if you did hate him, you got to know him well enough to. At least you had a chance to look at your father's face and recognize him, good or bad.

Yes, you're right, it was a long time ago and lots of people thought like you did, that it was better to keep things from children, to hide the truth, because it would make it easier. But for whom? I hear people all the time, even today in my work, convinced that if they don't mention the folks who are gone, their children won't miss them. Well-intentioned people, afraid of grief, believe that a father or a mother, even a family, can be replaced. As if those spaces in the heart, in our identity, are exchangeable. If they're allowed to speak, children will tell you it isn't true. It wasn't true for me.

I don't know how to say it more clearly. There must be a Spanish proverb you use that fits, but I don't know it. I think of my Jacqueline when she was a little girl learning to write, bent over our kitchen table working hard to manipulate the pencil in her small fingers, guiding it along the lines on the page to form neat rows of repeated letters, every one a new adventure. When she found one she wasn't pleased with she'd squeeze her little mouth tightly and make it anew, thrilled as she shrieked out her discovery, that the writing could be erased, but not the spaces.

You ask me why I was the only curious one in the family. Why I couldn't let things be. Maybe the others didn't need to search for answers. Maybe I'd been alone too long, and knew so little, that I had nothing more to lose. Or maybe the truth wanted to be told as much as I wanted to find it. After all, Nino was just one secret, wasn't he? You had so many. It wasn't my intention to expose them. What I wanted was my own history. Something I could pass down to my daughters that could be more than the awful legacy of incompleteness and separation I inherited.

Whether you acknowledged him or not, Nino never stopped being my father. Any more than you stopped being my mother during all those years when you wouldn't talk to me. I wanted to know about him simply because he *was* my father. I needed to claim him as my own. It was natural, and inevitable.

Doctor Ben and Mommy are baking a cake
it is Julia's fourteenth birthday
she will be going to high school soon
and is going to buy herself a new uniform
she isn't going to wear any more homemade uniforms
no way
she's tired of being a freak
everyone can tell Mommy makes our uniforms
the school emblem patch on ours is missing
Mommy says She can copy any dress but not the patch
why should She pay for something She can make
She needs to save money to pay tuition
and piano lessons and now my flamenco classes too
i didn't know it would make Mommy worry
just because i liked the dancers we saw
at the museum show
and i tried to do the steps in front of the kitchen mirror
Mommy said it must be in my blood
so She found lessons for me
Lola Bravo is from Spain and she says i have talent
i can roll the castanets real fast
and i learn the steps faster than the other girls in class
Lola says it's because i play the piano and i am musical
i get to wear my long skirt that Mommy made
and the red heel *tacones* Uncle Mickey brought
from Madrid
the studio is right on top of the Ed Sullivan theater
and there are never any wars at flamenco class
i wish i was there right now
Mommy is angry at Doctor Ben
She has turned off the Perez Prado music
maybe She is changing the record
they were dancing lindy in the living room before
Doctor Ben swings Mommy around first fast then slow
their feet move together and they laugh
Carmela and Julia can do it too they teach me a little
sometimes Mommy and Doctor Ben dance the tango

he dips Her all the way down just like movie stars
after the dancing the cooking begins
Doctor Ben looks like a chef with the big white apron
Mommy reads the recipe out loud and he mixes things
then he starts singing his favorite song *La Paloma*
even if he can't say all the Spanish words
it sounds pretty when Mommy sings it with him
si a tu ventana llega una paloma
tratala con cariño que es mi persona
then they start to dance again
and everybody waits for the food to be ready
but today he has made a mistake
Mommy said two cups sugar and two cups flour
instead he put in four cups sugar and no flour
it smells like candy and there is smoke in the stove
when Doctor Ben opens the oven
it looks like a science experiment
big bubbles everywhere
running down the sides onto the kitchen floor
it makes the girls laugh then i laugh too
Mommy starts to cry
You ruined it Ben you ruined it
Doctor Ben doesn't answer he just takes off his apron
the girls and i go into the bedroom
we can hear them arguing then the front door slams
Mommy is walking back and forth crying
Come out here she says and we go into the kitchen
Mommy is putting spoonfuls of cake blob into dishes
This will show you to mock me eat every drop
we try to do what Mommy wants
but the cake blob is very thick and hot
Julia gets up from the table
she says *I won't eat this crap* and takes Hamlet's leash
we can't believe it she is leaving with Hamlet
Carmela is trying to swallow but she can't
her cheeks look like balloons and she is scared
i finish mine then switch dishes with Carmela

i don't want her to get hit but Mommy sees me
She is even more mad now She gets the strap
She is holding my braids and hitting me
i try to cover my face but the strap hits my lip
there is blood in my mouth
i can feel my stomach shaking my heart is beating fast
the vomit is coming i start to cry
i try hard to stop it but it comes
all over the kitchen floor next to cake blob
Mommy is pushing my face into it
She is crying too and her eyes look like fire
maybe Doctor Ben will come back maybe Julia will come back
Sneaky one eat it eat it
i can't do it Mommy don't make me do it Mommy
then i see Carmela is under the table shaking
and i do it

7

one two
one two three
that's our signal for the bell Mr. Durant put in
so we can tell when someone is coming up
Doctor Ben made up the signal
the same as the dance he practices with Mommy
one two cha cha cha
we must use it when we go to his new office too
so he knows it's us and not another patient
Mommy says Doctor Ben works too late
ever since he moved his office
he can't say no to an emergency
so his big new waiting room is filled all day
the signal at home is so we won't open the door
when strangers bums or union men want to get in
or if it's unexpected company
which Mommy hates
She says *This is not Colombia*
where everyone has servants
and people have time for company
whoever rings the bell without the signal stays out
Uncle Paolo doesn't know the signal
he is coming today to take us to the circus
Mommy told us after Mass
to keep our good clothes on and stay put
yesterday Julia even shined all our shoes
we got up extra early to get our practicing done
one hour each except Carmela has to do two
but she likes it
Mrs. de Grab says she will be a very fine pianist
and Carmela should take the test
for a special high school called Music and Art
only a few kids are picked
Carmela practices all the time
even after the clock rings that her two hours are up
i like to watch when she plays the really hard notes
in the Pathetique Sonata she hums and sings

her chest gets all puffy and her head goes back
and she bends over the keys with her eyes closed
i think she is going to cry but she doesn't
Carmela can't hear us or see us
it's like she's far away from here
remembering something
probably she is remembering the big Macy's box
the one Uncle Paolo brought last year
it said Macy's on it and he said *Open it upstairs*
so we ran back up to show Mommy
three blue velvet dresses
with lace and long white ribbons and a bow
we put them on and we were triplet princesses
Mommy said they were very pretty
and that Nonna's eyes must be getting very bad
if she sent store bought
instead of making them herself
and no we couldn't wear them to the circus
so Mommy put the dresses back in the box
and we went back downstairs to Uncle Paolo
later She told us She took the dresses back
and bought green velvet ones in Klein's instead
we hate the green ones we cried when we saw them
Julia won't wear hers
She said *Too bad*
because the difference in price fed us for a month
but we don't care about food we want the dresses
i hope Uncle Paolo buys us those circus lights again
we get to swing them around in the dark
i think they would be good to have
in one of those shelter drills we have at school
when we line up in the hall and face the walls
we wait
just in case the commies send a nuclear bomb
i think i will be saved
my spot is right under the big brown crucifix
and Jesus looks down at me looking very sad

Uncle Paolo buys us cracker jacks and soda
and we're just like all the other kids in the place
i hate the clowns with faces like the bums on our stairs
but the trapeze ladies really fly
they hold on by their feet only and never lose their balance
after the circus Uncle Paolo takes us to Bickfords
we always ask for the same thing
vanilla milk shakes and hamburgers
it's American food and we love it
Uncle Paolo asks us about school
he says we are very smart girls who will go places
then he brings us home
and gives us each a five dollar bill and a kiss on the head
he says try to come visit Nonna soon she is waiting
it has been a very long time since she saw us
we say *Thank you for everything Uncle Paolo*
and watch him cross Union Square

Visita

"*Remójala*, Ronnie."

My mother looks over my shoulder and tells me to sprinkle water on the blouse I am ironing. I don't tell her I already have, hours ago, before she came downstairs, before the sun got its first peek through the woods behind my house, even before the blackbird who perches at the top of the big sycamore tree got her chance to squawk me awake. Sleep was hard to find last night. I've given Julia respite for the weekend and brought my mother to my country home. It is her first visit, ever.

"*Buenos dias*, Mom." I turn my head to greet her. "Did you sleep well?"

"I think so."

"I heard you washing up. Do you need anything?"

"No, no. Thank you Ronnie." She is still standing behind me. "You are very gracious."

I smile at my mother's formality. "Why don't you sit down while I finish? I'm almost done with this one." I motion toward the couch across the living room, where I can see her better.

My mother tiptoes slowly past me. "I do not want to scratch your wood floors," she says. In her paisley dress and heeled sandals her small frame and bounce could belong to one of my daughters' friends. She stops at the far end of the couch, glances through the open window, and quickly passes her hand under her thighs to straighten her skirt as she sits. The old creaky sofa doesn't make a sound as it receives her. We are quiet, and she looks at me intently as I work, seated behind my ironing board.

"*Peculiaridades,*" she says with a little humph. "Who sits while they iron?"

"*Yo,*" I say, and glide the iron across the back of the blouse in long strokes, along the shoulder line in shorter ones. "Ever since I was pregnant with Jackie. I discovered I liked it."

"You like to iron? *Que rara.*"

"Yes, I guess it is strange. But I do love to iron." I speak without looking up, aware that I am boasting a little. "Give me a basketful of wrinkled clothing, anytime. I lower the board and set myself up with a cool drink, put on a good piece of music, and I'm in heaven. Or I might turn on the television and watch a classic. One with Ann Sheridan, or Barbara Stanwyck maybe."

My mother doesn't answer. I turn the blouse around to its front and spread the collar open to retouch it. I stretch the material taut with my free hand and tilt the tip of my iron on its side, pressing gently up and away from the rim, careful to avoid leaving even the smallest pleats along the edge. I set my iron on its end and take a hanger from the few that I've jammed into the basket of clothes next to my chair. I feel my mother's eyes on me, and I like it. I drape the pressed blouse onto the hanger, careful not to wrinkle it, and lay it flat to close two of its front buttons. When I'm finished I hang it on the side rack of the ironing board with the six other blouses I've already pressed. I reach in my basket for the next item, a sundress, and spread it open. I give it two short sprays from the starch can.

"Use a little bowl," my mother corrects me. "*Con agua tibia.*"

I wish she hadn't spoken. I was enjoying the quiet between us, the sound of this rare August breeze rambling through the trees. I don't reply. I don't tell her that when it was still dark out and she was asleep in her granddaughter's bed I'd already taken out the white enamel pancake-mixing bowl, the one I use for salads now that the girls are gone, filled it nearly to the rim with warm water and added a drop of lavender oil. I laid each piece of clothing flat on my dining room table and scooped up a handful of liquid to sprinkle like a priest over a newborn at the baptismal font, then rolled each garment into a ball and set into my basket. I don't tell her there is another basket full of moist bundles on the bottom shelf of my refrigerator. I don't remind her this is the way she did it, late in the afternoons in Union Square, while I did my homework and pretended to need more time just to stay with her and watch. And I don't confess how often I've ironed, unnecessarily some would say, eager to catch the creases and rumpled sleeves, pant legs and collars as they tumbled out of the dryer, to feel the steam rise through the fabric and fill the air with each individual scent, no matter how much soap or bleach I'd used or how hot the setting's been, because this irreplaceable old iron in my hand has been my way to caress my loved ones, to soothe them, to soothe myself during all the years without her.

Instead I ask her if she is hungry. I offer to make some eggs. "No, thank you very much," she says. My mother doesn't accept food of any kind from anyone, no matter how hungry she is, when it is first offered. She sits with her hands folded on her lap, her face still. She could be someone else's mother. Not the smart and stylish powerhouse I knew, but a benign, aging *Colombiana*.

"I'll make *pericos*," I say.

"You know how?" her eyebrows rise.

"Sure. Caramelized onions, tomatoes, and scrambled eggs. *Y cilantro*. I make them all the time."

"When did you learn all these domestic skills?" She isn't looking at me, but out the window. "I never wanted my children to do housework. Or play those useless games like cards. Any idiot can do that. I thought it was a waste of time. Maybe that was a mistake. *Mi error*."

I shut my iron off and rest it on its end. I let her words hang in the air. Right now, I don't want to reassure her about her mothering or fill in any more missing information about the years we missed with each other. I want these few days of having my mother to myself to be full of ordinary things. I stand up and extend my hand to her.

"*A la cocina*," I say, and we walk to the kitchen. She stands in a corner, arms behind her back. I set a bowl, a fork and the carton of eggs on the counter near her. She looks at me, lost. I demonstrate for her, carefully cracking three eggs into the bowl, and I begin to beat them. I hand her the bowl. She takes it without hesitation and walks to the sink. She is suddenly confident. "*Yo se hacer esto!*" She's remembered how it's done. She stands over the sink scrambling eggs, making a lot of noise, her buttocks springing slightly from side to side as the fork in her hand hits the bowl. I can hear my sisters secretly mocking her for it as we'd watch from the kitchen table, and me joining in the snickering. I hear my own girls laughing at me for the same thing. A smile breaks across my face.

My mother looks up at me, still beating the eggs. Her eyes are sparkling. She is smiling too, in a wide, playful grin. She shrugs, "Ronnie, I cannot stop! You better tell me when!" My mother's laugh is deep and rich, like a slow knock at my front door, nothing like the quick ripples of woodpecker taps that escape me. The laughter echoes through the house and, even when I'm sure we've exhausted it, resounds. All it takes is one of my mother's gestures, a shrug, a smirk, a pause, which she repeats intentionally, as if to mock herself. But it's really just to make me laugh.

We're in my favorite part of the house, the screened porch, only a few paces from the woods that cover the steep hill the house sits on, sheltered on one side by the rock-filled garden that hugs the driveway up to the road. On the other, the slope descends to where the pine trees thin and a stream wanders randomly through large and smaller boulders, inviting a herd of deer to water each afternoon, just before sunset, and occasionally a black bear and her cubs visit. I sit back into my old rocking chair and watch my mother sip her third cup of *tinto*, unsweetened black coffee.

"*Sabor de Carlota*," my mother says, eyes closed and licking her lips. She might be referring to the eggs she's just eaten, or the coffee. I don't know which, and it doesn't matter.

"You say that whenever you taste my cooking."

She shakes her head. "*Es la verdad*. I do not cook like my mother. *Nada*. Not even coffee. That gift was passed on to you." She winks at me, lowers her gaze and looks directly at my breasts. "Among others."

She's thrown me off balance. I answer without thinking, swatting her words away. "What do you mean by that?" I don't like her glance or her remark.

"*Voluptuosa*. Even in a bathrobe with her hair uncombed, *la abuela* Carlota was something. Those big breasts, her full hips, and that tiny waist. I certainly did not inherit those attributes, *mi'jita*." She looks delighted. "My dear, you have the monopoly on breasts in this family. I am sure men love you for them."

I fold my arms over my breasts and make myself remember what I've read about Alzheimers and impulse control. How it affects sexual arousal and changes personality. But her impish grin is unnerving.

I change the subject to focus back on her. "You're very talented yourself, Mom. You speak beautifully, even in English. Better than anyone else I know." I go on. "You have a knack for finding the precise word for what you mean, in a split second. And with your accent, that's a great combination."

It works. She lets out a deep sigh and becomes still. She looks at the floor. When she speaks again, her playfulness is gone.

"That is a nice thing to hear. *Muchas gracias.* I learned English very early, you know. Since primary school."

"Really?"

"It was easy for me to learn languages. Especially *vocabulario.* Somehow I have it within my brain to grasp a word I have heard here or there only once, and never forget it. I got that from my mother. *Doña* Carlota. She loved words, and finding the right one. When she spoke you would think she was a college graduate, although she only went as far as the seventh grade. But she could make grown men tremble."

"Tell me about her."

"Have you been to Medellín? No? I will describe it to you because you were not taught Colombian geography in your American schools. *Absurdo.* All over the world students must learn this country's geography, but not the other way around. People in the United States call themselves Americans, as though the remainder of the two continents did not exist. Well, believe it or not, my dear, South Americans are also Americans. The rest of the world knows that, and just as immigrants came here, they also went to Colombia. All kinds of people."

The geography lesson continues for a few more minutes. I marvel at my mother's willingness to talk about, and defend, the country she spent her life denying. She tells me about Antióquia, the province in the Andes thousands of meters high *en la Cordillera Central,* where Medellín is. "Not like Bogotá," she says with a raised eyebrow. "*Diferente topografía.* Lush and isolated. *La zona cafetera.* The best coffee in the world. And the best flowers. Especially the orchid."

I don't tell her I know this already, that I have flown over the Cordilleras many times and seen their beauty. It all feels new, hearing it from my mother.

"People from that region are industrious, self-sufficient. And cunning, *se la saben todas.* They trust no one. That is what makes them good business people. Go to the shops in Jackson Heights, most are owned by people from Medellín. My mother was born there. Just a few years after Colombia became independent from Spain. *Diciembre 1906.* A Sagitarian, you say? *Será.* My father, my son, and I were all born under that sign. Do you think that means something? I do not pay attention to things of that sort. Breeding and education and character are what make a person."

She adjusts herself in her seat, crosses her legs and holds her chin up slightly as she speaks. The demented *viejita colombiana* has turned into a master storyteller whose memory doesn't falter.

"My mother had a difficult life, from the beginning. Carlos Barragán, her father whom she was named for, died a few months after she was born, of tuberculosis. I never met my grandmother, Ignacia, but my mother spoke of her being a beautiful, tall woman with thick black hair down to her hips. Her second husband was a Belgian business man named Brün, and they had two sons, red-haired with freckles and green eyes. But *el desgraciado* Brün the Belgian did not want someone else's child around, especially a girl. Ignacia had no choice. A woman without wealth of her own was at the mercy of men. My mother never forgot that. She was not yet five years old when she was sent away to live with a distant relative. She never saw her mother again. Ignacia died very young, probably of sorrow. So my mother was orphaned, *una huérfana.*

"Many years later, when she was already a grown woman, my mother met her brothers, here in the United States. I sponsored them. They were the only family she had, and I signed for my uncles to come to this country. It was not complicated then, there were no quotas, and I did all the paperwork myself. I used to read and keep up on the regulations. That is how I ended up helping many people come here. Your father used to say I should have gone to law school. I don't know what happened with her brothers. They didn't stay in New York very long. I think they went to California. They didn't keep in touch.

"Anastasia Jaramillo de Navarro was the woman who raised my mother. The Jaramillo people owned shipping lines that carried commerce, mostly bananas, throughout the Caribbean for the United Fruit Company. And of course, great wealth. That is probably why Ignacia believed her daughter would be better off with them. But it was not the case.

"The family business was based on the island of Jamaica, close to the Caribbean coast of Colombia. That is where my mother went to school, under the colonial British system. Very harsh discipline. Beatings. Whippings. My mother used to say that she learned to be brave in Jamaica. She would not cry, *pase lo que pase,* no matter what happened. But the Jaramillo people didn't see any reason to continue educating her past primary school since she was a girl, and not really their blood. She was about twelve when they returned to Colombia, to Barranquilla. That is where my mother lived the rest of her life.

"That Navarro woman was very strict. *La bruja*, my mother called her a witch. She had three daughters, older than Carlota, and they treated my mother like *la cenicienta*, Cinderella. They never let her forget they were doing her a favor by taking her in. If they ordered dresses made for all the girls, Carlota's dress was always of an inferior quality cloth. And she had to wear their old shoes. As she got older, Carlota's looks must have been a threat to them, because they kept her separated from the other girls, *las feas*, and excluded her from social events, so they could catch husbands. Very cruel people. My mother once told me that when she was very little and still in Jamaica, all the fruit from Anastasia's prized peach tree was gone. That woman was furious, *como loca*. She held an investigation, lined up all the servants, and when she could not discover who stole the fruit, she decided it must have been Carlota. As punishment, she ordered the servants to hang my mother by her braids under the peach tree.

"And the daughters were no better. When they were all finally married, Navarro built each of them a house on the same street the parents lived on. Four mansions along the *Alto Prado,* the most prestigious area of Barranquilla. But they would not acknowledge my mother socially. They turned their backs on her because of her background—she didn't have a European blood line.

"Carlota was a beauty. With that curly black hair and deep dark eyes, and her pearly white teeth. A different kind of beauty. Wild, like a *gitana*. I have nothing of her, physically. *Absolutamente nada.* Her skin was really something. *Piel canela*, like dark orange honey, and it glowed. Like your skin.

"One of *la Anastasia's* daughters, the younger and ugliest of the Navarros—they were all ugly—was being prepared to meet a suitor. A *criollo* of Spanish ancestry, from a powerful family. He owned a chain of *ferreterias*, building suppliers, in the province. It was arranged that he was to take the Navarro girl on an outing together with her whole family. But the girl got sick and could not keep the appointment. There were no phones then, so they sent Carlota to his office to deliver the message. Ezekiel Osorio took one look at my mother and asked her to go in place of the Navarro girl. That is how the whole thing began. How Carlota and Ezekiel became my parents.

"My father was all *español*, blue eyed and blonde hair. Much older than my mother. She was fourteen. He was thirty-six. That was not uncommon at the time. He was the youngest of four brothers. In Barranquilla the Osorios were *clase alta*, upper strata. They were devoutly religious Catholics. My father went to church every morning. The four brothers were educated men, went to *el Colegio Biffi*, only for high society families, and they did very well. One of my uncles became a federal senator, another a judge, and another a minister. My father was an entrepreneur. But he had another passion, a serious drinking problem. *La oveja negra.* He was the black sheep in many ways.

"When my father married my mother he broke all the rules of his social class. Carlota was not high society. She was not white European. She was not even a *criolla,* born of European parents. She had no family. No position. She didn't fit in. She never would.

"Two weeks before my mother's fifteenth birthday, I was born. Imagine that. *Como una muñeca.* I was like a doll for her to play with. Poor Carlota. She had a very hard life."

My mother turns suddenly in her seat to face the rock garden, then stands to get a better look. "Ronnie. You need to put some flowers here. *No hay color.* Too monotonous. A garden needs contrast. You need to plant roses."

I stand next to her and speak quietly. "We did Mom. Yesterday. You and I went to the farm store and got a rose bush. We dug a hole and planted it, near the plum tree. Over there on the left. Do you see it?" I turn her toward the plum tree. Once a sprout itself when my women friends gathered to plant it at the crest of the hillside the year I got the house, it is now tall and fruitful. I point to the newly planted rose bush.

She squints into the hillside. "*No recuerdo.* I get confused sometimes."

I know she doesn't remember these recent events. Not planting the rose bush or stealing it. She doesn't remember that while I loaded my car trunk with garden supplies, she wandered off to the rose bush display, lifted one and carried it into the back seat, and got in. Or that when I saw it in my rear-view mirror a few miles later, I drove back to pay for it, pretending I'd forgotten something inside the store. I don't tell her that it won't last, that the deer will eat it, roses and thorns alike, before the weekend is over, or that nothing can prevent it—not even fences, and that is why no one plants roses up here on the mountain.

I'm still hoping she will remember where her story left off. I sit her down again and refill her coffee. She takes a few sips without making a sound. "Tell me about *la abuela*, Mom."

She shakes her head and begins again.

"*Que vida.* My mother had a very hard life. My father's family did not accept my mother. They would not acknowledge her as part of the family. But they liked her children. *Hipócritas.* I remember being very little when my parents had large dinner parties. My mother prepared elaborate meals and was very busy supervising the servants. Sterling silver and crystal and linens on the table. I would help her, very excited. Then my father's family would come, and his friends. But only the men. They would not bring the women. I would watch them smoking their cigars, drinking and talking. And my mother would be alone in another part of the house. I could not understand, I was only a child then, why the aunts and cousins never came, why no one spoke to my mother.

"One of those men was my father's good friend Roberto Bornacelli. *Italiano.* A very nice man. He used to make me laugh, always brought a little gift for me. Roberto loved my father.

"I remember I could tell my father was home from work because I would hear his car. We lived on the Calle Murillo, and the property had a long driveway. He had a Roadster, a very long car, which he would park outside. One day, I was about five, I went out to the car and opened the door very slowly. I did not know anything about cars. I just remembered how my father would turn something and he would drive. I started touching all the knobs and things inside. I was going to drive! Suddenly the car started moving down the driveway. There was a neighbor across the street. He was as fast as lightning. ¡*Voló!* He flew into the car. People screaming. Then he pulled something, I guess the brake. My father said later that God made that man look this way, to save me. I never got behind the wheel of a car again in my life.

"Carlota never knew, of course, or she would have killed me. My father did not care. He was not materialistic or mean. I do not remember him ever being angry with me. He was a very soft spoken man and very aristocratic in his manner. Always well dressed, smelled sweet, and stood erect. They called him *El Mono* because of his shocking blonde hair. Like a Swede, almost white. And blue eyes. He was very generous, always plenty of food and fine things around the house. And of course, always lots of alcohol. Seagram Seven, Johnny Walker, and his favorite, Haig and Haig.

"He would get very drunk, but you would never see him stumble or raise his voice or act foolishly. He would become very quiet, and occasionally, very angry with my mother. Especially after my little sister died. Her name was Lili. She had big blue eyes like my father. I used to take her down the block in her stroller with her *criada,* her nanny. In South America every child has its own *criada,* sometimes until they are in high school. One day my little sister Lili got sick. From a bee sting, I think. They never told me exactly. She died the next day. My father got so angry. He was drunk for days. In the middle of the night he went out to the garden, poured gasoline on it and lit it. Burned the whole thing. My mother's special roses. She had worked so hard for those roses. She got us out of the house and took us to the neighbor's house. *Que desgracia.*

"My parents never lived together again. But my mother wanted to make sure that we all had a good education. That was the one thing she really cared about. I did the same with my girls. Good schools, music, dance, the arts. I never had my children mop a floor or cook or do anything domestic. Everything here in the brain. Even if they thought I was too strict. I wanted my children to be educated. So they would never have to depend on anyone. The same as my mother wanted for me.

"After my father left she opened a restaurant. Cooking was what she did best. She was terrific, never used recipes or measured anything. She could cook. None of the neighbors would talk to her then. They considered it a disgrace for a woman in her position to operate a restaurant. They shunned her. We used to get anonymous letters saying 'You Do Not Belong Here.' The neighbors would send their servants to walk up to me and give me those letters, for my mother. Imagine doing that to a six year old child. So she moved us to a neighborhood of a lesser class, El Barrio Boston. You would consider it middle class here. But my mother could not keep us with her. My father's family forbid it. They were glad my parents had broken up, but they wanted the children to stay in the family. My mother did not want to ruin our chances in society. So she agreed to putting my brothers and me into boarding school.

"I was in boarding schools all my life after that. There were only two months out of the year that I could live with my mother. She would rent a house in the outskirts of the city, *una quinta,* what you would call in English a vacation house, near the seashore, with servants and everything. That was the only way my father's family would let her have her children with her, so that it would appear respectable. In this way we were together, at least during vacation.

"Sometimes my father would come to see us there. Always when my mother was not home. I would hear his Roadster drive up. He would take my brothers and me out for ice cream, then to visit his family, to see my uncles and aunts, and my cousins. They were very cold to us. I did not let that matter to me. My father was very proud of me. He would call me *mi adorada hija*, his beloved daughter, and he would hold my hand when we walked. But he did not talk much. My mother would get very upset afterward, when she came home and found out he had come to see us without announcing himself. She was always afraid he would take us away for good.

"One day my father and his brother, *tio* Fortunato, showed up at my school. The *Colegio Americano Para Señoritas*. It was run by a Presbyterian minister and his wife. *Señor* Escorcia and *Señora* Regina. She had bright red hair, I remember. They were Cubans who spoke English. Most of the instruction was in English. And two hours of religion every day. They started us with English right from the beginning. Every command and greeting. They were right to do it that way. Small children pick up languages easily. My brothers were in the same school, but in the other building, for boys. I would see them once in a while, when they had joint events, like concerts or festivities.

"That day, when my father and my uncle came, they took me with my brothers out of school and put us into the car. They told us we were going for a ride. The next thing I knew I was in another boarding school, in another town. This one was Catholic. *Nuestra Señora Del Rosario*. Our Lady of the Rosary. My father's family did not want us with Protestants. So that is where I lived for another year or so. I made my first Communion there.

"I do not remember having any friends. The older girls teased me. They tormented me. The school was attached to a church, and the church had a grotto and a cemetery next to it. The girls used to tell me the dead people would come into the school at night. I was terrified. And of course the more scared you are, the more they enjoy teasing you.

"Sometimes I would get the special jobs in school. Like selling the *cocadas* at lunchtime. Because I was good at mathematics. So I would take the tray of cookies around the dining hall and, you know how I like coconut. So I would sell a few and eat one. The nuns never noticed. I loved sweets even then.

"My mother did not know my whereabouts for a long time. The Osorio family would not tell her. For nearly two years I did not see her. Finally she must have convinced my father. He was really not a bad man. He let her take us back to the American school, with the Presbyterians. I liked it there much better. We had to study English, Latin, and of course, Spanish, right from the beginning. I did well in languages and in sciences. I got to see my mother every two weeks, on Sundays, for two hours. She would hire a driver and take my brothers and me for a ride in the countryside. It was wonderful for us. But it was an awful life for her.

"Whose house is this?" My mother looks around the porch and back at me. She leans forward and whispers, "Who lives here?"

"We do, Mom." I am careful with my answer, as though I were speaking to someone waking from a long sleep. "We are in my house in the country. Today is Saturday. This is your second day here. We rode up together from the city on Thursday. I picked you up at your house in Queens and we drove up here in my car."

She considers my words, the little muscles contracting around her eyes as she listens. I wonder what she is thinking. How does she manage the waves of information that come and go, the complete blanks and detailed retrievals, playing a random game of hit and miss with parts of herself? What image is she digesting? Herself, her mother, me? Whose voice is she listening to? Who matters to her now?

I think of her stillness during the car ride up here. How she only glanced at the scenery as we passed, as though she were afraid to look too long and didn't want to be distracted for an instant from concentrating on the road ahead. Even my chatter about the classical music on the radio didn't interest her. She only spoke to ask *¿Cuánto tiempo toma esto, niña?* several times, as though I had not once answered that it would be another hour or so. And out of nowhere, in the final few minutes of the trip, she asked if Carmela was coming too, and I said no, she lives in Seattle now. And that look of complete surprise came across her face, the one I see there now.

She leans back into her chair. I let her rest for a few minutes. Then I say, "Come, Mom. Finish your story. Tell me about what happened when you were in school." She gives a little laugh and pushes her hair back from her face.

"*¿No sabes?*"

"No. I don't know your story. This is the first time you're telling me."

"By the time I finished primary school my mother had made money of her own. She had opened a beautiful restaurant, *El Normandí*, across the street from the Club Barranquilla. That was the most restrictive country club in town. They all went to my mother's restaurant. She knew exactly how to serve the upper class. She discovered that if she sold liquor she could make more money. She had to get a sponsor in order to get her permit, because she was a woman and not *sociedad*. My father's friend Roberto Bornacelli helped her. So she added a bar. She made a lot of money and started buying real estate. She had a sharp mind, my mother. Even without schooling.

"She wanted to take me far away from the *lenguas largas* gossipmongers in Barranquilla. They would have ruined my chances in society. You probably do not understand this. How could you? People in the United States hear Colombia and they see the low class element you hear about in the news today, the *ilegales* and the drug dealers. Some consider anyone who speaks with an accent as automatically ignorant, or a criminal. That has always been the case in this country. But *los norteamericanos* are the ignorant ones. They do not know Colombia is a very complex country with high standards of education—even a peasant with a fourth grade public school education is articulate and knows his history, even world geography. The *desastre* of Colombia is that class system the Spaniards left behind. That is what you cannot understand, because you have never lived it. Colombians are unforgiving, *no perdonan*. Wherever you are born, that is where you will stay until you die.

"That is why I never went back. People there spend their time worrying about what everyone else thinks and does, especially the women, because they have to depend on impressing each other. Everything you need has to be obtained through *palanca,* connections. I could not stand it. I like the United States, where nobody knows your business. Someone can live next door to you for thirty years and not know anything about you. You could be dead and they would not know for days. Not like Colombia, where anyone can drop in at any time of day to socialize and scrutinize. And you better be ready. You better have a clean bloodline, *ser decente,* with two decent last names. No privacy. Even the hint of impropriety can ruin your life. Even if you are a child. *Ach!*

"So, when I was twelve and had finished primary school, my mother took me by ship up the Rio Magdalena to Puerto Berrios, then by airplane to Bogotá. We stayed at the best hotel in the city at the time, *El Hotel Granada*. Through Roberto Bornacelli she had made contacts with the director of a school for girls. She named him as my sponsor. You could not get into one of those schools without an upper class name behind you. I do not know if my father was involved in any of it or not. He was already very sick by then, but I did not know it. No one told me.

"*Nuestra Señora de los Angeles*. Our Lady of the Angels School. *Interna*. I lived there and could not get out. I did not get close to anyone. Why bother? I knew already that there was a chance the same old thing would happen. Whenever I had made a friend, within a short time something would change and it would end. Plus, they were very cliquish. The girls were always jealous of my clothing. My mother had all my clothes hand-made in the latest European styles and fabrics. Maybe because I did not look like them? Who knows? They used to like my hair, because it was so blonde and wavy, and they would ask me to show them how I did my hairdos, but then they would get cold and rebuff me again. They were just using me. I knew by then that it would always be that way.

"And there were other things. The girls got to go home on holidays and school breaks. I would stay in the dormitories by myself, because I could not go home to my mother, except for the summers, and my father's family never offered. Even the teachers would go home. They thought I was very strange.

"How did I do it? It was not so bad. I got used to it. I read a lot. And I listened to classical music, and I would sing. With nobody else around I could sing as loud as I wanted. I would pretend I was an opera singer. Or I would dance alone. I had the whole place to myself. I would go down to the ballroom where they held the school functions and practice dance steps. If I got lonely I would write poetry.

"There were some kind people. The director of the school lived nearby and invited me to eat my meals with her family. She always encouraged me to continue with a career, which was not common for a woman at the time. She said I would make a great diplomat. I liked being alone. Without anyone prying into my family life.

"After a time my mother expanded her business. The property she had purchased previously was on the outskirts of the city. Later it became the red-light district. It was called *El Barrio Chino*, for some reason, but there were no Chinese there. I do not know if it still exists or not. Women could not go there. Except for prostitutes, of course.

"Well, one of my mother's customers at *El Normandi* offered her a partnership. He was high society with a gambling problem and wanted to make money off man's pursuit of pleasure. But he wanted a partner who would oversee the place without his having to be there, to save face that is. For my mother, she had very little left to lose. This was a way to make a great deal of money, which meant she could really be independent, and she wanted more than anything for her children to be free of that society trap. So she invested with this man.

"She never had anything to do with running the women's business. She put up the property, the silent partner hired a couple of men to run it. My brother told me years later how those places made money. They hired a band and a few young girls, teenagers really, as dancers or cocktail waitresses, to entice the customers to buy them drinks. But the drinks that were served to the girls were really cold tea, not liquor. The more the girls got the customers to drink, the higher the profit to the house.

"That is how they made money. For the girls, whatever they did in the back rooms had nothing to do with my mother. She would go there in the early mornings before sunrise, to see how things were going with the bar. She could never risk being seen there because that would surely ruin us. She had to be a tough woman to survive alone and keep her children.

"Of course, I never had any idea about this at the time. My brother Mickey knew what was going on. He loved my mother. He would not let anyone say anything bad about her. But word got out eventually. One of the girls in my school in Bogotá was from Barranquilla. Her father must have figured it out, probably one of the hypocrite customers. After that no one would talk to me. I did not know why. I was shunned, like my mother and grandmother had been. The girls would not even talk to me in the dining room. I got tired of trying to make them like me, of trying to figure out what was wrong.

"I showed them I was better than all their pure-bred high class. I was always the best in my subjects. Especially literature and philosophy, and mathematics. Also basketball. I played center. I loved it. Whenever there was an occasion in the school, an event, the director picked me to speak. If it was a public presentation or a celebration, like a professor's retirement, for example, or a death, or such things, they would say get Eva Dolores, because I spoke well in public. My mother trained me. She believed in the power of language, that it is one of the few things you can have completely under your control, that the way you speak can never be taken from you, and it determines to a great degree how you will negotiate the world. I liked public speaking. When we graduated I was valedictorian of my class. I showed them.

"My mother did not know what to do with me really. She had too many worries. That is why she put me in that boarding school, *requeinterna*. It means my mother signed for me to never leave the campus. She could not have me with her, so she sent me as far away from danger as possible. She would have liked to put me in a cage locked up if she could. Always worrying about my honor.

"But I was an adolescent, without any opportunity to meet anyone. You know what happens when you are confined. I found a way out. One of the teachers was a young woman, in her twenties, just a few years older than me. *Aura Rojas*. I asked her to do me a favor. She was a *Bogotana*, so she knew the city. I told her I would like to go out sometimes. Just for an afternoon or one evening every month. I would hear the other girls talk about the places they went to, and the people they met, like the Club Montenegro, a country club, where they danced to live bands or *orquestras*. It sounded luxurious. I wanted to see it too, why not? But because of the orders my mother had given, I would need—how would you understand this?—a female guardian. Someone who would be personally responsible for me. Even more than a chaperone. If I had a guardian my mother would give me permission. Aura agreed. I talked to my mother and she allowed it, as long as Aura was with me at all times.

"On one occasion the nuns took us for a *paseo* to a mountain village outside of the city. We had a big luncheon at a ranch, like a resort, and there was music for dancing. Colombians have music everyplace where there is a group of people, especially when it is a group of young schoolgirls. And there were other people there as well, tourists, people from the city who wanted to get away for a few days into the mountains. I loved to dance. Even the school chaperones who accompanied the group danced too. But the women from the interior do not dance well. Not as well as those of us from the coast. We have a different rhythm. Maybe it is from the sea. Or from the African rhythms in the music of the coast. Anyway, you can tell where a woman is from, especially if she is a *costeña*, just by watching her dance, the way her hips move. There is a certain flavor other women do not get.

"So I danced and danced, and this young man danced with me. He was very gracious and enjoyed my company. Being *interna* I could not receive telephone calls. So he gave me his telephone number on a little piece of paper.

"Gregorio Guitierrez Lindon. On the way back to the school, Aura told me about him. He was from a big shot family. British *criollos*. They owned department stores around Bogotá. After a few days I paid the secretary of the school five pesos to let me use the phone. I called Gregorio. I told him the next time the school had a big social event planned, I would let him know and he would join us if he liked. He said he would be delighted.

"Of course, I could not leave the school grounds unless I was with my guardian. Aura was responsible for me. We would go in a taxi to the Anglo American Club to meet Gregorio and his friends. I could not have liquor or anything. I just danced. What else is there for a young girl, anyway? I was very happy, seeing a different type of life outside the convent school. That is how it all started. The nuns took us to that resort. I danced. I met Gregorio.

"What I am saying is that we each have a destiny. No matter what it is, it is going to come your way. Gregorio was aristocratic and all. But he drank. You never know what a drunken person is going to do. I learned that from seeing my father.

"Gregorio really liked me. Introduced me to his family and his social circle. I had to have gowns made, which my mother sent me. He took me to *El Baile Del Año,* the annual society ball. Our pictures were in the newspaper a few times. He wanted very much to marry me. My mother was delighted.

"Then, suddenly, he broke things off. He sent me a note, saying how sorry he was that things could not be different. Apparently one of my own classmates from Barranquilla called his family. Told them about my mother. It was terrible. Terrible. I never got an opportunity to talk to him about it. It just ended with that note.

"You know, after many years he wrote to me in New York, saying he was coming to town. I was alone by then, and I went out and bought a mink coat so I would look nice. I used some of the money my mother had given me when I left Colombia. I wanted him to see I was doing well. But when he rang my bell he was so drunk I did not want to let him in. He looked awful. He would not leave. He fell asleep on the floor in the hallway outside my door, like one of those bums that used to sneak into the building at night. The next day he was gone. I never saw him again. He drank too much. Gregorio Gonzalez Lindon.

"Yes, there were other young men who pursued me. None of them attracted me. I was too broken-hearted about Gregorio. Although one stands out. Alberto Lleras Camargo. He was a very fine man. Also an aristocrat. But I was not physically attracted to him, he was not handsome, and there was no spark. Stupid me. He became the president of Colombia! A very respected world statesman. He was once being interviewed by the magazine *Visiones* in New York. *Por coincidencia,* your sister Carmela worked there at the time, as a summer temporary secretary. Somehow he spoke to her and recognized the last name. He asked to see me, but I would not. I was older by then, and so much had happened. Life has so many turns. When we are young we think only with our eyes. *La vida da muchas vueltas.*

"After I graduated in Bogotá, I had to come home to Barranquilla. It was a big problem. I was nineteen already. My mother had rented the summer home. But my father wanted to buy a house for my brother and me to live in. It was clear that we were an embarrassment to his family, especially now that my schooling was finished. I was the oldest, and a girl. They worried about whom I would marry, what position in society I would have, that it should not reflect poorly on them. My father really did not care about any of that. But he did not have much power to fight them. They wanted to prevent any scandal connected with the name Osorio. So my father came to my brother with the proposition about the house. My brother refused. He would never leave my mother. He did not care about the Osorio name or what that family wanted. For me it would be impossible to live alone in a house with just the servants, such things were not done by women. Everybody was a nervous wreck about what to do with me that summer.

"Then this handsome Italian showed up in town. *El destino,* once again."

My mother stops speaking and asks to use the bathroom. While she is gone I think about the yellow envelope with letters she once gave me, the newspaper clippings it contained of a young girl in long gowns and sophisticated men in tails at her elbow. I will look at those pictures again when I get home, and see them differently.

When she returns I watch her move slowly to her seat. I notice for the first time that the seat cushion is wet. So is the back of her dress.

"Mom, did you have an accident?" I ask as gently as I can before she sits.

"Where?" She has no idea what I am talking about.

"The cushion is wet. So is your dress."

"How strange," she says, staring at the cushion. I help her back into the bathroom and ask her to remove her dress and underwear. She hesitates. She holds her hands up at her sides, confused.

"But I washed them this morning, Ronnie." She is still not removing her clothing.

"Where? In the bathroom upstairs?"

"Yes. I did."

"Mom, did you put them back on? Wet?"

"I guess so." She shrugs her shoulders. I leave her in the bathroom and go get a clean pair of my own underpants and my robe. When I return she is undressed, covering herself with her wet dress. I give her the dry clothing and put hers in the washer. I tell her she will have her dress and panties back in an hour. "This is good," she says, as though we've exchanged clothing often. I lead her into the living room, where we started the day, and sit near her on the sofa. I prompt her to continue her story. She smiles.

"The day I married Nino was my last chance to show that whole bunch that I was just as much *gente decente* as they were. Especially those horrible girls from school. I got them back, alright. The day before the wedding I sent a messenger to two or three of the big mouth gossips who had started all the trouble for me with Gregorio, telling them that one of the other girls in our class was going to be married to that handsome American on Sunday afternoon at the cathedral. Well, they all showed up. Every single one of them. What a shock they got when they saw it was me walking down the aisle!

"My mother was so happy when she saw me in my wedding dress. She was so proud of me. She cried, and that was not like her. On the way to the church she did something. *De repente* she suddenly told the chauffer to make a detour. I did not know where we were going. She took me to that place, her business. To show me off to the girls there.

"I was horrified. I had never seen such a place. And on my wedding day, in my white dress! At first I was very angry. Then I saw how they treated her. They had great esteem for my mother. I had never seen my mother being treated kindly. She did not want to leave the girls out of the celebration, I guess. It was very strange. Decent women never get a chance to see such places. It was just like any Spanish house, red tile roof, an interior courtyard with a restaurant and a bar. We did not go in past the courtyard. All the girls came out from the back to see me.

"They were so excited, like children. They kissed my mother and hugged her and a few even cried. I understood my mother that day. I felt bad, you know, because none of those girls would ever get a chance to wear a wedding dress. They were so young, just teenagers really. I did not expect to see that. So terrible, what can happen to a woman when she is at the mercy of others. My mother ordered the bartender to serve them champagne and cook them up a special meal for that evening. They were so happy. I will never forget that about my mother, how she had such a big heart for anyone in a less fortunate position than hers. Those girls would be celebrating my wedding at the very same time, in that other terrible place. They were practically the only women in my mother's life. My poor mother."

The late afternoon light has filled the living room without our knowing it, reaching unembarrassed onto our legs and shoulders. I take a cue from it and touch my mother's arm. She turns to look at me and I see a rare confidence in her gaze. She places her own hand on mine and pats it.

After a little while I let go of her and say, "Help me with this Mom." I take the group of blouses I ironed this morning off the rack and hand them to her. I fold the ironing board and take it into my bedroom. She follows me and stands next to me as I make room in my closet to hang the blouses. When I'm done I reach deep into the back and remove, one at a time, several small garments made of silk, satin, velvet, and brocade, in deep reds and golds with fringe and lace trimming, ruffles and detailed bead work.

"Look, Mom." I lay the pieces on my bed. She studies them as though they were new to her, and doesn't touch any. I remind her. "You made these. Every one. My costumes. When I was a little girl. *Sevillanas, Valencianas, Jota Aragonesa, Bulerias, Paso Doble,* and the *bata* for *Seguiriyas.*" I name each dance and hold up its corresponding costume, bringing it close to her. She takes one and holds it up against my body. She is beaming.

"You kept them, Ronnie?"

"You did. In that little brown suitcase you gave me a few months ago." She doesn't know what I mean. She only sees the little dresses, doesn't know I soaked and washed each one of them by hand, and set them out in the sun to dry. She doesn't know how careful I was not to disturb the *mostazillas* and *lentejüelas* along the beaded patterns that once made me feel magically lovely on stage. She doesn't know that while I ran my iron along the seams she sewed decades ago, late into the nights in the midst of her worst, chaotic years, I understood why she'd never had the time to see me dance.

"They are beautiful," is all I can say while we both hold onto the same dress. "Such beautiful work."

My mother smiles at me and says, "My mother taught me."

i have marked off my calendar
just two more weeks then sixth grade will be over
and it will be time for Weedsport again
Mommy will send me to the Health Department
to get vaccinated
and i'll get my teeth checked by Doctor Ben too
then down to the Church of All Nations
all the way down on Houston Street
where the lady at the desk will look at all my papers
and give me the badge that says Fresh Air Fund
and she'll say *Don't lose this*
i want to tell her not a chance lady but i don't dare
i must be extra good so nothing can stop me from going
my report card is the only thing
Sister Claudia will surely give me a C in social studies
because my project wasn't beautiful like the others'
she wrote *Good content Presentation could be better*
maybe Carmela was right
i should have made drawings
but there's not very much to draw about the Supreme Court
i don't know where the other kids get the big posters
or how they make the letters so perfect
they all know about those things
it's probably because they go to Girl Scouts
and their fathers are in Holy Name Society
they don't have to practice piano and do extra homework
just to be as smart as kids in Colombian schools
worst of all they didn't get Sister Claudia twice
in third and sixth
Carmela calls it bad fate
at least Mrs. McLoughlin liked me in fifth grade
she smiled all the time and didn't make me scared
and the last day of school she gave me my report card
and she put her hand on my face
and said *Stay just the way you are*
hope i don't get Sister Thecla next year
she is the worst that is what Carmela says

especially about nails
Cleanliness is next to godliness
Sister Thecla makes fingernail inspection
every morning
and collects the dirt in a petri dish
just to show how bacteria grows into organisms
like worms and stuff
last year Carmela got a D in science
and she still got to go away
Carmela and Julia used to go on the train to Vermont
but not anymore
Mommy said the girls are too old for vacations
and this summer they will have jobs and earn money
Julia is so mad now and she doesn't talk to anyone
she never gets bad grades
but after what she did last summer in Vermont
when it was time to come back home
she took off all her clothes
even the ones in her suitcase too
and hid them in the woods
so they couldn't send her back home
she stood there just in panties and a bra
but it didn't work and they found her clothes
she had to get on the train anyway
now she can't go back
i think Mommy will let me go anyway even if it is a C
this is my third year going on the Syracuse train
all the kids cry when they say goodbye to their Moms
at Grand Central Station
not me i can't wait
even if we do have to get up before dawn
even if it takes ten hours for the train to get there
and the children are very noisy and you can't fall asleep
i count the stops
Poughkeepsie Albany Elmira Schenectady Utica Troy
the last stop is Syracuse
the Syracuse station is outdoors not like New York

and people are looking for each other
and there is Mr. O'Hara waiting
He is in charge of lots of children
he has all the names on a list
they come with us in his big station wagon
i get to sit in the front seat next to him
and read off the names
and we deliver the children to the families
the little ones are afraid and they cry
but i help Mr. O'Hara walk them in
we drive up and down the hills
out to the farms near Auburn
when there are no more kids left
he says *All righty lets go home*
i watch for the Lathrop house
i know once we pass it and the road turns left
we are in Weedsport
i see Main Street and the general store
and a little further past the library
we turn up Green Street
then we're in the driveway and i see the house
Mr. O'Hara carries my suitcase
and i go up on the big porch
say hello to Mrs. O'Hara and we shake hands
in a little while i will be unpacked
in my own room upstairs where it smells like wood
and i can use the whole dresser for myself
there is a big tree right outside my window
and i am allowed to do anything i want all day long
wake up any time i feel like
eat cold cereal and white bread with lots of butter
and walk across the back yard to Patty's house
she's on Maple street
i play dolls with her and the other grandchildren
they all have bikes too
Braunwyn is the oldest she teaches me how to ride
some days we hike to the outside of town

past the biggest and prettiest house of all
that's where the undertaker lives says Patty
and we can't step on his grass or it's bad luck
out by the brook we pick raspberries
she shows me how to catch tadpoles in a paper cup
they will become frogs' legs like we eat at Friday Fish Fry
when there are Little League games we get to help
Mr. O'Hara sets up the candy table
and we kids do the selling
he always lets us eat a whole bar for each of us
on rainy days we play canasta or gin rummy or monopoly
the kids teach me
and we eat chips
after playing is over everyone goes home
i wash up and wait for Mr. O'Hara to come home
we sit in the parlor and wait for supper
Mr. O'Hara asks me did i do anything new today
and what happened in the next chapter
of my summer reading books
then he tells me about his job in the Herald Tribune
and who he went to visit being the town supervisor
i wonder is that like what Mr. Durant does for our building
but for a whole town
but i am embarrassed to ask
i want Mr. O'hara to like me
then Mrs. O'Hara says *Supper*
and we all sit together on the back porch
with placemats and napkins and no straps or clocks
and you get to serve yourself
and say no thanks if you don't want any
after dinner it's one of Mrs. O'Hara pies
every day is a different one
i love the raspberry kind from the berries we pick
when i finish my piece i can have more if i want
then we clean up together and sit in the parlor again
Mr. O'Hara asks me will i play for them this evening
and i know he means the organ that i played one day

on my first visit
when i didn't know anyone was listening
and he said *Very Lovely*
so i play my Bach Two Part Inventions
or the Chopin Preludes
maybe this year i will play the Scarlatti sonatas
i know them by memory
it is terrible when the last days come
my stomach starts to hurt
i don't want any of it to be over
even though i already stay longer than the other kids
i want to tell Mr. O'Hara three weeks isn't enough
please let me stay here forever
please let me be your granddaughter
but i know Mommy will not let me
even last year when Mr. O'Hara wanted me
to visit during Christmas
Mommy said *No*
once before She looked very angry
because i said i love Weedsport
so i climb back on the train
and Mr. O'Hara gives me the bag
with cucumber sandwiches and cookies
Mrs. O'Hara makes for my trip
he shakes my hand
he says *See you next summer lovely girl*
and i try not to cry until i get inside
with all those noisy kids
all of them saying they can't wait to get home
and all the ten hours back i pray the train will break
or there will be a miracle or something to save me
you can tell we're back in Grand Central Station
it's so hot and the smell is awful like pee
all the kids scream Mommy Mommy
and they get big hugs and kisses
i look for Her but She is not there just like last year
i wait and wait

and all the children are gone home with their parents
there are only a few people in the waiting room
there comes the policeman to ask me
Where Is Your Mother
i have to tell him my telephone number
Spring 70892
and we wait some more
it's always a very long time until She comes
like She forgot me too

Search

I know you've questioned my motives. But really, the whole thing grew out of a conversation. I'd just started dating a man I'd met through work, and one evening as the inevitable questions about family came up, Jack asked me how my father had died. I didn't have an answer, of course, and when I mentioned Nino was from Little Italy, Jack's interest piqued. I told him he'd watched too many gangster movies and that he shouldn't jump to conclusions. But Jack wasn't thinking about that at all. If something shady had happened to my father, he said, I would have known something, because mob wives and children are usually taken care of. It was something else Jack wanted to know about me, and when he asked, he made it sound like an invitation. "Do you want to find out about your father?"

It was such a simple question, but I'd never heard it spoken out loud before. I told Jack I'd always wondered, and that several times I'd considered hiring a detective to find out. It had been thirty eight years since my father died, I said, the trail was pretty cold and it would probably cost a lot of money, so I'd let the idea go. Jack was an Irish Catholic. He was divorced and had a daughter the same age as Jackie. He'd been a gym teacher in an inner-city school and had spoken to a lot of people, cops and athletes and people he'd met in bars and on ball teams. He said he'd heard a lot of hard stories over the years but he'd never heard one quite like mine. Then he said something I hadn't thought possible. "Veronica, be your own detective."

The next time I saw him, Jack handed me a book. It was a guide for attorneys and estate executors on how to find missing heirs. He'd picked it up at a garage sale for a quarter. He said I should just follow the directions. "But in reverse, of course."

I thought about it for a few days. Maybe everything had been backwards all along. I'd expected to find out from you, that you would be the source of what I needed to know about my father. That wasn't ever going to happen. Maybe an heir looking for missing ancestors made sense. It intrigued me. So I read the book and made a plan. There would be records to search—birth and death certificates, civil and criminal court files, motor vehicle departments, the post office, funeral directors, coroners' offices. Letters would have to be sent to last known addresses, schools, hospitals, local churches, the Social Security and Veterans Administrations, and bar associations. This was before information was computerized, which meant that every one of these data banks would have to be searched manually. It looked overwhelming. I decided to put it off until the summer, when I'd have plenty of time.

But Jack kept at me. He'd ask me how much progress I was making on my search. "One call, one letter a day," he'd say. Until I told him that I'd made a call to my local police precinct and had a lead. I'd asked the cop how I could find out where someone was buried. He'd wanted to know who I was looking for. When I told him it was my father and it had been thirty-eight years, he asked me if he'd been murdered. I was a little shaken. The possibility hadn't occurred to me. Then he said I should ask you, because a mother would know what happened to her husband. You never talked about it, I said, and he was suddenly very irritated. He said if no one ever told me about my father, it was a sure bet there were plenty of secrets underneath the whole thing I was better off not knowing. "Lady, why bother?" He was nearly scolding me. "Just let sleeping dogs lie. You'll be better off." But the cop must have felt bad for saying that, because a few seconds later he said if I had to do it, I should go to the old neighborhood. "It's a gold mine. There's always somebody around that knows. Especiallly an old-timer."

Soon Jack had a proposition. Spring break was coming up. He offered to spend a day or two with me at the Bureau of Vital Statistics. His enthusiasm sparked mine and we headed for lower Manhattan. We had no trouble finding death certificates for Uncle Paolo, Nonna Guilianna, and my grandfather. But we found none for Nino. So we followed the book's next suggestion and walked through the New York County Clerk' offices, the City Register, the Civil, Criminal, Surrogate and Supreme Court buildings. We searched the case indices, enormous leather-bound tomes with pages the length of a newspaper's. Each volume held a year's worth of entries for legal proceedings—arrests, civil cases, probated estates, real estate transfers, bankruptcies, and family actions for adoptions, divorces, or name changes. Cases were listed by the defendant's surname. One page at a time, we looked for every member of my family I could trace since the year I was born.

I remember running my finger slowly down the rows of names, my pulse racing whenever I caught sight of a surname that began with the same configuration as my own, being very careful to avoid bending the pages as I turned them, keeping my hand from touching the meticulous fountain-penned lettering. It was all very odd, spending hours of tedious work inside those silent, musty underground repositories of information, waiting to stumble across a vital piece of my identity that might lay waiting for me. I kept trying to prepare myself, to stay one step ahead of each source I searched, vying between relief that I hadn't found anything disgraceful about my father and doubting the point of all this work.

I was grateful for Jack. I trusted his practical way of going about the search. It was good to have someone who cared about me and this very personal part of my life without making any demands on me. It was something I'd never experienced before with a man. The two days he offered became a week. Wherever I suggested we search next, he plowed on, scanning and cross-referencing along with me. He never lost interest, as though he was searching for something of his own, and I became accustomed to hearing his little gasps turn into sighs and fade into the silence of the rooms we worked in. We spent one whole day at The New York Historical Society reading through material about the Italian immigration. Then it was time to follow the cop's advice. We headed for Little Italy to find an old-timer to talk with.

Everything about Mulberry Street unnerved me. The crowds of merchants and tourists made me feel like a small child trailing behind my sisters. I half expected to look up at the tenements and see Nonna at her window, or to spot Uncle Paolo walking up the block holding his newspaper under his arm as he lit a cigarette. If I turned around I might see you standing on the corner of Hester Street watching as my sisters and I entered Nonna's building for a visit. Every door held the possibility of discovery, where complete strangers might know details of my own history that I didn't. Part of me felt like an intruder, excluded from the Italian order of life. The rest of me wanted to push my way in, figure it all out, belong there.

I went into almost every store in the neighborhood, with Jack beside me. I introduced myself to the shopkeepers in my unpracticed Italian, telling them that my ancestors once lived in Little Italy but had all died before I had a chance to know them, and that I would appreciate anything they could tell me about my family. Their reactions were surprisingly consistent. They'd stop what they were doing to quickly look me over, then signal me down the street to the next establishment. Sementa was not a name from their town, they'd say. I'd have to continue until I found the right block. It turned out that the streets of Little Italy were populated according to Italian provinces, with *paesanes* from the same villages residing in corresponding buildings. The Sementas' origins were listed on their death certificates as Avelino, Italy. I added that fact to my introduction as I made my way down the street. With each repetition my Italian pronunciation improved. I liked saying my grandparent's names, and of their village. The looks I was getting were friendlier as I went along. For the first time ever, I was beginning to recognize that I was Italian, too.

We were about a half block away from Nonna's building and still had no new information. But a storefront window caught my eye. A large statue of the Virgin Mary stood alone, adorned with faded plastic flowers at her feet, a dark drape in the background. The plain red door had no sign on it, and it was open. I could see a series of tables inside, and a group of men in the rear. I turned to Jack. He said it was a social club, and I wondered aloud how he came to know this. He just did, he said, and told me I should go in and talk to the men. But I protested. The thought of going inside a place so unwelcoming, especially for a woman, scared me. Jack said the men in there were about as old as my father would have been. They would know something. "It's just the contact you need. You should go in, and alone."

I took a look at Jack, leaning up against a parking meter with his arms crossed and a determined look on his face. He suddenly sounded too confident, and bossy, as if he were giving instructions to a reluctant boy standing before a swimming pool. There was something happening that Jack understood and I didn't. Something about men. Something universal about them that crossed cultures and races and ages, that made it possible for a person like Jack—younger and nothing like any of those men inside the social club—to sense from a hundred feet away what his next move should be. And I couldn't.

As I stepped inside I realized that I had been there before. The tables were laid out the same way, with a pathway to a kitchen door in the rear. It felt every bit like the gauntlet I'd been sent to walk as a little girl, when Uncle Paolo sent me down the six flights of stairs to buy him a pack of Camel cigarettes, alone, and I made my way through thick cigar smoke and tables filled with men sipping coffee. I felt just as nervous and scrutinized and out of place now as I had then.

At the back table four old men greeted me in unison, *"Buona sera signora,"* without stopping their card game. As I recited my introduction one of them looked up at me over his glasses. He said I should tell the fellow I was with to come in. The cop. I let out a loud, nervous laugh. Jack was a friend, I said, and no cop. I waved him in, but he hesitated, until another one of the men motioned to him, calling him Sonny and saying it was okay. Everybody laughed except Jack, and I felt vindicated.

We were invited to sit down and a waiter brought espressos. Jack spoke first and right to the point about how I'd wanted to do this for a long time because I'd never had the opportunity to know my family or my father. The old men looked at me some more, then resumed their card game. No one spoke until the game was finished, when the man wearing glasses looked up at me again. "See Tony Tenerielli. Down the block. At the Marechiara."

I thanked the men and walked down the street a little faster than before. Jack began to joke about how he'd thought the card game would never end, and how close he'd come to being killed, especially when the little guy brought out the coffee. It was good to laugh after all those days of damp record rooms and serious talk. But I could see that all my planning wasn't going to work here. Mulberry Street had a scheme and timing of its own. We weren't dealing with documents now. These were people, real characters we were meeting. I would do best to just go with it, and figure it all out later.

When I looked up we were in front of Nonna's building. The vestibule was smaller than I remembered. I showed Jack where Nonna's bell had been. The inside door was locked, but I peered through the glass panel and looked down the long corridor. I could see where the winding staircase began and hoped someone would come through to let us in. Jack turned to go, but I couldn't leave so fast. When I was ready, he said, "You look like you need a drink." I thought that was a good idea. And we should find this Tony who knew all.

I don't know if you remember the Marechiara, an old bar located between Nonna's building and the Café Roma. It was empty that day, except for an obese man who sat alone at the far end of the bar. He paid no attention to us as we took the two seats at the opposite end. I looked around and thought about what I'd like to drink in the middle of a warm spring afternoon. Nothing about the Marechiara was sleek or trendy, like its counterparts up the street. It was one large room, rather drab, with a dark wood bar on one side and a few bare tables on the other. A partition ran along the back, a series of ornate panels that reminded me of a confessional. Daylight came in through two large windows up front and on the far wall a few old sconces were lit. The smell of ale filled the room right to its tin ceiling. Jack said something about it having been a saloon before it was a *taverna*, and pointed to a Celtic crucifix on the wall behind the bar, just above an autographed photo of Ronald Reagan.

The big fellow stepped behind the bar and took our order. He didn't answer when I asked for Tony Tenerielli, just served our beers and rinsed out some glasses. When he finished he walked back to his stool and sat down. Then he said Tony had stepped out for a minute.

Mulberry Street didn't seem to exist inside the Marechiara. None of the noise or movement of people or traffic made its way through the heavy doors. I drank my beer and let the cold liquid soothe my throat. I thought of Julia and Carmela. We'd always been down here together. My sisters, not Jack, should have been with me doing all of this.

Jack wanted to talk about how far we'd come in the search. I welcomed the change of subject. I needed to be in my head, away from sentiment for a while. We pieced together the facts we'd collected so far. I knew that my father's parents left Italy as a married couple on a ship that docked at Ellis Island in 1908. He was a thirty-one year old tailor, she was a seamstress, five years younger. They settled at the southern tip of Manhattan in Little Italy with their infant son Paolo. There was no record of siblings for either of my grandparents, and they lived at the same address until they died. Nine years after their arrival, they had a second child, Nino, my father, whose fate positioned his childhood between the Great War and the Great Depression. The year I was born Nino was thirty-one, had graduated law school, married overseas, served in World War II, lost his father, and was a father himself for the third time. There was one more piece of information I hadn't found any evidence for, but I suspected the family had something to do with bakers because I remember Nonna had a connection to the Café Roma, next door.

As I talked with Jack, a man came in and passed behind us to the far end of the bar. He wasn't young, but moved with a self-assured, youthful bounce that caught my attention. The bartender pointed us out to one another. Tony Tenerielli gave me the same scrutinizing look I'd gotten all day. He spoke without coming any closer. "How can I help you?"

I swiveled my bar stool in his direction. His face was lean and smooth-skinned, free of the lines you would expect on a man in his seventies, with a full head of white hair. I told him a few people up the street had suggested I speak with him, because he may have known my family. I gave him my name.

Tony moved to one of the small tables near us. He pulled out a chair and straddled it, facing me, one arm resting along the chair back and his other hand to his chin. He studied my face again, as if he had nothing else to do, and spoke in an even, unrushed voice. "They lived upstairs. I knew them, yes. What would you like to know?"

I told him I hadn't known my family long because we were separated when I was a small child. Anything he could tell me would be appreciated.

"Your family were very fine people. The old man, your grandfather, was a tailor. Very respected. He made fine men's clothing. Suits for Mayor LaGuardia. People came from uptown, all over, to have their clothing made by your grandfather. All handmade, the kind of work you couldn't get anywhere today. Your grandmother, too. She made wedding gowns. Hand-beaded work. Made one for the mayor's daughter."

I wanted to know more about my grandfather. Tony dropped his arms to his side and smiled for the first time. "The old man? He used to come down-stairs in the evenings dressed in a fine suit and Arrow shirt, a Derby on his head, holding his walking stick in one hand and a book in the other. Back then people did that in the evenings, strolled up and down the block saying hello to each other. Your grandparents worked very hard. They were the first family on this entire block to have rooms with their own bathroom. That meant they had to combine two apartments, you know, which was unheard of at the time. Most people were crowding two families into one apartment."

As I listened, I thought of you. I remembered how you'd spend hours darning socks when I was very little and I'd sit next to you, watching the way you'd pass the needle through the cloth to connect one thread with another, patching up the ripped spot, and never break the light bulb you'd slipped inside to hold the sock in place. It was like that, listening to Tony, each detail he was giving me weaving something new for me. And I got the feeling it was like that for him too, that we were both changing with the telling.

I asked Tony if he knew my father, and he gave a short sigh. He turned his chair around and sat cross-legged, his hands folded on his lap. He spoke with the same steady voice as before, but slower, and never moved his eyes from mine.

"Your father was my dearest friend. The two of us and your Uncle Paolo were inseparable. Nino had something we didn't. He was smart. Maybe brilliant. He had talent. Nino could dance, play the violin, quote Shakespeare. He was a looker, too. He had girls after him all the time. He was a lawyer, one of the first boys on the street to become a professional. That wasn't an easy thing to be, around here. Certain people wanted him to work for things that weren't, let's say, above board. But he wouldn't do it. He went to work uptown for some fancy law firm instead. He spoke other languages, so they sent him to South America. It was supposed to be for a few months. But he was gone for years. We got word that he was married down there. Then war broke out and everything changed. We didn't see him again until after the war ended. For a while he lived upstairs with his mother and brother. You know, the old man had died suddenly, when Nino was overseas, so they never saw each other again. I know he took that very hard."

Then Tony stood up and stepped up close to me. "You look like him."

I didn't answer, because I didn't know what to say, but I felt my face get very warm. Then he asked a peculiar question. "How come you speak English?" I told him I'd lived in New York City all my life. That I'd grown up on Union Square and used to come to Mulberry Street to visit my Nonna and Uncle Paolo when I was small. He was surprised. "You mean you've been here, in New York, all this time? Your mother was from another country. Somewhere in South America. I only saw her once. A pretty blonde. People here thought your mother left your father and took the children back to her country."

For a few seconds I stopped listening. I was back in the courthouse a few afternoons before, running my hand halfway down the page of the 1949 Civil Court index until it touched your names, and next to it, *Matrimonial.*

I hadn't expected that. Seeing the official documents of your divorce made me feel more than betrayed and lied to—suddenly I was loyal to a man I'd never met. You'd ended your marriage before my father died, before I was born. I felt cheated, not only of a father, but of the image of you I'd always carried. You weren't just an unlucky widow anymore. You'd been a divorceé, like me.

Tony didn't know about the divorce. He didn't know how my father died or where he was buried. But he did know about Nonna and the Café Roma.

"Your father owned it. He bought it after he came home from the war. It was called the Café Ronca at the time. Your father changed the name, redid the décor, brought in new glass cases and marble tables. And that big mirror in the back. He wanted to serve customers out on the street, like they do now. But people told him he was foolish. Nobody did that then."

Tony didn't give me an answer when I asked why the café hadn't stayed in the family. He stepped away to the cash register, and in a few minutes came back to stand in front of me. His face had changed.

"You want to know. So here it is."

He began to pace, taking short steps before me, his hands back on his hips and his shoulders stiff with anger, his eyes on me.

"Your father was a dreamer. He was like that Elvis song, 'The Great Pretender.' He lost everything. He let the business fail. Nino with his great ideas. He could charm your underwear off without ruffling your pants. He disappointed a lot of people. Owed everybody money, his suppliers, the landlord. It was just before Christmas and his bakers hadn't been paid in weeks. He told them he'd pay them after the first of the year. And they were all family men. He made promises he couldn't keep. He got stupid. Borrowed money from the wrong people. He couldn't pay it back. On New Year's Eve, he walked away from it. Closed the café down and left town. That's how he left things. *Una disgrazia.* He disgraced his family. They couldn't look anybody in the eyes again."

Tony raised one hand to the back of his neck and turned to face the street. "Nino and his charm. It didn't do him a bit of good. Pretending everything was great. What a waste. He should have come to me. I was his friend."

I waited to see if Tony had anything more to say. He was quiet. All I could think to say was that my father had borrowed money from my mother, too. Tony took a step closer to me.

"Your father left no stone unturned."

Then he crossed his arms and walked to the back of the restaurant where I couldn't see him. Our conversation was over.

Tony's words hit me hard. I wanted to hide. I could feel my legs hanging off the bar stool but I didn't think they'd reach the ground. I felt Jack put his arm around me. I couldn't look at him. He said we should go, that it was enough for now.

We made our way up the block one more time, walking slowly, not speaking. It was already dark. We passed the restaurants with waiters standing like carnival barkers in their rehearsed Italian accents and their smiles that shined too brightly. Tourists pushed past, overdressed and rank with cheap perfume. Suddenly the street looked dirty, seedy. Someone in a sports car leaned on his horn.

I'd had enough. Of Mulberry Street, of secrets, lies, and betrayals. Of stories that all ended badly. I'd come here to search for facts about my family, but Tony Tenerielli had dislodged something I hadn't experienced before. The whole subject of Nino, my invisible father, suddenly disgusted me. I hated him for what he left behind, for the sorrow of his family, for the shame I carried for being his unknown daughter, a stranger needing to introduce myself to my own people, fighting to keep a connection no one else wanted.

I tried to speak and could only weep. That cop I talked to was right. It was too ugly. I wanted to get as far away from Mulberry Street as I could. I didn't want anything else to do with death or you or Nino or any of your awful story.

We turned back toward Spring Street, toward the garage where we'd parked, away from the shops, the social club, Nonna's building. We were near the Marechiara again and I saw Tony standing at the door. He was looking up the block at us. I thought of crossing the street, to get away from him, but I didn't have the energy. When we passed, Tony reached out and touched my arm.

"Come back next Sunday. Please. Come next door, to the Café Roma. Your father meant a lot to us. There are a lot of people, old friends who would love to meet you. Nino's daughter. They'll all come."

i have noticed
that big things always happen on Fridays
math tests and weekends
Doctor Ben moved to his new office on a Friday
He and Mom got married on a Friday
and now i'm rushing home from school just to see it
i'm going two steps at a time after waiting all day
Julia and Carmela are already home
and right there in the middle of the living room
is a basket with our new baby sister
she has one tiny finger in her mouth
and lots of black hair
Isabella
supposed to sound like Ben for her very own father
Mom is in the kitchen folding clothes
there is a crib in the corner behind the door
That Was Yours she says but i don't answer
She looks different back to how She looked before
with Her belly flat again
and Her long golden hair down on Her shoulders
the baby cries and She sits with it in the green chair
When you were a baby Doctor Ben carried you everywhere
To the movies and the park he even changed your diapers
i try fast to remember but it is embarrassing and disgusting
to think of diapers and be in junior high
anyway if Doctor Ben did those things
why isn't he my father too
later when we're all in bed i ask how does a baby get born
the girls laugh like they're keeping a secret
then Carmela says *A stork brings it*
and Julia says *Yeah right to the hospital*
and special nurses rub the mother's stomach
all night long until it goes down
and i don't know why but i laugh too
in the morning it's French toast for breakfast
Mom says She will not be going to work anymore
Julia will be Doctor Ben's new nurse

after school and on Saturdays
i think how lucky Julia is to be seventeen
Carmela is too she made it to Music and Art High
i'm lucky too Mom took me out of Catholic school
and baby Isabella has her very own dad
now we will go out again on Sundays like we used to
and have picnics and be a real family

8

You must do this Julia
Mom is talking very softly in the kitchen
She sounds angry but it's not at Julia
This situation cannot continue
they are standing around baby Isabella
She is putting the baby's coat on
Julia already has hers on and she is angry too
It's crazy what if they call the cops
Mom doesn't answer
just snaps the buttons closed and ties the baby's hat
after a long time Mom talks again
This is a very small apartment
It is inhuman to live like this
they are talking about Prince i think
Julia brought him home one day
when a lady stopped her in the street
stepped out of a limousine just like that with the dog
and offered to pay if Julia takes it for a few weeks
while she found it a good home
Mom said *No* first
but then she remembered how we cried for Hamlet
after he died Julia wouldn't talk to anyone for a long time
it wasn't anybody's fault just an accident
even Mr. Durant cried
he said he always locks that roof door for the winter
we didn't find out about it until after school
Julia hollered so loud i thought she would explode
screaming she never even got a chance to say goodbye
so now the lady's driver comes every Monday
with money for Julia to get beef bones at Sammy's
and Mom cooks them up
probably Mom has changed her mind and Prince must go
she is pinning an envelope on baby Isabella's coat
The third floor 3J next to the stairwell she says
Just ring the bell and leave Isabella in the stroller
Make sure you wait in the stairwell
Make sure you see them take her inside

And call me from the drugstore right away
baby Isabella is smiling but Julia is not
She sounds like she is going to cry now
I am his wife and this is his child and they will know it now
This secret life ends today
after Julia leaves with baby Isabella
Mom sits in the green chair in the living room
and She stares at Prince lying by the window

Hermanos

T he rich stacatto bass on my answering machine is a voice I don't recognize. "Friday. Try again." I play it back a few times until I realize
it is my brother's.

The usual image I have of Gabriel is of a little boy racing through the Jackson
Heights house in hot pursuit of an imagined friend or foe, his brows raised high
under a mess of blonde hair while he maneuvers a toy sword through the air.
He is conducting his own ensemble of groans, screeches, and roars and their
accompanying thumps and thuds, the clatter spilling through the windows, onto
the front porch and the neighborhood street. Gabriel was three when I was a
teenager, the last time we lived or played or spent time together.

I dial his number and hope he answers. I have no setting in which to
place him; I don't know where Gabriel lives or works. "He's very private"
was all Julia would say when I asked, which meant I shouldn't have asked.
These ten digits were all she would give me. A few days ago, I called for the
first time and reached a single beep with no greeting, not even the generic
prerecorded kind. It fits, I thought—the anonymity, the burden of secrecy
my family carries. I introduced myself to the silence on the other end of the
line. "It's Veronica, your sister," and recited my own ten digits.

Technically, of course, I am Gabriel's half-sister. It is an ugly term I
have trouble saying, even considering. I never heard anyone in the family
use it, which seems oddly noble of us. We were a group of people who used
language as the most preferred and most precise weapon of all, especially

the withholding of it. It would certainly have stung to be called half-sister or half-brother, as if one were half-something else, or worse, half-nothing else. I like to think it was overlooked because of the bottomless supply of proverbs and euphemisms my mother could summon and use instead, in less time than it took her to turn her head away. And because, in Spanish, all children born of the same mother are unequivocally *hermanos*.

I count three rings. I try to picture the grown Gabriel I met at his father's funeral. The manly, fit figure, the broad face that claimed Ben's strong cheekbones and our mother's full mouth. I recall his insistent gaze, hard to meet and harder to disengage from. The rings stop, and with his first word I am back in the chapel's flowered room crowded with people I'd waited decades to see.

"Speak."

My stomach tightens. I follow my little brother's now second command. "Gabriel, it's Ronnie."

"I know." How does he know? I wonder. Maybe he's very quickly recognized my voice from the four-word message I left on his machine. Or he has that new technology that identifies callers. I laugh to myself. The family secrecy, it has me on guard too.

"How are you?"

"Very busy." I glance at my watch. It says 10:15 p.m.

"Sorry. I only have this one number for you. Are you at work?"

"I'm an architect." Then he whispers. "A hostage to deadlines." I can't tell if this is his humor, or a genuine complaint, but I like this little glimpse of him.

"Oh, okay. I'll get right to the point then." There is apology in my voice again. I begin to question why I thought it important to call Gabriel at all. We are, after all, practically strangers. But he is my mother's only son. Without his consent, neither she nor Julia will allow anything to change in my mother's care. I tell him, "Mom's not doing well. She needs help."

"Help with what exactly?" I wonder when he's last seen his mother. "I was just at the house last week."

"Did you go into her room? She leaves it only if someone comes to see her. She doesn't even remember to eat, and she doesn't bathe."

But he has to know all this. This is Gabriel, the smartest of all my mother's children. This is whom Julia consults first, about any decision. Gabriel clears his throat. "It's very possible she's pretending."

"Pretending?" I can feel my fingers tighten around the phone. I hear the family's usual response to any display of vulnerability. "Why would she pretend? Why would anyone pretend to have such a condition, to live in a filthy room, in such chaos?"

"To get sympathy."

A sigh escapes me. I have believed, naively, that being a boy with a gentle father would have helped Gabriel escape my mother's harshness. Almost to myself, I say, "Julia thinks that too."

Gabriel doesn't hide his impatience. "What do you propose, specifically?"

"I think someone should go help Mom for a few hours a day. An attendant. Especially when Julia goes out."

"That suggestion has been discussed. Julia disagrees. She appears to have everything under control."

I search for something to say that will convey the urgency I feel. All I come up with is, "It will get worse, you know. As the disease progresses."

"Look," Gabriel modulates to *basso profundo*. "I'm not convinced this isn't premature. Particularly since there is no established definitive medical diagnosis for this alleged condition." He is enunciating carefully, taking his time. He is speaking to an audience, pacing before a planning commission. It is the same tone Ben used with his patients, talking as he worked, educating them on anything from a dental procedure he was performing to current weather patterns to politics, while their mouths were stuffed with cotton and metal instruments. Gabriel goes on. "Memory loss is common to a variety of conditions. Causality can only be positively determined posthumously. Through autopsy."

I am quiet. I've stopped listening to the Cal Tech graduate. I see the little boy and his sword.

He pushes on. "How reliable is this facility you took her to?"

"It's one of the finest geriatric institutes on the East Coast," I say.

"Who referred her there?"

I notice the words my brother, like my sister, avoids saying. I say them for him. "Mom has Alzheimer's. It won't get better or go away."

Gabriel is quiet. Just for a few seconds, enough for me to want to tell him it will be all right, to suggest we meet for a cup of coffee, or dinner one evening, he can come to my place, take the railroad, the way he does when he visits Mom, he can come with Julia, with anyone, bring Isabella, or Carmela if she'll come. We can sit together and talk this through. We are *hermanos*.

My chest swells. I bring my hand to my throat to keep it from closing. I am at the edge of the universe, watching my family circling its center—its awful cache of secrets. We are far from one another, solitary bodies spinning in our own orbits and fixed in place by something indefinably powerful. More powerful, I know, than my desire to make it otherwise.

I hear my mother's recent lament about her five estranged children. "*Que cosa*! It's hard to believe you all shared the same womb," as though she'd played no part in it.

I begin to cry. I don't want to cry, not today, not to Gabriel, not to this boy who's had five sorrowful women before him all his life. Then I see for the first time that the space between us isn't empty at all. It is vast, dense, and jammed with millions of unsaid words, with years of life not shared.

"Gabe," I start again. "Do you still play the piano?" I see the little boy sitting at the piano, feet dangling over the bench. I hear him practicing his first pieces, my mother's voice counting out the beats while I do my homework upstairs.

"Not any more. Not enough time," he says. Then his voice drops again. "By the way, how did you get my number?"

Doctor Ben is driving with Mom up front
baby Isabella is in between
she loves to sit in her car seat
and turn the little steering wheel that Doctor Ben bought
to go with his new Rambler station wagon
he is singing *In My Kiddie Car* again
this is the fourth time
when he's done baby Isabella says *Again Daddy*
and he does
she is so little
but she can make him do things for her like that
Mom looks happy up there with Her belly fat again
She says She can't sit comfortably anymore anyplace
but She is happy
because She's sure this baby will be a boy at last
a boy will make Doctor Ben happy
that's what She said when we were packing
wrapping all Her dishes up in boxes
if you ask me he looks pretty happy right now
singing Yiddish songs to the baby
i love when he does that
especially *Bei Mir Bist Du Shein*
at home he sings with his arms open wide
dancing around the kitchen snapping his fingers
then he kisses Mom and baby Isabella on the head
i don't think you can look more happy than that
Mom says if it's a boy it will be good for Doctor Ben
his mother and father will be satisfied and forgive him
they have been angry at him
for tricking them about marrying a Catholic foreigner
with three children
and for baby Isabella being born in secret
when we got to packing up Her pots and pans
She said *Every man wants a son*
For a son a man will do anything
then she looked sad and said
Your father thought you would be a boy

i wanted to say tell me tell me
but She was holding a tiny pot
saying She used to warm up my baby bottle in it
then She handed it to me to wrap in newspaper
inside one of the boxes with stuff She won't leave behind
not Her old pots or dishes or Her photographs
certainly not the old table in the living room
the one that opens up
No señor no way
no matter if Doctor Ben says to forget old memories
we are so lucky to have Doctor Ben
now we will have a house and big yard
and two floors and even a basement
Julia gets Her own room
Carmela and I will share
and i'll have the bottom bunk all to myself
i hope the baby is a boy so Doctor Ben never leaves
and i hope i haven't hurt the baby inside Mom
i feel scared when i think about it
Mom was very upset but it was all a surprise
when Tia Elena and Uncle Mickey came to visit
no one expected them
and it was all good at first
the grownups all in the kitchen talking and cooking
we could smell the *arepas* frying
everybody seemed happy that day just like today
we even got to play with our new baby cousins
all of a sudden Mom called me into the kitchen
she sounded real mad
and right there in front of everyone She asks me
Did something happen to you
when you went to Colombia
all of the grownups so serious not laughing anymore
Uncle Mickey won't look at me
then Mom drags me into the bathroom
She says *Take off your clothes*
i think She is going crazy for sure

i try to figure it out
does She mean about Edoardo
and how did She find out anyway
Mom is very upset She is standing very still
i see sweat drops on Her forehead
it's even worse than in the wars with Carmela
she isn't screaming but whispering right in my face
That servant in my mother's house
What did he do to you
i say nothing
i do not want Her to get more excited
You must tell me I know he did something
He hurt another little girl too now tell me
i say Mom nothing really nothing
but She's not believing me *Get undressed* She says
She is looking through the medicine chest real fast
Show me she says and hands my one of Her lipsticks
Show me with this what he did
Her hands are shaking and She is crying
so i say again nothing Mom nothing happened
She looks at me hard longer than i ever saw Her do before
i am cold and scared and naked
then She says *Get dressed* and turns around
i am glad She believed me
before She leaves the bathroom She says
All men are animals
They have a sickness even the good ones
Remember that you have to be careful don't get too close
then she stops and thinks for a minute
Even Ben is a man
after that day nobody ever talked about it again
but i think She is mad at me
i don't know what She means about Doctor Ben
i hope she didn't tell him about the lipstick question
it would be very embarrassing
i still would like to have him as my very own father
like baby Isabella up there in her car seat

he is the best man in the world i think
he is careful even when he is driving
now we have turned onto the Queensborough Bridge
and he makes sure
not to bump the trailer that is behind the car
i can see the girls out the back windshield
they are sitting on the boxes
full of dishes and pots and pictures
they are holding onto the sides of the trailer
the wind is blowing their hair all over the place
i wish i was allowed to ride back there with them
instead of sitting here behind baby Isabella
i bet they are singing Bye Bye Love
like they've been doing all week
bye bye bums
bye bye fluorescent lights
bye bye wars and fights
bye bye Manhattan bye bye
bye bye Manhattan bye bye

Café Roma

The Cafe Roma was empty when we returned, and there was no sign of Tony Tenerielli. The young boy behind the counter didn't have much to say except that Tony was sure to stop in as he did every morning, even on a Sunday. I sipped a black coffee and half listened as Jack read me headlines from the morning newspaper. My attention was on the checkerboard floor, the tin roof, the big grandfather clock against the back wall, and the pastries arranged like jewels in the display case. Nothing had changed. It could have been another long-ago Sunday at the end of a visit to Nonna, when I'd have raced my sisters down the six flights of stairs, pushing through the side door of the café, breathless and victorious. You would have been there, my young mother, waiting alone at one of the café's back tables in that red beret you liked to wear. I would have been grateful to Nonna for weighing Julia and Carmela down with bundles of leftovers from her table, so I could reach you first. And you would have looked a little startled, as though the onslaught of your three children were bringing you back, too, from someplace else you'd been.

When we'd waited an hour I asked to see the café's owner. A middle-aged man named Eli stepped from a back room, and when I told him who I was he untied his apron and gave me an eager hand shake. He was expecting me, which was a great relief. I wouldn't have to go through introductions again. Eli didn't have much information. He'd known my family, but the two boys were much older than he was, already grown men when he was a child. His eighty-one-year-old uncle Enzo, on the other hand, remembered everyone and everything about Mulberry Street. A little while later the waiter escorted a bulky old man to our table.

Uncle Enzo's face was a big wrinkled smile when he said he'd been waiting all week to meet the girl who had asked for his old friend Nino. I didn't have to prod Enzo to talk.

"Nino was a kind man, generous, he took an interest in people. If he saw you were having a hard time with anything, he'd cheer you up in a second. He'd make you laugh, or cook you a meal. Or bake. Nobody could make a Christmas cake like him. And he was smart. Always looking to bring new business ideas to the neighborhood. He even opened a foreign language school once, with two highbrows from the Upper East Side. He put his heart into everything he did, and everyone on the street loved him."

I wanted to believe Enzo, but I'd never heard anyone speak highly of my father. I had no experience of my own to measure such admiration against. Maybe all this affectionate talk was just the nostalgia of an old man.

"Mulberry Street wasn't for him. Nino wasn't like the rest of the men around here. He was educated. Elegant. He'd traveled, been places. Nino could have made a success of it, but after the war nobody wanted anything foreign. And you know, none of those uptown law firms would hire an Italian so easily. He tried business, but he had bad timing, that was all. His whole life Nino was cursed with it. He'd keep going, though, find something else to do. Such a fine man, easy to be with. He never had a bad day with anyone. He could talk politics or religion and never get into an argument. Only that one time he had trouble. He was just getting back on his feet. He got mixed up, in over his head with the bakery, that was all. He was young. Today it wouldn't matter. People lose businesses all the time. Back then it was a very big thing."

While Enzo spoke, more old men trickled into the café and quietly took seats at the tables around us. They also had good words about the Sementa family.

"People made excuses to go upstairs just to see the apartment. The boys each had their own room, and that bathroom! Paolo was quiet, a little shy, kept to himself. Nino was a sweet boy, the baby in the group. We were all together, since elementary school. Nino could read before the rest of us. Didn't they skip him a year? And he was artistic. He could draw anything, a person, an animal, a landscape. Just give him a piece of paper and pencil and ask him, and he'd draw it. No, no, never any trouble. He was a good kid. He didn't drink much, maybe a glass of wine now and then, and he smoked, like everybody else. You could see him in the afternoons walking with his violin around the corner to Hester Street, to his cousin Gracie's house, the girl with the piano, on the second floor. Other boys played stickball on the street after school, but Nino practiced music with his cousin. Never could get him to sit down for a card game or just hang around with the rest of us on the corner. He loved that fiddle. He'd give you his clothes, but don't touch that violin of his. The girls on the block loved him. You couldn't hold that against him. He was such a kind boy."

I didn't understand, if my father was so well liked, why no one, not even his close friends, seemed to know about his wife and children. After all, Uncle Paolo knew where we were. Didn't he talk about us? Why hadn't anyone made an effort to keep in touch? Only Enzo answered.

"We heard his wife left him, and took the children. We didn't pry into that kind of thing. It wasn't done back then. No one would mention it."

It was at about this time that I noticed Tony Tenneriello at the side door of the café, one hand on his waist and the other up against the wall, watching me. From time to time he'd send the waiter outside and the boy would return with another octogenarian for the group. Tony had been doing that all morning.

One of the last old timers to enter the café wore a red scarf around his neck and pushed his way through, nearly knocking over a few chairs on his way to a table at the far end. He couldn't settle himself down, squirming in his seat and tapping his fingers on the marble tabletop. At a pause in the conversation, he shouted out to no one in particular.

"They're all dead now. All of them. The father first. Then the boys. The mother went last. Ten years ago, maybe more. Dead now. All of them, dead."

None of the other men responded, as though they were accustomed to the man's outburst, and it put an end to our talk. But his words reminded me to ask about the who had cared for Nonna at the end of her life. Gina, the men said, and she still lived upstairs. But didn't come down much anymore.

I told the men how much I appreciated the things they'd told me. And, because I'd never had a chance to know my father, it would mean a great deal to me to know what happened to him. Where did he go when he left Mulberry Street? How did he die? Where was he buried?

The loud man at the end of the table shouted at the air again. "South! Brazil! The Bahamas. Bananas. Someplace hot." Then he turned to face me. "Who are you anyway?"

I said I was Nino's daughter. I asked if he knew my father. The man squinted across the room. He sat back and sighed.

"Sure I knew him." Then he stood up and quietly walked to the side door, and stepped outside.

I shouldn't mind Jimmy, Uncle Enzo said. He meant well. But it wasn't Jimmy the Red I was thinking about. I was watching the rest of the men sitting before me with their heads down, my question lingering in the air. A confessional, I thought.

"No one knew. Never heard. Everybody wondered. It was unbelievable. He just vanished. A terrible thing." A man who hadn't spoken before said he'd missed him all those years. "I wish I could see him now. I loved him. If you find out anything, come back and tell us."

As I said my goodbyes I couldn't help thinking, he would have been like them. If he was here now his hair would be white too, he'd be a little bent at the shoulders, slow to move, full of stories. I shook hands with each one. I hugged Enzo. His eyes teared up.

"The way you just did that, unexpected, was something your father would have done." For the first time, I felt I would have liked my father too.

When I stopped to give Tony Tenneriello a handshake, he waved it away. I wasn't finished, he said. I should come back later, after I saw Gina. He motioned to a tall young man standing next to him. Gina's son would take us up to his mother.

Outside, the air was cooler and fresher, and I breathed it in. The street wasn't quiet anymore. The regular bands of tourists and waiters were out. Four or five delivery trucks blocked the street and teams of Asian men loaded up at a produce warehouse. I tried to imagine the old men as young boys. A child would be out of place here now. Back then Mulberry Street would have belonged to them, to my father and Enzo and Jimmy and my Uncle Paolo. I thought of Nonna walking along these streets as a young mother, far from the people and places whose names I'd read on her death certificate. And I thought of you, doing the same thing when you came to this country.

We entered Nonna's building and I wondered aloud to Jack. Did my mother know how alone Nonna was? Did the two most important women in my father's life ever talk to one another? After all, there you were, each looking down at the city from your sixth floor apartments, three subways stops apart, three children linking you. How is it that nobody even knew we existed? Not even Tony Tenneriello, who knew everything about Mulberry Street.

Gina's son led us through the vestibule door and to the winding stairs. The indentations on the slate were deeper and the flights didn't seem as long as they had when I was a child. We reached the fifth floor apartment where Gina sat at the kitchen table in her bathrobe. She looked frail and weak, with dark circles under her eyes. She invited us to sit with her, uncovered a plate of cookies that sat on the table and offered us something to drink. She was sorry she wasn't dressed. She hadn't been doing well since the recent death of her brother. She took a good look at me, then she got right to the point.

"You want to know about your family."

As soon as Gina began to speak I realized we were directly beneath what had been Nonna's kitchen. "I lived in this building all my life. I grew up with your father. Your poor grandmother. She was alone a long time. It's not a good thing to live so long when you don't have family She was very fussy. The only thing she would eat all day was two hard boiled eggs. She wanted me to leave them on a plate on the chair next to her bed. She insisted on it, although she was blind by then. Toward the end Nonna would call Nino's name. I would talk to her, to calm her. Many times I asked if she'd heard anything from him all those years. Your Nonna said something very peculiar. She used to get telephone calls. The phone would ring, a long time. As if somebody knew she had to walk down the long hall to get to it. She would pick it up but no one would talk. She said she knew someone was on the line. Like they just wanted to hear her voice."

I felt a rush of heat cover my face. I was the one who had made those calls. And I admitted it to Gina. I would have said more, to explain what would make me do such an awful thing, but Gina's face was filled with judgment. As though she'd heard me admit to deliberately breaking the statue of the Blessed Mother that rested on the shelf behind her. Yes, I made those calls. When I didn't have you or my sisters to call, I'd dial Nonna's number—I still remember it, CAnal 6-0892. But when she answered I never knew what to say to her, or if she'd remember me. I hadn't seen her in more than a decade, since we left Union Square. I had no idea how old she was. I

always figured Nonna had people around her. Uncle Paolo, or all those others in her photographs. I didn't know she was so alone.

Jack changed the subject and asked Gina about Uncle Paolo, if he might
have known anything, and if there were other relatives.

"Paolo was a good son. He kept to himself. The only thing he did that
was unusual was that he took a trip every year. People talked about it, like
he must have had a lady somewhere he didn't want anybody to know about
and maybe she wasn't Italian. People around here didn't go on vacation. It
was very strange that he did that. Nonna had nieces, but they had all moved
away after the war. She had a nephew, Ray, who stopped by sometimes.."

I wasn't prepared to hear Gina mention your divorce. She'd accidentally
met you on Union Square one day, which surprised her because everyone
thought you'd taken the children back to South America. When she came
home she told Nino.

"He was so mad. I'd never seen him like that before. Don't forget, in
those days you kept those things quiet. Your father didn't want anyone
knowing his personal business. That was his way. A divorce in those days
was a terrible thing. Like having leprosy. But I kept his secret. I never told
anyone."

I asked Gina if she knew where my father went after he left Mulberry
Street.

"For years after he disappeared people said all kinds of things. Maybe
he got into trouble with the wrong people. Maybe somebody hurt him. I
didn't believe any of it. Not Nino. He was too smart to do anything like that.
I was sure he died abroad, because he never came back for his brother's
funeral, or his mother's. If he could have, he would have been here. You can
count on that. When he left that last night he was going down to work at the
café. He never came back home. Everything he owned was in his room. His
wallet, his glasses, driver's license, even his rosary. Right where he kept
them. Even his slippers under the bed. No one could believe he was gone. He
was such a loving man. How could he have disappeared like that? He always
looked well. But he must have been having a hard time. Harder than anyone
thought. You can't tell with people, can you? After all, he had his children,
didn't he? And your mother. Divorce or no, she was his wife wasn't she?"

She remembered you very well. "Oh, she was beautiful. When she first
got here, all the girls on the street came to see who your father had married.
He was very popular on the block, you know. When we heard he got married

in South America there were a lot of tears around here. Especially your Nonna. Then we heard he was sending his wife up here alone. I remember like it was yesterday. Everybody was shocked. The first time I saw your mother she was sitting in your grandmother's parlor with the baby, Julia. All the women in the neighborhood came up. Were we surprised. She was white! Whiter skin than any of us. And a strawberry blonde. A skinny little thing. And so fancy. Her clothes and things were so fine. See, years ago people around here didn't travel. We had never seen a South American. We expected her to be black, like one of the jungle natives. Nobody knew they had blondes down there."

Jack and I stopped to look at one another, and we laughed. What else could we do? Gina's answer was so honestly ignorant. She didn't understand or even mind our laughter, and just smiled back at us. Then her son returned with a message from Tony. Someone was waiting for us at the café. Before we left, Gina wrapped a few cookies in a napkin and insisted I take them.

"You know, my husband always talks about that last night, when he went into the café to wish your father a happy New Year. He was standing up against the counter with a strange look on his face. Like he was very sad. And he was never one to be blue. Always up, full of energy. So my husband asked him how he was feeling. Nino said, 'Tired, Sal. I'm so tired of all this.' My husband says he'd never forget the way your father sounded that night, looking out onto the street like that".

It was Ray at the café, my father's cousin. He looked very much like Uncle Paolo, but he seemed very nervous. His eyes never rested long on one place. As soon as Tony introduced us Ray asked for you. I said I hadn't seen you in a long time, and then I came right to the point. I asked him to tell me how my father died. Ray looked like he was about to cry, and his hands trembled. He said there had never been any news. He thought I knew, and that was why I'd shown up. Julia had come in to Ferrara's a few times over the years. He'd always expected she would have news. But no one knew.

I asked about the last time he saw my father.

"It was a very cold night. We were supposed to see him for breakfast the next day, all the cousins together that is, to start the New Year the way we always did. He was right outside the door here, closing up for the night. He wished me a happy New Year, and kissed me. I remember he felt cold, very cold. So I took off my coat, the new wool coat I'd gotten the week before for Christmas, and I told him to put it on. He didn't want to. He argued with me, but I made him take it. I didn't know where he was going to celebrate the New Year. It was such a cold night. I never saw that coat again."

So Ray was the last person to see my father alive. When I said it, Ray began to sob, holding a handkerchief over his mouth to muffle the sound.

"My cousin was a man who everybody loved. He got into some trouble with money. He must have thought he was ruined. He never knew how much love there was for him. *Scusi.* I don't mean to cry. This is what happens when you get old."

The café was very quiet. It was already late afternoon, between the lunch and after-dinner crowds. The group of old timers had shrunken to just a few, but Enzo was still there. Tony Tenneriello sat down next to me. I thanked him again, for making the day possible. My voice sounded tired, and I knew I wasn't conveying the gratitude I felt. Tony put his hand on my arm.

"Did you get what you wanted?"

I told him I'd gotten more than I expected. Then I laughed a little. "But I still haven't solved the Mulberry Street Mystery.

Tony glanced at the other men. Then he turned back to me. He held my hand.

"You're like him. So much like him."

His remark, like his behavior, made me suddenly realize what the day had been about. I had been tested. Been put through some tribal Italian examination.

Tony's face was close to mine. "Your father is alive."

I know he said it in his natural voice, but I remember it sounded like he'd said something from a great distance, and that once I heard them, the words moved me, quietly, quickly, irrevocably, into a different life.

"He's out west."

I looked around the table. I looked at Jack, and back to Tony.

"Out west is a big place," I said.

"Las Vegas. That's all I can tell you."

Tony Tenneriello held onto me for a long time when we said goodbye. I don't remember walking away from the Café Roma or up the street. I don't remember leaving Little Italy that evening. All I remember is Jimmy the Red saying, "Someplace hot."

i'm the last girl in school to get my period
they all announce it in the bathroom
while they tease their hair and put on eyeliner
which of course i'm not allowed to wear
Mom says that's the way *vagamundas* look
just because *americanos* can be very ignorant
and let their daughters dress like prostitutes
not Her daughters
no tight sweaters or skirts
and absolutely no black stockings
at night She picks out our clothes for the next day
this really pisses Julia off
after all she's in college already
she curses right at Mom now
and tells her to stay out of her room
and slams the door hard
but Mom goes in anyway it's Her house and Her rules
Carmela keeps secret clothes in her school locker
she buys them in the Village
i don't care about the hand-me-downs so much
it's my hair that's a mess
it already reaches my bottom and Mom won't let me cut it
it wouldn't be *decente* for a young girl to have short hair
so most of the time i wear it in braids or a pony tail
Paloma and i are the only ninth graders with long hair
she is the new girl from Spain
her mother wouldn't mind if she cut hers
but she thinks the other girls look like they wear helmets
and she enjoys having long hair
she says my hair is pretty
all the girls in Spain have long hair
she is my friend
just before the last school dance she helped me
i wanted to change my look to be like the other girls
Paloma teased every strand of my hair
we were hysterical in the bathroom
she used a hundred bobby pins to put it up

and almost the whole can of her mother's hairspray
she even put eyeliner on me
she lent me her pink sleeveless dress and black high heels
at the dance nobody recognized me
the girls kept whispering
Paloma's shoes were too small and hurt
so i couldn't dance very long
most of the boys were already coupled up
i really hated just standing around
i don't think i will be going back next time
we had to brush all the teasing out
before i went home
the boys change girlfriends every week or so
they call it going steady
it doesn't make sense to me 'cause nothing is steady
it's all the girls talk about in the locker room
who's making out with who
and who might go all the way
they pretend to have cramps to get out of gym
i would never give up gym not ever
even if i did have bad cramps
but i don't get them
not at all and it's already come twice
periods are really not so bad
except for the bother of washing out panties
we have to hide them from Doctor Ben
no panties or stockings hanging in the bathroom
once he gets home
Carmela says i don't get cramps because i dance
she wants me to choose Music and Art
that way we can be in the same high school
she says it's tough academically but i can do it
my new flamenco teacher Mariquita doesn't agree
she thinks Performing Arts is better
she says i will be a great dancer because i am tall
she sends me to dance at different places
i was even given the *soleares* solo at the Armory show

and i won first prize again in the school talent contest
Mariquita helped me prepare for the auditions
and she wants me to dance at the Spanish Pavillion
when the World's Fair comes to Queens
i like flamenco but nobody knows anything about it
not like ballet or tap
people always say flamingo or call it roach stomping
which i don't understand really
it's embarrassing
that's why i tried to fail the Performing Arts audition
all the girls there had ballet pieces
when it came time for my *alegrias*
the judges looked at me really weird
they didn't seem to know what i was doing
so at the barre i kept my knees bent on purpose
to make sure i wouldn't have to go back there again
She would never let me be a dancer anyway
it is not a career *Para una mujer decente*
You will be a lawyer she says
She can choose my career because she's my mother
and i don't know enough about life yet
i think really it's because of the boys
she must know about them
but i don't know how She found out
She has never come to see me dance
even though she makes my costumes
maybe Mr. Abbott told Her
he called last week to say i won again
i can't help it that my legs show
when i do the *quebrada* turns
and all the boys in the auditorium start to whistle
and clap loud
for me the best part is putting on the makeup
and the *sevillana* dress
it's like i am somebody else
no thick glasses or braids or sallow skin
and i'm not nervous or embarrassed or shy

not when i'm in costume
the kids in my class don't even recognize me on stage
until later when i win
they tease me for being teacher's pet
especially this year that's it's my third time winning
that's Mr. Abbott's fault
he always asks me to demonstrate steps in gym class
when we have folk dancing instead of calisthenics
sometimes we have to hold hands with the boys
and we swirl around
the other girls are always giggling about something
as if they know secret things about boys
but i just like to dance

9

Carmela teaches me how to stay safe
she is an expert in the subways
she rides to school every day all the way up to Harlem
i must be prepared
just in case i am accepted to Music And Art too
Carmela says Manhattan stations are no problem
there are always crowds
and nobody even looks at you
it's Queens you've got to be really careful in
especially on the Ely Avenue stop
that's where all the perverts get on
you can spot one early every morning
he'll stand behind a girl
and push up on her little by little
if Carmela sees one it makes her real mad
so she uses the hat pin she carries
and sticks him hard in the leg
or she digs her spiked high heels into his foot
the guys never say anything
they just get off at the next stop
that's how you know they really were pervs
if i go to M&A it'll be subways every morning
so i practice now on my way home
i don't have the courage to stick them with a pin
but i stand against the doors
i don't let anybody get behind me
right now i don't have to worry about subways
in the morning Ben lets me ride in his car
he takes me right to the schoolyard
he drives and finds shortcuts to the Midtown tunnel
while i read the Times front page and the editorials
out loud
when i'm done i fold the paper like he taught me
then we listen to WQXR
Ben asks me to name the composer
or which period the music is from
if i don't know he tells me

if nobody knows we each take a guess
before the announcer says it
the New World Symphony is his favorite
because Dvorak wrote it in an apartment
a few blocks from Ben's office
once he took me to look at the little plaque
right above the door
it looked smaller than Ben's dentist sign
he said *Yes but Dvorak's will be there forever*
i like the rides to Manhattan
they are the only time i get to spend with Ben
he doesn't get home until very late
then the arguing starts
it's usually about money
or because Mom has too much work
he says he'll get Her a housekeeper
She says She wants him to help instead
so on Fridays when his office is closed
he goes to the supermarket
when i get home from school
the groceries are on the kitchen table
Mom reads out the prices on the food
and Ben checks the receipt
then they put the food away in the cupboard
and into the refrigerator
she says *Things on the left side*
are for Ben's children
it makes me embarrassed when She says that
i want to disappear and be invisible
i know it is wrong and maybe sinful
but when nobody is looking
i drink his children's apple juice anyway
right from the bottle
it is delicious and cold and we never get any
except that one time Ben was feeding baby Gabriel
teaching him to speak
DaDa DaDa he says over and over

but baby Gabriel won't talk
and out of nowhere i hear myself ask
can i call you Dad too
Ben looks at Mom all confused
She turns away and starts to wash the dishes
it is very quiet and I want to get out of there
finally She speaks
Ben is not your father
then he pours me a glass of apple juice
You can call me Doc he says

Tesoro

I sit with my mother in her garden. We've just completed an unrushed walk around the perimeter of her house. She knows each of her plants and trees intimately but struggles today to name even a few. I am of no help to her here. I know very little about these living things my mother's hands have dug deep into the earth to make a place for, have fed, carried, cleared of debris, caressed furtively and roused from their unremarkable beginnings to the fecundity of fragrance and color that surround us now. I am jealous of them.

I take a deep breath, inhale the warm summer air and hope for a breeze. My mother doesn't mention the heat. She is busy at her potting table bundling flowers she has ripped off their branches without a tool. I see her strong limbs moving under her short nightgown. Her skin is smooth and translucent. Only her gnarled hands show her seventy-five years. When she is done she brings the bouquet to me and says *"Para ti."* She takes a seat with me at her crumbling patio set. I thank her for the flowers and picture them sitting on my dining room table in Nonna's vase.

"Hydrangea, hibiscus, zinnea." My mother grins in self-satisfaction. I can't tell if her pride is from her sudden ability to remember her flowers' names or for having grown them. Maybe it's from the pleasure she sees in my face. I set the bouquet on the table between us, next to the package I've brought with me. I reach for it, a manila envelope. It is worn, and the clip on the back is long broken, but it is large enough to hold what I slipped into it this morning.

"Que tienes ahí?" My mother is curious about what I have in my hands.

I open the envelope and remove the plain white binder. In it are a dozen or so discolored newspaper clippings and photographs, and close to one hundred pieces of correspondence written between 1941 and 1947. Notes, cards, letters, and cablegrams, some typed, others handwritten on fine onionskin, a few hastily scribbled on scraps of paper. Each is stored in a clear plastic sheath. All but five are directed to my mother. Most use her nickname, Cuchi, which I have never heard. They are from my father.

"Cartas," I say, and move my chair close to her.

"What letters?"

"Letters you gave me. A long time ago, one Mother's Day when I came to visit. When Michél and I brought the children to you for the first time. Do you remember that?"

She doesn't. But I do. It was on that day, when my mother told me she thought I'd ruined my life and I'd left this house feeling crushed by her absolute disapproval, that she'd quickly gone into her bedroom to get something just as we were readying to leave. *"Toma,"* she said, and handed me the yellow envelope I hold in my hands now. "You should have this."

I open the binder and show her the first page. It is a close-up picture of my father. He is sitting in what looks like the front porch of a house. He is in profile, features smooth and handsome, head tilted back, his eyes closed behind his glasses. He could be sleeping or enjoying the bright sunshine that lights the shot. My mother studies it carefully, brow bent.

"Where did you get that?" She is amused.

"From you, Mom. With all of these." I do a quick flip through the binder to show her. The purr of plastic sheets blows an insignificant breeze at us. I remind her that she gave the letters to me.

"I did?"

"Sí."

I don't tell my mother that I didn't look at the envelope for years. The night she gave it to me, I hardly glanced at the typewritten addresses and foreign stamps inside. I had more pressing things at hand—raising children, finishing school, my failing marriage, and, after the divorce, finding a job. The idea of plowing through an old envelope stuffed with my mother's mail made me angry. I didn't want her papers. I wanted her to welcome me back. I threw the envelope in the back of a closet, and it felt good.

The envelope moved to the back of every closet I owned. Until one afternoon in late spring, the year I discovered the truth about my dead father—that he wasn't dead, after all—I found myself sprawled out on my living room floor surrounded by the words of a man whose voice I'd never actually heard. I read each of the letters. I put them in order. I purchased this binder and slid each piece of the chronicle of the relationship that led to my birth into its own protective sheath.

My father's early letters are an amusing blend of Italianized Spanglish. The final ones are in nearly flawless Spanish. There are no letters from my mother. Perhaps they wait in the back of someone else's closet, somewhere, unread.

"Nino," my mother says, eyes opened wide. She touches the photograph I am holding and nods. I look at her and at the photograph of my father and I think, this is the only time the three of us have ever touched.

"Tell me about him, Mom."

She raises an eyebrow. "It was a long time ago Ronnie. Why do you care?"

"I want to hear about my father from you."

She sits back in her chair and sighs.

"There was nothing about him that you could not like. *Era bello.* So handsome, maybe the most beautiful man I ever saw. Tall, excellent bone structure, blonde honey hair with waves, and that olive skin. Perfect teeth, a little bit crooked like yours in the front, but beautiful. Big build, he was six foot three, slender and fair. *Puro Italiano.*

"Everyone loved him. *Mi mamá.* My brothers too. He was very humble, modest. In Barranquilla he would sit on the floor to play with the servants' children, the black babies. *Imaginate.* Playing with them. No white man did that. He loved children. How ironic.

"He was brilliant. Well-rounded. He loved to dance. He loved music, all kinds of music, but especially opera. Well-read, well-spoken. Yes, he was nice to look at, too. Was that all I saw? *Bueno*, everything enters through the eyes, sweetheart. When a man sees a beautiful woman pass by, does he think, I wonder how her brain works? The eyes are the beginning, even when you buy apples, or a dress. Some people believe it begins with the nose, *el humor de la persona.* Nino was perfect in that dimension as well!

"Who would not fall in love with him? He had the gift of words, you know. And he paid attention, noticed every detail—a new pair of earrings

I wore, a new hairstyle or shade of lipstick, the mood I was in. I should have said 'leave me alone,' but he was irresistible. Women were just waiting for his flattery. Especially an eighteen-year old just getting over a broken heart."

On the next page is a portrait of my mother, taken on her fifteenth birthday. She is standing with her father, who looks serious and tight-lipped. The photograph has been colored in, making my mother's eyes dark and her girlish cheeks rosy. I recognize my youngest daughter's determined look in my mother's face. Under her right eyebrow is a small beauty mark, faded now. Following her photograph are a few cropped news items from the 1941 society pages of Bogotá's *El Tiempo*, showing rows of young men and women standing arm in arm in formal evening wear. An X has been penned over the evening gown of the young girl who is my mother, when she was someone else, an elegant debutante living in another world. She is radiant.

"A broken heart? Do you mean about Gregorio Guitierrez Lindon?" I bring his letter penned in English close to her so she can see it. It is his message suddenly breaking off their engagement.

"Yes," she says, and waves the letter away. She grows quiet. I am afraid the stream of fertile memory that has begun to flow from my mother will stop. I turn the page to urge her on.

"Nino came to South America on business. The firm he worked for, Sinclair Robinson, sent him to close a deal with textile mills. Something to do with the Everfit factories in Bogotá. Colombia manufactured fine wools, you know. Nino spoke Italian, so they assumed he could manage in Spanish. They expected he would return in a month.

"You say it was Spring of 1941 when your father sailed? I take your word for it. The letters should say it, even if I cannot remember exactly. He left New York with his brains and his charm, those good looks and a few letters of introduction. Yes, that one is to Eduardo Zuleta Angel, who would become the Colombian ambassador to the United Nations.

"I have never known a man as well presented as your father. Everything about him was elegant. His carriage, his speech, his manner. He told me his friends from Little Italy went to the pier to see him off. You know, just a few months before he left, as a joke a few of them got together and sent a letter to a movie studio in his name, without his knowledge. They wanted him to be a movie star. But he had no interest in it. He was an attorney. He never answered that letter you have there from MGM Studios asking for a photograph.

"*Pobre* Nino, he did not know when he got on that ship with that trunk full of suits his father hand-made for him that he would never see his father again.

"Anyway, after a few ports in Central America he docked in Barranquilla. His final destination was Bogotá, *en el interior.* You know in Colombia there is great rivalry among the provinces. The Caribbean coast is on the equator, hot and humid, tropical. The people are of all colors and races, and they are more relaxed, less formal. In the interior, up in the Andes mountains, it is cooler, more remote. There is a big indigenous population and very few blacks. People are more reserved, guarded, in their demeanor. They believe they are better than the *costeños.* So, in Colombia we do not trust anyone, least of all another Colombian!"

My mother laughs at her own remarks, and I laugh with her. She is suddenly Colombian. The identity she has disdained as long as I have known her is undeniable now. She sits cross-legged and relaxed, sure of herself, her English never more fluid, the rounded inflections of her *Barranquillera* Spanish sweet and soothing as she blends her history and geography lessons into the story that holds my interest more than any other.

I show her a letter addressed to my father, signed "Lourdes."

"Apparently the captain of the ship was impressed with your father and introduced him to the daughter of a very prominent family on board, Lourdes Mercedes Santos. Old money. *Oligarquía,* cattle ranching. She had been studying in the United States and was going to meet her family at their vacation home in Cartagena, on the coast, very close to Barranquilla. She invited Nino to join her on his return trip from Bogotá.

"It was Lourdes Mercedes Santos who introduced him into *la rosca,* the inner society circle. He told me later that he actually did not like her. Apparently she was quite overweight and not appealing to his eye. That dancing eye, like my mother used to say, *le bailaba el ojo.* So in November he was back at the coast for the feast of *La Independencia.* He planned to be home in New York by Christmas."

My mother asks me if I have ever been in Barranquilla. I remind her that she sent me there when I was little. And that I passed through again when I went to meet my in-laws in Cartagena. I tell her that I didn't like Barranquilla, either time.

"I cannot blame you. In comparison to New York it is unremarkable, really. Except for one thing. It is a seaport, *estratégico,* on the northern coastline of the continent. It is the entryway from the Atlantic Ocean to the Panama Canal. We always had foreign ships, seamen, and tourists traveling through. Products and people coming from all over the world to enter South America. A little like Brooklyn.

"The United States was not at war when Nino left, but it was imminent. There was trouble in Europe and in the Far East. His parents were worried. They only had two sons. The older brother, your uncle Paolo, was too old to be drafted, past thirty already. But they did not want anything to happen to Nino. He was only twenty-four or so, their *bambolino*. When the U.S. entered the war they encouraged him to stay in Colombia to avoid getting drafted. I guess I would do the same for my son. I cannot say. But it made sense, once you knew him. Nino did not have a belligerent bone in his body. War was not for him."

I watch my mother as she speaks, her body animated, her gaze moving often into the distance, past the blossoms in her garden into a depth of memory that surprises me for its details. "People gravitated toward your father. One of his closest friends was Genaro Vargas, un *Barranquillero*. Also from *la sociedad*. They were inseparable. He encouraged your father to stay in Colombia and pursue a business in textiles. It was Genaro Vargas who brought Nino into El Normandi, my mother's restaurant across from the country club, after a round of golf. Your father was not a sportsman, at least his pastime was never athletics. He had other diversions. Of the two-legged, curvaceous kind. But the two men became regular customers at *El Normandí*. Apparently, Nino saw my graduation picture. Yes, the one you have seen on my dresser. My mother kept it on the wall in her restaurant. Nino asked Genaro Vargas to inquire about who that girl could be. When they spoke to my mother she said I was away at school and would not be back for several months. But Nino waited, and every time he came into the restaurant he would ask my mother again.

"When I met Nino, I was eighteen. I had lived in boarding schools most of my life. I was planning to continue my education, to go to university. All my professors recommended it. That was not a very popular idea then, for a woman. There were other expectations of girls. That code of behavior that governs a woman's life in Colombian society. Your appearance, your choice of companions, your opportunities. A respectable woman has one role only. To be the protector of her class. She has to watch everything she does very carefully, and she is being watched. In exchange for this, she never does any labor of any kind—not even to wash her own clothing or prepare herself a meal. That is what servants are for. And she will never handle money, even if it is her own. Hmph! Some trade-off. Like living in a prison with invisible bars. I hated it.

"When I came home from school in Bogotá my mother arranged for Nino to meet me. He came to the summer house she rented. After that there were invitations to tea or lunch. But we were never alone. It was unheard of for a man and woman to be alone in the same room, even family members, unless they were a married couple. So we always had a chaperone with us, *la criada*, an older woman my mother hired as my personal maid.

"He was so handsome, your father, and what a personality. He had a way of making people feel at ease immediately. And that laugh of his. It was contagious. You could not help feeling happy when he was around.

"Courtship was very different in those days. We did not have telephones everywhere. People communicated by messenger. A young woman had her own stationery and little calling cards she carried. If a boy liked you, he would write *un piropo*, a compliment, usually hidden in a line of poetry or the lyrics of a song, on your card. Like the one you are holding, with my name on it, where he wrote, asking me to meet him. Although I spoke English fluently, your father wrote in that half Spanish-half Italian of his."

Per favor Cuchi venga.

Venga a salir.

"I knew where he was staying, of course. He lived in a hotel owned by Italians, the Tivoli Natili. He preferred the Italian cuisine they served there, and of course they catered to him. He would even find his way into the hotel's kitchen to teach the chef new recipes! Nino did not care for Colombian food, at first. But once he tasted my mother's cooking, that was all he ate. He couldn't stay away."

Non esta bravo. Yo soy triste senza te.   I am not angry. I am sad without you.

Hagame felis y venga.   Make me happy and come.

Ti quiero. Un millione di baci.   I love you. A million kisses.

"Just a few weeks after we met the Japanese bombed Pearl Harbor. We were a continent away but it affected us seriously. Nino became very cautious. To begin with, he stood out everywhere because of his height and aspect. But once the United States declared war he was supposed to have reported to the American embassy. He gambled on postponing it for a little while longer. We courted for about six months, the customary period. One day he asked me to marry him and, *por supuesto*, of course I said yes.

"We were married in *La Catedral de San Nicolás*, which was on el Paseo Bolivar in the center of the city. My mother was delighted. She was glad to have me married to an American. I mean, she needed to get rid of this problem I presented being the only girl and without a home. Family honor and all that. When the daughter walks down that aisle to be married she carries it all on her shoulders, every merit and demerit of her parents and her lineage. No matter what else she accomplishes, it is her zenith to get married in a white gown, *con velo y corona*. It validates everything. Well, my dear, I did it!"

There is a jubilant expression on my mother's face. Her voice is loud and her hand is clenched in victory as she jabs her index finger into her chest and repeats her last phrase. It is as though there were a crowd of people around us she has convinced.

"My mother went to the best dressmaker in town, Eliza Gonzalez Rubio. There were a lot of people at the church. About two hundred guests. All the upper class big shots from my father's side of the family finally came. But not him. He was too sick, or too drunk, or something. My mother was afraid he would ruin my wedding. But he never showed up. So at the last minute his friend Roberto Bornacelli was the one who walked me down the aisle. It was such a terribly hot day in the middle of July, and very humid. I had trouble with my hair. Normally I could do any style with it, but that morning it was rebellious. Maybe it was nerves. Waiting to see if my father would show up. I kept listening for his car, but it never came.

"After the ceremony the photographer wanted us to pose for pictures, but he did not care for the way we looked, ridiculous really, because I was so much shorter than your father. So he made me stand on a couple of empty suitcases. Your father made a joke out of it, as was his nature, to set everyone else at ease. But he did not look well. He was very pale. It was a difficult day for him too. At the last minute he had had to borrow Bornacelli's shoes. You see, in Colombia shoes were only hand made. Apparently Nino's foot size was too big and a mold had to be especially cut. When the shoes were delivered that morning they were still too small. What a mess. ¡*Olvidate*! Then the Caribbean heat got to him, poor fellow. In the middle of the ceremony, he fainted. Such a big man collapsing, ¿*te imaginas*? They had to run and get smelling salts for him. The two of us were so nervous."

In their wedding picture my parents stand cheek to cheek, my mother's face just ahead of my father's, his long arms overlapped around her tiny waist, his hands meeting hers at the long stems of six calla lilies she carries elegantly across her body. Under her pearled crown she gazes dead ahead into the lens, her chin slightly raised toward him, his face bowed into her thick blonde curls, nostrils gently flared as though filling himself with her aroma. They are beguiling in their beauty. Yet neither one can muster a trace of a smile. I study the photograph and feel again its power to stir my yearning for these two people, and to enrage me with its uncanny prediction of the enormity of the loss that forged my family. Her feet do not touch the ground. He can't bear the heat.

"Then we went on the famous honeymoon. We left from Puerto Colombia and sailed up el Rio Magdalena to Bogotá, as I had with my mother en route to boarding school. A honeymoon? I do not know where they got that name. *Un desastre* is more like it. Your father was too rough with me. He wanted sex all the time. *Insasiable.* He would not even leave the *camarote* for meals. The pain was so bad I could not walk. Finally one night when we were docked at one of the ports, I put my clothes on and sneaked out while he was showering. I got off the ship. I did not know where we were. I saw some big boulders near the dock and hid behind them. Next thing I know your father and the ship's captain are searching for me with those big headlights shining. One of the sailors saw me and shouted *¡Aqui esta la novia!* and they were all laughing like it was a big joke. All the men laughing at the scared bride. *Idiotas,* all of them!

"But I know I was a big disappointment to Nino. He used to say I was missing a 'switch' that every woman has. He looked for it everywhere, but I just did not have it. I do not know, I guess I was defective. I still am. I never cared for sex. It is messy and noisy and something only for men to enjoy. Maybe it was all that stuff we were taught as children. That it was sinful to think about or do, or even to talk about it. A decent woman is not supposed to enjoy such a thing. That is for whores or prostitutes. Maybe I had a complex or a trauma. Maybe things that happened between my mother and father. Who knows? Too late now to worry about it.

"Men are just not happy unless they get all the sex they want. From eight to eighty, it does not matter. I tried to make up for it in other ways. I took care of the home and everything else. But with men, if you are no good at sex nothing else makes up for it. You are a failure as a woman and as a wife.

"My mother was not like me. She seemed to like being sexual. She attracted men's attention anywhere she went. There was something about her. She could be dressed like a nun and she still exuded passion. I remember when I was very little I would wake up at night sometimes and hear noises in my parents' bedroom. It would frighten me. I thought she was being hurt. We never spoke about that, of course. I certainly did not inherit any sexual appetite. I was a failure in that department. I was not a complete woman.

"I suppose, now that I think about it, that was why I was such a jealous person. I questioned Nino's fidelity. I still question the capacity of any man to be faithful. I do not trust men, *punto*.

"Your father loved Colombia. He wanted to stay there for the rest of his life. He had already made important contacts before we were married. There were big opportunities for him. He was skilled. He knew how to design patterns for garments, how to lay one out and cut a cloth without wasting an inch of material. He learned that with his parents. Colombia had no such thing as ready-made suits or shirts or dresses at that time. Everything was hand made and custom fit. The opposite of what is in demand today. A factory-made suit was a novelty, a luxury. Big companies like Everfit and Arrow wanted to open factories in Latin America. They had been getting Colombian textiles all along. But with the war going on they began to look at locations closer to the States for cheap sources of labor. Colombia was an excellent spot."

I take a yellowed newspaper clipping out of the envelope and pass it to my mother. It is an advertisement, in Spanish, with the image of a man in a suit and hat. Clocks mark time in the background to show how quickly the gentleman can add to his wardrobe.

> A NEW SUIT IN JUST 6 HOURS!
> At 10:30 am you get invited to a party.
> At 11:00 am you select an EVERFIT suit.
> At 4:30 pm it is ready for you to pick up.
> No fittings. No bother.

"Yes. Several prominent businessmen offered your father partnerships. He worked with *Sastrería American Gentleman* for a time. Then he accepted an offer from Industrias Rendon in Pereira. So we moved inland to Pereira, mountainous and a very pleasant climate. My mother helped us get a very nice apartment. Your father even joined the country club. That clipping is from the society page announcing our arrival. Gossip by another name.

"We were in Pereira for a time and then had to make a trip to Ecuador. Nino needed a visa to work in Colombia. It was necessary that he leave the country and reenter to claim it. We made that long trip by car through the Cordillera. Those winding Andes mountain roads were endless. I got sick all the time.

"When we returned to Pereira I found out I was pregnant. Nino was very happy. It was a good pregnancy. My mother would come up from the coast to visit us, to help me. She was delighted with becoming a grandmother. You see, she had been very worried because I had trouble getting pregnant. More than a year passed since we were married and nothing. And it was certainly not because of lack of sex.

"I had to go to doctors who made me take all kinds of things, vitamins, especially calcium, because I was always too skinny and anemic. I weighed ninety pounds. My mother took care of me. She ordered special creams for me to use to avoid getting stretch marks. She gave the cook instructions on what to prepare for me. She was very happy. My father was thrilled too. But he was very sick with stomach problems and could not come to Pereira. But he was happy for us."

I never knew my mother to throw salt over her shoulder or avoid black cats crossing her path. She possesses a core of brazen courage that is her defense against all threats to her security, real and perceived. It is her unshakable pessimism that compels her to expect and prepare for the worst, always. So that when times are bad she perseveres, and when they're good she detects certain disaster ahead. It is a lesson she learned well in 1943, she says, during what was to be the second in a string of doomed Decembers.

"We never had any peace of mind. Your father was persecuted because of his name. Government officials were always stopping us, asking to see his documentation. They were concerned about having fascists in the area, thinking he was an Italian, but when they saw he had an American passport they left us alone for a while. But it did not last long.

"One day a group of military police knocked on our door. They were from the American embassy. It was December 7th, exactly two years after the first surprise attack. We were as unprepared as the sailors at Pearl

Harbor. They police came to arrest Nino. He was an American living abroad during wartime and had not reported to the embassy. He believed, because he was twenty-six and married, he could not be drafted. He was wrong.

"I was pregnant with my first child. They took him, just like that. First they flew him to Bogotá, and my mother and I followed, to be with him. Within a few days, he was back in the United States for basic training. We had no time to arrange things. We said a very quick goodbye at the airport and he boarded a big U.S. Army plane with no one else on board but him and the flight crew. I felt like my life would never be right again.

"Things got even worse. A few days later my mother told me that my father was dead. It had happened on the same day that Nino was taken away. Esophageal cancer. From his drinking, I am sure. He had been receiving treatment, radiation, in a hospital in Bogotá. The treatment produced severe vomiting and he developed a strangulated hernia. They did emergency surgery but he did not last. Peritonitis. I was in the same city that day. But I was not told. They kept it from me because of the turmoil with Nino's sudden departure and my pregnancy. So my mother stood next to me at the airport as I waved goodbye to my husband, and she had lost her own husband a few hours earlier and said nothing. *Doña Carlota.*

"There I was, pregnant, living alone in Pereira, my husband snatched away from me by the strongest military power on earth, not knowing if I would ever see him again. And I did not get to say goodbye to my father or to see him buried. My uncle Fortunato sent me a very nice letter of condolence, I remember."

> . . . Your father's thoughts were of you, as you are the being he loved most in life. Yours was the image he took with him into eternity...During his final years of isolation he felt deep sorrow for his failings, for which he was not entirely at fault, inasmuch as he was a victim of an inherited and wretched affliction. He died peacefully, willingly . . . after having received the sacrament of confession and absolution. My brother lived a life too intensely lived . . . I believe sincerely that he is forgiven by God, and by you, his loving daughter.

"So it was just my big belly for company. My mother told me to come back to Barranquilla. She found me an apartment and took care of me, as much as she could.

"Your father and I had terrible luck. Things just happened to us with disastrous timing. We had no peace. I had no idea where he was. I did not hear from him for nearly two months. The army had taken him to New Orleans for basic training. It was wartime and I was a foreign spouse. Letters were censored, you know. And since he wrote to me in that mixture of languages, that slowed them down considerably. But he wrote sometimes three letters a week."

Fort Amador, 27 February 1944
Sweet and Beloved wife,

I am truly happy today, because yesterday was positively miraculous, for three reasons. First, I scored highest in my class in target practice. (It was your love that inspired me to win.) Second, when I returned from practice I received your letter. You can't imagine what a letter from you means to me. Suffice it to say that I sang all morning. And third, the real miracle, our commanding officer, Major Carlisle, a serious man to whom one cannot speak without special permission, saw your picture during inspection and said he certainly understand that I must be with my wife when my child is born. I will tell you in my next letter what date I will be able to visit you.

I'll sign off now telling you that everything you wish will surely materialize. You must believe in me. I am so happy about us. I weep, like a small child, knowing that you continue to love me. I need you still.

The next sheath holds two plain cards bordered in green. I pull them out and show them to my mother. She points to one and tells me to read it.

Here is the album I promised you for the baby. It is the best I could find here. I hope you are taking good care of yourself and loving me still. When I recall the beautiful life we had together it seems like a dream. Good night with kisses sweet wife.

I pronounce my father's words and think of my mother being dutiful, obedient, keeping the news from her husband that her father is dead. It is an utter reversal of what she would do later with her children.

"My mother said it was best to keep that news from Nino until we were reunited. It would be too hard for him to learn about in a letter. He knew my father. They liked each other.

"As time went on, your father's outlook grew more positive and I became more of a *pesimista*. I was terrified of giving birth without him. When the time came, my water broke, and my mother had her driver take us to the hospital. It was a very long labor, more than eighteen hours. If my mother had not been there, I would have been completely by myself. After the baby was born she sent a cable to Nino in Louisiana: *Es una niña!* But he had been transferred to the Panama Canal Zone, so there was a delay in getting him the message.

"My mother got a *criada* to help me take care of the baby, as was the custom. Everybody loved Julia. She was so fair, blonde, and chubby. My mother was crazy about her, and had all kinds of clothes made for her. I named her after Nino's mother, which was what he wanted. The baby was already two months old by the time Nino got to see a photograph of his daughter."

> Fort Sherman, Colon
> 5 May 1944
> At last I have seen my daughter! Thank you, my love. You have made me very happy. Our daughter is beautiful. I look at her picture incessantly. Please tell me it isn't true that she has my eye problem. I want so much to hold her in my arms, to play with her. I see in the snapshots how magnificent you are. That makes me very happy, because you are my life.
>
> Thank you darling for reminding me of Mama's birthday. I'll send her a cable in both our names. Do you know that twenty-two months have passed, twenty two moons have come and gone since that morning when we became married in the cathedral? And four months since that horrid day when the plane took me away from your side. But this will all soon be in the past for we shall be together very soon. The General Consulate is proceeding with the necessary papers. It looks

like in just a few brief weeks you will be here with me, with the *cherubina*.

Darling I got a ten-dollar raise. I get paid forty dollars a month now, so you'll see when you get here that things won't be so bad, actually I see them as being great. I am sure we will be very happy. It is important that you take care of yourself as well as the baby. Eat well.

I've had no news from my folks since my last letter. I've asked my cousin to write to you. I'm very sleepy now. I will say goodnight praying that we three will live long lives in harmony and peace. I send you everything that is beautiful from this man who loves you so. Kiss my daughter babyJulia. I need to see you.

"I could not take it anymore, having a newborn, separated by a war and a passport, and knowing my husband was right over the border in Panama. I looked up a friend of my father's family who worked for the ambassador of Panama in Colombia. Estrellita García, a truly lovely person. She contacted Nino on the base, and he was able to call me, which was not so easy then. He was very concerned about the baby, and that he had not been there to see the birth of his first child. He was always very tender like that, full of little caring details about my health, my mental outlook, encouraging me to have faith. After that, he called every week, on Sunday afternoons."

20 May 1944

My dearest,

This will be a long letter, because I have many things to tell you. First, your letter of 24 April only arrived today, because you must write SPANISH on the envelope so that it can get through the censors more quickly.

I don't know why, and it is difficult for me to believe, that although I have loved you deeply and always make an effort to show it, now that we have a daughter, you doubt me. This causes me great pain. I believed we had gotten to know each other well, and that we had become sincerely united. I am at a loss for words. I was convinced that you knew how much you mean to me. But I can see now that my wife still harbors strange ideas. Help me to understand this. I have the right to know what you mean. You ask me if I love you? That is not a question. It is a punishment. One I do not deserve. I have done nothing to merit your distrust. My love, be patient, I beg you, until we are together again and you will see these torments leave you.

Please Cuchi, talk to your mother about this. I knew your mother before I met you, and she surely knows my nature. Ask her about these things that trouble you. She will help you, because she is a woman who has suffered greatly, more than any woman I have known. In my heart there is a place where sculptors have carved 'Carlota', because she has given me her beloved daughter. Talk with her.

Darling, I hope you are teaching the baby to love me. I like the idea of showing her my picture. I'm glad to hear that you both have good appetites. How do you feel? Are you well, ready to travel? Have had no news from my family since last month's letter from Paolo. Can you send them snapshots of Julia? My parents will get a thrill seeing her.

In my last letter I sent you two documents you will need for your trip. There is one pending, which is being processed.

P.S. Another raise. My salary is fifty dollars a month now. Good, isn't it?

There is an airmail envelope that catches my mother's eye. I pull it out and hand it to her. She reads the list of names written on one side. She counts them.

"Nino sent me this list of names, twenty-two of them, people he said I would meet one day when we traveled to New York. He asked me to send each of them an announcement of the baby's birth."

Third on the list, after my father's cousins, is the name Dan Tenneriello, whose son would break the biggest of my family's secrets to me forty years later. Further down are the names of other old men and women who shared their stories with me in the Café Roma. I remove two notes from the envelope and begin to read them to my mother. Before I get too far, she interrupts. "They are from your Uncle Paolo."

My dear Eva,

At this time I am forced to let you know because you'll be wondering how my Dad feels about you and the baby. He passed away on the morning of February 28th. It was a terrible shock. My mother and I were both home at the time. There is not much that I can add to what my brother has told you about him but that he was a fine man and we loved him. He enjoyed living and knew how, but how he felt about being a grandfather I could never tell you, I could only imagine that. I'm sure you can imagine why I kept this from you till now.

Last night I received a letter and a cable from Nino. I haven't told him yet, but for the first time he said that he feels something is wrong and wants me to let him know what the trouble is. I do not know how to tell him and I wouldn't want him to know, not for the present, because he has you and the baby and the army to think about now and the shock may do something to spoil a lot of things.

Let him be happy with you and the baby. Please keep this from him and I'll love you for it. I won't say more . . . The thought just came to me that the good book says: The Lord gives and takes. He took our Dad and He gave us you and the baby.—Paolo

As I begin to read the second of Paolo's letters my mother remembers it arrived the day before her departure to Panama.

We received your cable and I trust the sad news didn't upset you too much. My mind will be at ease again only when I will have found a way to tell my brother. And that for the time being is far from my mind. When he is together with you again it will make things so much easier and I'll be able to think better.

In his last letter Nino wrote that he intends to return to the States together with you and the baby for a while when the war ends, but eventually his heart is set upon returning to Colombia where he feels he can make a go of it. What do you think of this plan? All we do is talk about you and the baby. It would have been swell if you were here with us.

"Nino was working on getting entry papers for me and the baby to go to Panama. But it was taking a very long time. My friend Estrellita helped again, to get me a temporary visa and a hotel in Ciudad Colon, outside the base. I fixed my suitcases and flew out of Colombia, with money my mother gave me. I wanted to surprise Nino. It was our second anniversary. I sent him a cable from the airport in Barranquilla. He was shocked. Especially at how I managed to get to him under such harsh circumstances."

When they meet again at Albrook Air Field my parents look very different from their last time together in Pereira. He is a soldier in uniform. She is a plump mother holding an infant.

"He was so happy to see me, and the baby of course. But, you know, I never believed he wanted me to be near him. He wanted his freedom. He liked the army, being an officer. He was a big wolf, always chasing women. That is what he did all his life.

"Anyway, the next day he said he was going to speak to some people to get us housing on the base. He filed some papers and after a few days he moved us into a small bungalow on the base. He was trying to do something heroic for us, I guess, since he was not around to see the baby's birth. But it did not work. After about a week, the military police was at our door again.

"Nino was not home that afternoon. They were very rough, those men. Shouting at me 'Who are you?' I told them I was the wife of a U.S. Army officer. They did not believe me—my accent, my visa—and ordered me off the premises immediately, saying that nonmilitary personnel could not occupy those quarters. Your father had not gotten the necessary clearance under wartime conditions. So I had to leave, right then and there, with soldiers and their guns watching me pack. With a baby right in front of them. I was not an American citizen yet, officially. All because of paperwork. Technically, I automatically became a U.S. citizen when I married your father. But they did not give me a chance to speak.

"Nino was very upset when he came to see me at the place where they took me. It was the only time I ever saw him visibly angry, raising his voice at the other officers. They were going to arrest him again. Luckily, they let him take me off the base, back to the hotel in Colon. They said I had twenty-four hours to return to Colombia. They brought disciplinary charges against him. But he wrote a legal brief to the base general, defending our situation."

When my wife arrived here in Panama . . . we proceeded immediately to the Minister of Foreign Relations . . . to the Polizia de Extranjeros in Colon and to the Governor of the Canal Zone. I understood that quarters on the post could be obtained, and I made a request for same. At no time did I act under false pretenses . . . nor did I intend at the time to commit a crime.

I have with me now my wife and child. The baby is really too young to be subjected to travel such long distances again. It is only for her that I beseech you people to allow and permit that my wife and child be afforded to remain here in the City of Colon at least until I can make arrangements to send them both to my folks in New York City.

I repeat that if I committed a wrong I am indeed sorry and I offer repent and apology. But whatever the result, please let them remain for at least a period of time, because they have just arrived . . . and more travel at this time might have serious consequences on the health of my child.

In the event that my plea is denied, I make a request that my wife and child leave for the United States.

"Nino and his beautiful words. They worked. They let him go. They even gave us a nice little house on the base to live in. Right on the beach."

Of the images inside this collection of letters, the sweetest is of these months my parents spent together in Panama. This is the second beginning of their marriage and the closest they would ever come to conventional family life. They are secure in their roles as enlisted man and army wife, protected within a military compound in the midst of world turmoil. Pictures of them during this period show a relaxed, broad smiling father playing with his baby girl and a mellow young mother in tap shorts and an upswept hairdo.

Perhaps because I would never know my mother and father together, and because soon their lives would take a swift slide downhill from which we never recovered as a family, the time in the Canal Zone stands out as the only evidence that we might have made it. Had circumstance and timing been kinder, I'd like to believe my father's affectionate joy for living and my mother's determination to succeed might have blossomed compatibly. But at the very least they would have needed continuity, a requisite they were repeatedly denied.

"We lived in the Canal Zone for about half a year. Of course I had not told him about his father, or mine. Nino was so happy with the baby. Julia looked just like him. He wanted to send his family a picture of us. So one day he had us pose for pictures, right in our back yard, which was a few hundred feet from the ocean. He used to love to take the baby into the water. Not me. I do not swim and I hate the water, even though I am from the coast. Well, the baby had very unruly hair. It would fly in all directions. So I took her down to the water's edge to wet her hair down so she would look cute in the photograph. Suddenly a big wave came and knocked me down. I saw the wave take the baby out into the ocean. Your father was inside the house loading the camera. I screamed and screamed. Out of nowhere three soldiers came running and saw the baby in the water. With their uniforms and shoes still on they swam out, right into the ocean. They got her. Julia was all red, holding her breath. She had floated on the waves. I was so scared. It all happened so fast.

"I couldn't help it, though. I believed it was a *mala seña*, a bad omen.

"Very soon after that Nino got orders to ship out of Panama. There were rumors that the war was about to end. He asked me where I wanted to go— back to Colombia, or to meet his family in New York? He himself was torn. He had not seen his family in six years, but he loved Colombia. Of course I picked New York. I wanted to see everything I had read and heard about it. So different from Colombia. And I wanted to meet my in-laws. Nino wrote to his brother. I wrote to my friend Flor, whom I knew from boarding school in Bogotá. She was living somewhere in upstate New York. I was very worried about the winter, how to prepare myself."

> *Querida amiguita* Cuchi,
>
> What a delightful surprise you've given me. Your daughter is absolutely adorable, and you look as beautiful as ever, and as elegant with your hair combed up like that. With your handsome husband you make a beautiful couple. I imagine how busy you must be now spoiling the baby, and attending to the big boy too. Housework certainly keeps one busy doesn't it? I've had to learn to cook, and to do laundry and scrub floors. Domestic help is scarce and very expensive here [in the States]. I think you are the happiest woman in the world,

with your child and your husband who [must be] everything to you, father, husband, brother, friend.

Your plans to come to New York are welcome news. I will certainly travel down to see you. You see Ithaca is quite far from the city. I do hope we can spend time together reminiscing and catching up on the past two years. Life here is quite interesting, there's always something new to do, but I must warn you it is very cold. Colder than you have ever felt. I looked into the matter of your suit and found that the model you sent me is not in style this fall. A pity, because I think it quite elegant. I found two styles which I am enclosing. I think the first will suit you very well, especially as it trims the body more than the second and I don't know just how heavy you've gotten. You must choose the color carefully as being a blonde and so fair-skinned the blue or light brown would complement you best. I am enclosing samples of the wool and prices. Believe me you will need a heavy cloth in New York.

It will be quite a change from the hours I imagine you spend at the beach. You know how beneficial the warmth, the sun and the sea are for your baby Julia. You tell me she is afectionate and smiles a lot. Not surprisingly, she is identical to you.

Come quickly, dear friend, I have so much to tell you. We could see one another, and now, with a baby! How delightful. It would be even better than in Bogotá.—Flor

"A few weeks before I left Panama I had a surprise. I found out I was pregnant again. I had fallen for that old wives' tale about breast-feeding being effective birth control. So when the time came I traveled to the United States with one baby and expecting another. They put me on a military plane that stopped in Miami. I was supposed to continue to New York, but it was wartime. The Army made the civilians surrender our seats to the soldiers. They did not care. I had to find my own way to New York. There were so many soldiers coming home that I could not get a seat on any flight, even commercial airlines. And it was December, just before Christmas. They said I could stay in Miami at a hotel and wait. In my condition, and with a baby, I was not going to stay in a strange place. I decided to take the train. It took two days anyway. When we reached Pennsylvania Station I was exhausted, and in shock. I had never seen so many people. I had no idea how I would find Paolo. I had never seen him. And I had never seen an escalator before. A nice man helped me get on. As it was going up, I saw a man holding a photograph high over his head. It was our wedding picture. The man called out, 'Wow you really are a blondie!'

"That was your uncle Paolo. I did not know what he meant by that remark. But he was very kind, genteel, well educated. Like your father, but not as charming. And not handsome at all. I liked Paolo. After it all happened, he used to come to take you girls to the circus. Do you remember, Ronnie? That night he hailed a taxi on Lexington Avenue and took us to Mulberry Street. To my new life."

I picture my mother climbing the winding stairs at Nonna's house for the first time, my grandmother waiting at the top. Two women from very different worlds thrust together by the fate of the man who wasn't there to introduce them. For my mother each step is one further away from the constraints of a place and social order she was glad to leave behind, toward a new life with a new family in a new culture in the greatest city in the world. She is filled with illusions.

For Nonna, the woman and child climbing the steps are reminders of her son, who she'd sent off on what was to be a brief business adventure. Nearly six years later he hasn't come home. He sends a wife instead, a woman from a place he prefers to Mulberry Street and wants to return to. All of it too late for Papa to share.

For both, each represents a part of Nino the other does not know.

"It was a nightmare from the very beginning. Not because of Paolo. But that lady, *La Signora Guilianna*, your Nonna. From the minute I stepped into her home she would not talk to me. She sat in that kitchen and cried. She was very angry. She hated me. Because I was not Italian, I suppose. She spoke very little English and no Spanish. Her dialect was impossible for me to decipher. I had to go through Paolo for everything. Even to get milk. Maybe she was jealous. She was a widow and I took her son away. I never really knew why.

"Her home was filled with women all the time, dressed in black. *Un funeral perpetuo*. All of them examining my every move. It was early in my pregnancy. I had terrible morning sickness. More than with Julia. Every time I got up to go to the bathroom I would put on my robe, a *pieza* of lingerie my mother had especially ordered for me. Silk and lace. She always wanted me to have the finest things. Well, these funereal women would be sitting in the parlor from early in the morning to the end of the day. Did they have nothing else to do? You remember Nonna's apartment. The bedrooms opened onto the parlor, so I would have to go through it to get to the bathroom. The women would watch me when I passed, and whisper. So rude. I did not understand most of what they said, but I could make out certain words that were the same in Spanish. *Vestiti de putana.* Was that a way to welcome me? Those women never saw a negligee in their lives! I was not some sort of tramp Nino had picked up in a cabaret or something. I was his wife. The mother of his child."

"Paolo was very nice. So were the people from the apartment below. Nonna's *paesani* from Italy. They tried to interpret for me. I wanted Nonna to understand that it would not be too long. The war in Europe was over already. It would be just a few months or so until Nino would come home. But she did not care about me. She just loved the baby. She was very possessive with Julia. She would not let me carry my own child.

"It got so bad all I could do was stay in my room and cry. I did not have anyone to talk to. I would not tell my mother. Why worry her when she was so far away? I had to tell Nino. He did not know what to do. First he said I should try to wait until he was discharged.

"The problem was Nonna disapproved of everything I did. Our customs were different. I was not raised to be domestic. I had servants. I did not cook or even boil water or clean anything until I came to New York. I was willing to learn, but she was very cold to me.

"The biggest problem was with the baby's diapers. You see, in South America they did not use bleach. There was no need to. The *criadas* would scrub the diapers and then drop them into boiling water in special, large pots and hang them in the sun. That Caribbean sun made them white. Who needed bleach? I had watched my mother's servants work. So I did the same thing. I boiled water in one of Nonna's big pots and put the diapers in. Well, she had a fit! Screaming and throwing the pots in the garbage. She pointed to the door and told me I had to get out. That is when I went downstairs crying, to the neighbor's apartment. They let me stay with them until Paolo came home from work.

"I asked him to call Grace, Nino's favorite cousin. She was a pharmacist and lived in the Bronx. She had written to me a few times in Panama, and when I first arrived at Nonna's she came to see me. Nino told me to call her if things ever got very bad. She would help me.

"Well, she did. She came right away with her husband. They talked with Nonna. But I had had enough. My first winter and I had to spend it with that woman, trapped in that apartment. She was spoiled. Living with three men who catered to her. She would not share her kitchen or anything else. And then to throw me out. *A mi no me la hacen dos veces.* That would only happen to me once! *Basta.* I was not going to go back for more. Grace took me and the baby out to an area near Mount Vernon. I rented a room from a very nice family for a few months, but then they raised the rent and I could not stay. The landlord was afraid that I was due very soon and did not want two babies with me in one room. Grace helped me again and I found another room on Southern Boulevard in the Bronx."

> Fort Benning, Georgia
> 1945 May16 PM 4:50
> Your letter has made me weep STOP Forgive me STOP I love you with all my heart STOP For God's sake darling move right away STOP I am doing everything I can to come to you STOP Letter follows STOP Kisses STOP Nino

I ask my mother for a photograph from this period and she says cameras were not something people pulled out in those days as easily as today. She asks me what I'm looking for, what would a picture explain better than a letter? My father's face, I tell her.

These are the final months of World War II. My father is due home on furlough, his first return to New York since he embarked for South America. He arrives at the Breslin Hotel, a popular place for service men and their families on short stays. But whatever enthusiasm he brings is quickly stifled as he learns that his father is dead. With his wife and mother at odds, he spends his four days leave traveling between his grieving mother downtown and his anxious, very pregnant wife and baby daughter who wait for him uptown.

"Nino changed after that visit. He was not prepared for what he found. He never said it, but I knew he wanted me to return to Mulberry Street. But I liked being away from the family. In the Bronx I was on my own, nobody to criticize me or make me feel unwanted. Anyway, our plan was to return to Colombia as soon as your father was discharged."

Camp Shelby, Mississippi
8 June 1945
Delicious Woman and Beautiful Wife,

It is 7:15 in the evening. All my thoughts are of you my dearest, and my beloved little doll. It has been over two weeks since I had had news from you. Such silence worries me very much. I prefer to think it is due to my transfer. Today more than ever before I miss you and the baby, immensely. I am again in a new place. I feel alone, forgotten, melancholy. Here on my cot I think of you and the baby and a deep sorrow comes over me. This terrible disgrace of being so far away. To make it worse I have never felt such immense heat in all my life. More than Barranquilla. It is a veritable hell. Paolo is working hard at helping me get an early discharge. Soon it will be our anniversary. Try to remember all the good things, my love, like I do. All the good we have done in three years of marriage, our journeys, our adventures and whims, the thousand kisses I have given you when I held you in my arms. Think of the lovely things, please forgive me all the bad. All this time lost.

"He was very worried about me living alone and being so close to my delivery date. But I had made arrangements. I would call Grace when my time came. I knew she would help me."

13 June 1945
Cuchi my love,

Your lovely letter arrived yesterday and set me more at ease since I hadn't heard from you in a while. I love to read everything you tell me about the baby and yourself.

How I wanted to be able to see you getting heavier with the new *bambolino*. We have already produced two children and I have not had the blessed luck of seeing you carry either of them. But this time I will be there when our child arrives. Even if I have to go AWOL. I promise you this on the souls of both our fathers, who I am sure look after us always and will intervene on our behalf so that we may be together. I'm glad you've found a doctor you like and trust. That's important, darling. And really, forget the difficulty you had the first time. This time you will see everything will be much easier.

You will probably want to do it again. But not me. With two we are golden. A perfect family.

One month later:

14 July 1945
Beloved wife,

I am again in a new place, Camp Campbell, Kentucky. At least it is nearer to you. Don't forget darling to have the doctor cable me here when your time comes.

How do you feel my love? Keep eating well, the baby too. It is not as warm here in Kentucky. I am relieved that you have at last found a bit of peace and rest. With luck we will be able to find an apartment when I come on furlough. That way we will have a place of our own to enjoy and we will not argue as much. And you will stop doubting me. We will be together with no one to bother us. Did you get the slippers I sent you and the toy for the baby? And the wallet? I am still looking for the ball for Julia. I didn't find it in Shelby, or the pots you want. Maybe I'll have more luck here. Don't be upset with me. I'll find them.

You know what tomorrow is, don't you? A sacred day in my life. I hope it equally is so in yours. Tell the baby about us and our three years together. I love you.

19 July 1945
Dearest Cuchi,

This morning I wrote you a very short letter. I was half crazed without news from you. But at noon I got your beautiful note. You know, you write English divinely. My darling listen, I don't want to hear any more of this about losing me, much less about separating. I have no desire to leave you. Where do these ideas come from? I married you before God and vowed to stay with you forever, to love only one woman. I love you very much. I can't say it more clearly. You must learn to trust me. So the subject should be dropped. Please darling, enough.

There is so much hypocrisy in the world. Politicians talk about democracy and the conference of San Francisco, the need for fraternity among people. But in truth they are as evil and ungrateful as the enemy. It is difficult to tell sometimes whether the principles for which we fight such a wicked war aren't themselves lies and propaganda we're being fed for the gain of a few over many. Soldiers die to make the world free. But how do we distinguish between the conquering Allies and the brutal Dictators, if all are guilty of the same sin? Greed.

Forgive this indulgence and have patience with me Cuchi. You and I are capable of everything good, together. I'm thrilled that Paolo sent you an anniversary cake. Did you tell the baby about our three years together? What did she answer? Soon we will celebrate together, all three of us. I'm still searching for the ball. Take care. I await your cable. I love you very much. Hugs to baby Julia and kiss her for me. Your husband.

"A few days after our third anniversary Carmela was born. I was alone, but Nino flew home on furlough to see us the next day, then he went back to the army. He was stationed in the south again, I think Mississippi. He tried to talk to his mother about things. I thought I should give in and try again, for him. But when I thought of my mother-in-law, how she threw me out, I could not do it. I could not go back to a place where I was not accepted. She never accepted me. All because I am not Italian."

My mother has saved three greetings from Carmela's birth. I hand one to her, a yellowed card that offers congratulations for the new baby and is signed "Sincerely, Paolo." A post-script reassures her that "Baby Julia is very well [with Nonna]." On the back of the card is a penciled list of forty girls' names in my mother's writing. The third name is checked, Carmela. It was a popular name at the time, my mother tells me, but not her first choice, Aida. She yielded to her husband's family tradition again, naming this baby after his maternal grandmother. I sigh, remembering the months I too spent finding the right names for my children, only to bend to the tradition of my in-laws at the last moment and let the elders name them. I sigh again, silently recognizing the growing number of similarities between my mother's story and my own.

In the next sheath there is a lengthy letter from cousin Grace.

> Dear Eva,
>
> I received your letter last week and was just about to answer it when I heard the surprising news that you had given birth to your second baby girl. I hope everything turned out well for you.
>
> I had not seen my aunt (your mother in-law) in a very long time. Yesterday I decided to visit her and bring her some clothing she is going to send to Italy. Imagine my surprise when I opened the door and saw babyJulia. She is a little doll. My aunt is very excited over her. She was wearing a red dress with a red bow in her hair. She looked adorable. Her Uncle Paolo bought her new white shoes and she was all excited about them. Do not worry about her. She will be very well taken care of. Paolo sent Nino a telegram informing him of the baby's birth.
>
> I know you wanted a boy. But do not be too disappointed. It is nice to have two of one kind when they are so close in age. I hope I shall get an early opportunity to run up to see you soon. I'm glad you sent Julia to her grandmother. Somehow I feel Paolo is very cold toward me and I don't know the reason. It is best that the baby is with them. I don't want to interfere with your relations too much as Paolo blames me for the rift with his family. I think you should try to patch things up with them, Eva. For your sake and your husband's. They are trying to be very nice to you and I think you should meet them halfway. I hope with the birth of the new baby conditions will be better.

I turn over a small gift card with a baby design on it. It must have accompanied flowers my father sent to my mother when he arrived at Lincoln Hospital in the Bronx. He speaks to her lovingly and with Bogotá formality.

> Thank you my beloved and forgive me.
> I am downstairs. I'll be right up. I love you.

In a few days my father begins his final letters as a soldier, from Camp Campbell, Kentucky.

Thirteen Headquarters Detachment
2nd Army Special Troops
28 July 1945

Darling, tell me, do you sincerely want to return to Colombia? Because if you do, I do too. But remember also how once you couldn't wait to leave that place. We will see how things develop. As for me, I will close my eyes as soon as I finish this letter and I will rush on board the boat that sails up the Magdalena River, to be once again in Salgar and Bogotá on our honeymoon. That's how I'll spend the evening, cool and contented traveling with you beneath the Colombian moon that is like no other. Sleep well, my love, I'll see you on board, and please let's not argue this time, because now we have two children, and we want, and will make this a splendid journey.

3 September 1945

Congress will reconvene in Washington this week to decide the number of personnel to be discharged monthly. Fathers will be first, and I am one, double! I've lived like a monk in a monastery, please stop worrying yourself and imagining otherwise. You are all I think about. You know your blonde hair is always in my eyes, and everything I see seems painted yellow, like yellow corn.

So my Carmela is eating well. I like that, because a good appetite is a sign of good health. It seems we are all blessed with a good one, especially you who are the mother and work the hardest. My little Julia is helping you, you say. Tell me when she helps you with the first dish, at least to dry one. I wish I could see her. As soon as I get paid I'll see about getting them toys, a doll for each. I'm going to try to get you the pair of red shoes I saw in Shelby, and I'll send you more sheets this week and another blanket.

Oh, I almost forgot. I got my haircut even shorter than when you saw me on furlough. You see no woman would even bother with me now. Don't worry, by the time I get out it will be long again the way you like it.

Remember I am also alone, maybe that will help you in your loneliness, because I share those moments with you.

25 September 1945

You are truly an inimitable woman, with your beautiful words you say things that make me feel more than regal. No darling, not even Napoleon's ladies or the mistresses of Simon Bolivar in their time could describe so perfect a man as you do me. 'An idol among women.' Why do you joke so? I tell you again there is only one blonde for me. I am a poor man without much to offer, except for a sincere affection for my wife. I am simple, and that is how I want to be. The two of us alone, uncomplicated. I your lover and you mine. That will make me happy.

Yes, M'am. I will arrive in civilian clothes, wearing my wool suit so we can have our picture taken as you so much desire. I don't know the exact date. It doesn't matter. It will suffice to be able to touch, kiss and see you once more. To play with my daughters, to be together, the four of us. A beautiful family, unique in this imperfect world . . . I feel like a child who is getting a new outfit. I am happy and I want to sing. Take care my love, kiss the *bambolinas*. Tell my Julia that Papa will be with her soon, and that she should open the door when I come home.

I remove a snapshot from its sheath and study it. It might otherwise look like an average family portrait. My mother and father stand together facing the camera. She carries Julia and he Carmela. Their formal clothing matches their pose. She is in a tweed suit and open-toed heels, a beret angled on top of her long, ungathered blonde hair. He stands in suit and tie, arms open to contain his family, a hat in his free hand. Julia wears a dark coat and bonnet and stares at the camera. A snug cap covers Carmela's head as she ignores the lens to stare at her father. My parents smile into the sunlight, but their bodies are stiff and awkward. It is December 1945. The world is at peace. My parents are not.

"A few months after Carmela was born, Nino was discharged. But for some reason it took him weeks to make it home. That bastard. He was having fun with his friends. And women, I am sure of it. When he came back I found all these little things crawling on me. Crabs. He thought it was funny. He laughed and laughed when I got mad and accused him of being with whores. He said it was from the Kentucky heat. What a liar! Who is he telling about heat? Did I not come from Barranquilla? Since when does heat cause venereal disease? He just laughed. He thought I was overreacting. I had to spray him with Fleet insecticide, all over his body. I was disgusted. I never trusted him after that.

"It was hard on him too, I guess. His mother wanted him to stay with her. She had not really had him home since he left for South America. She wanted Nino to herself. He was her baby. A Mama's boy. But he was a married man, with two children. She did not want to let go. She would not accept me, but she wanted him and the grandchildren to be there all the time. We never had any time to be free, by ourselves.

"There he was going back and forth between his wife and children in the Bronx and his Mother on Mulberry Street. She spoiled him. When he was with his mother he was a king. She even made his clothing. The whole neighborhood knew him there. When he came come to us there were noisy babies and diapers and obligations. He had just come out of the army. He needed to find work. He came back to a completely different life than he had left.

"But your father never complained. He was always happy to be with us. Never an angry moment. He just stopped coming home. He would stay out late. Then all night. Saying he was at his mother's. I never believed him. He was too handsome to be at his mother's all night. He was having fun, making up for all those years in the army. And I could not join him because of the babies. Your sisters were only fifteen months apart. It was very difficult for me. In South America we would have had servants, and our life as a married couple would have been easier. *¡Que horror!*

"To his credit, one of the first things he did was to open an office with his brother Paolo and another partner. Import/export business. Nino signed up for a course at a business school. He wanted to be prepared for the move.

"Nino always wanted to go back to Colombia, to the business he was starting up before he was taken into the war. He loved the life down there. He wrote to Industrias Rendón and they were thrilled about having him return. He spoke with my mother too. He loved my mother, and my brothers. Everyone was happy that we were going back with the children.

"So we made plans. I would go back first with the girls. I would stay at the Tivoli Natili hotel, like he had when we met. He would follow after a month or two, after he spent time with his mother and brother, and got everything in order for the business. I still had the money my mother had given us when we were married, so we went shopping. We picked out a new stove, refrigerator, and deep freezer, items that would be difficult to get in Colombia. He made arrangements to have them shipped to Barranquilla. We would have the most modern house in the country, he said. So I packed up the children, gave up the apartment on Southern Boulevard, and returned to Colombia."

On letterhead marked "Sementa Brothers Import Export Agents" just twelve weeks after his discharge, my father is writing to my mother again.

> My dear wife Cuchi,
>
> Your cable came today. I was very worried but now I am at ease knowing my doll and two *cherubinas* have arrived safely. I called Tuesday morning with some difficulty getting a line through the Miami operator, but the hotel manager said you'd just gone out. So I've been a bundle of nerves since, until now that I know you are well.
>
> The furniture went out yesterday and should arrive in Barranquilla in about a week, depending on how long the ship gets delayed in Panama. The refrigerator hasn't been delivered yet, since the teamsters strike was only settled two days ago. But I should have it in two weeks time.
>
> I received a letter from our contact in Cartagena and it looks like we'll be doing business. I've sent him a price list today. Hopefully things will work out well. Darling, listen to me carefully. Eat well, eat an egg every day and give the babies one too. Give all my kisses to Carmela and Julia. Nonna cries a lot for Lala. Please send her a few photos of the children together, when you have time. Paolo sends kisses to all three of you. I am off to classes.

"In the beginning I was happy to be back in Barranquilla. My mother was delighted. She could have her grandchildren with her. My brothers were away at school, but they wrote and called. They were very happy to have us back. They were excited about Nino coming to join us soon. We were going to be a happy family."

Today, this day of darkness and bitterness for me, is nevertheless my beloved daughter's birthday. Dark because I haven't the right to have her in my arms to kiss and say Happy Birthday to my sweetheart and may God keep you all your life. I feel very bad, because I hear Julia's little voice everywhere saying she 'wants with Papa.'

I'm glad you are getting a much deserved rest at last. How odd that Carmela cries so much. Here she was always contented. Maybe the change of climate? Take good care of her, and of yourself as well.

I am enjoying my classes. They keep me busy. Forgive me darling but things have not been good with the business. I have not been able to find work. I am trying everywhere and something will turn up soon. It must.

Please tell your mother that I am filled with gratitude for the way she has received and cared for you and the children. Some day I will be able to repay her.

I will write to you again soon. And I hope I will be able to tell you that I have work. Kiss my girls for me. And for you, everything you want.

P.S. Did the furniture arrive? No need to use Fleet darling. I swear it.

"Your father. At first he wrote and called every week, sometimes twice a week. Then the letters stopped. He stopped calling. I called him at Nonna's, and I could hear the operator say 'Person to Person International Long Distance' and she would say 'Not Home' and hang up.

"Months went by. Then a year. I was miserable. There is no place in Colombian society for a married woman with children and no husband. No invitations, no social life. Just being at home waiting for letters and calls that never came. My mother began to get crazy. She knew what it would mean if I stayed in Colombia like that. It would be open season on me. I would be considered *abandonada*. A disgrace. A woman alone with children is easy prey for men.

"So she sold the stove and refrigerator and freezer. She bought me a return ticket to New York. That was the last time I saw Colombia."

My mother's tone has become harsh. Her lips are pursed to one side of her face, eyes wide and dark. Her voice punctures the air around her. She gestures toward the floor, sweeping her past out of her way to bury it with all its good and bad, as though the mention of its faces and places has been an awful transgression.

I thank my mother for remembering; there is nothing more I can do. She becomes quiet, still. She has been talking for nearly three hours without lapsing into her dementia. I wait, not knowing what she will say or do next.

"I never told your father I was coming back. When I arrived at Mulberry Street, climbing those awful steps with the babies, it was your father who opened the door. His first reaction was to start laughing. Everything to him was a laugh. 'Finally! You've come!' he said. Like it was just yesterday since he'd seen us. He was really very happy to see us. He even cried. That night, in that bed where your father was born, in Nonna's apartment where he grew up, you were conceived. Maybe that is why you are so curious.

"We stayed with Nonna very briefly. In a few days Nino moved us uptown, to Union Square, into the apartment, for fourteen dollars a month. Imagine that?"

In my mind's eye, I do imagine it. I see the room in Nonna's house my mother speaks of. The tenuous stream of light pouring in through a transom, the wardrobe with my father's suits and hats, the dresser with his glasses neatly laid near his pen set, the single brass bed, his desk and armchair. I see our place on Union Square, too. The apartment my father finds for his family. The wide open living room, the windows looking out onto the square and Klein's Department Store, the long, low-ceilinged kitchen and beyond it the hallway to the bathroom and single bedroom. It is the place where I will spend my childhood, the place where he will leave us when he goes.

"He said he had not followed me to Colombia because he talked things over with his brother Paolo, and he had decided it would be foolish to go down to meet his family without some kind of security, without money to invest or a position waiting. A few months before I returned he had taken a position with a law firm in midtown.

"But there was more to it. All that time I was away he had been having a good time. Living with *La Mamma*, no responsibilities, no food bills, no wife and children around. When we moved up to Union Square it was the same thing all over again, coming home late or staying out. I suppose he could not help it. He was so handsome the women threw themselves at him. Of course, I did not want to make things worse by telling him I was pregnant again. But I kept hoping that if this baby were a boy, he would change. A man would want to stay home with his family if he had a son.

"As time went on I got more and more disgusted. He wanted to live the high life, as though he were still living in South America. Restaurants, shows, nightclubs to dance in. He got spoiled in Colombia, and in the army he did not have to worry about taking care of anyone else. When I went away it was even easier for him. He could claim a wife and family without doing any of the work. His mother did not help either. What did she care? I was out of the picture and she had her son back.

"I got fed up. Years of up and down, packing and unpacking, together and apart. *¡Basta! ¡Ya!* Enough! I was not going to spend my life with an unfaithful man. After one of his nights out I told him not to come back anymore. I did not care that I was pregnant and had two children. I would find a way.

"As it worked out, my two brothers came to visit, Mickey and Agustín, on their way to aeronautics school in Shenandoah, West Virginia. Then I got a roommate, a wonderful Mexican woman, Madelaine. She is your godmother, *mi comadre*. She was working as a bilingual secretary, and she gave me the names of schools. That is what I did while I was expecting you. I took secretarial courses, typing and shorthand. That was a very difficult time, during that pregnancy. Sometimes I think you turned out so sensitive because I spent most of that pregnancy crying.

"After you were born, Madelaine helped me get a job. I was entirely fluent in two languages, so jobs were not difficult to find. I started in mid-town, at the Mony Building, with an insurance company. That is where I opened my first bank account, on the corner of Fifty-Fifth Street and Broadway. I was glad to earn my own money, not depend on anyone else. My mother helped me too. It was very hard. A foreign woman, three children, and alone. But I did not care. I was not going back to living with a philandering husband, and I was not going back to Colombia ever again. In America I could have my own life. I liked that. It was exhilarating. God bless this country."

Before her dementia I'd heard my mother describe my birth only as a passing comment, usually made during a heavy snowstorm, compared as "nothing" to that night. By the time I came into the world, she had taken legal action against my father on the grounds of adultery. According to the transcript I found in the dusty courthouse Record Rooms decades later, my parents separated in August 1947, just three months after my mother's defiant return from Colombia, in the beginning of her pregnancy.

"The night you were born there was a terrible blizzard. Seventeen inches of snow fell. Everything was stopped in New York City. No trains, no buses. In those days plows were not common or reliable. When my water broke, I sent your sister Julia downstairs to get Mr. Durant, the super of our building. What a wonderful man he was. He went into that snowstorm and waited for a long time, until he stopped a truck on the Square. The driver did not want to help at first, probably because Mr. Durant was a black man, but he convinced him. Then he came all the way back up to get me and brought me down again and told the driver to take me to the hospital."

I imagine my mother making her way down the six flights of stairs of our pre-war building, dropping off my sisters at Mr. Durant's, pulling herself across Union Square and up into the cab of the truck. The anonymous driver reassured her along the way, she says. But she was quiet as she held on to the belly she had tried to abort and hadn't been able to. "I had no contacts, no money, no family in this country. How could a Colombian immigrant arrange such a thing on her own in 1947?"

Bellevue Hospital was desolate that night and the doctor she'd grown familiar with didn't make it. So, from the beginning, I have known myself as hers, only.

"Anyway, your uncle Mickey was taking a flight course in Mineola, Long Island, so he was able to come to see me a few days later. He called Nonna's house, and your father came to see you in the hospital the next morning. Your eyes were small and almost closed, like a China doll. When he saw you he called you *Tesoro.*

"I had a sitter for you, a Puerto Rican woman named Patricia. She loved you. She would spoil you from the minute I dropped you off each morning. Her son was a year older than you. Do you remember Humberto? He became an assistant district attorney in the Bronx. My mother wanted me to send your sisters to her for a time, until I could get on my feet. They stayed with her for about a year. She loved having them there. Later, when they came back, I sent you too, when things became so difficult for me.

"Your father sometimes came to see us. Most of the time he lived his own life down on Mulberry Street. He did not put up a fight to make things better. It was as if somehow he was actually relieved by the separation. I had made a few friends at work and sometimes I would leave you with Madelaine and go to a dinner, or a party. Sometimes I even took you with me.

"I was very lonely. Your sisters were away. You were all I had with me during that time. My little *compañera*. You were always so sweet, so good. *Veroniquita*.

"Yes, there were invitations from men to go on dates and things. Of course I never said I had three children. But I was not interested anyway. I was glad when the girls came back home and started school. I was not as lonely because I was so busy. Less time to think about things that made me miserable.

"Then I met Ben. I started to work for him. Once we began to see each other romantically, he suggested I speak to an attorney, because the situation I was living in was not favorable to me. I was not married but I was not single either. I found an attorney who explained divorce procedures to me. There were only a few grounds for divorce. Not like today with that no-fault divorce and people changing partners like they change their underwear. You had to prove abandonment or cruelty or adultery. I think also insanity. Even if both parties wanted it, someone had to win and someone had to lose. That was the way it was then.

"Of course, the obvious grounds were adultery. But it was not so easy to prove. You had to have pictures, letters, hotel receipts, witnesses. Or an admission. Your father was not going to admit anything, forget it! The attorney suggested something they used all the time then, *un testigo falso*. A false witness who swears in court that she saw so-and-so in bed with a woman who was not his wife. These people were paid for their testimony. My attorney hired a chambermaid at the Breslin Hotel. That is where we had stayed earlier when your father came home on furlough, because the room I had in the Bronx was too small and too far from Mulberry Street. She testified that she saw him with a dark-haired woman in one of the rooms, in bed. It was the only way we could prove adultery. Although if I had wanted to, I could have hired a private detective to follow your father around and they would have had plenty of evidence! But I did not want any photographs or things like that.

"I told your father what I was going to do. At first he laughed it off, as usual. He did not believe me. He thought I would change my mind and take him back. Divorce was a terrible taboo then. Today it would be like admitting you have a deadly disease. He really did not believe me. Always trying to romance me. But I was not falling for his charm anymore. All I could think of when I got near him were the women he spent time with instead of with his family. *No gracias. A otro perro con ese hueso!* Sell it to the marines, Mister!

"And your father was not exactly concerned about providing support for his children. In our separation, the family court had specified an amount he was to send me every month. He was never on time. Always an excuse. But I fixed him. I presented myself at his office and sat there in the waiting room until he took me to the bank and got money out. I did not care. I even nearly had him arrested once. They were going to put him in alimony jail. Yes, they had that then. His children were not going to starve while he was sitting in his fancy suits in his fancy law firm impressing people with his fancy ways.

"Of course that made things worse for him. The law firm he worked for asked him to leave after that. It was bad enough that he had an Italian surname. With a divorce action against him too, and a wife making scenes, they wanted no part of him.

"Nino was very upset. He said he would be ruined. And his family would be disgraced. No Italian was ever divorced. It was a terrible thing, a personal catastrophe. He probably also worried about his chances after the divorce. The way matrimonial law was written then, if you were the loser in a divorce, you could not remarry again. Not within New York State.

"Your father would not show up in court. The case was adjourned several times. He figured I would give up. He never heard any of the testimony. The day he finally did show up, he testified for about five minutes and walked out. He only had to answer a few questions my attorney asked him. He was so angry, so ashamed. He called me afterward, crying. He told me that he did not want anybody else to know about the divorce. Nobody. Never. Except for his brother, Paolo, he would not tell anyone. Not even his mother."

I tell my mother that the divorce was granted on the day of their eighth anniversary. It is one of the details I remember reading aloud from the transcript the day I found it.

"It was our destiny, I suppose. I did not despise your father. I just wanted my freedom. I did not want to disgrace him, so I agreed. I would keep the divorce a secret. He told everyone I had returned to live with my family in South America because I did not like it here. Only that time when I was shopping in Klein's with you, and I heard somebody shouting my name, it all came out. It was Gina, one of your father's neighbors on Mulberry Street. They had been childhood friends. She came running over to me, talking a mile a minute. She could not understand why I was shopping in Klein's. 'What are you doing here?' She kept asking stupid questions. When I told her that we lived across the street from where we were standing, she nearly fainted. I think she went back to your father and told him she saw me. He called me, very upset. He did not want anyone to know. But what was I supposed to do? Disappear?

"It's funny. Your father was not a bitter man. Even after the divorce he would call me, embarrassed, apologetic. Always with the sweet words. Yes, I was tempted to reconcile with him. Several times. He was the father of my children, after all. We saw each other a few times. Especially that last autumn. He had bought the Café Roma and seemed to be doing well. I was tempted to give Nino another chance.

"Just before the end, around Thanksgiving and my birthday, a delivery came to the apartment. Three men came in carrying a new washing machine, a television set and a piano. From Nino. I was overjoyed. And very tempted.

"We even went to a Christmas party together that some friends of mine were having. I remember I got very dressed up and wore my mink coat. But when I sat next to him at that party he seemed quiet, blue, not his normal self. He was never a morose man, never showed the world his worries. So it struck me that night that he seemed different. But I did not want to make him feel self-conscious. We were at a party together, divorced after all. I took his silence to mean he did not want to be with me in public. So I left him alone most of the night. After the party he just dropped me off at the door of the building. We said goodnight and I reminded him that we planned to spend New Year's Eve together. I was very confused by his mood that night. I actually left my coat, my mink, in the cab. Luckily, your father took the same cab home."

I take out and show my mother a Western Union telegram, my father's final communication.

> I have your coat STOP Telephone will be in order tomorrow STOP
> Call me if you can STOP Love Nino

"A few days after Christmas he asked me for money. He wanted to borrow it, he said, for a business investment. A fantastic opportunity to expand his Café. I never understood why a man with a degree in law would want to operate a café on Mulberry Street.

"But I did it. I got three thousand dollars from my savings account at the Union Square Savings Bank. You remember it? Where you used to get a lollipop from the guard when you were a little girl? I cleaned out what was left of the money my mother had given me when I left Colombia for good. That was a great deal of money then. A great deal. Enough to buy a house.

"I was so stupid! So naïve. I let myself be talked into trusting him because of his charm. I never thought the father of my children would jeopardize my future like that. He even signed a promissory note. Some promise. *¡El papel aguanta todo!* What a laugh! He even went to the bank with me, watched me get the money. Then we took the subway back to Little Italy. To some back room in a restaurant. He wanted me to see that he was using the money for business. Business! What did I know? There were two men there, he spoke to them in Italian for a few minutes, then gave them my three thousand dollars. That was the last I saw of my money.

"No, I have never believed he was involved in anything criminal. That is *una calumnia*. An ugly stereotype the *ignorantes* use. Your father wanted to get away from all of that. He was very proud of being an attorney. He would not jeopardize it.

"Anyway, his vanity would not let him gamble with that beautiful face!

"It is paradoxical, yes. Nino was a playboy and borrowed money from me, but he would not steal. He promised me he would pay me back in a few days. I believe he believed he could keep his promise. It would be right after the New Year, he said, when the holiday receipts were in and he had paid the bakers.

"I believed him. Completely. But I never saw him again."

I think of my mother as a thirty-one-year-old immigrant, alone in New York City with three children, facing the worst of her Decembers. The woman who imposed years of silence and secret-keeping on herself, determined to hold back misfortune at any cost. That is the mother I recognize.

"I knew something was seriously wrong the day after New Year's. I was puzzled that I had not heard from him for New Year's Eve. I told myself he had had a change of heart. Two days after that, Paolo came to the apartment looking for him. He seemed desperate. He said Nino had disappeared. People were looking for him everywhere. Even his mother did not know where he was. He owed money. I did not know what to think.

"A week or so later three men came to take back the washer, the television, and the piano. They gave me back that promissory note you have there with your father's signature. Some trade. I remember you girls standing there crying while they carried the things out and down the stairs. I really did hate your father for that. *Cobarde.*

"Then I began to panic. After a few weeks I looked in the yellow pages and hired a detective. I was out of my mind. I called everyone who knew him. He was gone. Without a trace. It took me years to accept that."

> Dear Madam:
>   In view of the fact that all available clues have been exhausted in the matter in which you are interested, please advise us whether you are agreeable to the use of publicity in newspapers or magazines. You may reply by mail. By publicity we mean that we seek someone and why. No cost involved.
>
> National Detective Bureau
> 105 Nassau Street
> New York 38, N.Y"

"I kept thinking he would show up. Every time the bell rang unexpectedly I thought it would be Nino. Then people began to say he was dead. That loan sharks got to him. It actually became easier to think of him dead.

"No, nobody ever told me anything. No one ever said a word. There was an occasional call from Nino's cousin Ray asking if there was any news. Finally, I got fed up with it. I could not continue waiting like that.

"Nino did not deserve his children. He was a coward. He did not even honor his poor mother, or his brother, sitting there waiting for him. I never felt compassion for him, no. Not for what he did. But my mother did. She used to say that it must have been terrible for him, a man who loved people so much, who was always careful to please others and do the right thing, to turn his back on his entire life.

"I would do it again. Telling you he was dead was the best way to keep you from being hurt. What would have been the use of waiting? You would have wasted your whole life. I believe I did the right thing.

"To me he was dead. Dead. And good riddance. Until you dug him up from his grave."

The sun is coming low over the back of the house now. Neither of us speaks. The sounds of distant children and lawn mowers that have accompanied us these few hours are now stilled. The birds have retreated. My mother's oak trees extend their shade over us. The day is readying to harvest the final hours of light for itself. The air is warm, dry, and a little aroused.

My mother's sundowning will soon begin. She will play with the button or hem of her nightgown. Her gaze will lose its focus and wander restlessly. She will retreat to her inner world and be inaccessible again.

I offer her a drink of water. She declines. There is no harshness in her, no plea for vindication, none of the need to legitimize herself that once drove her mercilessly and kept her racing, ever the disbeliever, battling life's capriciousness as much for her children as through them. She sits before me now, vulnerable, powerless, spent.

I slide my father's letters, this evidence of family, back into the yellow envelope. The trio of our voices stirs inside me still. I am flooded with images of my parents when they were half my age. The neglected society girl and the handsome adventurer, the burdened young wife and the longing serviceman, the anxious mother and ineffective father. They are young and flawed, as fallible as I am. I have trouble finding anything to say. I feel the urge to thank her, and him. I want to weep for all we lost.

"So, Ronnie. What did you accomplish? Did finding your father satisfy *una añoranza,* some deep longing you felt all your life? Did he make up for anything? I don't understand, you never even lived with him. You only saw him once or twice as an infant. None of the other girls expressed an interest."

A strong temptation envelops me to repeat my mother's gesture of waving away what she cannot abide. Or to follow my father's lead and leave this place to never return. Maybe I too should keep their wretched story neatly wrapped and tucked away, undisturbed for another half a century.

I flip through the pages to find my father's last army letter. It is written from Fort Campbell, Kentucky, just days before his discharge. I want to read it aloud to my mother, still grasping to make her understand. But I stop, and read his words again to myself instead.

> Kiss my girls and take good care of them for me. Tell them Papa is ailing because he cannot see them. How much he wants to see them. Tell them that many times their father has wanted to give up, because everything seems to go wrong for him, but that having them has given him a new ideal to live for—to become a man truly deserving of his children. And that he asks their forgiveness now, for the worst sin of all, for not being there.

My mother speaks again, her voice is almost tender now.

"Ronnie, are you satisfied? You got to see his handsome face. His beautiful hands. Just like yours, long fingers, nice nails with half moons. You got to hear his kind voice, his happy laugh. His impeccable manner and style. His brilliant mind. You probably fell in love with him. Your father."

it's really Ernest Hemingway's fault
in English class Mr. Howard had us do an exercise
not too wordy
and in the style of A Farewell To Arms
describe a place where you spend time waiting
of course that would be Mrs. deGrab's bathroom
on Tuesdays after school i go for my piano lessons
at her studio on West Eighty Seventh Street
it is a brownstone with a plaque outside
The Music House
it has studios on three floors
i think there are bedrooms on the very top
but i've only seen the first floor where the pianos are
that's where she teaches
each week after my lesson i tell Mrs. deGrab
i need to change my clothes into my dance gear
she slides open the pocket doors into her study
then the second set past the double harpsichords
her bathroom is just beyond them
it is bigger than any other i've ever seen
with a full wall of closets
and a separate tub and shower
it's all white tile
and the pedestal sink has porcelain handles
best of all is the long mirror at the far end
that's where i practice my postures and arm positions
and get warmed up for flamenco class
it starts in a few hours
it's better than warming up at the dance studio
even though it's only a few minutes downtown
if i get there too early there are always wierdos around
like the perv who kept telling me i have beautiful legs
she wanted to put cream on them
right there in the dressing room
but i ran out quick
Mrs. deGrab's bathroom is even bigger than Nonna's
it has beautiful pictures of women's faces

and fresh flowers on a little table by the window
different ones every week
while i'm in there i experiment
with the new shades of eye shadow and rouge
i buy them with my Saturday money
from helping Ben and babysitting
it would work if i didn't have to wear dumb eyeglasses
once i tried one of Mrs. deGrab's lipsticks
she keeps them on the glass shelf
but i didn't like how it felt on my lips all sticky and oily
i puckered my lips and pressed them together
like the girls do in the locker room at school
i've been watching them ever since that Friday
a few weeks ago when the Cuban missile crisis started
they really went wild
that was when we all heard the news
that there might be a nuclear war over the weekend
and they all vowed not to die virgins
i wonder when i look at them
if it's true that it shows on your face
when i'm done with the makeup i wash my face
and change into my dance gear
i sit on the floor and take out my dinner sandwich
it's been in my school bag all day
while i eat i think about Mrs. deGrab
how all the time i'm in there she never bothers me
she just keeps on teaching her next lesson
and the one after that
i can hear her soft voice over the music
her words just pour out of her mouth
in her Belgian accent
explaining the fingering
or how to use the wrist on a certain line
she is never angry and never rushes you
not even if you don't get it
she'll just sit down at the second piano and play
right along with you

i like it when we begin a new piece
she plays it for me from beginning to end
i stand next to her and turn the pages
and watch her hair
with browns and grays and blondes and reds
it sways back and forth
she tells me about the music
and what the composer was going through
when he wrote it
This will be for your repertoire she says
i'm always afraid it will be too difficult especially Chopin
but after a few months i can play it pretty well
the thing about music is that it make you feel things
once while i was playing Debussy my eyes got watery
before i could control myself
there were drops on the keys
when i finished Mrs. deGrab sat next to me
she said she knew
that sometimes life was very hard for me in my family
but that i am a strong person
and when i have my own children it will be different
i will be able to read books about being a parent
and learn how to do things better
It was like that for me she said
the whole thing was very embarrassing
i wanted her to stop talking
but at the same time it felt good that she knew
i couldn't think what to say without crying some more
and anyway how does Mrs. deGrab know anything
maybe Carmela told her
that the wars have started again
late at night when she comes home
from Mannes Conservatory of Music
she's hours late for curfew
and i know she has been with Eliot
he is her boyfriend since senior year at M&A
even though he goes to Julliard they stayed together

Eliot says i am like the kid sister he never had
sometimes they come to M&A to meet me
and Eliot takes us places
to the Museum of Natural History
or a Broadway matinee
or to see Leonard Bernstein's Young People Concerts
at Carnegie Hall
once he took us to Coney Island on the Cyclone ride
near his house
and another time we saw President Kennedy
at a rally in Sunnyside
i love being with them except for one part
it's not much fun
with them holding hands and kissing
and me walking behind watching but trying not to
plus everything has to be a secret from Mom
i have to make up stories about where i've been
Carmela says she's old enough to stay out
til midnight if she wants
but Mom does not believe in American morality
especially for women
Nine o'clock or nothing She says
so that's how the wars begin
i try not to listen
because i have to get up early for school
so i bring my transistor radio into bed
and listen to Chubby Checker
and pretend i'm doing hoola hoops
singing Let's Twist Again and counting
usually i just hear the thumping sounds against the wall
little Isabella and baby Gabriel never wake up
i always wish Ben would stop them but he doesn't
he just stays in the bedroom
if i wasn't such a coward i would tell him
all about Mom
and how she hits baby Gabriel
when he doesn't eat his baby food

i ask Carmela to please try
to get home on time to avoid the wars
it would make everything better for everyone i say
she says she'll be moving out as soon as she can get a job
it seems like everyone is just waiting to escape
but then on weekends
sometimes Ben's family comes over
Mom cooks stuffed cabbage and chopped liver
and matzo ball soup
his sister and brother and his parents like it
they think She is a great cook
they carry baby Gabriel and twirl little Isabella around
everything seems happy for a while
but i know it won't last
after dinner when they want me to play the piano
i stay in my room
and say i have to do my English homework

Vegas

I t was another example of what you liked to call, *mi destino.* Tony
Tenerielli's revelation, *your father is alive,* sent me searching through
the Las Vegas telephone records. But there was no listing for Nino. That
made me think he might have been living under another name, especially
because of the way he'd left New York, and that was why you and the
other people on Mulberry Street weren't able to find him. I would have
another long search ahead of me, I was sure. So I made a list of places
where he might be working. In Las Vegas, the first place to look would
be the hotels.

Maybe it was what I said to the hotel telephone operators—that I hadn't
seen my father in a very long time and I believed he worked there. As it happened the woman at the second number I called asked me what he looked
like. I quickly pictured the old men at the Café Roma. I used their words.
Tall, slender, elegant, seventy-ish, very kind. The operator didn't hesitate.
"Oh, you must mean Mr. Sementa."

Before I could react she began to commiserate with me. "What a pity,
how awful, terribly sorry but Nino left the hotel a few years before." She'd
heard he was at Caesar's Palace now, and she went on about it, telling me it
was the grandest hotel on the strip, a must-see. She seemed to want to stay
on the line with me, which I actually found reassuring. I asked her name,
Beverly, and thanked her. Once again I heard the words repeated. "Your
father is a real gentleman, a real sweetheart."

When I called Caesar's Palace the operator was ready to connect me to him right away. My mind began to race. What would I say, how would I know it was really him, and why would he believe me? I couldn't do it, so I hung up. It had happened too quickly. In no more than it would take to play the final chords of Chopin nocturne, an anonymous voice on the other end of a telephone repeated what was probably one of a hundred unremarkable tasks in her day, and closed the last link in my search.

I rested my head in my hands for a few minutes. I needed to slow the whole thing down. Then I made up my mind. I wasn't going to meet Nino on the telephone. No matter what the outcome. When I introduced myself to him, I wanted to see my father's face. And I wanted him to see mine.

The first friend I told disagreed with me. I was making a mistake, she said. A colleague agreed with her. I should consider the impact. Simply walking up to an old man and introducing myself, the child he left behind a lifetime ago, could have a severe consequences, physical and emotional, for both of us. It could go very wrong. I should wait a few months, to be sure of what I was going to do. I should at least call to let him know I was coming. But I didn't listen. I was certain.

My girls were happy for me. In their adolescent excitement they helped me prepare how I would approach him. We rehearsed the moment. Until I left for airport the next week, it became what we did, in the middle of supper, while we shopped for a dress for me to wear, while I packed. I would practice introducing myself and one of the girls pretended to be him—Nino turning away, Nino collapsing, Nino saying he didn't know what I was talking about. Every time, I froze. I didn't know how to react. I had no frame of reference for walking up to my own father and introducing myself. What could there be about such a scene that was predictable?

I was even less prepared for the spectacle of Las Vegas. At thirty-nine, I had never been inside a casino before. I found myself standing in a sky blue linen dress surrounded by glitz and sparkle and half-clothed waitresses who handed me free cocktails in the middle of the afternoon. I walked past rows of old men watching televised horse races, clouds of soured cigar smoke hovering over roulette wheels, young men and women in business clothes leaning silently into Black Jack tables, the whispering croupiers at baccarat, and lines of middle-aged women who sat charmed by slot machines—all oblivious to anything else, intent on beating the odds. It was the background noise, the incessant dropping of coins and clicking of chips, that made the place feel like everyone there was alone. I circled the room, skimming along carpet so thick I was never sure I was actually walking on the ground, scanning a hundred faces to locate one I didn't even know. A strange place, I thought, but fitting. Here, in the midst of illusion, it made sense that I would utter the most unnatural words I'd ever say to anyone.

In my nervousness, I'd forgotten to ask the hotel operator what it was Nino did at Caesar's. I tried to imagine him as a dealer, or a cashier, or maybe a bartender. But as I crossed the room I could see that those jobs were in the hands of young men. Then a burly, well-suited man stopped me, arms crossed over his chest. I had unknowingly stepped too close to someone who turned out to be one of the pit bosses. The big man asked who I was looking for. When I told him, he dropped his arms to his sides and told me Mr. Sementa didn't work in the casino. "He's a vice president in the hotel." Then he very politely pointed me in the right direction.

The passageway that connected the casino at Caesar's Palace to the hotel lobby was opulent, like everything else in Las Vegas, boasting an oversized statue of Cleopatra standing on a floating barge, perfectly balanced on the waters of a simulated Nile as she escorted passersby away from their games of chance toward certain comfort ahead. That plaster empress was the first thing I saw when I stepped out of the gaming room. And it was there, at the end of Cleopatra's passageway, standing a few steps above the hotel lobby, when I looked down for a second to mark my step and then looked up again, that I saw him.

He was about a hundred feet away, moving across the lobby deliberately, but not rushing. He had one hand in his pocket as he walked, a long, easy stride that didn't quite fit with the bend of his shoulders. And he was wearing a cream-colored suit, the same as in his picture at Nonna's house.

I wanted to catch up to him, but in those first seconds I couldn't get myself to move. My eyes were fixed on him as he stepped behind a column. When I couldn't see him anymore I made my way to the reception area. A young woman at the front desk began to speak to me, but I interrupted her. I said I'd like to see Mr. Sementa, and she said something, but I couldn't hear her, or my own voice, or anything else, as if the volume in the room had been turned off. It took a few seconds until I could make out what she was saying.

"He's just stepped out for a moment. He'll be right back. And you are?"

I turned away without answering. I headed in the direction I'd seen Nino go and reached an open area near an elevator bank. No one was there. But a minute later the cream-colored suit was walking toward me.

I wanted to extend my arm to stop him, but my hands suddenly felt large and clumsy, too heavy to lift, as if they didn't belong to me. So I took a step into his path.

"Excuse me, Mr. Sementa?"

He stopped short, looking a little startled. *Yes.* He seemed to be agreeing with me. Then he quickly moved his hands up in front of his chest and broke into a playful smile.

"Whatever it is young lady, I didn't do it."

I don't know what I saw first. There was so much to take in at once, but I remember most his voice. A little raspy, but rich, like the lower strings of a cello. He was looking right at me, eyes wide and curious, and I noticed they were dark brown, like mine. I couldn't tell you specifically about anything else on his face then. It was a collage of Nonna and Uncle Paolo and Julia. I knew him. He was familiar.

I never felt so still before, as if I weren't breathing. I had the sensation that I was standing very straight, much taller than my normal height, caught inside an indistinguishable fissure in time, like the instant or two after a deep sleep, when you first open your eyes, before any sound or sensation reaches you.

And I said it. "I'm Veronica, your daughter."

Then no one else was there. Nothing visible in my periphery. Nothing moving. Only Nino's eyes circling my face, in delight and disbelief, the way people look at something splendid and inexplicable. My father moving toward me, slowly, until the soft skin of his cheek was next to mine and he was placing the lightest of kisses, the ones I gave my newborn babies, on my face, my eyes, my mouth.

He whispered. "It's been a thousand years."

Mr. O'Hara will be waiting in the lobby
like he always does
sitting in one of those comfortable-looking chairs
wearing a jacket and tie holding his hat on his knee
my heart was thumping the whole way on the train
it was much easier when we lived in Manhattan
no subway dirt and crowds to rumple my clothes
it's important to look clean and neat for Mr. O'Hara
he comes into town on business with the Herald Tribune
and takes special time to see me
it's usually in January which leaves half a year to wait
before it's time for Weedsport again
when i get home from school Mom tells me
Mr. O'Hara called he wants to see you
i wonder on the subway ride what they talk about
and why She never wants to meet him
but once i see the Biltmore Hotel sign i forget Her
Mr. O'Hara stands up and shakes my hand
and we do a lot of smiling
then we order lunch in the restaurant
he lets me order first i always get a club sandwich
then he tells me about the weather in Weedsport
and about the grandchildren and new things in town
the mailman retired
they might move the little league to another park
there's a new third grade teacher at the school
later he asks did i bring my report card
he looks at it carefully
and says *Very fine work indeed*
he asks me questions but i only tell the good stuff
like about my new friend Elise from France
we have music theory class together
Elise lives down the block from the Guggenheim
and practices two hours a day but on voice not piano
between classes we sit on the steps outside the school
Elise and Amy and Laura Nigro and i
we harmonize to the Beatles songs which is easy

or we practice sight singing which is not so easy
sometimes i can't stay on my part
because i get distracted
by sitting right in the middle of their beautiful voices
other times Elise sings French songs by herself
she sounds peaceful inside
like she's never going to make a mistake
i could never have the courage to sing alone
Mr. O'Hara says i seem happier in high school
than ever before
i tell him it's because at M&A
people are different
nobody teases their hair
and everybody practices something
so i'm not an odd ball with my piano lessons
and with dance classes
it's not really what i thought high school would be
you can hear music rehearsals everywhere
the art floors smell of linseed oil
everyone carries portfolios or an instrument
i tell Mr. O'Hara that i have a job now
every Saturday i work for Ben
just like Mom and Julia used to
i get to wear a nurse's uniform
and prepare the patients
and pass the instruments to Ben
when he's doing procedures
i try to anticipate which one he'll need
especially during extractions when every second counts
i get to answer the telephone and make appointments
Ben teaches me how to do the filing
he says i am very organized and a fast learner
he says *Never be afraid to ask questions*
i like Ben because he helps people
like the men and women who come in hurting
with only one or two teeth left
he tells them how their lives will improve

with a new set of teeth
i get to write Full Upper Full Lower on their charts
and a few appointments later when he's finished
they look like new people all smiles and happy
and if they can't pay the hundred twenty dollars
he lets them take years to pay
i don't tell Mr. O'Hara
that some of the patients ask Ben if i am his daughter
or that he says *No she is the nurse*
a professional's private life must be kept separate
that's what Ben says
Mr. O'Hara says i'm very lucky
to be growing up in New York City
and i want to say not really
but i say thank you instead

10

i think Andrew likes me
i wish i knew for sure but he doesn't say
he has a big smile whenever we meet in the hall
he spends extra time after orchestra rehearsals
or during breaks when we practice piano duets
i like to listen to him improvise
especially the Dave Brubeck Take Five lines
he is very serious about music especially composition
but he always says something to make me laugh
i feel tingly around him
especially when he stands close
Elise is sure he likes me
she says he laughs at things i say
and he doesn't seem as happy around other girls
i know Amy has a crush on him too
and it is very hard
she is my favorite friend
and so much prettier than me with beautiful hair
Amy can bring friends over to her house anytime
her mother is sweet and never screams or hits
no crazy family and she can buy her own clothes
she is Jewish like Andrew which he probably prefers
just to avoid wars with his family
like Ben had
and the same thing is happening to Eliot too
Carmela says his parents made him choose
tuition for Julliard or the *shiksa*
it is all backwards
first she has curfew wars for seeing Eliot
then she gets locked out and has to sleep in the garage
next thing you know she moves out
to live with a friend on the west side
but it winds up being Eliot who has to choose
his parents say either tuition or Carmela not both
Carmela won't go back to finish school
she is heartbroken and working in an office
so Mom makes Ben call Eliot's parents

to fix things
but it doesn't work
Eliot is at Julliard with another girlfriend now
and everyone is miserable especially me
i wish i could ask Julia what to do about Andrew
but she is always studying or working
usually she is angry and won't talk to anybody
just comes in and locks herself in her room
since Carmela's been gone the wars have changed
they're with Julia now
she hates pre-med and does not want to be a doctor
but Mom says she has to finish another year
Like It Or Not
so Julia stopped talking and stays locked up
once Mom got so angry she took the door off Julia's room
i was afraid that day that they would kill each other
pulling each other's hair and slapping and punching
little Isabella was crying scared so i took her for a walk
all the way to Saint Joan of Arc's church
i told her it is a place to go to feel safe and peaceful
then we lit a candle
and she liked blowing out the match
when i grow up i think i will take little Isabella away
so she won't be afraid or lonely or think she's ugly
Julia has a boyfriend too i know it
because i saw him once
they were talking at the subway station
and holding hands
when they saw me she introduced me
his name is Neal and he's at college like her
of course Mom's not supposed to know about Neal
but she'll find out she checks everybody's drawers
and book bags and pockets
that's how she got Carmela's diary
and found out about Eliot
i'll never do that
won't write things down about Andrew or anything

just keep it all to myself
like i do about peeing in my bed
i can't help it
it's stupid to be fifteen and still peeing in bed
i try not to but it's always the same
i'm having a nice dream
but somehow i end up sitting on a toilet
next thing i know i'm not dreaming anymore
and there is this puddle of hot pee under me
so i jump up fast as i can and strip the bed
if i tiptoe to the bathroom fast and wash my sheet
and spread it out over my desk chair
it's dry by morning
same with my panties
the hard part is sleeping on the wet mattress naked
but it's better than having Her find out
anything is

Perdida

"*Tres empanadas y cuatro arepas de queso, por favor.*" I ask the clerk at the Colombian bakery for three meat pies and four cheese-filled corn cakes. I've come directly from work to this particular shop in Jackson Heights to get them for my mother. It is her birthday. The place is warm and smells of good coffee, a refuge from the bleak and chilly November afternoon.

I wait on the long line for my order and recognize the various regional inflections as people speak—Bogotá, Cali, Medellín, the mountain areas. No *costeños* here, with their relaxed low-country usage like the *ajá* and "swallowed" consonants of my uncles. The people I am on line with speak as formally as they dress—suited and tied under their heavy overcoats. *Tenga, su merced*, the clerk hands a bag to a customer ahead of me. I watch the man carry his tea and yucca scones out of the store as he says he's rushing back to his job. Some customs die hard.

"*¿Algo más?*" The young woman behind the counter wants to know if I want anything else. She doesn't smile. She doesn't make eye contact with me. She is busy serving customers, running the cash register, calling out instructions to the bakers in the back, talking with her boyfriend on her cell phone. I say no, and thank her. But really, I do want something else, something more than the array of *delicias* in the showcase. I want time, abundant and unmeasured, sufficient for long conversations over an afternoon cup or an evening *tertulia* with friends and a bottle of *aguardiente*. I miss my in-laws, Michél's large family, their sunny house in Cartagena, the heat and smell of the tropics. I am in the midst of an inevitable nostalgia that surfaces whenever I visit this store.

I wish my mother were here. I imagine us sitting together at one of the small round tables sipping our *café con leche,* celebrate her birthday the way we never have. Now that her memory has eroded, she might have no problem joining in with other Colombians. I could get to see her, this once, enjoying herself, being addressed as *Señora* or *Doña* by these working class men and women she was trained to look down on, to distrust. She might follow my lead, see me at ease here, and even engage in conversation with them. We could relax together, in Spanish.

I could take her for a walk along Roosevelt Avenue to window shop at the Colombian-owned stores, hear the latest *bachata* melodies, touch the fabric of a wool back pack, maybe buy one for her. It was just a few blocks from here that she and Ben bought their first house, when they moved us from Manhattan. She wouldn't remember that, or how much they hated that house and the way the neighborhood began to change, or how they decided they'd made an awful mistake and fled to Douglaston. But she would see the thriving commercial center the neighborhood has become, at the hands of her very own *compatriotas.*

I could tell my mother about the restaurant review I recently heard on WQXR, New York's finest classical music station, the one she listened to for more than fifty years. Right between the Brahms First Symphony and a set of Scarlatti sonatas, Frank Rizzo raved about his new discovery—*arepas*—recommending that everyone rush to eat these tasty Colombian delicacies. I imagine her face, eyes and mouth wide as these corncakes in disbelief, saying *imposible,* because, of course, the world could not have changed *this* much.

When I arrive at my mother's house I put the bag of food on the kitchen table. My sister Julia looks through it. "Fried stuff. Clogs your arteries."

"It's Mom's birthday."

She pulls out an *empanada* and bites into it. "Good. Mom used to make these. With *Tía* Elena!" She smiles. "But why so small?" I don't answer her. I'm enjoying watching my sister devour this treat she hasn't tasted since we were children. She finishes it and reaches for another. I regret I didn't buy more.

"Where's Mom?" I ask.

Julia answers me through a full mouth. "With you."

"No. I just got here."

"What?" Julia swallows hard and locks eyes with me. Her friendly tone is gone. "What do you mean? She's been out for hours. You took her somewhere."

"Uh-uh. I was at work all day. Weren't you here?"

"I went out. I had things to do. I can't stay cooped up in here all day." Julia closes the bag and steps to the sink to wash her hands. Her loud voice is a warning that I should back off. But I don't. I'm alarmed, too.

"Are you sure Mom isn't in her room?"

"She is not." Julia dries her hands and faces me again, hands on her hips. "I just looked in there."

"Well, when was the last time you saw her?"

"Early. She was up in that cave of hers all morning, as usual. I had things to do." Julia jabs her index finger in my direction. "You took her somewhere."

"If I had, she'd be with me. Did you check her room when you came home?"

"What's the point? She only comes out of there at night. I went upstairs. I just came down a few minutes ago when I heard your car."

"So you haven't seen Mom since this morning?"

"You took her somewhere." Her repetition, I know, is to convince herself. But it's getting on my nerves.

"I'm worried, Julia. It'll be dark in a few minutes. Mom hasn't been out by herself in a long time. Where would she have gone?"

"Who knows?" Julia walks out of the kitchen to the front door and steps out onto the porch. I follow her. "She probably went to the bank. That's what she used to do."

"Where is the bank?"

"Northern Bloulevard."

I mentally track the distance. "That's over a mile from here."

"That won't stop her. She walks everywhere." Julia steps back into the vestibule and grabs a jacket. "Idiot."

"Wait, where are you going?" I follow my sister out to the front porch.

"To find her. You stay here." Julia gets into her car and pulls, screeching, out of the driveway. I walk back into the house. I check the first floor rooms, the bedrooms, the bathrooms, the basement, the garage. My mother is not in the house.

I am back in the cold kitchen. I notice the bag of *delicias*. At this temperature they will harden soon and loose their taste. My mother will be hungry when she returns, I'm sure, because she never eats food outside her home. I find aluminum foil. I wrap the whole bag in a sheet of foil and put it on the stove, above the pilot light, to keep it warm.

I see my mother's green chair. The leather seat has a tear across it, covered with duct tape that is curled at the edges. I sit in it. I wonder where my mother is. I try to think like she might have, if she'd had a period of clear-mindedness, if she'd forgotten her illness for a few hours. But I don't know any of her neighborhood routines, where she shops for groceries, her favorite vegetable market, her drug store. I don't know which of the two nearby churches she goes to. Or which library. Maybe I should walk around the block to see if I spot her. In her condition, she could easily have gotten lost in the labyrinth of streets around here. No, I think again, someone should be here when she returns. Does she know it's her birthday? Is that why she went out? Maybe I should call the police. Would they take a report now? It hasn't been twenty-four hours. And I don't have any idea what she's wearing today.

I hear Julia drive in. I walk to the door, hoping she's found my mother. Maybe she saw her at the bus stop, and, without upsetting her, gave her a lift home, the way she used to, before the illness, when things were difficult only because they were routine and predictable. Not like this.

Julia flies past me. "No sign of her. She wasn't anywhere near the bank or along the Boulevard." She sprints up the stairs and into my mother's room. She comes out holding my mother's telephone book. I follow her into the kitchen. She picks the receiver off the old wall phone and puts it at the fold of her neck. She holds the telephone book open with one hand and turns the rotary dial with the other.

"Who are you calling?"

"Some Peruvian woman she used to visit in Kew Gardens or someplace."

"I didn't know Mom had any *latino* friends."

"Not a friend. She was helping her with immigration papers. She was always finding people who needed help." I see my mother in our Union Square kitchen, sitting with one unknown woman or another, a pile of papers on the table before them, my mother reading out loud from the forms in English, repeating herself in Spanish, explaining the laws carefully, as sure of every regulation as if she'd written them herself. I see myself sitting across from her, marveling at her ability to translate, feeling a rare safety being with her like that, watching her help people, proud of how smart she was.

"When was that, Julia? I mean, when did she help this particular woman?"

"Last year some time." Julia waves me away with the telephone book and turns toward the phone. "Hello? Is this Ernestina? This is Eva's daughter. *La hija de la Señora Eva. Sí.*" I break into a smile. I've never heard my sister speaking Spanish before. She has a distinct American pronunciation. Of course, I think, Julia has never lived with any *latinos,* other than my mother. "*¿Mi Mamá está con usted?* Is my mother with you? She may be lost. *Sí, perdida.*" After a few seconds she says *muchas gracias* and hangs up the phone. "She hasn't seen her." Julia pulls out a chair from the table and sits down. I do the same.

"What now?" I ask.

"We wait. What else?"

A minute passes. "Shouldn't you ask the neighbors?"

"They would have called by now."

"Julia, do you think she might have gone back to Union Square, or Jackson Heights?"

"For what?"

"I don't know. She might have woken up thinking she was back there."

"Nah. She's probably sitting in a park somewhere yapping with some foreigner. Giving somebody advice about where to learn English or how to become a citizen."

"Which park?"

"Who knows? The only one around here is Alley Pond."

"I can drive over there and look."

"It's getting dark already. She can't still be there."

"She probably got confused on these winding streets. She's probably lost."

"She's lived here for thirty years. How can she be lost?"

"But, doesn't she usually tell you where she's going? I mean, when she went out before?"

"Usually."

"Would she have gone to visit a friend?"

"Nobody's left. The few she had are all dead."

"Maybe she went shopping in Great Neck. I could check the shops there."

"Never goes there. Too expensive. She goes up to Northern Boulevard. I told you that already." Julia shakes her head and pouts her lips. Worry lines surround her eyes and mouth.

"Okay. Tell me what her regular route was when she went shopping. I'll follow it in my car and loop in and out of the side streets."

"What shopping? She doesn't remember how to shop. She doesn't remember how to write a list. She doesn't have any money. And why would she go shopping today out of the clear blue sky?"

"It's her birthday. Maybe she's confused. She might think it's your birthday, or mine. Maybe she went to get a cake."

"Ridiculous. She doesn't buy cakes. She bakes them."

The telephone ring startles us. Julia answers. She listens for a few seconds, then hangs up without saying anything. "Damned telemarketers." I glance at the clock. Five forty. It is dark out.

"We should call the police, Julia."

"What good would that do? You think they're going to issue an all-points bulletin for an old woman?"

"I don't think we have a choice. Mom isn't thinking clearly. She's been missing for nine or ten hours. She had no destination, no appointment to keep. She has no money. We don't know if she has a coat on. Or clothing, for that matter. Or any identification."

"Her coat!" Julia jumps up. "Let me check." She goes to the hall closet and seconds later calls out, "Dammit! It's here. So is her pocketbook."

I go to my sister. I look at my mother's coat, gray tweed with a fur collar and belt. I think of my mother walking the cold streets, unclothed, delirious. "We can at least call and ask if she's shown up at the precinct. Someone might have brought her there."

"Fine, then. Call. But no police here." Julia closes the closet and goes back out onto the front porch.

I get the number of the local precinct from my mother's handwritten list taped next to the phone. The officer on duty listens to my request and puts me on hold. He comes back on the line and tells me no one has come to the precinct answering my mother's description. He suggests we wait a few more hours, she'll probably find her way home. Maybe I forgot about an appointment she had? Or maybe she told me about it and I didn't hear her? It's not uncommon with the elderly, he says. I tell him again that she has Alzheimers and is cognitively disabled. He offers to send a squad car to the house. I think of Julia and turn him down. He says I should call back in two hours. I tell him I'll call back in one. He suggests we get a tracking bracelet for my mother, similar to a dog's identification collar, to wear around her wrist. That way she can always be brought back home by anyone who finds her. And, he adds, one of those alarm necklaces you see on television is a good idea as well, in case she falls or something.

I go out to the porch. The wind has picked up. Julia and I stand a few feet apart, our jackets zipped high, our hair blowing. We don't speak. We look out onto the road ahead, where it begins its steep bend to the right and continues a few hundred yards to intersect with a small side street. My feet and face are freezing. Tears well up in my eyes. Julia sniffles, holding back a sob. We won't surrender our watch, we know this, until our mother is home.

In time only the silhouetted magnolia trees in the front garden are visible in the moonlight. Until the small shape of someone appears at the side of the house, moving slowly, silently, up the steps and across the wide porch, passing us by without a glance, until she reaches the front door, the whimper of a small child escaping my mother as she steps inside her house.

ninety words per minute
that's even faster than Carmela types
the lady wants me to interview for a permanent job
Kelly Girls believed the lie on my application
that i'm eighteen
i was scared when She sent me to do it
the same trick Julia and Carmela had to play
put on lots of makeup and dress older
then impress them with your typing
and they'll never guess you're sixteen
she was right
the test part is easy
after all the typing She made me do
an hour a day every summer since eighth grade
while everybody else is at the beach i'm stuck inside
copying from some ancient typing manual
the same one She learned on
the clock is ticking
and i'm setting margins for business letters
last summer it was night classes for steno
next summer it'll be dictaphone school
She has it all planned out
because i'm too old now to be babysitting
or working for Ben or going to Weedsport
it's a waste of talent She says
A woman has to have office skills
so she can support herself without a man
but now that Carmela works in an office
She changed her tune
Office work is a dead end without a degree
i don't care about all the Without A Man stuff
i just like working
you get your own desk a typewriter and a telephone
it's like being a real secretary with a real salary
if you get a mean boss that makes you make mistakes
it's only a one or two week assignment so who cares
the best ones notice your work and compliment you

then the agency gives you a raise
i already have three hundred dollars saved
which i'm not allowed to spend
because it's college money
i heard Her tell Ben i will be going away
he disagrees
says i'm too young to handle the pressure
but She spends all day reading catalogs
She is going to find a college
one that has a good music program
and strict dormitory rules
i guess i don't have to be a lawyer anymore
She doesn't talk about it much and neither does Ben
which is fine because i'm sick of hearing her
Ben thinks you are the smartest of the three girls
i hate them both
i want to tell Her to shut up
to stop making everybody hate me for being smart
and him to shut up too
making it feel like The Three Girls are lepers
like i have to prove something
something i don't even know about
but i don't really want to be a musician either
when i think about being grown up
all i want is to run away to Weedsport
and if i can't be there then i'll be a secretary
to somebody important
and have my own apartment in Manhattan
maybe one of the empty studios that nobody uses
upstairs in Ben's building
anyway it doesn't seem like it's up to me to choose
being a dancer is *Out of the question*
not just because She says so
but because i am a coward about it
i can't do it like i used to
now i hate everybody looking at me
i even tried having courage like Priscilla

nothing stops her
even though her footwork and castanets aren't great
and her mother doesn't sew her costumes
she's never scared
her mother tells her she will be a star
wherever we perform Mrs. Lopez is in the audience cheering
so there goes dancing
mostly i like reading books and writing stories
and speaking other languages
but that won't make you a star in my family
in school the others are going away too
Elise wants to go to Brandeis to study politics
Amy wants Buffalo for English
and Laura Nigro is going to California to write songs
their parents let them decide for themselves
i guess i'm stuck
i'm not like other girls even after all this time
they seem to know so many more things than me
about boys about the world about regular things
like shaving your legs or shopping for clothes
maybe there will be a miracle
and She'll pick Syracuse so i can be near Weedsport
anyway it will be good to get out of here
away from wars and snooping and put downs
eat what i want
sleep till i want
pick out my own clothes
read and study and practice when i want
everything i want
except boys
She can still control that until i'm really eighteen
can't fake that in college
Restricted Permission is what it's called
She is requesting this because i am under age
younger than the other freshmen because I was skipped
i won't be allowed to leave the campus after dinner
but it doesn't matter to me

as long as i get to leave Queens
i can't figure out what to do about boys anyway
i like them a lot but things don't ever work out for me
Andrew doesn't talk to me much anymore
he's swamped he says
taking six regents classes
actually nobody spends time together now
it's like something invisible has changed us
we haven't been together since midterm half-day
we all went to the new James Bond movie Goldfinger
Elise Raymond Amy Paul Andrew and me
all of us having fun on the way down to the village
doing the Two Thousand Year Old Man routines
and cracking up on the subways making noise
talking about college interviews and auditions
Raymond telling us he heard Malcolm X speak
Elise talking about an NCCJ rally in Washington
it was nice in the movies Andrew sat next to me
his knee kept touching mine and he didn't pull it away
and twice he put his arm around my seat back
that's where it got confusing
i don't know if a girl is supposed to do something
or wait for the boy's next move
Elise says i should just kiss him
which is what women do in France
but i keep thinking it will end up like that party
she took me to
about a hundred kids in somebody's apartment
first there was talking and laughing going on
like everyone was best friends
everybody drinking wine and smoking pot
i don't mind the wine but trying pot scares me
people get so stupid after they smoke
and what if i wouldn't be able to stop
so after a while the necking starts
lights off and everybody groping somebody
even if they don't know you

some guy with bad breath puts his hand on my breast
i shove him off
and try to find Elise to see if she wants to leave
all i see are kissy-facing bodies
on every piece of furniture
and wall to wall on the floor
i make my way to the bathroom
there's people inside the tub
i walk into the kitchen
and right there on the dinette table
somebody's naked ass is bouncing up and down
on top of somebody else
my heart starts pounding like the Union Square days
all the way down the elevator
and on the subway ride home
all i think is i'm so glad Andrew was not there
i try not to think about what i saw in the kitchen
how ugly it sounded like animals grunting
i think how i want it to be special when it happens
not with some stoned smelly stranger
and not in front of a hundred people
then i wonder if there is something wrong with me
maybe because of what happened when i was little
in Colombia
i don't ever think about it
but maybe it's true
maybe it made me damaged goods or something
none of the other girls at that party got scared and left
i wonder if Andrew ever thinks about me that way
i know it wouldn't be ugly like that with him
sometimes when i'm in bed
i hold my pillow between my legs
and i think of Andrew holding me
but in the movies only his knee came close
when it was over we talked about the movie special effects
then we all said goodbye at the subway
i go to Mrs. deGrab's but my lesson is very strange

i can only think of Andrew
i can't even concentrate on scales
then there's a knock
Mrs. DeGrab goes to the door
and i am grateful for the interruption
i hear her give a little yell *Dear God no!*
she comes back in the room and closes the piano
Go straight home she says *Straight home*
her face is pale and her bottom lip is shaking
Something terrible has happened to our country
i never saw her cry before so i don't ask questions
on my way to the subway it gets stranger
there are cars stopped on Broadway
with doors open and radios on
in the train an old man is crying
people look so sad but nobody talks
it's like we're in a silent film all the way to Queens
maybe it's another scare like the Cuban Missle Crisis
and there will be a nuclear war
and i will die a virgin
i get home and She and Julia and Ben are in the den
it is a Friday
and the television is on in the middle of the day
but little Gabriel isn't watching Bullwinkle
or Soupy Sales like he's allowed to
She looks like she's been crying and says *Un catástrofe*
Someone has killed President Kennedy
everything is stopped
and for the next three days
we sit together
at the TV
no wars no practicing no homework
we watch his wife and little children say goodbye
all of us cry
even more than when Hamlet died

Sundays

I see, looking back now, that it was a bad idea to call you, out of the blue like that. It's true that we hadn't spoken in years, but you were the first person I wanted to tell. I sat in that plush suite of rooms Nino had arranged for me at the hotel, my mind turning over the images of meeting him just hours ago, my senses tagging every morsel of information they'd just been given. Even my heart was beating differently, not racing, but strong enough to get my attention. I was sure you'd be happy with my news. We had him back.

The thing is, you didn't hang up. You didn't interrupt while I told you how I walked up to him and introduced myself. You didn't ask what you ask now, why I searched or how I found him. You were quiet, and I took it to mean that you were interested. So I described him to you, as though you'd never met him yourself, because to me, you hadn't. I told you about the two hours we spent sitting on the couch in his office. He asked me questions—how old was I? Was I in good health? Married? Had I gone to college? And I was tongue-tied and giggly with my answers.

I'd memorized every detail. The sure, steady eyes, the mouth always a little pursed while he listened, the line of his nose, like mine. There was a warmth about him, his arm around my shoulders, his face close to mine, how he gently pushed my hair away from my eyes. I was comfortable with him, as though I'd known him a long time. Even the feel of his clothing set me at ease—the silky fabric of his suit, the French-cuffed shirt, the neutral tone of his tie and tie pin. He held my hands, turned them over, put them up against his and compared our long fingers. He said the same thing you'd told me, that I had my father's hands.

Still you asked no questions. So I went on. When I stumbled on what to call him, he gave a little shrug. "I'm your father. Call me anything you like. Curse me, beat me if you must. You're entitled. It doesn't change who we are."

He never asked how I'd found him, and when I began to tell him his eyes widened. "I assume you work for the FBI."

We both laughed, and it surprised us that we did it the same way because we'd never heard each other laugh before. I told him an old friend of his had helped me, Tony Tenerielli. All he said was that he was grateful. He didn't make excuses or offer explanations, and he didn't apologize. He just received me. In that brief amount of time, being his daughter was entirely contradictory to being your daughter. I felt like a school girl opening a present, wanted and accepted, all at once. Any questions I had didn't matter. I almost didn't want to speak. I was relishing what I had come for—to look into my father's face and be seen by him.

I'd brought some photos to show him. The one of you sitting out in the back yard of the Jackson Heights house in your white halter dress, hair up and tanned, and the only ones I had of Julia and Carmela, their high school pictures. He looked at each one for a long time, but he didn't say anything.

Was it the idea of the photographs that ignited you? I couldn't tell, it happened so quickly. You began hurling words at me deliberately, hurtfully, your accent worsening their sting as you mocked me.

"You are suffering a delusion, my dear girl. This man is an impostor. You have been fooled. Which is to be expected of you. Once again you are attaching yourself to some stranger for a morsel of attention."

You slowed down only to make pronouncements. "What you have is a case of misplaced loyalty. You have forgotten who you are. You have betrayed Ben, me, the whole family, again. You are not to be trusted. It is what happens, my dear, when you are ruled by your glands and not your brain."

I started to say something. Not to defend myself—I would have needed more time and a different kind of courage for that—but to make you see what I saw. Your logic didn't make sense, and I wanted it to, to stop your fury. I asked you to think about what you were saying. Why would anyone want to impersonate my father? But you hung up before I could finish.

I remember the jab of the dial tone in my ear. I looked down at the telephone with its pearl-white plastic panel of buttons. Just a few minutes ago, I'd been too happy to figure them out, so I'd rung the hotel operator to place the call. I extended my hand out to touch them, to call you back. But what would be the point? You wouldn't answer. You'd let the phone ring all day, all night. You wouldn't budge. I knew that well enough. I slammed the receiver down hard on its cradle, but missed it and struck the nightstand instead. I picked it up and slammed it again, hitting it hard. Hard enough so it would break, and you would break, over and over until the little plastic buttons weren't on the panel anymore, but on the carpet next to my face. I shrieked back at you across the continent for soiling everything good in my life, intentionally, always, knowing all the while I screamed that none of it would ever reach you.

I lay there a long time, spent, all the warmth I'd felt with Nino gone from my body, until an unfamiliar stubbornness took its place. I would have my father, with or without you.

After our first meeting my father called me every week. It surprised me, too. Sundays, between two and four in the afternoon, the phone would ring and I'd hear his warm "Hi sweetheart," or "*Tesoro mio,*" and after a few months, "It's Dad."

At first, they were brief but gratifying chats to see how I was, and we used the weather or latest news to fill the few minutes of connection. Later, I began to prepare myself. I made mental notes of things that happened during the previous week, to tell him. A car problem, a good movie I'd seen, a difficult case at work. I liked it, having this exclusive time with him, being important enough in his life that he'd regularly interrupt his work to speak with me.

If my daughters were home when he called, he'd ask to speak with them. They never knew what to say after the initial hello, but he'd engage them in conversation and make them laugh. Later, they'd tell me it was weird to have a grandfather they'd never met. Sometimes when he'd call, Jack was with me. They'd make small talk too, Jack truly happy that things had turned out so well.

The telephone visits always ended the same way. He'd ask me about my plans for the evening, what I'd be having for dinner, a new book or piece of music I was learning. He'd say something to make me laugh, and say he loved me. "*Ti voglio bene*. Until next week, then." It was easy to believe things would be like that for a long time.

All his calls came from his hotel office. Sundays were a work day for him, but from that first day I met him he'd made it clear why he didn't call from home. "I have a wife." When I asked if I would ever meet her, his answer was swift.

"No. Ask me anything else. This is one thing I cannot do. I am a coward. I cannot tell her this. It would be disastrous. Of course, I can't stop you in anything you need to do. I just ask you to consider the circumstances. This is an innocent person. A delicate situation. She's been very good to me for many years. She has no idea that I have children."

I'd never imagined such a scenario, that after unearthing my mother's secrets I now had to keep my father's. I felt trapped. I didn't like it, but I wasn't willing to lose him. Without considering it very long, I acquiesced. I told myself that his wife was none of my business. I never asked again to meet her, nor for his phone number, nor to be included in his life in any other way. It didn't occur to me, then, that I was entitled to.

I knew where he lived. The day before I met him I'd searched through Las Vegas public records and found his address. I drove there, to a house on a wide corner with a high stucco wall around its perimeter, juniper trees reaching over it. The wrought iron entry gate offered a glimpse of the front courtyard. A Chinese fan palm high above shaded the roof of the house—a Spanish tiled roof, like yours. I sat across the street in my rented car that afternoon. Part of me felt like a stalker, another part wanted to get the whole ordeal over with, quickly. Just walk up to the gate and ring his bell. Meet him here, in his home, in view of any family he might have.

I couldn't get myself to do it. I drove back to my hotel and called the only telephone number I'd been able to cross-reference for his street, someone named Anne Walken. I told her I believed my father was her neighbor, and that I had never known him. She was pleasant, and described him the way so many others had. Nino was a lovely man, as was his wife, Marnie. Nice people who keep mostly to themselves. They had no children, Anne said, and she knew my father worked at Caesar's. She apologized for not having more to tell me. I gave her my phone number and thanked her.

A few months later my father told me Anne had paid him a visit at work and told him about our conversation. He wasn't completely surprised. I'd told him from the beginning that one of his neighbors had my phone number. Still, I thought her visit would have upset him. But it didn't. In some ways, he said, it was a relief.

I went back to see him several times. They were short trips, two or three days, and each was a variation on the first. I'd meet him in his office. He'd be elated to see me. He'd have a suite of rooms reserved and an itinerary of activities for me to enjoy—a day at the hotel's beauty spa, a trip to Hoover Dam, a ticket to a show. I refused them. All I wanted was to spend time with him, and he indulged me. He'd clear his schedule for a block of hours to sit with me at one of the hotel's restaurants, where he'd arrange for a quiet table and especially prepared meals. He'd speak directly to the chef—an *osso bucco* cooked in rosemary and white wine, or a *bolognese* sauce that was close to Nonna's flavoring—and had me write down the recipes, so I could make them when I got home. The only distraction was the beeper he wore on his belt that signaled the occasional urgent call from his office. He would attend to it quickly and return.

Our early conversations were about your life together. I had expected him to tell me your relationship had been awful. So it surprised me that he spoke kindly, and called you by your nickname.

"All the time Cuchi and I were married I believed things were good. We got along well. The normal things between man and wife. Nothing terrible. Certainly nothing irreparable. I never dreamed she would want a divorce. Not after those years in Colombia. They were wonderful. We were going to go back there. It was paradise. The easiest place in the world to live in. I felt like I'd been dropped into a Cole Porter musical. Family, friends, good work. We knew everybody, from the peasants to the gentry. We went to the best places. Traveled through that whole marvelous country. We had a good life."

I was absorbed in his stories, especially how much he liked Colombia, so different from anything you'd ever told me. He talked about the war and how it changed everything, separating you from one another before you'd been able to get settled, and when it was over he wasn't prepared for what he'd found at home.

"Cuchi had it in her head that I was intending to leave her in Colombia and not return. She was so wrong. What happened to us had nothing to do with my children or my wife. Nothing. It was never a question of being a husband or a father. I loved that. I loved my girls. It was about the mess I made of everything, especially handling money. I was a complete failure. Everything I touched failed. Eventually Cuchi had me served with divorce papers. I never really believed she would go through with it because we kept seeing each other, even during the legal procedures. And we were expecting you. I thought she would want to reconcile once you were born. I delayed everything. I intentionally didn't show up in court, just to have it adjourned. But I was wrong. She did finalize it. She was going to get married again. To a dentist she was seeing. You know, it's sort of funny, whenever she saw me she reminded me to take care of my teeth."

He seemed to need to tell me these things as much as I needed to hear him. But I was more interested in other events. Why had he left New York the way he had? Where had he been all that time? He never balked at my questions.

"I kept trying to make things right. I'd finally found a position with a good firm uptown. But there was an incident one afternoon with Cuchi coming up to the office demanding the alimony money. No one wanted an attorney with sloppy personal problems. Especially a divorced man, and Italian to boot. They said it reflected poorly on the firm. They let me go. I was thirty-four. A man with no position, no money, lost his wife, his family. And I was living with my mother. Things got pretty bad. I was even put in jail, overnight. Another surprise. I hadn't been able to pay alimony for a few weeks. They had that then, alimony jail. It was horrible.

"Only my brother Paolo knew how bad things had gotten. When he heard the Ronca people were selling the café downstairs, he gave me the money to buy it. But I was short three thousand dollars. By pure coincidence your Uncle Mickey was in town—he always stopped by to see me, even after the divorce—and he suggested I ask your mother for the rest. He said he'd get her to give it to me. And he did. I never believed she'd do it. She had me sign a promissory note, notarized, with interest. She even went down there with me to pay the Ronca people.

"I got the café running. I learned everything there was to know about baking. We were doing well. We had a couple of very successful months. I began to pay your mother back. I even bought her a piano—she always wanted one—and a washing machine and television set. I had them sent to the apartment, on her birthday.

"But after a few months everything turned. My bakers began to leave. First the most experienced one, then the others. I didn't know what the devil was going on. I found out it was because of a rival down the street. Another café, past Grand street, relatives of Ronca. My bakers had been with Ronca for years. They were loyal to him, not to me. Within days I had only one baker, the worst of the lot. Customers began to stay away too. Only one or two a day. I couldn't pay the baker. Or the rent, or the suppliers. I started to borrow. No, not from loan sharks. Worse. From friends, acquaintances. I kept saying to myself, if I make it to Christmas, I'll be alright. And those last few days of the year business did pick up. We had holiday tourists. I worked day and night. Baking, serving, cleaning. I made it through the week. I had promised to pay everything by the first of the year. I didn't have it all, but I had something.

"Then, New Year's Eve, I got more bad news. I was just locking up the Café. It was so cold that night. I had planned to go uptown to the Square, to the apartment, to see Cuchi and all of you. My cousin Ray came in looking scared to death, and said some people were looking for me. Some rich girl said I'd burned her with a cigarette. My cousin had known me all my life. He knew better than to believe such a thing. The woman was a singer I knew, from a small jazz club on the west side, the Show Spot, which was run by some shady people. She was upset that I'd stopped seeing her a few months before. I had to, because I was broke, but I couldn't tell her that. She made up this story. I never found out why. All of it piled up together. That was the final straw. I didn't know what to do. I stood there in the dark, exhausted. And it was so cold. I couldn't go to my brother with this. I was already ashamed of my life. My cousin Ray said I should hide for a while, until it died down. I remember how he insisted. Go now. Take my coat. He'd just been given the coat for Christmas. It was cashmere. I never forgot that. There wasn't enough time for me to go upstairs to get my own coat, or my wallet. He gave me some money. I went to the train station, with ninety-three dollars in my pocket, and left town.

"I didn't see it then. It would have been easier to face that crisis, the despair, than to do what I did. In another year, it would have been resolved. I would have made it. I wanted to make it. But I panicked. To do what I did was despicable. The most horrible decision I ever made in my life. Not only for what I left behind and all the people I hurt. But for the life I had afterwards. Nobody likes a drifter. You understand? That's what I became. From a professional man to a drifter."

He went on to tell me that for over a year he drifted across the country doing any work he could get. In Los Angeles he found steady work in a restaurant, worked his way up to chef and learned the business. He met

Marnie, and they tried their hand at their own restaurant. But they didn't do well.

"This time I didn't wait. I sold. And that was my last attempt at being an entrepreneur. We came to Las Vegas and began to work for the hotels. That was twenty-five years ago. I married Marnie. Bought a home. I settled into a simple life, a routine. I work. I go home. I swim in my pool every morning, I read, listen to music. My big enjoyment is cooking. I have a public side, yes, what you see here. But I've never cared for parties or crowds of people. All my life—your mother knew this about me—I've preferred to live my life simply. I'm with Marnie because she is a wonderful companion. I don't go inside any other casino or accept invitations from anyone. It doesn't attract me. I prefer to live my life privately.

"In the beginning I nearly died of sadness. I had no one to talk to. I couldn't get acquainted with anyone. I always thought someone would come to confront me about the business debts or maybe Cuchi would find me. But that didn't happen. Of course I wanted to go back, but how? What would I say? How would I make an entrance? Not an entrance like you're thinking now because of how you see me here. Not the kind of entrance with a band and a welcome banner like a war hero. How would I go back without a penny in my pocket? Like a beggar? That's how I left, as a beggar. No one wants a poor man. I left disaster back there. I kept saying, I'll make a little money here and one day I'll go back and make things right. When I finally did have enough money, too much time had passed. I was too ashamed. If I had only succeeded at something—well maybe your mother would have divorced me anyhow—but at least I would have stayed in New York. I would have seen all three of you grow up.

"I'm not heartless. I was a fool, certainly, but not a villain. Whenever I could, I called Paolo to find out how things were. I asked him to look in on you. He took you to the circus. He bought you gifts. I knew you went to visit Nonna. Then you stopped. You moved to Long Island. I lost touch. I would think, one of my daughters will show up. But eventually I gave up hope of that, too. Then one day, there you were."

Nino took my hand, but I didn't know how to respond to what he was saying. He was my father, and his story had shaped my life and my family's life. But there was more to him than his story. I was the only person hearing all of it. His wife, at least, should know. It felt wrong. This wasn't the way I wanted to have a father, being the *other woman* in his life.

I thought of Ben and how often I'd stood at the side of his dental chair dressed in a that nurse's uniform, working hard to prove myself to him, keeping quiet while he matter-of-factly denied me as his daughter. "No. She's the nurse." There I was, a grown woman, being a secret daughter all over again.

I didn't let my doubts sink in. It would be later, years after, that I would be able to acknowledge the flurries in my stomach and the quiver of my legs for what they were—alarms going off to alert me to the ugly side of my father. He was a man who could lie effortlessly and ask his child to cover for him, coldblooded and unscrupulous, and not think twice. His whole perspective on things—his marriage to you, his desertion of his family and a business, his need for a private life because he had something to hide, the façade he maintained with his wife even as he sat and spoke intimately with me—was skewed. My father could admit his mistakes and even ask for forgiveness. But in all our talks he never acknowledged the toll his actions had taken on anyone, least of all his children.

I should have spoken. I should have said I felt cheated, swindled, robbed. I should have demanded some sort of compensation, retribution, for the decades of deception. At least I should have made a scene, called his wife, hurt him back. Or I should have done what he'd done. Left him, without a word. But I'd see his beaming smile, he'd kiss my head and call me *Tesoro,* and I'd call him Dad. I did what I'd done all my life, pushed it all aside, let myself lean into his embrace, and indulge in being his daughter, whatever the cost. To have my father in my life I would have to ignore the nagging feeling that it was all contrived, that our relationship would not exist if I hadn't presented myself to him.

He wanted to see you. He wanted to see my sisters. "If you can arrange for the whole family to meet, I'll fly back east."

So I told him about us, how you hadn't spoken to me in years, how angry you'd become when I called to tell you I'd found him. He offered to try to fix things. "I'll call, then. Give me your mother's number."

Instead, I let him record a message for you, in case you'd ever want to hear it: "Eva. This is Nino. As hard and difficult as it is to believe, I'm alive and well. I'm sitting here with our beautiful girl. I tell you it was one of the happiest days of my life when I saw Veronica. Believe me, not that I always told you the truth, I'd like to speak with you. If you allow it, I can call you. You can hang up on me if you like. At least say hello. And, if Julia or Carmela are in the house with you, tell them I'd like to speak with them also. God bless you all."

On one visit I brought my girls. He was thrilled, escorting them arm-in-arm through the hotel. It was odd, but he told everyone who spoke to him that they were *mie nipote*, his granddaughters. When Jackie said she felt like a mafia princess, he doubled over in laughter.

"For whatever I'm entitled to say as an absent grandfather, I must tell you that the girls are wonderful. I expected typical ill-mannered, difficult teenagers. But your girls don't match any young people I've seen. They are smart, talented, refined. And funny. When I look at the world today, I know the young people have a very hard time. You raised two good people. I am proud of you.

When we gathered in his office to say goodbye, he was different. He fumbled for his glasses, gave repeated instructions to bell hops about our luggage. He took the girls' hands and kissed them.

"Forgive me. I have been a terrible father to your mother. I regret deeply that I didn't get to know her sooner, and both of you. That is a terrible loss."

Then he turned to me and I could see he was crying.

"Be very careful. They are so beautiful. Terrible things can happen to girls."

A family friend is coming
He will be taking your sister out tonight
that's what She tells me just as i walk in from work
and before i can get my shoes off She gets me
He is meant for Julia but you will chaperone
it doesn't matter to Her if i'm dead tired
or if i hate the thought of being a third wheel again
or if i've never even heard of this Family Friend
it's all so phony
our family doesn't have many friends
and chaperoning my older sister is ridiculous
anyway Julia isn't even home yet
and i have studying to do for Regents exams
but of course i can't say no not to Her
She is always plotting something
i hear Her on the telephone trying to convince Ben
he doesn't like the Family Friend idea for Julia either
but that doesn't stop Her
I know my daughter
they talk for a long time they way they do late at night
when Ben sits at the table and She scrubs Her pots
he listens to Her complaints about ungrateful children
and he tells about new drugs that will calm Her nerves
Ben doesn't get it yet
it's useless to talk to Her
no matter what he says She has the same answer
I am not an americana
I don't believe in spoiling children
they go on and on every night
She wears out Brillo pads
while he reads out loud to her from some article
or the latest book he is reading about disciplining kids
then he gives Her a few pills
like She's his patient and he can reason with Her
he's trying the same thing now on the telephone
but She will not change Her mind
Julia must forget that riff raff boy from Brooklyn

She repeats it to Ben all over again
Neal has nothing to offer
he comes from the projects
no daughter of Hers will marry into an inferior class
not after all the sacrifices She has made
it's really pathetic
She sounds like Desi Arnaz and looks like Lucy
except nobody's laughing
She still tries to convince Ben that it's a good idea
Julia will forget about Neal
after she experiences an evening with a grown man
An educated man well positioned in society
The upper class she can never experience here
She seems so sure of Herself like She can't be wrong
She hangs up and explains it to me
This gentleman lives in New York now
He is familiar with old-fashioned customs
And proper courting
i think all of it is crazy
even if it is only for one evening
and he will show Julia the New York nightlife
dinner dancing a show
and good conversation with a gentleman
it is the kind of evening She used to have
when She was young in boarding school
nothing Julia could ever experience
not with that riff-raff boy
i play with baby Gabriel and wonder about Julia
i wonder if she will really forget about Neal tonight
or if she'll be strong enough to resist Her schemes
if it were me i wouldn't care i'd never give up
not if i had a boyfriend
there will be a war for sure when Julia gets home
She orders me to *Go upstairs and put on a dress*
Take one from your sister's closet
i know She means the ones Carmela left behind
ugly homemade dresses she hated and so do i

i don't want to have anything to do with them
they remind me of how much Carmela suffered
no matter what she put on or how pretty she looked
She would call her *flacuchenta* or *narizona*
it's true Carmela is skinny
and her nose used to be enormous
but even after it was fixed She still called her names
She has a name for each of us
Julia is *antipática* because she talks loud like Italians
mine is *bizca* to mock my lazy left eye
i really hate Her when i hear those names
i think Carmela is beautiful in anything
with legs that go on forever
Julia has the prettiest coloring so fair
and her little nose that has no bumps at all
i got stuck with this dark hair
and black eyes that don't work without glasses
and these braces on my teeth
but it isn't my fault
that i'm the only dark one
She says i get my coloring from *La Abuela*
it makes my skin crawl
i don't want to be anything like that woman
that's the reason Julia hates me
because i'm dark
when Julia's really mad she calls me names too
stinking indian nigger
i can't see why she has to be so cruel
so what if i'm different from all of them
that doesn't make me bad
i try my best to have courage
last week i asked permission to have my hair cut
even after She wouldn't answer me
i asked again but still no answer
so i went ahead and did it at Macy's beauty parlor
the first female in the family to ever have short hair
if it weren't for Ben She would have killed me

he told Her not to hit me
to find another way to punish me
when he finished talking to Her he came to me
Your Mother will forgive you
once she's used to it
but he was wrong
She just looked me up and down like i was a mannequin
Ordinaria She said and walked away
next day i hear Her calling Mariquita
My daughter will not go she has been disobedient
Mariquita tries to talk her out of it
but it doesn't do any good
it was supposed to be my first paid dancing job
all summer on a cruise ship back and forth
dancing flamenco between New York and Spain
but She hangs up and looks at me and says
Keep it up and there will be no college either
i was really mad and cried into my pillow really hard
i figured i couldn't have done it anyway
me with my motion sickness on a boat no way
it's alright now
i stopped thinking about it and just look at my hair
it's short and cute and i feel like a regular girl
i pick out my black dress for Orchestra Concert
with rhinestones around the neckline
and i go over my plan again
if She doesn't send me to college i'll move out
just like Carmela did
i figure i can make sixty dollars a week typing
and live on English muffin pizzas
the recipe is on the back of the package
all i'd need would be an eight pack of muffins a week
one can of tomato sauce
one package of mozzarella cheese
and one piece of fruit a day and lots of water
that will be about ten dollars
thirty dollars for rent and five for carfare

i will have money to save
probably i could move in with Carmela at first
until i get a job
it's a good plan
i think about it when i'm walking to the subways
and when i have time to kill before dance class
i stop at the Hit Parade record store on Broadway
it's always crowded
so nobody minds if you don't buy anything
they play the latest top ten hits through a microphone
i wait to hear Bobby Darin sing Mack the Knife
and i think about my plan
it's a good plan i'm sure Ben would say so
She is vacuuming the living room now
i finish getting dressed and go downstairs
the place looks like House Beautiful
She has put out the good sofa cushions
all the lamps are on and She's changed the tablecloth
this friend must be from Hollywood or something
when she looks at me She says *Change Your Shoes*
Red Is Immoral And Sends The Wrong Message
they are Carmela's high heels
i stuffed them with toilet paper so they'd fit me
now i have to change into my low black plain ones
and wait for the end of Her war with Julia
they are upstairs screaming and slamming doors
i escape the noise and practice instead
next month will be my senior recital
it means playing nine or ten pieces by memory
Mrs. deGrab says she will invite all her students
she is sure i will play very well but i'm not so sure
it's more likely that i will go blank while i'm playing
so i pretend there is an audience in the living room
i ask little Isabella to sit and listen
while i play the Bach French Suite
she likes it and claps her little hands hard
i go on with the Scarlatti sonatas

it sounds like the war is over so i play the Ravel
little Isabella claps again
she wants me to practice bowing
we do it together and giggle
but it's her bedtime and i am alone downstairs
for a long time i play my favorite Chopin nocturnes
i never worry about playing this music
it just comes to me
it is as if Chopin and i had been friends once
and i am far away from this place
somewhere in Paris maybe
sitting in a large room with beautiful windows
and plants and a piano just for me
the doorbell rings
She yells down that i should get it
there is a man standing there in a suit and tie
Hello I am Michél
he has eyes like the perfect sky
on a Weedsport afternoon
i say hello too and apologize
for the rest of my family not being ready
Was that you playing he asks *Please go on*
Michél sits where little Isabella sat
and i play Chopin for him
he listens he watches me he asks me about the music
i want to tell him
it is written by a young man who had great sorrow
and he made his suffering sing
all i can do is smile
into the pools of blue that watch
like they have been waiting all day to meet me

11

nobody knows except Carmela
she found out by accident
but i know she will keep my secret
she caught on this afternoon at my senior recital
because of the way Michél looked at me
all the while i was playing
i didn't even know he would be there
or that Carmela would be there either
Mrs. deGrab said friends and family
i didn't bother asking anyone
Amy and Elise probably couldn't come anyway
the family part was up to Her
it was all a big surprise
especially how the place was set up
all the pocket doors opened and rows of chairs
so many faces i didn't know
even a program printed up with my name on top
the second piano had a vase with tiny yellow roses
it was embarrassing
that Mrs. deGrab did all those things just for me
when i started to play i thought of Ben listening
he likes the Scarlatti sonatas
i wanted to be a good example for the little ones
but during the applause i realize they aren't even there
they're going to be late as usual
i begin the Bach Sarabande and i see Michél
sitting across the room on the loveseat
legs crossed arms folded eyes nonstop almost smiling
i played my program just for him and Mrs. deGrab
i didn't care about anyone else i wasn't nervous at all
it was during intermission that i noticed Carmela
way in the back seats near Mrs. deGrab's bathroom
just as She and Ben arrived
they missed the whole first half of my recital
and now they're making a scene
Carmela and Her crying hugging making up
Ben getting the kids seated

i hide in the bathroom
Julia comes in and says Mrs. deGrab planned it
neither one knew the other would be there
now they are making peace
at my piano recital
i wish they would both go away
the second half of my program is for Michél only
i play easily especially the Chopin nocturnes
when i take my bows i see little Isabella bowing too
she is clapping loud like we practiced
Mrs. deGrab has kept the best surprise for last
she asks everyone downstairs
where i have never been
it is lovely
a big sunny kitchen opened onto a garden
and a long dining table covered with food
it is a reception
in my honor
little finger sandwiches and melon balls
tiny cakes called Petite Feurs
all kinds of cheeses and stemmed wine glasses
in the center of the table more tiny yellow roses
Mrs. deGrab comes to me and smiles
i have played my repertoire beautifully she says
i should be very proud of what i have accomplished
she introduces me to the other students and teachers
her husband is there too
he enjoyed the way i played the Bach very much
over his voice i can hear Her explaining
how difficult it was for Ben to find parking
Mrs. deGrab changes the subject
and asks Her who Michél is
i wonder how she knows his name
She is doing that phony laugh
explaining her Julia scheme
how She'd hoped Michél would find her attractive
she laughs more and says She hasn't given up on it yet

i am very mad
i could scream
Mrs. deGrab turns to look right at me
i want to tell her that Julia couldn't care less
even on that first night when i chaperoned
the whole time in his car and at the Copacabana
all Julia did was sit there with her arms crossed
it was me he danced with
me he talked to all evening
me he enjoyed being with
it's me who knows all about him
how he loves to sculpt more than anything
how he came from Paris to Cartagena then New York
he stayed because he knows his destiny is here
i want to scream to Mrs. deGrab not to listen to Her
but i don't have to
Michél has come to me with a plate of food
he is telling me how lovely i look
and how well i have made the piano sing
he would like to take the whole family out to dinner
i laugh and tell him he's making a terrible mistake
he looks confused and we both laugh
i feel dizzy with liking him liking me
no one is looking not even Julia who already left
She is talking with Carmela about her job
Ben is arranging lessons for the little ones
later they turn down Michél's invitation
i am glad because i will have him to myself
he has given me his card
hoping we could spend an afternoon together
visit a museum or walk in Central Park
maybe a lazy lunch in a French restaurant
i do not tell him about Her rules
or how much i want to break them
i put his card in my pocket and let him kiss my hands
when everyone has gone Mrs. deGrab comes to me
she is sure i will do very well in college

we hug for the first time and she doesn't let go first
it makes me think how much i will miss her
Mrs. deGrab tells me
i must take the tiny yellow roses home
because she can see how happy i feel
with the gentleman who sent them

Tormenta

The clock on my nightstand says two thirty-three in the morning when the phone rings. "Ronnie!" my mother is whispering into the receiver. "*¡Están aquí!* They are here! They are coming in!" This is her third call tonight. She doesn't remember the others—have I seen her slippers, do I know where Julia is—each more anxious than the one before. Now she is desperate. "*Por favor mi'ja, ven.* Come help me."

I am at her house in fifteen minutes. Despite the single digit temperature outside, the door is ajar. It looks like every light in house is on, competing with the holiday decorations of the other houses on the street. My mother is at the top of the center hall steps. She is in her frayed nightgown, barefoot, one hand on the railing, the other clutched to her chest. Her hair is loose and tangled. As soon as she sees me she hurries down the steps to me. "Ronnie!" I open my arms to receive her and feel something hard pressing against me. "What do you have there, Mom?" She reaches into her nightgown and pulls out a stick, about a foot and a half long with a jagged-edge on one end, probably broken off a broom.

"I am going to find them!" She is loud now, nearly wailing. "*Están escondidos.* They cannot hide from me!"

In a second my sister appears behind my mother. "Drop it! Lunatic!" she yells. Julia's face is pale, her eyes small. My mother swerves toward her. I grab the stick out of my mother's hand and slide it along the floor toward the dining room. Julia circles around our mother to my side of the hall. She is in a tee shirt and long johns, also barefoot, and as panicked as my mother.

Her hands are at her side, in fists. My mother's head is down, clutching her midriff, bent before her daughters.

"Please! There are men here! Get them out!" She pulls at her hair. Julia moves closer, directly behind me now.

"She's a fucking maniac!" This isn't Julia's usual daunting yell meant to overpower an opponent, but a frantic supplication. I don't know my sister like this. I want to help her. I want to help my mother. Who first? How? I am caught between them, heart racing. I make an effort to speak as steadily, as neutrally as I can.

"Julia, she's hallucinating."

"I don't give a crap! It's three in the morning. She's been at this for hours!"

"¡*Ayúdame!* They are upstairs. Look, Ronnie." My mother is turned around toward the stairs. I step closer.

"I am helping you, Mom. Right now. I've come here to help you."

"Yeah? You're going to help her?" Julia's voice cracks behind me and she begins to cough. She keeps talking, struggling through the spasms. "She's putting on a show. Don't you see? She's a fruit cake!"

I turn to my sister and reach toward her. "Julia, do you need help?"

"Leave me alone!"

"¡ *Ahí van*! Look at them!" My mother points toward her bedroom. She is shaking.

"What men? What the hell is she saying? There aren't any men here! Stop this act!"

Now I want Julia to shut up. I want her to be my big sister, lead the way, not fight me.

"This isn't acting." I've raised my voice. I'm scolding her over my shoulder. I've forgotten that my mother's doctor predicted Julia would vehemently deny this disease, precisely because she's lived with my mother all her life, because the loss would be different for her than for me. I don't care. I scold her again. "Can't you see Mom is suffering?"

"Suffering? I'm the one that's suffering!"

I coil around to look at my sister. She is breathing through her mouth. She has released her fists, her hands fallen alongside her body. Without her high heels, she seems very small. She looks haggard. Only her broad shoulders contain strength. She is a motionless girl in oversized shoulder pads. I look away. I want to hide, not let her know I've seen her vulnerability.

"*Rápido!* They are coming in the windows!" My mother crouches to the floor. I go to her. She sees me and jumps to her feet. She moves to the stairs again, pointing up. "*Ahí! En el cuarto de Isabella!*"

Julia slaps her thighs, the way I do when I feel beaten, and cries, "When is this crap going to end?"

Again I modulate my voice, this time to calm myself. I must help these women. They are my women, the only family other than my children that I have left. "Julia, call an ambulance."

"No! That will only make her worse."

"All right. Call her doctor."

"At this hour? What is he going to do to help?"

My mother grabs my shirt and pulls me with her as she starts to climb the stairs. I don't resist. I call down to my sister who stands at the bottom of the stairs. "These men are real to her, Julia."

"Hallucinations my foot! You're just indulging her."

"*¡Ahí van!*"

"Where, Mom? Show me."

"*Aquí.*" My mother is whispering again, tiptoeing into the room that used to be Isabella's, with me in tow. The twin beds are overturned, both mattresses and box springs flung over the sides of the beds. The closet door is open. Girl's clothing is strewn on the floor, skirts, slacks, dresses, neutral-colored and unadorned. A few of the hems are visible, basted with satin ribbon and double folds, the mark of my mother's sewing. I think of my little sister living here in this room two decades ago, a teenager wearing reconstructed hand-me-downs, before she moved to the Midwest, before I was allowed to enter this house. I put my arm around my mother's shoulder and lead her, still attached to my shirt, around the mattress pile to the open closet.

"See, Mom. Nothing. No one. They're not here anymore. The men have gone."

She seems briefly satisfied, then turns and pulls me out into the corridor. We cross the hall and enter Gabriel's room, still intact. She lets go of me and moves quickly to the bed and, in one swift and astonishing motion, turns the box spring and mattress over the side. She stands for a few seconds looking through the empty bed frame at the carpet. She moves to the chest of drawers. A large telescope sits on top. She's told me before that it was Gabriel's favorite toy; he spent hours looking out into the sky through it. She pulls out one drawer from the dresser and empties it on the floor. She does the same with the others. The telescope doesn't budge. She goes to the closet and reaches above her head to pull down the clothing hung there. Her eyes are wide open, her jaw clenched. She isn't saying anything. She is all motion, pulling, yanking, throwing. I repeat myself, slowly, loud enough for her to listen. "See, Mom, they're not here anymore. No men. They've gone away."

I realize I've lost track of Julia. I don't see her or hear her. I don't dare turn away. I call out as loudly as I can without startling my mother. "Julia?"

"Leave me alone!" It sounds like she's in Isabella's room. Maybe she's cleaning up. My mother pulls us out of Gabriel's room. She heads down the hall, her chest heaving, but I don't try to stop her. I recognize my own, old panic. The kind I felt for her once—so did Julia, we all did—when we waited for her to turn the key in the door, not knowing what mood she'd be in when she walked in. But this is more than panic. There's no way I can stop her unless I overpower her physically, and I won't do that. Julia hasn't even tried that. And Julia will never call an ambulance. My mother will have to exhaust her terror. All I can do is interrupt it, make sure she doesn't hurt herself.

Julia reappears. We're in the room Ben used as a study when he was alive. Pictures of him with Isabella and Gabriel line the wall over his desk. The scene repeats itself: my mother overturns the sofa cushions, spills drawers, empties the closet, Julia yells, I offer reassurances. When she's done, my mother heads for her own bedroom. I notice she's walking slower. She's getting tired. At the end of the hall, she stops abruptly and looks around. She sees the upholstered chair outside her bedroom and slumps into it, hands on her lap, head down. I stand near and watch her until her chest stops heaving. I notice her hairline is moist from sweat. I kneel on the floor beside her and carefully take her hand. It is cool, a good sign. Her body is regulating itself. She could be anyone now, a woman in a waiting room, or on a bus, weary, disappointed, lost. Julia's footsteps pound her retreat up to her bedroom in the attic. I wait with my mother. I stroke her hair. Silence settles in by degrees, until the house is mute, no clocks tick, nothing creaks, not even the refrigerator purrs.

"Mom, would you like a glass of water?"

She doesn't look up. "No, thank you *mi'ja*."

"Can you get up? Let's go into your room. It's nearly your bedtime." I glance at my watch. It's four thirty. She can still get some sleep in before sunrise. Maybe we all can.

I help her to her feet. She lets out a small groan and moves gingerly again, unsteady. It is cold in her room, colder than the rest of the house, but I am relieved to see that her bed is undamaged, drawers are in their place, and the closets are closed. I lead her to her bed and help her in. I go to her bathroom and get her a glass of water. She drinks it eagerly. "*Tengo sed.*" I bring more water to quench her thirst. When she is finished I pull the covers up and sit next to her. She is calm. She smiles. I am exhausted.

"Ronnie," she speaks tenderly.

"Yes, Mom."

"What are you doing here?"

I take a breath. "I came for a visit. Now it's late. It's time to get to sleep."

"*¿Y Julia?*"

"She's upstairs in her room."

"Ronnie."

"What, Mom?"

She makes a circle at her temple with one arthritic finger. "I think Julia has lost her mind."

"How so?" I hear my absurd question and ready myself for the answer.

"She brings men in here. *No le digas.* If she knows I told you that, she will be very angry."

"All right, Mom. I won't tell her." I should let it go at that, but she is so calm, and I am curious about this newest apparition. "When did this happen?"

"*De noche.* Every night, she gets naked and brings men in here."

"Here, where?"

"*Aquí.*" She points to the foot of her bed. "Right here."

"Here, on this bed? And where are you when this happens?"

"Right here where you see me. I do not want to look at such things." She puts one hand up to shield her face and turns away. "I close my eyes. But I hear them. Terrible things." She looks back at me and whispers. "Sex."

"Mom, do you know who these men are? How many are there?"

She shrugs her shoulders. She shows me four fingers of her hand.

"Do they speak to you? Do they try to hurt you?"

She shakes her head "No. They do not look at me. Only at Julia."

"Did this happen tonight?"

"Yes. Earlier, before you arrived, they came here. She brings them in."

"When this goes on, does Julia say anything?"

"No. She only laughs, *la desgraciada*. She has no shame. All that Catholic school and this is what she does. Do not let her fool you. *Doble cara*. She is one way during the day and another at night."

I've had enough. I need to change the subject. I look around the room. On the nightstand beside her radio is a small blue book. I turn it over to see its title, *La Santa Biblia*. I am surprised. I wouldn't have expected my mother to keep a Bible close by. I pick it up and show it to her.

"Mom, is this yours?"

"*¿Qué es?*"

"The Holy Bible. In Spanish."

"*Sí*."

"Do you read it?" I know she doesn't. The disease took away her ability to read months ago.

"Sometimes."

I go with my impulse. "Could we read a little of it together?"

"I did not know you were religious, Ronnie. Are you planning to become a nun?"

I laugh, and I can't believe I can actually laugh again. "No, not at all. I thought it would be interesting to hear the Bible in Spanish. I've never read it in Spanish."

"I read the Bible every day in boarding school. It was very comforting."

"Let's see." I thumb through the little book. "What is your favorite part?"

"*Los salmos*."

"Any psalm in particular?"

"All of them."

"All right, then." I open to the first psalm I find. I begin to read out loud. "*Salmo 41. Salmo de Gabriel. Bienaventurado el que piensa en el pobre: En el día malo lo librará Jehová...*" I do a mental simultaneous translation: Psalm 41. Psalm of Gabriel. Blessed is he that considereth the poor: the Lord will deliver him in time of trouble...

My mother interrupts. "*El Señor lo preservará, y lo mantendrá vivo, y el será bendecido sobre la tierra, y no será entregado a la voluntad de sus enemigos.*" The Lord will preserve him and keep him alive, and he shall be blessed upon the earth, and he will not be delivered unto the will of his enemies.

I flip through the pages to find another psalm. "*Salmo 59. Líbrame de mis enemigos, o Dios mío...*" Deliver me from my enemies, O Lord.

I stop, to see if she continues. She does. *"...Ponme en salvo de los que contra mí se levantan."* Defend me from those that rise up against me.

"Mom, do you know all the psalms by memory?

She shrugs.

"Which psalm did you pray most?"

"The twenty-third. The most popular one."

"Say it for me Mom."

"El señor es mi pastor. Nada me faltará. En lugares de delicados pastos me hará descansar..."

I listen to my mother pray. I watch her lips construct the words she has secretly depended on all her life for comfort and I have never heard her say before. Her hands are folded over her chest. Her placid face belongs to someone else, not the tormented woman of half an hour ago. I let myself know this woman who is here now, for these few minutes. She is my mother, too.

When she is finished, I kiss her forehead and tell her I am leaving.

"Mi'ja," she says, softly. "Be careful. *Que La Virgen te acompañe."*

I accept my mother's blessing and leave her. Before I go, I listen at the bottom of the attic stairs. There is no sound from Julia's room. I walk into each of the other bedrooms and turn out the lights.

Ben has come up with another new idea
Family Outing Day
his friend Mister Cantor got him into it
ever since they've been going to the Astro Gastros
pretty awful if you ask me
a bunch of grown-ups hanging around
they bring food and most of it tastes worse than Hers
then they take turns showing off
singing old songs or reciting poems or telling a story
all the kids have to perform too
the first time we went She made me dance Sevillanas
it was very embarrassing
people touching the ruffles on my costume
and talking right through my dance
asking stupid questions about my castanets
i told Her i'd rather play the piano
at least people keep quiet and listen
some other kids dance and sing stuff they've made up
they aren't shy at all and everybody claps for them
people tell them how wonderfully talented they are
even though they aren't
it isn't so bad when they do it at the Cantor's house
Mr. Cantor and Ben are friends since childhood
back during the Depression
when they did homework and studied by candlelight
now Ben is a dentist and Sidney is a lawyer
they make sure to tell us each time they are together
that they are bosom buddies
when it's Mister Cantor's turn we prepare ourselves
he sings Old Man River
but it's so flat it hurts your ears and everyone scowls
still they clap for him and say *Wonderful Wonderful*
his wife is the kindest woman in the world
always has a long hug for each of us
she is tall and slender and seems so happy
doesn't really match with Mister Cantor
her hands are long and soft and graceful

no matter what goes wrong Gertrude never gets mad
people spill things on her rug
once even broke a chair in two
she just said *Don't make yourself sick over it dear*
sometimes Gertrude jokes with us
that if we ever want to run away
she'd love to have girls
it's because she only has two sons
they are teenagers and nice just like their mother
while the grownups talk the boys teach us games
Concentration Scrabble Charades
at first it felt stupid
because we didn't know any of the games
but the boys never make fun of us
if we make mistakes or forget the rules
they still want to play another game
even Julia has fun and says she'd run away anytime
i wish we could all run away to the Cantor house
but we'd have to tell them what was really going on
and they'd never believe us anyway
because when we are with the Cantors
everything is good
Ben and Her sing together *La Paloma*
Begin the Beguine too and Smoke Gets In Your Eyes
then Ben's solo I'll Be Seeing You
and She has this smile on her face
looking at him like She adores him
She really looks pretty with Her short hair
She clipped it all off herself one day last week
to look more American for her in-laws
just left her long blonde braid lying on her dresser
like it was dead
everybody thinks we are one big happy family
that's how we look today
all of us piled into Ben's new Rambler station wagon
a Family Outing to the World's Fair
as if we do this every Sunday

as if She hadn't had a big war with Julia
just to make her come with us
the only one missing is Carmela
but the worst possible someone is here instead
La Abuela
here on a visit with Uncle Mickey
his pilot's uniform is gone and now he wears glasses
and his voice isn't kind like it used to be
most of what he says doesn't make sense anyway
he gives this short hard laugh all the time
i can't tell if he's trying to be funny or making fun
there aren't any suitcases full of secret presents
and no sign of Tia Elena or the three little girls
just some talk about a divorce
and a new wife in Florida
of course no one tells me about this visit
i just walk in from school and there she is
sitting on the Do Not Enter living room sofa
like it's her throne
the hair is all gray but the eyes are still hot coals
and that row of perfect whites still peek out
behind the mean mouth
i must look horrified because She glares at me
Say hello to your grandmother
but it's not like she's Nonna or some nice old lady
so *Hi* is all i can get out
She glares at me again saying *Un beso de respeto*
there's no way i can kiss that cruel face
so i offer my hand instead
which is the worst thing to do
La Abuela crosses her arms and turns away from me
Ingrata malcriada
i don't care if she calls me ungrateful or ill bred
or that all week she's been saying mean things
even now sitting next to her in this car
i don't care how long she talks about Americans
and how they don't know how to raise children

to be respectful of their elders
i don't care
because none of this matters to me now
i'll just sit here and look out the car window
wait for Ben to find parking
and hear Her call him *El Doctor*
follow them from one pavilion to the next
and think about how different things will be soon
at the end of the summer i'll be out of here
off to college
even if it's for a whole year
until i can marry Michél
after that i will spend the rest of my life with him
he said so
i can't let anything ruin it for me
just have to make it through the summer
without Her finding out

Valentine

He died on Valentine's Day, eight years after I found him. It was his neighbor, Anne Walken, who called. She said my dad was taken to the hospital early that morning with chest pain and died a few hours later.

I'm sure Anne spoke in her normal voice, but I remember her words sounded hollow and stilted, as though she were speaking through a long tunnel. Maybe it was my own mind slowing down her message. As soon as it registered, I thought of the other deaths in our family, and how they'd happened on holidays, too. Christmas Eve, when Nonna died. That anonymous voice mail message on Rosh Hashanah saying Ben was dead. And of course, my father's own first "death," on New Year's Eve. We were slowly filling up the calendar, I thought, and it surprised me that I could find humor in this news.

Anne said my father's wife was with him when he died. She was certain Marnie didn't know about me, because she'd made no mention of expecting family or children at the wake the next day, nor for the cremation the following morning. As I jotted down the funeral arrangements, I found myself having a mental dialog with him that continued as the day progressed. *We never discussed your dying, did we Dad? We spoke of so many things, why not this? There won't be a resurrection this time. No second chance to explain yourself.*

The more I thought about it the more certain I was about what to do. I wanted a last visit with my father. It was the only thing that made sense to me. I wasn't going to cause any difficulty for his wife, but it was my right to be there. I wouldn't be cheated out of him again.

I took the overnight flight to Las Vegas. It was dark and hushed in the cabin, miles above the ground, and I imagined telling you that he was dead, and the comments you would make. *Good riddance. It's about time.* I could see you raise an eyebrow in ridicule. *This has all been nothing but a farce.* I told myself I shouldn't think of you today. It had nothing to do with you. There was something else at hand, more compelling than any of the old hurts between us. Today, not even you could stop me. I was sure of myself in a way I'd never experienced before. And suddenly I wanted to tell my father about it, to hear him say *Brava, figlia mia.*

I paid the taxi driver and noticed there was only a single car parked in the lot of the funeral home. It was very early, just after dawn, and already hot in Las Vegas. The viewing wouldn't begin for two hours. I would see my father briefly before anyone else arrived, and get the noon flight home. As I stepped inside it struck me that I'd once walked up to him without warning, and changed his life. Now he was changing mine, just as quickly.

A young receptionist greeted me and offered me a chair near her desk, but I didn't take it. I told her who I was, and that I'd traveled a long distance to be there. I wanted just a few minutes alone with my father. Just a few minutes would do. She looked puzzled, and I explained that it would have to happen before the rest of the family arrived. It was important, because they did not know me, and I didn't want to cause them any disruption. I only needed a few minutes, and then I would leave. She seemed to be thinking about it for a second and then reassured me that it would be all right. Before she stepped away to open the viewing room she handed me a heavy leather-bound book and said I could sign the visitors' log while I waited.

I opened the book and saw that mine would be the first name entered for the day—a record that I'd been present to mourn my father. The family was sure to see it. I didn't have to sign it. I could choose instead to remain forever his silent, secret daughter. The woman returned and asked me to follow her, and I put the book down on the desk, unsigned.

The viewing room was large and softly lit, and once the receptionist left I was grateful for the privacy. My father lay in an open casket in one corner of the room. He was in a dark suit and white shirt. There was a tiny gold pin on his tie. His face was blank, with none of the affection I'd come to know and look for. A folded American flag lay near his head in honor of his military service. At his feet were three small, gift-size white boxes, unmarked. A brown rosary draped his hands. I thought I should say a prayer. But all that came to me was, *None of this is you, Dad*. I waited, because it was what I did most in our family, as though waiting would somehow make a difference, and I might find the right words.

It was then that I saw the ordinariness of my father's other life for the first time. He was someone who prayed and voted, argued with his wife, dressed casually, had headaches, read the Sunday papers, threw out the garbage and went to the drugstore. I wanted that, to be a part of that ordinariness. I wanted us to be a father and daughter like any other. I had longed for it all my life. Now it would never be. I saw how willing I had been to forfeit any sense of peace, just to have him in my life. The intrigue, the separateness, the lost time, I had accommodated it all. It was the cost of being his daughter, your daughter, and all of it became transparent to me as I stood near my dead father.

I don't know how much time passed. I sensed someone standing next to me. It was the receptionist, apologizing. "I know you asked for time alone with the deceased, but Mrs. Sementa has arrived. I told her you were here."

I didn't have time to react. Over her shoulder I could see a tall red-head walking toward me, fast. She was saying something I couldn't make out until she came closer and I heard her repeat it.

"Outrageous. My husband didn't have a daughter. I would have known that."

She stopped in front of me, her head lifted, her green eyes filled with disbelief as they circled my face. She looked much younger than my father, with a plain, round face that was distorted in anger. I remember she held a tissue in one hand, and it shook nervously. Anything I could say would be inadequate for the anguish I knew I was causing. I was sorry, I told her, very sorry about this.

"Who are you? And what do you mean you're Nino's daughter?" I told her my name, and that I hadn't intended this to happen. She shook her head hard, as if to shake off my words, and me, and started again. "My husband didn't have a ..." But she stopped in mid-sentence and reached up to pull a stray strand of hair from her face. She took a step closer to me. "Yes. Of course you're his daughter. You look just like him."

I'd never felt anything close to the relief Marnie's words brought me. I'd been acknowledged, and by my father's wife. I didn't have to hide anymore.

I watched to see what she would do. She walked to the coffin. She looked at her husband and back to me. I expected her to lash out. But she didn't speak. She began to pace between us, her elbows tight against her body as she moved, as though whatever it was she needed would only come to her if she kept moving.

I thought I should give her room. I'd had a long time with family secrets. It was obvious that Marnie hadn't. She stopped pacing and leaned on the back of a nearby couch. I moved to a seat across the room from her, and watched her tremble. She put her face in her hands, not crying, but rocking slowly. I felt terrible. In another circumstance I would offer comfort. Here, I couldn't. I looked over at my father in his casket. *What a horrible thing to do.*

After a few minutes a man and woman arrived and went to Marnie. They spoke softly to her, then turned to look at me. I edged forward on the seat, ready to move to another part of the room and out of their view, when the woman stood up and came to me. She had an English accent when she introduced herself, but I don't remember her name. I noticed she wore very high heels. That reminded me of Julia, and I felt a surge of anger at her, and Carmela too, for not being there with me.

The English woman sat next to me. My husband and I have known Marnie and Nino for more than twenty years. "We were together very often. We were good friends. Surely if Nino had a child, he would have told us."

I didn't have an answer for this woman who had spoken her accusation so politely, whose skin was as white and flawless as porcelain. I hoped she would go back to Marnie. Instead, her husband joined us, taking the chair on the other side of mine. He had an accent too, but not English. It sounded like Mrs. DeGrab when she made a correction in my playing, you remember. A mixture of French and Belgian. The man leaned in close to me and spoke slowly, as though he were an old friend. He kept his eyes on me.

"Veronica, we hope you'll understand that this is terribly difficult for Marnie. Perhaps you can help to make this easier for her. You are quite a shock to her. And she's just lost her husband."

I began to say that I had just lost my father, but he went right on.

"You can see, can't you? Your presence here is too much for Marnie to bear right now. She needs time to accept the situation. After all, she's the innocent one here, isn't she?"

I didn't understand. What did he expect me to do? He didn't hesitate with his answer.

"It would be best if you would leave."

Leave. That message, again. Your old message. And now from a complete stranger, at a time and a place like this. The English wife echoed him. "Yes. You should go."

I might have started to cry. I might have become defensive and said that I'd planned to leave anyway, that I'd done what I came to do and was going home in a few hours. I might have gotten angry and made a scene. Or I might have said nothing and left. But that feeling came over me again, that certainty I'd felt on the airplane. I looked straight at the man. I said no. I wouldn't do that. I was Nino's daughter.

No one said anything. No one moved. The man looked very tired. He sat back in his seat and dropped his hands on his lap.

"Very well. Then please, could you give Marnie, say, a few hours? Could you go now and return this afternoon?"

I took a cab to a nearby diner. It was noisy with the breakfast crowd, but I was able to get a back table near a window. I settled in to wait. I didn't know what would happen when I returned to the funeral home, but I was obviously not going to make my noon flight home. I found a public phone, called the airline, secured a room at a nearby motel and called my girls.

Then I called Jack. He'd been with me on my search. With me when I talked to the old men at the Café Roma. With me when I discovered that my father was alive. It was Jack who encouraged me to meet him, and once came out to Vegas with me. Except for my children, Jack was the only person who had seen me with my father.

"I'll take the next flight out. I can be there by dinnertime," he said. But I thanked him and turned him down. I had to do this myself.

The waitress didn't rush me and wasn't chatty. Instead, she left the local newspaper and a pot of coffee on the table, as though she knew what it was like to wait. I tried to read, but after a few pages I stopped. I ordered an omelet, but couldn't eat it. I rested against the booth, looked out at Las Vegas, and waited for the morning to end.

Marnie was alone in the viewing room when I returned. As soon as she saw me, she motioned for me to join her where she sat. Her face was serious but without the pained look it had earlier.

"Please, I want to know about all this. I'm entitled to know."

I told her again how sorry I was, that it hadn't been my intention for things to happen as they had. She wanted to know how old I was, where I was born, where I lived. She knew Nino had been married before, long ago, before the war, somewhere in South America. The marriage was still young when the woman died.

I could hardly believe what Marnie was saying. My father had done the same thing you had. You'd both made each other dead, as though that would have solved your family problems, as though such lies wouldn't do damage. I told Marnie you lived a few miles away from me, that you'd been married to my father for eight years, and you were separated before I was born. Then I told her I was the youngest of your three daughters. I wondered how much more I should say and how much Marnie could take. She seemed pretty calm, except for the tissue she twisted around her finger. I told her I hadn't known my father was alive until a few years before. He'd been very surprised when I found him.

She didn't ask me anything more and hardly looked at me. I guessed Marnie was in her early fifties, but at that moment, in the line of her shoulders, with her head bent and hands crossed on her lap, she looked like a young, mournful girl. I held back my own questions, and we sat like that, in silence, just sensing one another, Nino's wife and Nino's daughter.

A long time passed. Then I stood up and walked to the coffin. I wanted him to be alive for a minute. I wanted him to see us together. See the absurd situation he'd left behind, for the second time. Marnie came to stand beside me. I asked her what the three little boxes were for.

"Those are our girls. Nino and I arranged it this way. Whoever died first would be buried with their ashes. Our three Yorkies. He loved those little dogs." She tapped each box. *Lala, Cookie, and Baby.* And I thought, he gave our names to his dogs. He walked around his house calling out our names, every day, all those years.

People began to arrive. Marnie received the mourners. Most of them were businessmen who gave her a handshake and a business card. It seemed she was meeting them for the first time. She said very little, and had a way of bowing her head slightly as she accepted each condolence. The couple who had been there in the morning didn't return. Marnie didn't introduce me. She never glanced my way. No one else did either. I sat at the far side of the room, unnoticed, negotiating my old realities of belonging and not belonging, simultaneously.

Around midafternoon three young women arrived with their parents. They each embraced Marnie and sat with her. As soon as the mother spoke I recognized her voice. She was Anne Walken. She was very much as I'd pictured her, a plump woman with curly brown hair and a kind, unremarkable face. I turned away, not wanting to chance calling attention to myself. I'd brought Marnie enough pain.

In a few minutes I heard Marnie's voice. "You know? What do you mean, you know?"

Anne followed, saying she felt awful about it, but Nino has asked her not to tell. She didn't think it was her place to make trouble between a husband and wife.

Marnie's voice grew louder. "What are you saying, Anne?"

I turned, to see. Marnie was on her feet, shouting over Anne. "How long have you known about this? Does the whole world know? Am I the only idiot, then?"

She looked across the room at me, and I stood up just as Anne did. Anne and I exchanged glances, hers full of curiosity, mine of dread. She took a step toward me and said my name. Marnie cupped her face in her hands.

"My god! Do you two know each other?"

Anne began to speak at the same time her husband and daughters did, all full of apologies and reassurances for Marnie. I didn't move from where I stood. Marnie grabbed her purse and rushed out. Anne looked like she might cry. She thought she'd been doing the right thing. She was sure Marnie would understand in time. She was awfully sorry for my loss.

In another minute it was over. I was in the viewing room, alone with my dead father and my thoughts. No one else came during the rest of the afternoon. Later, the evening mourners arrived, more businessmen. I was the only person there to receive them, so they came to me. Over and over I said I was his daughter and no one seemed surprised. No one asked for Marnie. None was a relative of hers or of my father. Of the business cards I was handed, one was from his doctor. The others were from men who worked with Nino. One man, in his thirties, was teary as he approached the casket. "Your father was my role model, the gentlest man I've ever met."

A dark haired man with a large build lingered after he gave me his card. He spoke to me without letting go of my hand. He said he knew my father very well. They'd been close friends and this was a great personal loss.

"Your father didn't have an enemy in the world. I never knew anyone with such kindness, such elegance. Real class."

After he stepped away I glanced down at his card to get his name. I wanted to connect it to his words, so I wouldn't forget, Jim Logan.

At around nine o'clock the funeral director approached me. The viewing was about to end, and he would be closing the casket. Yes, I said, I wanted to be present. Marnie couldn't be reached, and had not returned or called. He would proceed with the original arrangements.

I'd never seen the closing of a casket before. I remember feeling very protective. All the anger I'd felt before was gone. I wanted it to be done carefully. My father's doctor was there, and the young man who cried. The funeral director stepped in to remove my father's jewelry and his rosary, which he placed into a plastic envelope and set aside. I stood before my father. I reached to touch the supple cloth of his jacket. *I can't let you go without words, something needs to be said.*

I remembered I carried a copy of "Desiderata" in my purse. I read it aloud as the top of the coffin was lowered. "Go placidly amid the noise and the haste, and remember what peace there may be in silence. As far as possible, without surrender, be on good terms with all persons."

The last sound in the room was the cranking of the casket key.

i follow Michél's directions carefully
make sure to get on the first subway car
and off at the Lexington Avenue stop
so when the doors open
i'm just a few steps from the escalator
it's always a surprise that he is there waiting for me
every morning on the way to work
i believe he will wake up one day
and decide to forget about me
i'm just a teenager probably just a summer fling
who has never even been to New Jersey
and he is a man twice my age
who finds adventure in everything
i cannot resist Michél
he takes me to that world out there
where things are new and interesting and safe
away from the million complicated rules
and the No Fun Allowed life She's made me live
it's just the opposite with him
Michél puts pleasure into things
even riding the F train to a boring summer job
the crowds and the heat and the pervs don't exist now
only the counting down of minutes until i see him
he will be standing near the railing
handsome and impeccable and smelling good
in the beautiful clothes beautiful men wear so easily
the dark honey waves of hair falling onto his neck
just above his shirt collar to show his olive skin
when he sees me his face will lose its seriousness
he'll give me a smile
and the inside of my chest will get warm
his arm will slip around my waist like it belongs there
we'll ride to the next stop together like that
then walk down Fifth Avenue to the Pfizer building
at the lobby coffee shop he'll buy me breakfast
we'll say goodbye at the elevator bank
he'll go off to his studio

i will ride fourteen floors on his kiss
one gentle taste of his lips saying we will meet again
it will last all morning while i sit at the typing pool
lunch break comes and i run to the public phone
Michél will make time to talk to me
no matter how busy he is
maybe he'll invite me to his studio for lunch again
last week he walked me through the place
showed me how jewelry is made
he liked it when i asked questions
and he said he will teach me to sculpt
i will be good at it he says because i notice details
i recognized some of his tools
dentist's instruments i said
he was surprised and happy with me
all day i type letter after letter waiting for five o'clock
and there's Michél waiting for me
so we can ride back to Queens together
i wish i could tell someone but they are all gone
Amy Elise Paul Andrew
i haven't heard from any of them
they probably have exciting lives now
backpacking through Europe or something
and have forgotten M&A
at graduation there wasn't time for long goodbyes
everyone busy with their families and pictures
so i was really shocked when Paul said he loved me
he just grabbed me and looked right at me and said it
like he'd been holding it back since forever
he looked like he would start crying
everyone started hugging and promised to keep in touch
but i don't believe them
maybe what She always says is true
There are no such things as friends
but i've told Carmela about Michél
and she will keep my secret
since my recital she's been coming to the house

there is a lot about her that has changed
she's stopped wearing makeup and her stutter is gone
when she speaks she shows off but in a good way
about music or her job
or how she's against the Viet Nam War
she seems happier too
because she has Eliot back again
when his father died last spring
all the stuff about choosing died too
i think they will be together forever Carmela and Eliot
and i am happy for them
especially now that i have Michél for my own
i don't feel so left out around my sisters anymore
we all have boyfriends and that make us equal
i keep imagining we can all be together
maybe go on a triple date
but none of them ever suggests it
not even after what happened
it's been a whole month and nobody will talk about it
that's the way we are about everything
like it never occurred
but it did
Eliot started it
with his concert at Queens College
and Carmela saying what a great chance it would be
for them to meet Michél
so after the concert we find each other in the crowd
and everybody gets along okay
Michél and Eliot talk like they've done it all the time
and somebody says it's a nice evening for a walk
then we sit on the benches along the quadrangle
and we start looking at the sky not a cloud around
then the coincidence happens
Michél says his first New York address was Brooklyn
it turns out to be right down the block from Eliot's
everybody is happy about that
i know it's a good omen

we are all meant to be together
then Carmela starts talking to Michél about us
tells him she's worried about our age difference
eighteen years will work against us
may not now but what about in twenty years
what will Michél do
if some day i want to run through a field
and he can't keep up
Michél smiles
and says he will wait for me to run back to him
i don't like it
Carmela talking to him about me
like i am invisible or deaf or stupid or something
but Michél puts his arm around me and i'm better
all of a sudden Eliot says *Isn't that your sister*
and there's Julia walking up the path with Neal
another coincidence
Neal shakes hands with everyone
he doesn't seem nervous at all
and Julia isn't saying a word
they sit on the benches with us
and Neal says the sky is really clear tonight
he starts telling us about the stars
he knows how to track them
he says man will be walking on the moon very soon
everybody talks about it and i watch them
and i think how great this is
the three of us together with our men
Michél reads my mind
I want to know he says
Why don't you do this more often
You are sisters aren't you
no one answers we all stare at the ground
you can hear the crickets and passing cars
then Eliot says *They don't know how*
and Neal says *They were never allowed*
in a minute someone makes a whimpering sound

it is Carmela covering her face
i look at Julia she is biting her finger
and tears are coming down her face
i don't expect it but seeing my sisters cry
makes me cry too
it is not easy
it is like that old way
the way we cried in Union Square
together in the bottom bunk
the night Hamlet died
Julia gets up to walk away and Neal stops her
then Eliot gets up and Carmela too
we're all on our feet
marking the steps of a *soleares*
Julia stands still
Carmela moves toward her
me in between
the men around us
we are embracing
i am embarrassed and uncomfortable
but i stay
and i want them to stay
and we do
for a little while
Julia is the first to break the circle
Neal looks up at the sky again
Michél touches my hair
Eliot hands us his handkerchief
and just like that it is over
everyone talks at the same time
about how late it is or how good the concert was
and i can tell
that what just happened
never happened
they will let it slip away
and i will always want it back

12

i feel like a beggar
when Michél talks about his family
how they do things together and help each other
he knows so much about them
but i am ignorant
all i know is rules and wars
and hurting and nobody talking
he asks about my family
i feel awful an awful i can't explain
not to someone like Michél who knows himself
when someone asks me what i am
i try to find an answer like other people give
fast simple and just one thing
but i can never find one thing that fits
and anyway i'm not just one thing
so which do i choose
am i Italian like Nonna
Spanish for my mother
or Jewish for my baby brother and sister
one thing alone doesn't fit and all three is worse
i've tried saying Mixed
but people make strange faces
like they've just heard you say Leper or Wierdo
Michél says it is a sin
that i don't know my history
that no one has told me stories
that i do not know where my relatives were born
or why we never visit them
especially that we don't visit Nonna the elder
i cannot answer him about these things
all i can tell him about is wars
and Michél won't want to hear about that
he says we should be all right especially as sisters
i don't want anything to spoil what i have with him
so i just think of the happy times instead
i remind him about our first real date
how i heard Her on the telephone when he called

after my recital
Her telling him i am too young for romance
and She has plans for me
i will become a professional woman
and he should not call anymore Thank You
but i couldn't let that happen and neither could he
so i made arrangements
letting Her think i was doing a dance show
but really went to dinner with Michél
he let me order anything i wanted even an artichoke
and when i didn't know how to eat it he showed me
the two of us laughing the whole time i made a mess
afterward we went to the Worlds' Fair
so different from the Family Outing Day
walking through the whole place holding hands
knowing everything in the world would be okay
i had to tell him i would not accept any gifts
because She would find them
so he gave me a kiss to keep instead
thinking about him makes everything else disappear
all i need to know is that i will see him soon
every evening after work i race down the elevator
and there he is always ready with a treat
a grenadine or fresh dates or a yellow pepper
teaching me things like the pleasures of food
exotic new ones and fresh delicious things
nothing old or stale
if i can arrange to stay out late
we will go to his apartment in Woodside
and he'll cook for me
dishes his family eats chick pea stew and Kibbee
he will show me how to work in the kitchen
how to hold a cutting knife and slice the onions thin
how to flavor the olive oil with garlic cloves
or prepare a chicken in lemon and oregano
and never criticize me for my mistakes
we will eat together slowly like it is a holiday

and later we'll listen to music or watch a sitcom
i will explain American humor to him
he will imitate the different American accents
and we will laugh until tears come out of our eyes
if his friends come over we will play cards
Michél has all different kinds of friends
New Yorkers Cubans Arabs Jews even a Japanese couple
and they all like me
sometimes we spend the evening alone
we end up on the sofa and i end up confused
it is his smell i think
spicy and earthy and somehow very familiar
it fills my head and clouds me up
i like the kissing and when he touches my breasts
but i am afraid of what will come next
i don't know if i should tell him
if it is his right to know about the Edoardo thing
i'm not sure whether i am a virgin
but i am sure he will expect me to be
all the sex stuff confuses me
could all the things She said really be true
are all men like animals
i think it could be something good with Michél
safe and kind like in the movies
but i believe She will certainly kill me
so i remember what the girls in gym class said
how the best way to stop boys is a long-line girdle
so when Michél's hand wanders under my skirt
i hold my breath and he stops
he laughs and says my mother trained me well
i'd like to explain to him how wrong he is
but that would ruin everything
so we just kiss and pet and i get dizzy
at ten o'clock he drives me home
i ask him to drop me off a block away
so She won't see his car
it feels so sneaky and wrong but in a way i like it

being with Michél is all mine and no one else's
it is the one thing She cannot boss me about
nobody can

Sangre

I share the look of surprise on the school secretary's face as she calls me out of a meeting to answer the telephone. "Your sister?" Her question is reasonable, since I've never received a call at work from any relative other than my daughters. "She says it's urgent." As I reach for the telephone, for a split second I think, which sister?

"You better get over here." It's Julia. She sounds frantic.

"What's happened?"

"There's something wrong with her, is what. She's a complete freak."

"I'm speaking to you from a crowded room. Let me move to my own office where it's quieter. I'll call you right back."

"I don't give a crap where you are. Get over here. Right now!"

I take a breath. "Tell me what's going on, Julia. Start from the beginning."

"Fine. We'll do this your way. She's a zombie. I went in to give her breakfast and she doesn't answer me. She's not moving. And there's something rotting in her room. It smells like a dead animal or something. Is that enough? What are you waiting for? Get over here!"

My stomach cramps. The two worlds I separately manage well have collided. I'm standing in the middle of a place where I am generally at ease, a competent, self-assured professional, with people who admire and respect me, being hollered at by my big sister. At the same time I recognize a solidarity with my sister. When we're scared, adequate language escapes us. I become mute. She yells.

"Is she awake? Is she breathing?"

"Yes. But she's just staring into space, like she's in some lunatic asylum."

"Have you tried getting her to move?"

"No, thank you. I don't touch her. That's your department. And there's something red on her fingers."

"Red? You mean, nail polish?"

"When did she ever wear nail polish?"

"Maybe it's food, or juice."

"Blood. I think it's blood."

"What? Call an ambulance."

"You get here first."

"Julia, I'm in Brooklyn, twenty-five minutes away from you if I speed. In the meantime, call an ambulance."

"Get over here!

I hang up, make my excuses, and rush out of the building. In my car I try to imagine what might cause my mother to have blood on her fingers. I can't come up with anything medical. Except for the Alzheimer's, she's is good health. Intrusive images of my sister and mother battling each other flood my mind. I reject these, remembering that Julia said it smells like a dead animal. There have been reports of raccoons in the area. Could one have gotten in somehow? This is a worse idea, too awful to hold.

Maybe she went outside. But no, she wouldn't do that again. My mother hasn't left her room for months. Not since her birthday, when she slipped out of the house unseen and reappeared after dark, like a phantom walking out from behind the shrubs. All she had on was her gardening jacket over her nightgown and a pair of slippers, trembling from the cold and sobbing like a child all the way back to her room. We still don't know for sure where she'd been. I suspect it was her garden she went out to work in. Confused by the bare branches, her blossoms vanished, the soil stiffened, she hid, until she heard Julia and me calling her name into the night. No, she wouldn't go outside again.

Maybe the red is from fruit juice after all. My mother likes cranberry juice. Maybe she made her way to the kitchen in the middle of the night, like she used to, and spilled it on her hands. But cranberry juice doesn't stain skin.

I check the time. Almost nine thirty. Ten minutes ago I was diffusing a hostile encounter among a set of parents, a teacher and two administrators.

I was thinking clearly, finding the right words to calm everyone's nerves. Now I've made the wrong turn and missed the parkway entrance I've used for more than twenty years. I click on the radio. More snow is predicted for tonight. I avoid the side streets, stay on the main avenue where it's been plowed and salted. I catch the next entry ramp. Traffic is light. I switch stations. Good, I say to myself, I'll let Franz Liszt guide me to my mother's house.

this college business is awful
i'm practically the only big city person here
my roommate Cory hardly talks to anyone
and acts like she's afraid of me
she's never met a person from New York City
her graduating class only had twelve kids in it
but she's very neat and she's a studier
i like that about her
the way our schedules work we hardly see each other
i spend my evenings practicing or in choral rehearsals
those are the only times i enjoy myself
i don't seem to match the people here
they make freshmen wear beannies everywhere
and the upper classmen get to haze us
they stop us and tell us which footpaths to walk on
and you can't refuse an order from an upper classman
i think they're idiots all of them
if the dining line is too long they get to cut in
last week they woke us up at midnight
had to empty the dorm just to do exercises in the rain
i got really pissed and i cursed a lot
that made Cory cry
i wrote a letter to the senior class president
i asked to be excused from the whole freshman thing
so he calls me on the dorm phone
says i don't have any class spirit
i tell him i think the hazing is a form of fascism
he says i think that because i'm from New York City
i tell him it is within my civil rights not to participate
he says a decay in civic pride is destroying the country
but i am excused from having to participate in hazing
i'm the first person ever
in the entire history of the college
now the other freshmen point me out to one another
i don't care
i don't plan on making any friends here anyway
in four more months i turn eighteen

then She won't have anymore power over me
i can leave this place
and all the girls whose clothing match
with perfectly cut hair
and care packages from home every week
all they talk about is pledging sororities
or going into one of the bars in town with frat boys
i didn't even know what pledging meant
until Naomi explained
thank God for Naomi
she's a sophomore
and has actually been to New York City
we were friends from the first time we saw each other
on the dining hall line
waiting for seconds of macaroni and cheese
the woman serving us says *It's as good as home*
then Naomi and i blurt out *Uh uh better*
at the same time
she liked my eyeliner so i showed her how to use it
she likes the long tail ends
now she calls me Spider
we help each other with music
i show her notation and she drills me on dictation
sometimes she comes into my practice room
and listens to me play
she agrees it's not fair that they hold me back
they won't let me skip the foundation classes
no matter if i've been taking theory since forever
my piano teacher told me to speak to the chairman
because she thinks i'm very talented
at my last lesson she called in other teachers
to hear me play Chopin nocturnes
six old women in cardigan sweaters and gray skirts
it was very weird but they liked my playing
but it didn't help
the music chairman said i must be retrained
their way

so i spend all day in beginner classes
with people who can't even make a G cleff
if it weren't for chorus and anthropology i'd go crazy
but i found a good way to make it through
i write a letter to Michél in every class
short notes
i tell him how miserable i am without him
he never writes back to me
but he calls me every evening
and spends most of telephone time making me laugh
Michél always has a joke or a funny story to tell me
he likes to hear me laugh
every time the hall phone rings
i listen for my name to be yelled out
then i go running down to get it
on the days when we don't speak i am very unhappy
the sorority hopefuls tie up the line all night
and the switchboard gets cut off at eleven
weekend nights are the hardest
the whole place empties out everyone goes into town
and i am the only girl left in the dorm
except for the R.A.s
they come up to my room to check on me
they ask me if i'm all right
and i have to explain again about C permission
it's like they can't believe i'm still here
they must expect me to break the rule and run away
but i just read or listen to Judy Collins
or i listen to Cory's records of Barbra Streisand
and wait for the phone to ring
the R.A.s are probably the reason
i had to go see the Dean of Women
i thought i was in trouble about my hazing letter
but when i walked into her office
she was very nice to me
she didn't have blue hair at all
and she had a Van Gogh poster on the wall

and fresh flowers on her desk
what she wanted to know was why me
why am i the only woman on campus
to have Restricted Permission
i tell her it's my mother
She doesn't want me going out with boys
the dean says Restricted Permission is very rare
and has almost never been requested
i tell her she doesn't know my mother
then she does something strange
she says the restriction is valid until i turn eighteen
so in four months i can determine my own curfew
then she gets even more weird
and asks me if i know about birth control
i lie and say yes
she doesn't believe me
she starts to explain how important it is
she tells me the safest method is the pill
and that today women can choose to have children
it is our privilege and good fortune
as modern American women
she says she's inquired about me
she has seen my school records
You are bright and talented woman
Do not waste your gifts
i'm sure the next question will be about careers
but she surprises me again
she asks me do i have any money of my own
and gives me the name of the lady
in the college business office
i can have a job at the switchboards in the evenings
so i won't be alone and bored
A woman should have money of her own she says
and never says a word about hazing

Julia is waiting on the front porch, pacing. She is coatless, wearing just the blue quilted vest she uses indoors all winter over a red turtleneck and jeans, her plaid scarf thrown around her neck. As I step closer I see that she is shivering. "Get in here," she says, and pulls me into the house. "You have to see this." I follow Julia up the stairs and ask her if she's called an ambulance. She stops short outside my mother's room and stomps her foot, her silent No.

The odor in my mother's room is thick and heady, not the usual one nor any I can identify. I look around. The usual clutter doesn't look disturbed, nothing is broken or overturned, no sign of a struggle. I stand next to the bed. My mother is sitting up, eyes wide open, strangely still, but doesn't notice me. She holds the bedclothes over her chest, like a child preparing for sleep. The tips of her fingers, her jagged nails, just as Julia said, are stained red.

"Hi, Mom. It's me, Ronnie." My mother turns very slightly in my direction, her face ghostly, as though she were looking at me through frosted glass. I ask, "How do you feel?" She doesn't react. I touch her forehead. It is very warm. "Fever," I say to Julia, on the other side of the room. I move to open one of my mother's hands, but she won't release her grip on the sheets. I see that her pajama has a few red stains on the collar. I gently lift her hair from her neck. It is soaked and sticky. I look at my hand. It is red with blood. I am nauseated. I reach toward the foot of the bed with my other hand and pull back the bedclothes. My mother isn't wearing pajama bottoms or underwear. She sits in the middle of her bed, small, defenseless. Her legs, like her sheets, are covered with blood.

"Jesus!" Julia calls out. "What the hell is that?"

I look for cuts or marks on my mother's legs and groin without touching her. I can't see through the smudges of dried and fresh blood. I pull up the sleeves of her pajama top and look for marks there. Her skin is clear, smooth and hairless. I think, how impossible this is. This is how I might examine a schoolchild for signs of abuse. "Mom?" I snap my fingers near her ears. "Can you hear me?"

My mother throws an unfocused glance in my direction and another toward Julia. It is as if she were listening intently to something else, a sound in another room, or upstairs, and trying to track it. She bows her head a little. Then she lifts both hands to her neck and begins to scratch, hard. A second later she is doing the same thing to her legs.

"Mom! Don't! She's cutting into her skin. My God, call 911!"

"Do we have to?"

I shout at Julia. "Either you call or I will." My sister hesitates, then hurries out to the kitchen. I hear her dial the telephone and recite her address.

I look through my mother's dresser drawers for something to put around her hands. I find two pink pillowcases. I fold one around each hand. I go quickly into her bathroom and look in the medicine chest. I find a small pair of manicure scissors. I spot a package of gauze, the wrapper long faded. I wash my hands off, grab the gauze and scissors, and head back into the bedroom. I will trim her fingernails and bandage her hands. I cut a few strips of gauze and lay them on the dresser. I notice the pillowcases are on the floor. I glance at my mother. She sits as she was, dazed, but isn't scratching.

Julia returns. Behind her are two paramedics, a man and woman. I pick up one of the pillowcases from the floor and lay it across my mother's naked lap. I don't want her to be embarrassed, even if she doesn't know how to be, right now. I wait for Julia to say something, but she moves silently to the corner of the room. I tell the medics my mother has dementia, has a fever and is scratching so badly she's bleeding. The man calls to her from across the bed. The woman moves closer, near me, and also calls to my mother. She doesn't respond to either.

"Mom," I speak close to her face, fighting my queasiness. "You're not feeling well. There are two doctors here, friends of mine. They want to examine you."

My mother takes no notice of the paramedics. They measure her blood pressure and temperature, and visually examine her body. She is placid, as limp as a broken branch on one of her azalea shrubs. She doesn't respond to their questions. After a few minutes they tell us they can't determine what has caused the scratching, but she needs to get to a hospital. Julia steps forward and tells them which hospital she wants. They don't object. While she looks for my mother's medical papers, the two paramedics transfer my mother onto a stretcher. They are being careful, speaking to her calmly, as if she could understand them. I watch their gloved hands buckle the straps across her body. I watch them lay a heavy brown blanket over her. They lift her, and for an instant I think I catch her glance, but it disappears behind her glossy eyes.

The street is quiet. The ground is covered in old, dirty snow. I ask the medics if we can ride in the ambulance with my mother. They say yes, but

Julia says she'll follow in her car instead. The wind starts up and sprays a mist of icy snow over me as I climb in beside my mother. The ambulance doors slam shut and we slip out of the driveway. No one is around to see my mother leave her home.

please God i hope Ben is there
if he's home it won't be so bad
and it's Friday so there's a good chance
i'll know by his station wagon
he never puts it in the garage when it snows this bad
just six blocks to go and i'll see the house
goddam slippery sidewalks
should have worn my boots
not enough time to think of everything
especially about how hideous snow can be in Queens
a few inches and the whole place is paralyzed
worse than at college
they get a foot at a time but it's cleaned up overnight
damn snow is blowing right into my face
no buildings around here for protection
just rows of look-alike house and car dealerships
Carmela and i could never have played refugee here
maybe she'll be there too
now that they are friends again
Carmela could stand up for me
she ought to
this whole thing has blown up because of her
her and her dumb appointment book
that stupid car just blew slush all over me
but i'll take it
i'll take anything you want to give me
just let that Rambler be there when i turn the corner
let Ben be sitting at the table reading his paper
or talking to Her maybe trying to save me
i know he really can't save me
or any of us
couldn't save his own kids when he should have
he's been right there and seen it happen
seen Her hitting baby Gabriel because he wouldn't eat
seen Her making baby Gabriel eat until he vomits
and shove it back into baby Gabriel spoon by spoon
he's seen Julia scream Stop It

and throw the milk bottle against the wall
seen it all and still couldn't save his own kids
not from Her
but it still will be easier to take if Ben is there
no matter what She does to me
getting in will be the hardest part
not knowing what mood She's in
maybe sunk into Her green chair staring into space
or ironing and singing the old songs on the radio
or pedaling full blast on Her sewing machine
with her face all wrinkled
maybe the whole house will be dark
with Her locked in her room upstairs asleep for hours
or She might be wild
i bet this time She'll be wild for sure
i swear if She comes at me like that night last summer
i'll run out
just like a vampire coming at me out of the dark
it wasn't even past my curfew
and i was extra careful too
made Michél drop me off two blocks away
but i didn't see her
perched under the porch lamp
like some supernatural creature
wild hair and nightgown blowing
whispering Spanish insults at me
all i see as i pass her is the baseball bat
then a quick flash of light
and i'm down on the living room floor
can't hear or feel anything
just the throbbing left side of my head
i try to get up
i wonder if i'm dead
but i see Her walking up the stairs so i can't be dead
then everything is quiet again
as fast as it all began it ended
still don't know what made Her go crazy that time

She never talked about it either
five days later i left for college
like it never happened
but this time i'm really afraid
She'll kill me for sure
what do i do if Ben isn't home yet
if only i had Carmela's guts or Julia's mouth
if i was like them i wouldn't let Her hurt me
i'd answer or hit her back
but i don't have guts like the others
i am a coward and She knows it
the only thing that will save me is Michél's plan
walk in and calmly apologize for disrespecting Her
then let Her go off but keep my distance
for thirty minutes stay in another room if i have to
until he comes
he said he will come in thirty minutes
i am trusting him
what i really want is for him to walk in there with me
but there's no way to tell him how bad She gets
he'd have to see it to believe it
and what difference will thirty minutes make anyway
i must believe in him
he knows how to handle people
he will know what to say to calm things down
he will make everything better
it isn't so bad when i think of Michél protecting me
they will be shocked
and Ben will know i've been lying
but i don't care now
in three weeks i'll be eighteen
She can't touch me then
all i have to do is make it through thirty minutes
please let it be just insults and threats
i can take that
as long as She doesn't touch me
She sounded mad last night

Union Square mad
making whimpering sounds
like Hamlet would make just before he'd growl
She didn't even say hello
and i never expected her to call
She hasn't called all year
there i was racing down the hall
happy to get my Michél call
and it's Her voice instead
You are no longer my daughter
You are disgraceful
not yelling just cold and slow
the way She talks when She's about to flip
it's worse than hearing screaming or crying
Indecente Imoral
You have behaved like a common tramp
Just as my mother predicted
then silence
i'm racing to figure out why She's so mad
but my gut knows before She says it
Tell that individual he has twenty-four hours
to show his face here or else
Ben will file charges against him for statutory rape
the first thing i think is that rape is what happened
a long time ago when i was little and it's too late now
but She was so mad and hung up
i never got a chance to ask how She found out
and what She knows
or even defend myself or lie or anything
but as soon as i told him Michél figured it
then he confirmed it
it was Carmela
during one of her visits
she told him she feels terrible about it
hadn't meant to leave the appointment book open
during one of her visits
right on my mother's dining room table

right to Monday's page
Lunch with Michél at twelve thirty
i can't believe she did such a dumb thing
i didn't even know they'd been meeting for lunch
she told him she's heartsick about it now
a terrible mistake
Michél thinks she did it on purpose
but i can't bother to figure it out right now
i have to figure out what to do when i walk in
it's all so crazy
Michél is the only one i really need there
but i have to make it through thirty minutes of hell
this damned February snow is exhausting
been in it since six o'clock this morning
racing to get the first flight down here from school
Her twenty-four hour deadline ticking away
that tiny rattling plane scaring the hell out of me
but it was a lot faster than the bus
nine hours on a bus would've been unbearable today
at least on Thanksgiving and Christmas breaks
i had something good to look forward to
coming down one day early
and spending a whole night with Michél
without anyone knowing
no curfews or restrictions
just us
when this is all over i want to sleep
the kind of sleep I only get when I'm with Michél
warm safe uninterrupted nowhere-to-go sleep
even if we don't fool around just laying there together
i really think Michél should walk in with me
that would stop Her from making a scene for sure
but he didn't think that too wise
the sight of us together might make things worse
and we have to think of the future after we're married
when all of this blows over and we are all a family
i didn't contradict him

it seems impossible She will ever be all right with this
but i must put all my trust in Michél
after all he knows much more about people than i do
i wonder what will happen with exams this week
maybe i won't even be going back to school
maybe everything in the world will be different
after tonight
there's Ben's car right in front of the house
and there are a lot of lights on inside
like She's expecting company
i'm afraid to use my key and just walk in
better ring the bell
it is so strange
standing here on the porch preparing for battle
little Isabella opens the door
her braids have gotten so long
baby Gabriel right behind her walking on his own now
little Isabella smiles when she sees me
but then looks away
like she's remembered something
maybe she doesn't like me anymore
i want to hug them both
but they've already started going upstairs
i see Ben coming from the kitchen
he looks at the floor shaking his head
Your mother is very upset
You better wait in the living room
i can't believe he's telling me to sit on the couch
but i do it
he leaves me there and goes down to the basement
i can hear my mother talking in the kitchen
She is on the phone with someone speaking Spanish
it must be long distance because She's talking loud
maybe Uncle Mickey or maybe *La Abuela*
they are talking about me
i am a disappointment i was the sweet one
She'd never suspected

i am evil
She doesn't care how good Michél's family is
She doesn't care how much money they have
or what his intentions are
She did not raise her children to be whores
or concubines to older men
it's funny to hear her say *Si, Mamá*
yes She will try to make Michél understand
that Her children are American
that they will not be running into marriage
not with anyone
they will finish their education become professionals
but *No, Mamá*
whether Michél understands or not
She will send me back to Colombia or to Spain
interna for a year in a strict boarding school
that will be plenty of time for me to forget him
my stomach cramps and my hands are trembling
She's finished talking on the phone
but doesn't come out of the kitchen
i wonder if She knows i am here
it is so weird sitting alone on this leather couch
like company
and no one talking to me
i wonder if Carmela and Julia are upstairs
i look at the piano
the Utrillos on the wall
the pattern on the Persian carpet
i watch the light cross the chandelier's crystal drops
i wonder how much time is left for half an hour
no matter
i am certain
Michél must take me away from this place forever

Julia walks up the hospital corridor toward me, moving with unusual resignation. She is returning from her latest check of the flow chart on the emergency room wall. "Still third from the top," she says. She looks weary, her eyes sunken. I must look as bad, I think, as I lean against a pillar I've appropriated as my own. My legs hurt. In the sixteen hours we've been here, we haven't been able to sit down. It's been a particularly busy day in this E.R., not an empty seat in the waiting room, but we've been allowed to stay with our mother.

"Look at her," I say to my sister. My mother lies on a gurney across the corridor, forty feet from the hospital's emergency entrance. "It's a good thing she can't see herself like this." I think of my mother in her yellow taffeta dress, her blonde French twist, her high patent heels and white gloves. Now she is clothed only in the open-back hospital gown that was slipped onto her by a morning-shift nurse, after she cut away my mother's clothing, cleaned her up and took her for a MRI, after the attending resident made his diagnosis. "Herpes zoster," he announced, face serious and quick-talking, as though he were dictating a letter. "Shingles. It's a form of chicken pox. Viral, not contagious. She must have had it in childhood. Stress reactivates it. She's delirious because of the high fever. And because of the acute pain and itching from the blisters. Zoster can be very painful. We'll give her something for the fever until a bed becomes available for her in the hospital."

I check my watch. Three thirty in the morning. It will be my turn next to take the walk down the corridor to the nurse's station and review the list of names on the electronic board. Julia and I do this every hour or so, looking for an improvement in the odds that our mother will be admitted to the hospital before the night ends. She's been third from the top on the list for nine hours. It feels, at this time of night, like we're following the ranking of a sporting event, or looking for the digits to change on the departure schedule at the railroad station. We've given up asking the nurses. They seem as frustrated with their answer as we are. It could be hours longer. But we don't stop checking. Vigilance makes us feel like we're doing something.

The sheet that should cover my mother is on the floor again. She's repeatedly kicked it off, and Julia and I are tired of retrieving it. My mother has managed to move her feet far enough up along the wall so that she's become inverted, legs above her and open. Her head hangs off the side of the gurney, her matted hair aimed toward the floor. She mumbles to herself ceaselessly, unintelligibly, oblivious to the bursts of frigid air that rush in each time the emergency doors fly open, and to the hundreds of strangers that have walked past her old, exposed body.

Three times, in increasing urgency, I've requested restraints—the ones I remember were placed on my wrists when I was in labor—to prevent my mother from falling off the gurney. Each time I've been offered reassurances from the nurses. Restraints cannot be applied to a patient without a prescription. As soon as a psychiatrist can come to examine my mother and write the order, it will happen. But that probably won't be soon. There's no psychiatrist on duty tonight. There is a call out for one. We just have to wait.

Julia and I are caught in the undertow of the emergency room. We won't go home. We won't leave our mother like this. We don't want to miss anything important—a change in her condition, a doctor's visit, another test, or the coveted transfer to a room. We haven't said it, but we won't leave one another either. So we fight exhaustion and hunger and boredom, together. We're getting punchy.

"These geniuses better keep her here for more than a day," Julia says. Tonight there is something likeable about her sarcasm. Maybe it's the relief from the dullness or because it isn't aimed at me. I laugh, and then she laughs at herself too.

"Please, yes. We need to get some rest. So does Mom."

"Who cares about rest? This is my chance. Demolition time!"

"What are you talking about?"

"I'm going to clean out the cave tomorrow. I'm getting rid of all that crap."

"Are you kidding?"

"Nope."

"You mean the stuff under the bed, the cans of food and the papers?"

"All of it. All that junk she's been collecting for her 'hundred years' war."

"Can't that wait?"

"No. This is my window of opportunity. Carpe diem!"

"My god. That's a lot of work."

"It gets done tomorrow. I'm on a mission." My sister takes a few steps in front of me, in small circles. Her arms are by her side, fists clenched. "I'm dragging that crap out."

"You mean all the boxes of shoes in her room, and the clothing racks, and Ben's clothing too?"

"You got it."

"Where will you put it all?"

"I'll get those heavy gauge trash bags and dump it. All of it. I'll have to stagger the bags along the curb on garbage days. I don't want to get a summons from the Sanitation Police."

"You don't mean Mom's clothing? The things in her closet and drawers?"

"Everything."

"What's the rush?" I hear myself asking questions that seem ridiculous to me.

"Rush, Veronica? I've been living in that museum for thirty years. I can hardly breathe from the dust and the mold. If I don't get it done now, it'll never happen. I'll wake up one day covered with mold myself."

I laugh again. "You can't do all that alone, Julia."

"I don't need any help. You can't lift anything anyhow. You'd collapse." Julia steps close to me and lands a little punch on my arm, playfully, but it hurts. I instantly remember the rough playing she'd do with Carmela when we were girls.

"Ouch. Take it easy."

"That hurts? That little tap? You need to get to the gym. Do something useful with your time. Instead of wasting your life digging up the dead."

I'm thrown off by her remark. I was enjoying the banter between us. I know what she means, and it's the first time she's made reference to our father, her father. From the look on her face it's caught her by surprise, too.

"I was wondering when you'd get around to that," I say.

"Never mind. It doesn't interest me. You're the one who can't leave that stuff alone."

"Aren't you interested, Julia?"

"Who cares? Nobody cares."

"I care."

"You must have a father complex or something." Julia rolls her eyes, half playing again.

"Yes. Or something," I half-tease back. "Do you want to know about him?"

"Forget it. Whoever you found back then was an impostor. It couldn't be him."

"The man I found was our father, Julia."

"You're so gullible. Anyone could sell you a bill of goods."

"Aren't you curious? Even a little?"

"No. Not at all."

"Hold on. I'll show you something." I reach for my wallet, where I've kept a small picture of my father taken on the day I found him. It is creased now, a small corner piece torn off. I hand it to her. "Here, look at this. This is your father."

She looks, but doesn't take it from me. "That's not him."

"Of course he's much older in this picture than what you might remember."

"It's not him."

"Julia. It's Nino. Why won't you believe it?"

"Why? I waited for him, that's why." Her tone isn't playful anymore. "If he'd been alive he would have kept his word."

"What do you mean?"

"Uncle Paolo told me he'd be back. That he had to go away, but he'd be back. He said I should wait five years. 'When you're thirteen,' he said. 'Pappa will come back. He gave his word.' All lies. I waited. He never showed up."

I see us at the window in Union Square combing the crowd for a tall man in a cream colored suit coming down the street. I hear my big sister's angry voice slamming the window shut in the awful disappointment I didn't understand then, but do now.

"So all those years, you knew he wasn't dead?"

"Of course he was dead. He had to be. That's why he didn't show up." Julia's jaw is set, her voice strong but, oddly, not loud. I know she's fighting against everything I'm saying, all the while wanting to hear it.

"Julia, listen. When I found him he asked about you. He wanted to see you, and Carmela."

"Too late. What would that have fixed? Nothing."

"Take the picture, then."

"Nah. It's your picture."

"I have others. Take it, it's yours." I hand it to her again.

"Fine. If it makes you happy, I'll take it." She slides the photo into her pocket without looking at it.

"It does. It makes me happy that we're finally talking about him."

"What's the point in talking, now?"

"Because we're sisters. We share the same father, but you knew him differently than I did."

"A lot of good that did."

"You know, Julia, he was a very kind man. A terrible contradiction to what he did. But very affectionate. Do you remember that about him?"

"No. I don't look back at this family crap. You do."

"You would have liked him. Really. He was easy to like."

"She always said that about him, that he was a gentleman and very kind."

"And you look like him. Same face."

My sister bows her head. "Yeah, well." Julia turns away and begins to walk toward the gurney where my mother lies with eyes wide open and startled. "I've got other things to think about right now. I've got to get that house cleared out before she comes back."

"I'll come over in the afternoon tomorrow," I say.

"What for?"

"If you're going to go through Mom's things, I'd like to be there."

"To do what?"

"I don't know. I guess I'd like to see what you decide to throw out."

"It's all garbage, Veronica. Moldy, smelly, crap. Everything in that room stinks. So does the rest of the house. Or should I say mausoleum? Never mind. Tomorrow I begin. First, the cave!"

"Julia, you won't have energy tomorrow."

"Watch me."

"Just don't throw any of her personal things away. This isn't fatal. Mom will be back home in a day or so."

"The first thing I have to do is to get rid of that putrid, stinking mattress of hers."

"Yes, I agree. Especially now with the blood stains on it."

"Yuck! That thing will probably disintegrate when I touch it. She's had it since Jackson Heights. I'll have to go first thing tomorrow. Assuming we're out of here sometime tonight. Oh! The dogs! If these people don't get this show on the road pretty soon I'll have another disgusting mess to clean up when I get home."

"You can buy a mattress by phone. Just dial the letter that spell mattress."

"Just like that?"

"Yeah. They deliver a new mattress to you and haul away the old one. God, I sound like the commercial."

My sister's eyes are sparkling. "What about paying for it?"

"Credit card."

"Great idea. Let me find a phone. I'll do it right now."

Julia scurries down the corridor and out of sight. I think about her dismantling my mother's room. I think about my own bedroom, my papers and jewelry and books being taken apart someday, perhaps by my children, maybe by some stranger. I should stop Julia. What she wants to do may be right for her, but it's not ethical for my mother. She will go home again and she should have her personal things around her. Her clothing shouldn't be touched. It wouldn't be right. The junk, the clutter, yes. Not her clothing and personal things. I should demand Julia leaves those undisturbed.

But I know I won't. I don't feel entitled to make that kind of demand. I haven't lived in that house. I don't know which of my mother's possessions are her most valued. I'm not a part of all that. It's Julia who's lived with her all these years, Julia whom my mother authorized to make her decisions for her. Who am I to know how they have lived, their private understandings? All I can do is hope Julia changes her mind once she gets some sleep.

"I did it!" My sister is back, and ecstatic. "They're coming tomorrow afternoon. They're going to take away that deadly, smelly piece of crap and bring a new mattress."

"See, it was easy."

"And she'll never know the difference." Julia claps her hands together and chuckles. She leans into me, eyes glittering and a smile like an impish child. "You can never tell her we did this. Never."

"Why not?"

"If she finds out, we're dead."

"Dead? Julia, Mom has dementia. She won't notice her mattress."

"Are you kidding? She'll know. Nothing escapes her. She's a witch."

"What about all the stuff you're getting rid of? Won't she know about that?"

"No. That's a different story. She'll know about her bed. She'll sense it."

"And what could happen? What would be so bad?"

"She'd never forgive us. We'd be guilty of killing her mattress."

"Oh. We're committing mattresside."

We burst into laughter. We fill the corridor with it. We don't care about the noise we're making. We can't hold back. A nurse steps out of her station to take a look at us. We are bent over. We are in tears. Every time we look at our mother, we laugh more. We are never more sisters than this, cackling like guilty schoolgirls.

Give me back everything I have ever given you
it is what She said and what i am doing
folding every piece of clothing She ever gave me
out-of-date homemade hand-me-downs
moth ball smelling sweaters and ugly pleated skirts
Carmela's dresses and Julia old school shirts
i hate them all
the horrible shoes are going back too
and the broken down bras held together with pins
all of it
i'll only keep my books my records my earrings
stuff i bought with my own money
i'll call the trucking company
one stuffed trunk direct to Jackson Heights
twenty three dollars and good riddance
then i'll unpack the box that came yesterday
it was like finally getting a care package
but it's from the Montgomery Ward store in town
the greatest place to spend your eighteenth birthday
Naomi went with me
we spent the whole day looking through the catalog
she showed me how to plan a wardrobe
how to pick fabrics that suit me
she says i am just the right proportions
and that i have great luck because i am dark
so i never have to put on makeup just be natural
after we shopped she took me to a bar in town
it's some crazy college ritual
you have to chug mug after mug of beer
until you get to your birthday number
i was flying after the first gulp but i kept on going
people were laughing and shouting me on
i only got to four mugs
but it was the most fun i've had in college
now i get to unpack my new clothes
i will look completely different
a new haircut and no glasses

kissed them goodbye at last
even the eye doctor in town was impressed
never had a patient adapt so quickly to contact lenses
it's supposed to take a few weeks
but i wore them home the very day they were ready
and no problem since
i hope Michél likes my new look
i told him about it and he's sure it looks terrific
that's what i love about him
how he always encourages me to try new things
i want him to be very proud of me
he is coming to take me home in June
i'll have one year of college finished
and be legally free
i can start my new life as his wife
we haven't talked much about the wedding
Naomi says i should start planning now
there isn't much time before Michél comes she says
but i don't know anything about a wedding
never even been to one
and no one talked about weddings at M&A
Naomi got me some bridal magazines
in the evenings i look through them
i imagine what it would be like
to have a long gown
and ushers and bridesmaids and favors
but that stuff is for girls who have families
and mothers to help
all kinds of etiquette rules and formalities to follow
it's not really for me
i'm sure Michél will take care of everything
he'll plan something with his family
it wouldn't be right if i lived with him not married
since i can never go back home
when he takes me out of here in June
i'll be staying with Carmela
that will give us time to plan

something small maybe at a restaurant or something
i'll only have Carmela and Naomi on my side
Michél will have American relatives from Brooklyn
and all his friends
he really believes things will change
and that She will come around when we get married
he's sweet to think that
even Carmela believes it
i don't
i know Her and how long She hold grudges
the way She did with Her friend Olga
She stopped talking to her last summer
never gave anybody an explanation
just said we weren't to answer the phone
but it rang and rang all weekend
She wouldn't answer it
then on Sunday morning a man came to the door
with a telegram from Olga's husband
she was killed in a traffic accident
after that She stayed in Her room for a whole week
never came out even to cook
but it hasn't changed Her
and that's how She'll be with me
Michél doesn't understand
a mother so angry with her child
and i can't explain it
but i would like Ben to come
maybe walk me down the aisle
and little Isabella and Gabriel
they could be the perfect flower girl and ring bearer
Julia and Carmela could be bridesmaids
maybe Michél is right
maybe She'll have a change of heart
it would have to be one of those miraculous moments
like Sister Claudia used to talk about
because after the way things turned out in February
there is no real chance She'll change

it was me waiting on that couch alone
nobody talking to me
until Michél came
right on time thirty minutes behind me
Ben let him in
everybody being polite and really serious
asking Michél about his morality and his intentions
trying to make him feel small and ignorant
like he didn't know that he was getting into
with such a young girl
talking about the difference in our ages
and how we're from different cultures
but him not falling for any of it
calm and sure of himself saying over and over
I love your daughter
and every time he said it making me stronger
She getting wilder and wilder
like She's the one in trouble waiting to be punished
going on for over an hour trying to scare Michél
then turns to Ben
saying *Do something Ben do something*
until he is calling Michél a liar a con artist a playboy
and Michél is looking hurt but still calm
saying *You are very wrong Sir*
in his beautiful french accent
then it's really getting to Her so She changes tactics
She stops talking and goes to the kitchen
brings out food and wine
all charming and maternal
trying to convince Michél
One year surely you can wait one year
Since she is so young
and Michél not knowing about Her scheme
falls for it
agrees
Yes we can wait one year with your blessing
they're pouring wine and coffee

they are laughing and shaking hands
it's like they're mocking me
all the while i have not been allowed to speak
Michél doesn't see what's really going on
he is too good too trusting too foreign from this
he doesn't know this kind of family
he's fallen for it
and i will be sent to Colombia or Spain
someplace where i'll never escape
i cannot let this happen
i won't be sent away again
i won't
so i beg
on my knees in the forbidden living room
i beg Michél not to believe them
there is a hurt on his face that embarrasses me
No no don't do this he says and lifts me to my feet
he asks if it is true that they will send me away
She says *It is for the best*
You will have time to think things over
Time to find someone else
Who will make a better wife for you
and like never before i see Michél angry
he steps very close to Ben
his voice is deep and strong but not nervous or loud
This agreement is broken
I will marry your daughter
with or without your blessing
She starts crying and yelling at Ben at me at Michél
at the walls
Ben shakes his head like he doesn't know what to do
then he tells Michél he must leave at once
and Michél takes his coat and before i know it
he is out the door
Ben follows Her into the kitchen
i sit back down on the couch and wait
nobody talks to me

i think about what i should do next
i hear Ben in the kitchen he sounds nervous
He'll never go through with it
You'll see he's all talk he's a big bluffer
She has stopped yelling and crying
She is quiet for along time then answers Ben
You ignorant man
You can't see he's in love with her
i get up from the sofa and walk to the kitchen
they do not look at me
i ask if i should get the midnight bus back to school
i have exams tomorrow
Ben says *Yes that would be best*
i start to go upstairs
to say goodbye to the little ones
to see if Julia has been there all along
but Her cruelty stops me
Leave this house and never come back
You are dead to me and to this family
You don't belong here
Just give me back
Everything I have ever given you

My body is bulky and sluggish as I walk to the room my mother's been assigned, way at the end and rear of the hospital's sixth floor. I need sleep. The cat nap I took while my mother was being transferred out of the emergency room will have to get me through until Julia comes back to relieve me.

When I reach the room there is a man outside its closed door, mopping. I wait a moment to let him finish. He looks at me and speaks to me in Spanish. This is a separate unit from the others, he says, medical staff must wear gloves and facemasks when they are with this patient. Maybe *la familia*, too.

I thank him and walk back to the nurses' station to ask about a facemask and gloves. There is no one there. I return to my mother's room and decide to go in anyway. I am surprised by the size of it. It could easily hold four beds, and with its high ceiling it feels vacant. It is very quiet, no machines sounding or beepers going off, and even at mid-morning, it is dark. The blinds are closed and only a few renegade sunbeams break through, streaking shadows along the floor and onto the single bed.

My mother is not in the bed. I imagine she's getting other tests done, or perhaps she's being toileted. The bathroom door is open, a small light inside lets me see that no one is in there. I turn to leave, to try again to find a nurse. As I reach for the door I see something in the shadows, a figure I don't recognize. It is someone seated in an armchair; the body is arched forward, the head down as if in a deep, reverential bow. I can't see the face, only the back of a shaved head. The feet are in white hospital booties and the heels are off the floor, like a dancer preparing to leap. Something is missing. This person doesn't seem to have arms. I must be in the wrong room. I take a few steps closer. It is my mother, tied in a straightjacket.

"Mom! Oh, Mom." I crouch to the ground. "Not this." I want to tear off the jacket, release her. I want to erase this hideous scene. My chest is heavy, caved in. I feel beaten, as immobilized as my mother. I need Julia to be here. I need my sister's voice. I don't realize it but I stand up yelling, "Nurse!" The loudness of my own voice jolts me. I open the door and run toward the nurses' station. Halfway down the corridor a nurse steps out of another room. I tell her who I am. I ask her, please, to come to my mother's room, there's been a mistake made in the way she's being treated. The nurse walks with me, quickly. She says nothing until we enter the room, where she grabs a pair of gloves from a box on the wall and slips them on as she moves to my mother. Gently, she lifts my mother's chin. She has a dreamy look, between sleep and wakefulness, and there are dark brown circles under her eyes.

"She's fine." The nurse sounds confident. She slowly steps back and stands next to me, gloved hands at her sides, as we both look at my mother.

I am breathing hard. "How can anyone be fine in a straightjacket?"

"We don't call it that anymore. It's a bunny. A restraining halter. It was ordered because of the scratching."

"This is barbaric."

"She was pretty wild, scratching the doctors and the nurses."

"Then just clip her nails."

"They've been clipped. But while she's still delirious she'll need the bunny."

"The what?"

"That's what we call the halter." The nurse repeats herself, her voice steady, undisturbed.

"Can't you use restraints on her wrists instead?"

"No. Not in this unit. They do use mitts sometimes. But not until she's lucid. She'd just tear them off now." She continues to stand with me, watching my mother, unhurried. My breathing has relaxed.

"She won't be tied up like this all the time, will she?"

"Only when she's out of bed. Thirty minutes every four hours." The nurse checks her watch and walks to the bed. She turns the sheet and blanket down. She returns to stand next to me. "Your mother can't stay in bed with all those lesions. She needs to move, for circulation."

"It's so dark in here."

"Light hurts her eyes."

"Is my mother in a lot of pain?"

"Yes, she is. But she's probably not aware of it. The meds she was given will kick in soon. She should get sleepy."

"Please, can we get her out of that thing now?"

The nurse takes a step toward my mother again and says, "Yeah. She's done."

Together we undo the Velcro strips on the halter and remove it. We carefully lift my mother out of the chair. She walks gingerly, only on her toes, and we practically carry her to the bed. We help her lie down, bring her legs into the bed, lower the header, and cover her with the sheet. I see that not all her head has been shaved; the top and a few side locks are intact. I stroke her forehead, the only part of her that is unharmed. My mother doesn't respond to any of this.

The nurse is at the opposite side of the bed. It is only now that I notice her face. She is a redhead, trim and fortyish, and doesn't smile, but I am comforted by her presence. I don't want her to leave. "Your Mom will be here for a while," she says and turns toward the window. She reaches for the blinds and adjusts the wand to change the angle of the slats. No sunlight enters now. She turns the switch on the lamp on the wall above the bed, and this, with the small light in the bathroom, bring a pale glow into the room.

"We haven't been told anything yet," I say.

The nurse tucks the sheet in around my mother, beginning at one side of the bed and working her way to the other. I step out of her way. "Being sick takes a lot out of the elderly," she says as she passes me. "It might be months before she's better."

"Months?"

"Her doctor will know more. Talk to the doctor." I sense wisdom in this woman. I want her to keep talking.

"If it's going to be months, does she stay here or go home?"

"Usually they send patients like this to rehab."

"Why is that?"

"She'll be very weak. She might not be able to walk again. And the dementia will probably be worse. It happens after a hospitalization."

"But she'll be able to go home again, won't she?"

"The doctors will tell you. They'll watch her progress." She pulls my mother's chart from the rack at the foot of the bed and begins to write. A part of me wonders why she is being so forthcoming, but I like it, so I don't question it.

I wait for a few seconds. "What part of the hospital is the rehab in?"

"Not here. Rehabs are in outside facilities. You have a while to go before that happens. A social worker will help you with all that when your Mom is ready to be discharged." She puts the chart back in its rack and moves toward the door. "No matter where she goes, though, she'll require a lot of care. Round the clock."

"My sister and I will do it," I say. "I'm sure of that."

She stops before she reaches the door and turns around to look at me. "Does your Mom live with you?"

"No, my mother lives in her own home. My sister lives with her."

"It's not so easy. It's like having a baby to take care of."

"I've done that. Twice."

"How old are your kids?"

"Adults." I smile a little, grateful to be reminded me of the other parts of my life, outside of this room.

"Taking care of babies has a lot of rewards," the nurse says. She looks vibrant, athletic inside her white pants uniform. She's about Isabella's age, I think. This could be my little sister. "Babies are cute. Their skin feels smooth, they smell good, and it's fun to watch them grow. Someone who is sick and old is a different story."

"My sister and I can do it. Between the two of us we'll find a way."

"Don't you work?"

"I do."

"And your sister?"

"Retired."

"Hire a home attendant. It'll make all the difference."

"I don't know about that. My sister doesn't believe in having strangers in the house."

"She'll have to do it eventually." The nurse opens the door and steps out into the corridor. She calls over her shoulder to me. "Either that, or a nursing home."

After the nurse leaves I pull the armchair my mother was sitting in close to her bed and sit in it. She is on her side, facing me. Her eyes are open, but she isn't reacting to anything. I sit with her for a long time, saying nothing, hoping she'll sleep. I think of Julia. I should call her, to tell her what has happened, but the room telephone hasn't been connected yet and I can't use my cell phone inside the hospital. Someone should let Gabriel know, too. Yes, I remember, Julia said she would, after her "demolition work."

I imagine my sister taking my mother's bedroom apart and I think about what she said, that my mother would sense the change. I look at my mother. I try to find something recognizable in her expression. She is far away, out of my reach. I take her hand. Her nails are trim, spotless. I reach my fingers to her face and stroke it. Her skin is silky. Her white hair shines. I feel drawn to her, to be close, just the two of us, safe, like this. An odd feeling for a grown woman, I hear myself think. But I ignore my thoughts. I lower my head onto my mother's bed. The sheets are soft. They smell clean. I give in, and rest there.

it is a Jonathan Logan dress
white linen with a voile over-slip and long sleeved
just to the knee
a baby pale pink bud resting over the breast bone
on white velvet ribbons
picked it out right from the bridal mail order magazine
Delicate Sophistication
Perfect For The Intimate Daytime Affair
when it arrived i showed it to the girls on my floor
the only snotty remark came from Cory
You're going to regret not wearing a long gown
You only get married once
but she was wrong
Michél and i will be married twice
yesterday in Judge Fink's chambers
and in three years when i turn twenty one
we'll do it all over again in church
none of the three priests we went to would do it
not without parental consent
but i could tell by their faces it wasn't about that
it was really Michél's age they didn't like
so we will wait three years until i'm legal
then we won't need anyone's permission
and i can walk down the aisle like other girls
Michél says it works out better this way
the second time we will have a real wedding
he thinks his entire family and mine will come
because all will be forgiven by then
and i can have an official wedding gown
that should show Cory about New Yorkers
Michél has made us beautiful wedding rings
sculpted lines that weave into each other
i keep checking my hand to see if mine is still there
Michél laughs at me
and says i am like a little child with a new watch
people have started to arrive
all i have to do is put this ribbon in my hair

i'm not wearing any flowers after all
dumb florist got it all wrong
i wanted only lilies of the valley
and one baby rose bud like on my dress
but he sent ugly carnations instead
Michél said next time everything will be perfect
i will make the best of it like he says
make it an offering for good luck
maybe they will all be there when i walk in
Her and Ben
Julia and Neal
Carmela Eliot little Isabella and Gabriel
and if not maybe they'll come late as usual
of course it could also be a bad sign
that She will come to make a scene
Michél must think that too
he's asked two of his friends to stand by the door
just in case
maybe it's not a sign at all just a stupid florist
it's just so miserably hot i can't breathe
i wonder if She got the invitation
nobody has answered or called not even Julia
and Carmela bowed out too
that leaves just Naomi and her boyfriend
i don't know what made Carmela flip out
just two days ago
with her name already printed on the invitations
Requests The Honour Of Your Presence
At The Marriage Of Her Sister
out of nowhere she calls me and says
I cannot attend this wedding
it would be hypocritical against her better judgment
she says it's a doomed marriage
we have too many things working against us
Michél talked to her for a long time but it's no use
i won't even have a bridesmaid standing up for me
i should have been prepared for something like this

first her appointment book fiasco
then the change of plans when i left school
after Michél drove all that way to pick me up
the girls on my floor being nice to me at last
saying Michél looks like a movie star
all of them helping me load up the car
waving goodbye and good luck
and me having nowhere to go home to
because Carmela lets me down again
telling me i can't stay with her
her roommate won't agree to it she says
all i needed was a place to stay for a few weeks
while we got the wedding planned
but she said no and hasn't called me back
i can't figure out why she's changed
Michél said there was no choice
i had to live with him in the meantime
it could have been very awkward
but it's been pretty nice really
his brother Georges has come to be the best man
he is just as kind as Michél
and both of them always look after me
making sure i am never uncomfortable
giving me the bedroom while they sleep on the sofa
even been teaching me more recipes
he says i will be a great cook
i like to watch Michél with his brother
no fighting or name calling or sarcastic remarks
just sharing things easily even the housework
Georges calls me his little sister like Eliot used to
Michél doesn't want the rest of his family to know
that we have already lived together
he says they would not understand such a situation
and loose respect for me
we haven't even had sex all the way yet
but i guess nobody would believe that
this will probably prove to Her i am as bad as She says

Michél must have been embarrassed about all this
maybe that's why he arranged things so fast
he has a knack for finding solutions to problems
no priest to marry us so he found Judge Fink
no formal reception place available
so he talked to his building manager
now he'll let us use the empty apartment next door
he found a caterer to set up a table for twenty
and even supplied a wedding cake
Michél did it all
he got Judge Fink to waive the age restriction
and marry us at the State Supreme Court yesterday
and paid him two hundred dollars
he's even booked a honeymoon for us in Mexico
now it is done and i am a wife
no matter that we had to use the judge's secretary
a perfect stranger who couldn't pronounce our names
no matter that this isn't a real wedding or real wedding dress
no matter if She thinks me dead and will forget me forever
i am a wife now
and everything is safe and brand new and mine

Treasure

The morning after the funeral I opened the Las Vegas paper and read an item on the obituary page that quoted Jim Logan speaking about my father. "Everybody who knew him loved him. He had the power to make people happy in life. He was a caring person." I looked through the business cards I'd received at the viewing and called Jim. He was hoping I'd call, he said, and suggested we meet for breakfast before I left town.

Jim was very warm to me, and told me my father had only recently confided in him that he'd always expected one of his daughters would find him. When I showed up, he was elated. Jim was very surprised, disappointed in a way, when he discovered at the mortuary that my father had kept me a secret. Jim had assumed my father would have been happy to have had his child back in his life. It was out of character for him, Jim said. How could a man be able to connect so deeply with people, and still keep vital parts of himself hidden? I remembered my conversation with Tony Tenerielli years earlier, how he'd criticized my father for that very defect. I thought of you and my sisters, how Nino had betrayed his friends, his mother, all of us. Jim said something about how all men make big mistakes.

"You can be sure of one thing about your father. In a town like Las Vegas, Nino was one of the most honorable men I've known. Here, at least, he was a man of his word."

I smiled to myself, too weary to object to the absurdity of what Jim had just said.

On the way to the airport that afternoon I made the cab driver turn around. I couldn't leave Las Vegas yet. I wanted to see my father's house once more. But as we approached his street I began to second-guess myself. Maybe it wasn't such a good idea. I should leave it for another time, say, in a few months or a year, when my feelings weren't so raw. We stopped in front of the house. This time the outside gate was open, and I could see the front path to the door. I thought of getting out of the taxi and walking up that path. I didn't want to cause Marnie any more harm; I hated being part of this awful mess. Of course, I knew a moment like this would never come again. I knew I wouldn't be coming back to Las Vegas.

I asked the driver to wait and rang my father's bell. I stood at his door thinking, this is what I should have done in the first place. It would have saved years of heartache. There was no answer. I rang again. I looked at the Chinese fan palm tree that loomed over the house. I remembered where I'd seen one like it before—in the photograph on Nonna's wall, in the picture taken in Barranquilla. Did he have the tree planted there intentionally, I wondered, to remind him of you, and us?

The door opened a crack and I saw Marnie's long red hair. Her voice was barely audible, like a small child's, asking who was there. I told her I wanted to speak to her for a few minutes. She didn't open the door any wider.

"Please. This has been very hard."

"I'm sorry about all this. I'm going to be leaving Las Vegas in a couple of hours. I won't be back again. I know this is horrible for you. It is for me, too."

"What do you want?"

"I've never seen where my father lived. If I leave without at least trying, I'll lose my only chance to see how he lived, forever. I know it's a terrible thing to ask on a day like this, but I have to ask. Then I'll leave and I'll never bother you again."

She closed the door. I turned to leave, but Marnie opened the door again.

"I'm not dressed, but come on in." She was in a long robe and barefoot. As I stepped inside she took my hand and quickly led me through the house. In each room she stopped to recount something about my father, things he'd picked out on a trip, his favorite drawing, recordings, a pattern in a quilt he'd liked. She didn't let go of my hand. I was so surprised by her kindness, and it was all so fast, that I don't remember most of what she said.

The house wasn't as large as yours, but it had plenty of open space and, off the living room, a set of French doors lead out to a patio and pool. I remember it being very elegant, with very few adornments and dark wood furniture, but I couldn't describe any details to you now. I tried to see my father there, sitting in a chair reading, walking through the rooms, involved in conversation at the table.

The room that stood out was my father's bathroom. As large as a bedroom with an oversized tub in the center, it had a chaise lounge and coffee table to one side, and potted plants and skylights on the other. His dressing room was beside it, and Marnie opened the built-in cabinetry, one section after another, to show me my father's belts, shoes, ties, and handkerchiefs. A little beyond were his shirts, hung and arranged by color, and racks of his suits.

"Take anything you want, dear, anything." Marnie repeated that in every room we walked through. "Here, take his shirts, maybe some of his ties. Maybe your husband would like them." I told her I didn't have a husband. She squeezed my hand and showed me the floor-to-ceiling shelving that held my father's shoes. An oval mirror hung above a bank of drawers. On the top, neatly arranged, rested his gold pen, his glasses, and a grooming brush in the shape of a small duck. I reached to touch it, but pulled back.

When we walked into their bedroom Marnie let go of my hand. She removed a drawer from a tall chest, emptied the contents onto the bed and sat beside it.

"Come, dear. This is your father's jewelry. Pick what you want. Take it all."

I leaned in to study my father's adornments: a set of initial diamond cufflinks, a gold Saint Christopher medal, a few watches and gold bracelets. I didn't touch anything. But I looked for the ring and tiepin the undertaker had removed, and they weren't there. That made me wonder about his ashes, and whether or not Marnie had gone back to get them. I didn't ask her about any of that, there was so much going on already.

We were back at the entry hall of the house when Marnie took my hand again. She spoke softly, but with the urgency of new grief. "Do you have time for a cup of coffee? Let me make you some." I followed her back into her kitchen and sat at her table.

"You know, I've looked everywhere. I haven't found anything with your name on it. Not a book or a piece of paper. Not in his telephone book or his pocket agenda. I've searched everything. There's nothing written down about you. I've been asking myself why I didn't suspect anything. Were there clues I missed? The only thing I come up with is that one time Nino took me with him on a business trip to New York for a few days. I found it strange that he didn't have anyone to see, since he grew up there. He said they were all dead. But on the last day, before we went to the airport, he asked the driver to make a detour. We stopped in front of this very old building. It was ancient. He never got out. He just sat in the limousine. I thought he looked like he was going to cry. After a few minutes he told the driver to go ahead."

Marnie served me a cup of coffee and opened a can of diet coke for herself.

"I want you to know. Your father and I were very happy. If he didn't tell me about you, it must have been because of something inside him he couldn't bear to open. We were very close, very happy. We did everything together. He was an easy man to live with. We had a good life."

I didn't know what to make of it. My father was a man who confided in a friend, a neighbor, even his child, but not his wife. Still, she held him in high regard. So did I. So did everyone. Maybe Marnie was the kind of wife who didn't ask questions, the way I'd been with Michél.

I thanked her for letting me come inside her home, for receiving me the way she had. She shook her head. "It's awful, when I think about it. I couldn't have children, you know. I wish he had told me about you. We could have had you out here. We could have celebrated holidays together. Like family."

When I finished my coffee I asked Marnie if I could take just one thing. She walked me back into my father's dressing room. At his dresser I reached for his grooming brush, the little painted duck. Then I left.

A month after I returned home I heard from Marnie. She asked for my address and the names of my children. She wanted to put them in her will. Weeks later I received a box from her. Inside were my father's rosary, his glasses, his gold pen, two of his favorite books, and several pieces of his jewelry, including his ring and tie pin. His agenda was there, too. On the last page, in very small writing, was a list of names. Near the middle of the page, next to the letters *VP*, were the unhyphenated digits of my telephone number.

i want to tell Her
about all the things i've learned to do
write checks and pay bills
Michél taught me
bought me a whole set of cookbooks too
i can make great saffron chicken and season a salad
Michél says i am an excellent *señora de casa*
anyone can come to our home anytime at all
it is clean and neat
i have learned it all from Michél
how to shop for meat sweep a floor fold laundry
even wash a bathroom and cut flowers
we do all of it together
Michél says it is too much work for one person
he doesn't mind that i didn't know anything
when i ask him how to do something
he enjoys teaching me
as if he were giving me the answer to a great mystery
Michél says i won't be doing it long
soon we will have a housekeeper
and i should know how to direct her
but i like doing these things myself
i like how it feels to keep everything in order
no piles of papers no clutter of old things here
nothing rotting in the refrigerator no day old bread
i can look in every corner and open every drawer
no you-have-tos no you-can'ts
and no fighting either
when things go wrong Michél speaks calmly
like the time i lost my contact lens down the drain
just a few minutes before company came
he got that look on his face
one eyebrow up and his lips tight
he was very quiet for a few minutes
then he walked over to the hall closet
i was sure he was furious and about to leave
but he was really thinking about how to find my lens

he took a wrench out of his toolbox
opened the drainpipe and there it was
next day he got me a spare set in a pretty little case
another time i thought it was the right thing to do
with Michél gone to work
and me alone in the apartment every day
pressing his shirts got me thinking
how it was August
and She's always better in the summer
and maybe no one had called
because they were waiting for me to call first
so i did
She sounded okay when She said hello
i was thinking fast to find something to say
so She wouldn't hang up
like we just got back from our honeymoon
or i'm happy now and couldn't we just make peace
couldn't we be like regular families
who visit and help each other
but She spoke first
Never call here again
and then hung up
i should have known She would react like that
i was ashamed to tell Michél about it
but the next day when Her letter came
he brought it to me
all happy because he was sure it was good news
standing there in the kitchen waiting for me to open it
but when i saw the beginning
To my disgraceful daughter
i couldn't say the awful things she'd written
in that angry scrawl
things about me being tainted and immoral
and the betrayer of the family
and ugly words worse than cursing
illicit sexual relations with that man
and calling me a nymphomaniac

saying Her mother's curse was on me
and telling me again that i don't exist for Her anymore
it ended with *You are dead consider me dead too*
i couldn't read it to him my chest was too heavy
so i put it back in the envelope and cried myself to sleep
the next morning Michél said he read the letter
Your mother is not well in her mind
You are better off away from her
This is your home now this is your family
so i haven't told him about the Candygram i sent on Her birthday
and the Christmas card and the flowers on Mother's Day
or that they all came back Refused Return To Sender
he wouldn't understand such things
still there are so many things i'd like to tell my sisters
about Mexico how in Acapulco the hotel was beautiful
just like in a movie
but i found myself crying in the bathroom every night
and didn't know why
wondering if my sisters cried too their first time
and if the things She said about me and sex are true
i do believe there is something wrong with me
Michél says i don't seem to enjoy it like a woman should
i know it is my fault
he says i will learn to like it
that i am under stress by being newly married
i do well at everything wifely but sex just doesn't work
and it is expected so often
there are so many things i didn't know about
places on his body and mine that frighten and disgust me
i am strange because what i really want is cuddling
but Michél is not a cuddler
sometimes i just want to hold hands or lean my head on him
but right away he changes and wants sex instead
it is not the way i expected
not like the movies or the songs or the books i've read
or the stories the girls told in college
no whispering or romantic talking or kissing or holding

Michél doesn't do those things
probably husbands aren't supposed to
probably that stuff is all make believe after all
anyway it is surely because of that thing that happened
when i was little
i am damaged
i am a very big disappointment to my husband
and of course it isn't fair to him
that is why i told him
because he has the right to know
so he can understand
anyway there shouldn't be any secrets between us
i thought if he knew he would make it all better
like he does with so many other things
so after we finished one night i told him
we just laid in the dark
he was very quiet and didn't say a word for a long while
then he got up and went to the bathroom
when he came back he was very serious
You must put your past out of your mind
We will never speak about this again
then he went to sleep
so we don't talk about any of that stuff anymore
not my mother or my sisters or Edoardo
or that Irma woman
and when i iron now i remind myself
about how wonderful the rest of it is
how when i wake up i'm not back there
and i don't have that stinging feeling
in my stomach anymore
because no one here is going to hurt me
best of all i never have to worry about being sent away
i am safe now
so i keep my thoughts to myself
and enjoy the good times
there is lots of company and we laugh and have fun
Michél says our home must always be hospitable

and prepared for guests
so there is plenty of food to cook up
ice in the freezer for drinks
card games and music and dancing
all of our friends are older than me
i like to listen to them talk
about worldly things that are happening
like the Vietnam War or Women's Liberation
but when is see the crowds of people marching
i remember Elise and Amy and the others
and i wonder are they out there too
most of the talk is about how different things are now
the men say everything is much more complicated
the women like it because things are faster and easier
but nobody ever gets mad even if they disagree
the best times are when Michél recites
a story or a poem Rumi Garcia Lorca or Neruda
i feel warm and calm while i listen to my husband
sometimes i imagine that they will surprise us
She or Ben or one of the girls will just show up
just ring the bell and join us
All is forgiven She'll say
i want to tell Her about the abundance
food drink sweets books paintings
piles of towels to use two at a time for each of us
one for the body another just for the hair
sometimes Michél takes me shopping for clothes
even when i don't need any
he is patient and picks things out
in colors and fashions that will suit me
it is important that i be modern and stylish he says
he never comes home empty handed
even when he's been out for short while
there is always a surprise package for me to open
maybe fresh bread or flowers or a book
or a record he thinks i'd like
the best is when he brings pictures he has taken

he is a good photographer
i arrange them into albums so they are ready
if She ever comes to visit
soon we will get new furniture
for our next apartment
we won't need Michél's bachelor stuff anymore
we will throw it all out especially the bed
it doesn't feel right
to sleep on a bed Michél used with somebody else
especially not since that Irma woman called
telling me she was Michél's girlfriend first
right up until the day we got married
and she left her clock radio behind and wanted it back
since then nothing about the bedroom feels right
Michél doesn't want it mentioned anymore
Irma was just a woman he knew
while i was far away in school
she never meant anything to him
he loved me even when he was with her
and anyway he was a single man then
i don't understand how that can be
how he could be with her but still love me
maybe it's because i am just a teenager
and Irma is a woman
the clock radio is gone now
and Michél has forgotten about Irma
i am trying to forget too like he said i should
but sometimes i still hear the sound of her voice
so angry and hurt
and I wonder if she is the reason
for all the letters being in his bottom dresser drawer
my letters from college
unopened

13

Watch the clock
nurse Anna says it every time the pain comes
it would be hard to miss
the biggest wall clock in the world right in front of me
it's the only thing i can see besides her and Dr. Mayes
watching the clock isn't bad it's the counting i hate
i don't know why they want me to count
it seems a ridiculous thing to have to do
at such a time
i can only get to two or three at most
and then i can't anymore
so nurse Anna counts for me
in her strong German voice
in between she talks to me and holds my hand
this woman's timing in incredible
like she knows
just when the pain is going to take hold of me
she says *Lady beautiful lady*
You are doing a great job and strokes my hair
i don't want to scream i'm afraid to hurt the baby
there is a woman in the next room
yelling her head off and cursing
Get me out of here
I'll get that motherfucker
If he comes near me again
I'll cut his dick off get me out of here
why doesn't someone help her
i have seen nurse Anna at Dr. Mayes' before
i don't know why she is here now
there are plenty of regular hospital nurses around
but when they wheeled me in there she was
smiling like welcome home
talking to me like i was a movie star or something
Beautiful lady your time has come now
The best time of your life
then she strapped my hands in the restraints
Nothing to worry about

Nurse Anna is here just for you my lady
We will do this together
her accent reminds me a little of Mrs. DeGrab's
it's like she's teaching me
even though i read the book
about the different stages and all that
once the pains started i forgot everything
how lucky that nurse Anna is here
it's good to have a familiar face with me now
i was afraid of having to be with strangers
the screaming from the next room is spreading
women in other rooms are screaming too
it sounds like a horror movie
i don't want to scream
those women wouldn't scream
if they had someone like nurse Anna with them
i must thank Dr. Mayes for bringing her
i'm grateful for Helen too
she said not to listen to everything people say
a woman's body knows what to do even without help
Helen has had four babies
which makes her wise in these things
that's why i picked her from the start
when i told Michél about the baby he cried
and twice said Thank God
then he worried about who would help me through it
You will need a woman to talk to
so i picked his cousin Helen in Brooklyn
he probably thought i would want it to be Her
or maybe one of my sisters
but that couldn't happen
not after i saw Julia on the line in Macy's last year
when i was buying a lamp
she said she and Neal had eloped
right after graduation
but a few months later he'd decided to join the army
in a few weeks she was going to meet him

in Germany
Julia will teach English on the army base
while Neal is in Viet Nam
when i asked about Carmela she said she is gone too
broke up with Eliot
met a hippie artist in Greenwhich Village
they were living out of a van
and going to live in San Francisco
but She insisted they get married first
She made a party at the house for them
and then they drove off
Julia says nobody thought of inviting me
She would have had a fit
now only little Isabella and Gabriel are left
i gave Julia my address
but i haven't heard from her
don't know where to write to her in Germany
or to Carmela in Seattle
so i picked Helen
i am grateful to her because she has been my friend
when we didn't know a doctor
it was Helen who recommended Dr. Mayes
He is marvelous she said with a big grin
like she knew a secret
it didn't matter that it was a trek to Brooklyn
every month for checkups
Michél was happy because it would give us a reason
to visit the family more
Helen helped me with things
when i got sick on the way to work all over the subway
she told me to stick a cracker in my mouth
to stop the nausea
she gave me her maternity clothes
and explained about baby layettes
Helen says everything will come naturally
and i don't have to be afraid
she is here right now waiting with Michél

and the rest of the clan
it has been over four hours
a few minutes ago they gave me an intravenous
i hope it doesn't hurt the baby
nurse Anna said it was something to speed things up
induced labor she called it
but now the doctor said it wasn't necessary after all
so they took it off
this baby has a mind of it's own
it must have heard Dr. Mayes talking this morning
at my checkup
telling me that he plans to be out of town next week
right on my due date
must have heard me saying no i don't want that
please no other doctor
i have been with Dr. Mayes all along
he is a good man
I knew since that first time
when he asked me about my mother
his waiting room was filled
with pregnant women and their mothers
he wanted to know about my family history
about her pregnancies and deliveries
and was She with me
i said no my mother doesn't speak to me
Dr. Mayes' face looked very sad
That's okay he said *You'll do a great job*
without her
i don't understand how he can tell that about me
but i trust Dr. Mayes
so does this baby
that's why it did not wait for a special appointment
just decided to begin its journey into this world
on its own time
not during my walk
from Dr. Mayes office to cousin Helen's house
not during the whole afternoon of soap operas

or while we waited for Dr. Mayes
to call back with the arrangements
but right in the middle of our meatball dinner
with one sharp turn of its shoulder
this baby let everyone know
that it was taking control of its own birth
not waiting for grownups to figure out schedules
or medicines to speed things up
the contractions aren't the worst thing about all this
it's the other stuff that goes on when they come
everyone moves fast
lights glare in my face
Dr. Mayes yells *Push! Push!*
me trying to figure what he wants
because i can't push any harder
nurse Anna wiping the sweat off me
saying *Bravo Lady Bravo*
then the whole thing passes and i'm exhausted
there is no memory of the pain
so that each time it grabs me by surprise again
Baby is almost here nurse Anna says
more *push pushes* from Dr. Mayes
i can see my hands in the restraints
there is no wedding band
i remember Michél has it
and my contact lenses and my cross
the nurses handed it all over to him
when they made him leave
he kissed my forehead
he looked very pale and said *Don't Worry*
then he turned to Dr. Mayes
Take care of my wife I don't want her to suffer
i watched him walk down the corridor
and push through the doors
it seems unfair that he cannot be here for this part
he has been a good partner
attentive to everything i needed and wanted

fed my cravings and massaged my back
listened to the baby's heartbeat
poured through lists of names
doesn't care if it is a girl or boy
and wants me to stop working
to take care of the baby
he will be a good father i know it
We see the head the doctor is saying
Excellent Excellent nurse Anna yells
now i remember it's called crowning
just another twist of the shoulders and it will be born
i picture this baby
doing this brutal work
sending the last of its silent signals to me
not the quick hello flutters of the beginning
or the happy dance steps late at night
tonight it sends me lightning bolt announcements
our face-to-face meeting is here at last
i'm not afraid only excited
to know this new person who will transform my life
to see myself transformed
i know that i am ignorant about mothering
but i am eager
i want to do this right
no lying no broken promises no hurting this child
keep it far away from what i knew
never let it see ugliness
just treasure it
it can be done
other women have done it
Mrs. O'Hara Mrs.DeGrab Michél's Women Helen
even nurse Anna
they have stayed sweet and good and caring
so can i
this baby will be loved
it will have plenty and not know loneliness
a father of it's own

aunts uncles cousins who already love it
friends who wait downstairs right now to welcome it
i will be a good mother
no matter if i am the only woman here
without one of my own
no matter if She has forgotten me
i trust Dr. Mayes

Cante Hondo

The smell of rubber is inescapable, even inside the elevator. I count to a slow ten between floors and remind myself that the elevator has to move at this snail's pace to accommodate the wheel chairs, and that the dense smell comes from the nursing home brand of rubber sheeting. I think about these things each time I come here, a ritual that helps me take the trip to the top floor. That is where the nonambulatory residents live, the ones who need constant supervision. My mother lives there now.

It is quiet as I step onto the floor. No gurneys whining along the corridor, no moans or supplications coming from the corner rooms—those incessant, unnamed cries I once found heartbreaking, until they, too, became part of the mix of piped-in rock 'n' roll music and the Caribbean talk of the attendants. The large wall clock at the end of the corridor tells me the midday feeding has just ended. Drowsiness has set in among the residents, which explains the lull.

The duty nurse is alone at the station, bent over something he is reading. I don't remember his name. I don't try to. He isn't Pauline. Pauline was the nurse who greeted my mother when she was first brought here, seven nurses and as many years ago. She could prompt a chat with her smile, and I could never resist. Other people's dementia didn't seem to weigh her down, and her accounts of my mother's daily antics could become belly laughs, a few moments of respite I could count on. I miss

Pauline. I throw a quick glance at the nurse as I pass, but he doesn't notice. I head for the Day Room and prepare myself to see my mother, Pauline's instructions in my ear. "Don't ever quit talking to her. Remind your mother about her life."

It is stifling in the Day Room. I take off my coat—the old, worn one I use only to come here, to save my other coats from getting impregnated with the smells of soiled linens. I drop it on one of the empty chairs up front near a young attendant who sits, arms crossed, beside one of the few male residents. Both are asleep. For a second, I envy them. At the other end of the room, Faiza looks up at me. She is an old-time attendant, kind and careful in her work, and still addresses the elderly residents with the title of Mr. or Mrs. before their surnames. Her younger colleagues omit titles and first names altogether. I nod to Faiza and guiltily turn away, to avoid looking at the row of gurneys and recliners next to her. Those hold residents whose limbs and eyes have finished moving, lined up now along the back wall like naughty time-out children in a classroom. I keep my gaze in the center of the room and scan the clusters of wheelchairs and white-haired heads, looking only for my mother. I tell myself she is years from being placed along the back wall, even longer from confinement to a corner room on the floor.

"Re-iss!" The front attendant awakens just as I reach my mother, who is slumped to one side of her wheelchair. "Wake up, Re-iss!" My mother isn't asleep. She is looking at the floor. "Look who here. Is your daugh-tah come see you. Wake up now!" I stand before my mother and feel myself shrinking, inevitably, a child stretching out her arms, not knowing which mother will greet me today. Will she be the alert and talkative mother who smiles when she sees me, blurting out, "What a surprise!" "How did you find me?" and "How did you know I was here?" Will she weep when I touch her, despairing in whispered Spanish that she is being abused, molested, fondled—*Es terrible, terrible*—and sob as she tells me there are terrible, dirty women here who put their hands 'down there' and pinch her nipples—*¡Sucias! ¡Lesbianas! Sácame de aquí, te ruego*—begging me to take her home? Or will she be the muted, unreachable soul who doesn't know me or herself, orbiting her solitary mental path, unstoppable, her return unpredictable?

"Where are my mother's glasses?" I ask no one in particular. This would be the second pair gone this year. Faiza tells me my mother hasn't had them all day. She must have lost them. I don't tell Faiza she's describing another old woman, not my mother. One who can dress herself, move about, and hold a pair of glasses in her hand long enough to misplace them. Maybe she is thinking of her own mother, whom she's told me about: eighty-four and feeble, at home in Guyana with her youngest son and his wife while the other seven siblings send money each month for everything their Mother needs, and never a thought of a nursing home. I make a mental note to call my sister about the glasses. She probably knows already. Julia comes every day.

"Hi, Mom." She doesn't move. I bend to her ear and repeat myself. She looks up at me, her eyes traveling across my face, working hard. "It's me. Ronnie."

"What do you want?"

"Not much." I ignore the panicky tone of her question and place a light kiss on the smooth skin of her forehead. She flinches, raises one arm to wipe away the kiss. I step back to get a better look at her. Her eyes are clear and her face has its natural blush, both good signs. "Just came to see you." I rearrange the two pillows under her, to straighten her out. This requires that I slide my hand along her back and under her legs. Her body is tiny and solid, but she doesn't resist my touch. I wheel her out of the Day Room and down the quiet hall.

"Where are you taking me, Miss?"

"To where you live."

"How do you know where I live?"

"I'm very smart," I say. "My mother made sure I studied and learned."

We reach her room, just past the elevators. Kate, her roommate, is asleep and snoring softly behind the divider curtain. My mother has the window side of the room, which saves her from the usual traffic and harsh light of the corridor. I position her to face the window, near an armchair and small sink. I pull the blinds up and slide the window open an inch, enough to ventilate the room but avoid a draft of cold air.

"Look, Mom." I motion toward a white clapboard house with a green roof that sits at the crest of a hill across the way. A row of bare apple trees hugs the driveway through a wide, yellowing lawn and up to the roomy front porch. "There's the house you like." She doesn't, really. Even on the long-gone days when she was able to decipher images that far away, she only commented on the trees. I'm the one who likes the house, very much.

Especially on late afternoons when the waning sunlight skims the tree tops and floods the porch. I've never seen anyone go in or out, but I like to imagine it a home filled with conversation and music, and a big dining room. I pull the armchair under the window and sit facing my mother. "Never seen any children in that house, have we, Mom?" She stares at a spot on her lap.

I pull out a tube of lavender scented baby cream I carry in my pocketbook. I pour a few drops onto my palm, rub my hands together to take the chill out of it, and push up the left sleeve of my mother's shirt. I apply the cream in small circles along her forearm. She watches my motions but shows no expression. I dot the top of her hand to form a smiley face with the cream, the way commercial manicurists do before they massage my hands. It doesn't register. We both stare at her clenched left hand, frozen from lack of movement and wrapped around a bundle of gauze. Her hand is her only bodily defect—she has no medical complications, not even high blood pressure. I take her other hand, the one that still opens, and glide cream over the bumps of our interlaced arthritic fingers. When I finish I roll up her pant legs one by one. The skin on her legs is silky and radiant, like a child's. I move the cream in short strokes to avoid bruising her. "How'd you get these great legs, Mom? Not a mark on them. No spider veins or age spots for you." She doesn't move.

I stand up and clean my hands at the sink, then reach to the dresser for her hairbrush and comb. As the comb moves through her hair she turns her head to look up at me. "Who are you?"

"I'm Veronica."

"Yes?" She pauses. "That is my granddaughter's name. Do you know her?"

"I know both your granddaughters, Jacqueline and Lissette." I insert a small clip in her white hair, cut short now, but still thick and vibrant. I sit back down and use two fingers to gently lift her chin. I wait for her eyes to meet mine. "Veronica is your daughter."

"Oh." I could have just told her the price of strawberries or the news of the worst oil spill in history along the Louisiana Gulf coast. She brings her clenched fist to the place on her chin I just touched, and leans on it. "How do you know so much about me?"

"I'm an agent for the Immigration and Naturalization Service."

A few years ago my mother would have been indignant: "Young lady, you have the wrong customer. I am an American citizen. I was a citizen long before you were born. I did not have to wait in line to get into this country, either. I was escorted. I was the wife of a United States Army officer. You are not doing your job very well, Miss." Pauline would have laughed and encouraged me to confuse her, provoke her, use anything to keep her mind working.

Today she is quiet, gazing at the floor. There's no way to tell whether she is struggling to find a rebuttal or if she's retreated to that other place I'm not privy to. I lower her fist and pat it gently. "Sorry about that, Mrs. Reiss. I believe you're right. My mistake. We will correct the records."

"Ayyy!" The sound travels from one of the corner rooms. It is a deep, guttural yelp that startles me for a second, but not my mother, although she turns her head in the direction of the cry as it repeats.

"*¿Quién canta?*"

"One of your neighbors across the hall, Mom. She sings like that all day."

"She knows *flamenco*?"

"*Sí, seguro.*" I muffle a laugh. It's too good to resist, this arbitrary association my mother has made with *cante hondo*, the deep, soulful song style of gypsy music that typically begins with mournful arpeggios much like the ones we're hearing. I urge her on. "This woman is a great *cantaora*. I think that's a *Seguiriyas* she's doing now." I raise my hands and lightly clap a few *sordas* to set the beat, the way I did when I was a child at our kitchen table.

"*Bien.*" My mother gives her approval. In a few minutes the wails stop. Softly, I begin to sing a lyric she was once familiar with.

> *a primer rayo de la luz de la mañana*
> *despierto siempre preguntando ¿dónde va?*
> *y con mi aliento empaño el cristal de mi ventana*
> *y veo a mi barquilla echarse a la mar*
> *navega sola, navega sola*
> *mi barquilla velea sobre las olas*

My mother's face relaxes as I sing. She lifts her head and looks out the window. I want to believe the wistful melody and words have reached her, even for a few seconds.

"Ma. Isn't that a lovely *cante*?" She turns her head to me and sighs. "It's the one about the little boat sailing off alone at dawn." She leans back against the headrest and closes her eyes. Very soon, she's asleep. The room is still. The corridor is silent. Chilled air drifts in through the window and touches my face. I hear the faint squawking of geese in the distance. I'd like to sleep too, here in this quiet with my mother. But I'm due back at work within the hour. A quick cat nap, I think, indulging myself, five minutes' worth, would do me good. I let my head rest against the window sill and half-close my eyes. I look at my mother and try to match her breathing.

Sleep doesn't come. I see only the incongruities before me: my mother's placid face, her healthy body, her ravaged mind. Finally and without obstacle, whenever I want her, she is here for me. I wonder again and against reason: how much does she know of her life now? Does she see herself, reduced to this half-room, robbed of every personal decision by a disease—the first she ever had—even to the very people and images she looks at? No books to read, no radio or television, no choice in what to eat, what to wear, when to bathe or brush her teeth, what time she awakens or goes to sleep, the bed she lies in, or when to shut the lights off. What would the decade-younger Eva say?

I tell myself what I've been told: she doesn't know any of this. She isn't suffering. Alzheimer's has wiped away her capacity for insight. It's not like in the beginning with her frantic pleas to take her home. She complained about the amount of work she'd been given to do, how she'd stayed up all night but was never be able to finish, and she called the attendants *ignorantes*, incompetent women bosses who did not notice or reprimand the other "lazy bureaucrats," meaning the immobilized residents around her. A year later she only shrugged her shoulders when I'd ask about her "work," and had to be roused into conversation. Then came her silent hours spent sitting in the first floor recreation lounge, oblivious to all others, as though she was waiting for something to happen, staring at the bingo card in front of her—a task as foreign to her as eating the tasteless food she was offered. I'd stopped coming every day by then. Instead, I planned late afternoon interludes after work a few times a week, when the recreation room wasn't used, and wheeled her next to the upright piano in the back and played for her. For an hour or so she'd listen to Scarlatti Sonatas, Bach French Suites, Chopin Nocturnes, Mozart, Beethoven, Debussy, Ravel—the music she'd heard her children practice and had known well. She looked only at my hands, as though she were watching magic, and it didn't matter how badly or well I played. Later, when she couldn't sustain interest without turning away or repeatedly blurting out, "Miss, I need to get out of here," the recitals stopped.

My mother has succumbed, the fight no longer in her, as though she had never lived differently than this. To anyone who doesn't know her past, she would appear peaceful, serene. I see her as she must have been back in her childhood boarding schools, obedient and institutionalized, waiting to be freed. Yes, I miss her feistiness. On the rare day that she is verbal, I allow my imagination to negotiate my loss. One of these days she'll get up out of that wheelchair to rectify her life, I say to myself, toil in her garden, argue with my sister, stand at her front door to let me in.

"Ronnie?" She's awake and looking at me. I must have dozed off after all.

"Hey, Mom." I straighten up and smile at her. "You look pretty today. Who combed your hair?"

"Pat? Is that you?" It is Kate's voice, quick and fretful, from behind the divider curtain. I wait a few seconds, hoping Kate will go back to sleep. "Pat? I combed my own hair."

"No, Kate. It's not Pat." I rise and look behind the curtain. Kate's eyes are closed, her hands pulling at her bedding. "I am visiting my mother at the next bed."

"Oh, I'm so glad you came! This is no good, Pat. No good. Get me out of here." She doesn't open her eyes. "You can't be the only one having fun. I need to get home and get dressed. I have a date tonight."

"It's all right, Kate. Your sister will be here soon."

"You saw her?"

"Yes, down in the lobby. She's on her way up." This is my usual answer to Kate, because it quiets her down. I've only once seen her sister Pat, but I know from the attendants that she rarely comes. Kate opens her eyes and repeats her plea, looking up at the ceiling. "Take me home, Pat." I step out into the corridor and spot the medication cart nearby, but not the nurse. An attendant I don't recognize steps out of one of the rooms. I wave to summon her. When she's within earshot I tell her Kate is awake and agitated. The attendant comes to the door of the room and calls out firmly, but not loudly, "Mackenzie, relax now. Yah not be feelin' well lately. Don't want to be gettin' sick again, do yah now?" Kate stops moving. She looks like she's instantly asleep. The attendant nods to me and walks back down the hall. I sit in front of my mother again.

"I'm back."

My mother looks at me and asks, "Where is your boyfriend?"

"My boyfriend?"

"I heard him."

"No. That was your roommate, Kate, I was talking to."

"What happened to your boyfriend?"

"Don't have one. Not right now."

"He left you?'

I can't be sure, but I believe she's referring to Jack, the only man other than my ex-husband she's seen me with. "Jack moved away, Mom. He'll come to see you soon." In fact, Jack retired early and left New York before my mother ever lived in this place. On occasion when he's in town, he's asked to visit my mother. She doesn't recognize Jack, but her eyes light up whenever I introduce him. Maybe she associates his deep hello with another male voice—Ben's or Gabriel's. Maybe the rare sound of a man and woman in conversation pleases her.

"¿Sóla? " Her face contracts into a scowl. She doesn't have to say another word. I can feel my hands perspire. She looks down and shakes her head, as if she'd never before considered the idea of a middle-aged woman living alone, not her daughter, not me. Why didn't I just go along with her and say my boyfriend was in the bathroom? Why didn't I see this coming? My jaw tightens against my mother's uncanny ability, even now, to pinpoint the very thing about myself I find most distressing, and with one lone word make me feel hopeless. Why don't I just tell her how unwarranted her concern for me is now, at this late date?

When I look back at her, her hands are shaking, and her arms. Tremors are a recent development, and likely coincidental at this moment. Her neck and shoulders stiffen, she throws her head back, the shaking quickens. I touch her leg, knowing I can't stop her flailing, afraid it won't stop at all. She looks more helpless than ever. A short moan escapes her. Whatever damage this woman ever did, I want to say to someone, anyone, this disease has extracted enough atonement.

In a few minutes her body is still again. She looks at me as if I'd just arrived, her eyes bright with curiosity. I could tell her that I'm okay, because I am, and that she doesn't have to worry about me. But really, I want to tell her how hard it sometimes is to live alone, coming home to a silent house every night, not to be desired or touched. I want her advice, her blessing, for finding a loyal partner. Then I see that I am daydreaming again. My connection to my mother has never changed, and never will. I smile at myself.

"I'm working on it, Mom."

She waits, then says, "Do I know you?"

I should be used to the question by now. But the timing of it can feel like a pinprick in my chest. I take a long breath and say it again. "Yes. I am Veronica."

She smiles, exposing the few teeth she still has, stained and decayed alongside the dark gaps where others have fallen out since she stopped allowing anyone, including Julia, to brush them. "That is my daughter's name."

"Oh? Tell me about her."

"Veronica is very kind. Smart."

"Go on."

She says nothing. I wait. "What about your other children?"

She turns away, disconnecting. I hear myself name her five children in birth order, a roll call of my missing siblings. The recitation feels like a cruel reminder, since Julia and I are the only ones who come to see her. Does she sit here waiting for the others?

Julia doesn't have such doubts. She carries on like a warrior on a mission. Once a day, usually mid-morning, she marches down the hall carrying a thermos filled with strong coffee and an American cheese sandwich, cut into bite-sized pieces. She knows the names of each duty nurse and attendant, and makes a point of saying hello to each as she passes. Occasionally she brings sweets or flowers from my mother's garden to leave at the nurse's station. After she wipes my mother's face and hands with the towel she has also brought from home, Julia inserts bite-sized pieces of sandwich into my mother's mouth. All the while she talks to her, scolding, prodding her to eat more because she has to get stronger, has to stay alert. My mother groans and writhes to avoid the food and Julia's heavy hand, sometimes cries out "Leave me alone!" but always acquiesces when she tastes the coffee Julia brings to her lips. The nursing staff applauds Julia's determination because she gets my mother to eat. There is rarely a time I'm here that someone doesn't stop me to say, with admiration, "Your sister comes every day."

I, too, admire her diligence and devotion. But lately I avoid coming when Julia is here with my mother. I cannot watch their struggle any longer. My presence does nothing to mitigate their distress with one another. And Julia makes it very clear: without the distractions of house and garden and feasible conversation, we three are overcrowded in this room.

"Mom, did you have a good visit with Julia today?"

She shrugs. "I have not seen her."

"She was here earlier," I say. Today, Julia's name was a half-dozen lines above mine in the registry book downstairs. "She gave you food. And coffee."

"When did she get home? Is she upstairs?"

"Not right now. She's gone out to do some errands."

"She is busy."

Julia is always busy. True to her intention, my sister spent more than a year clearing out my mother's house of clutter and trash. She pulled up the carpets, had the ceilings repaired, and walls cleanly painted. Closets and drawers were emptied, and old clothing thrown out. The last time I saw it, my mother's bed was made up in new, floral linens, seemingly waiting for her return. Except for the roof repairs, Julia insisted on doing it all herself, turning down my offers of help, or hiring workers. In the first months after my mother came here, Julia joined me for a weekly evening of dance, and even signed up for tango lessons. We had fun and laughed together, buying each other hair ornaments and dance shoes, and sharing stories about the men we danced with. When she met a steady dance partner and brought him to holiday dinners at my home, I was delighted. We'd roll up my living room carpet and put on the latest salsa music to show off our new steps. But a time came when she stopped accepting my invitations or suggestions that I stop by at the house, even to meet at the coffee shop up the block from here. She was busy, she'd say—always a house project looming—and had no time.

I'd like to think that Julia is in the midst of a passionate affair with her dance partner, liberated from duty and obligation, her time consumed with love. But if she were happy, wouldn't she want to tell me about it? It's more likely that this long goodbye to our mother has fatigued us. We've run out of things to do together, or talk about, to distract ourselves. To thrive under such a regimen as this, no victory in sight, our sisterhood would require a ready, uncompromised ability to find solace in each other, and we never developed that.

Occasionally in the evenings as I prepare for sleep, I picture my sister in that cold, cavernous house. I think of picking up the phone to call her, and then don't. She wouldn't answer anyway. Even when I have left friendly messages or inquiries about my mother's condition, Julia's replies have come in brief email explanations about not being home or not hearing the ring. I've stopped pursuing her. More often, I think of the day we transferred my mother to this nursing home, when we understood she'd never live in her own house again. We were both quiet when I drove Julia back home. Before we knew it, we were sitting on opposite sides of the new bed she'd ordered for my mother's room, crying together, unashamed, in little girls' sobs. I thought then that our sisterhood was indestructible, comprehensible only to us. Now this half-room is our only remaining common ground.

I hear the buzz of my cell phone vibrating in my pocketbook. I scramble to get it, but I'm too late. One missed call, from Jackie. I flip the phone open and hold it up to my mother's eye level. I click a few buttons and pull up a photo.

"Can you see the picture, Mom?" She squints into the phone. "That's Lissette and her baby boy, Erik."

She frowns, but keeps looking. In a minute she asks, "¿Se casó?"

"Yes. Jackie is married too. And she has a baby of her own coming soon." I give her time, in case it will help her grasp what I'm saying. "What do you think it will be, Mom? A boy or a girl?"

"Who?"

"Jackie's baby." She shrugs. "The doctor says it's going to be a girl. Her name will be Lilah Grace."

A smile crosses her face again. "That's nice."

I pat her shoulder. "You're a great-grandmother."

"Who, me?" She lets out a nervous laugh.

I close my phone. "Yes, Mrs. Reiss. You." I slip the phone back in my pocketbook, and catch my image in the mirror above the sink. Tonight, I promise, I'll get a good night's sleep. I swivel the wheelchair and roll my mother out of the room. Kate is sleeping soundly. Down the hall, I spot the duty nurse assisting a resident with medication. We exchange glances.

"Seventy-two." My mother begins the random calling out of numbers, a signal that she is very tired. I tell her where we're headed. "Forty-nine," she says.

The very loud sound of a television pours out of the Day Room. I ease my mother back into her spot. The attendants have changed rotation, and the new ones are discussing an item on the Oprah Show. My mother doesn't seem to notice the television, although she has a full view of it. She looks out the window. I carefully run my hand along her hair, her face. I bow my head to kiss her cheek. "See you later, Mom."

I grab my coat and head for the elevator. I think I see Faiza walking into another room, but I can't be sure. I give a little wave anyway. On the first floor I go to the sign-out desk and record the time. Just enough minutes left to make it back to work. As I step through the front door, someone calls out. "Hey, there, Miss Vee." It's Dave, the head cook for the nursing home, standing under the canopy in his shirtsleeves, his tall and lean body shivering as he takes a deep puff on a cigarette.

I smile and say, "I thought your wife made you quit those things." We exchange hugs, an old and easy confidence after he once found me weeping in the lounge after a visit, believing I was alone in the room. He came to sit next to me and waited, then spoke only to offer me a cup of coffee. Today his dark face beams as he speaks in his Louisiana drawl, "The Mrs. thinks I did. But that's another story. How is Momma doing?"

I say what has become my ready answer, "Still here, but a little further away every day."

"Not to fret." He pats my hand. "She's just the way she's supposed to be. And seeing you has to have brightened her day."

I thank Dave for his kindness and beg off his offer to stay for lunch. "Always good to see you, sweet lady," he calls out as I walk to my car. I sit for a minute in silence as the engine warms up, letting myself feel flattered and a little disappointed that I don't have more time to chat with Dave. He has a way of lightening me up.

Traffic is surprisingly light as I turn onto Northern Boulevard. I click on the radio and hear the forecast for continued cold temperatures, but no snow. I remember Jackie's missed call and reach for my earpiece. But I hold off when I recognize the opening chords of the Chopin Berceuse. I follow the elegant, simple melody which in the hands of a lesser composer could have been a child's tune, turn into an unbroken, soulful story. I see Carmela at our piano, her fingers cascading across the keyboard, her face transformed, as if she were in a place of splendor and great peace, where she took us all when she played, each from our different room in the house, listening to the music together.

My phone buzzes again. It is a text message from Jackie. *My water broke. Going to hospital.* I wipe my eyes, make a U turn, and head toward the highway.

this is our moment
nobody else's
wrapped in each other's arms
in the middle of the night
we make detailed crossings of one another's faces
out through time and back again
closing some anonymous ancestral circle
that has drawn us to one another
you stare at my hair
a smile suddenly breaks across your tiny lips
and stops to hold them poised as if to kiss me
as if you knew what a kiss from you would mean
they tell me it is the darkness of my hair
that holds your interest
because you cannot focus
what do they know of the wisdom in these gray eyes
they have come to teach me something no doubt
directly from the source
untouched
to me
i wait all day for this time with you
to feel the sway that soothes you and me
both of us together on this blessed chair
its arms always open to receive my confidences
things no one else will know about
because no one asks
its white oak spindles curved to fit my back
and give it ease
a respite from intruders who keep me from you
who will again at dawn demand
that i appropriate myself to them
and under worthless protest i will submit
bundle you up against the cold and hand you over
to people who say it will not matter years from now
that two weeks is old enough
that you are ready
like my first was ready

to be held by strangers
i will die a little
at each repeated surrender to their greed
as if work and money and worldliness mattered
more than this
but we know you and i
these moments are what counts
and i have already missed so many
stored them away since my first time
each one stacked and neatly labeled
like survivors who will one day demand retribution
they are saved inside my yearning
to hold my babies more
here in this chair
its rhythm as certain as its memory
someday it will tell you
when you come to it for solace
how we waited for you
your big sister fallen asleep on my belly
exhausted from months of impatience
to see you already
your father working at his bench late into the night
sculpting himself into a jeweled offering for you
and me knowing with every to and fro
that what ever else may come
more good than this i dare not want

Epilogue

My mother died peacefully in her sleep nearly thirteen years after her illness was diagnosed. When I touched her hand for the last time I had nothing but love for her, and deep gratitude for the gift of redemption we found together. I continue to discover more and more gifts she gave me, and it is plenty.

Every morning as I begin my day I see my siblings in my heart. As of this publishing, it has been 48 years since we were together. I thank Julia and Carmela for treading the path before me and for bearing the blows that didn't reach me, and I extend my hand to Isabella and Gabriel. I see us feasting at the table. We share stories, we laugh, we cry, we make music, we sing, we dance.

Until we meet again, I hold them close, and bow to our fate.

Acknowledgements

I'd like to thank the members of my writing community, especially Darlynne Davenny, Anna Kushner, Rebecca Cooney, Lisa Freedman, Jenny Van Horne, Dorothy Randall Gray, Hannelore Hahn, David Siegerman, Karol Nielsen, Jennifer O'Reilly, Betsy Feist, Beverly Magid, JoAnn Kawell, and Jonathan Wallace. Each one contributed generously in time and spirit, and with great care for the integrity of the story.

My deep appreciation to Amy Rothman for her steadfast devotion to the book and to my sanity during the process. A special thank you for their early and constant support goes to Laura Sayegh, Vera Slamka, Shain Fishman, Joanna Carmosino, Joy Vanegas, and Cathy Santiago.

A special debt to Robert Moteki, Robert Sherman, Peter De Vries, Ben Cirlin, and Nancy Turret as life teachers and friends, to Bert Hellinger for his work, and to all the friends of Lois for showing me tools and their loving support.

My enduring gratitude to Sean Wrenn for his unshaken belief in my story and its importance, and for walking through it with me.

I can never adequately thank my children, Jacqueline and Lissette, for the faith and enthusiasm they had in the book throughout the long years of writing.